Redistribution to the Rich and the Poor

The Grants Economics of Income Distribution

Redistribution to the Rich and the Poor

The Grants Economics of Income Distribution

Edited by

Kenneth E. Boulding
University of Colorado

and

Martin Pfaff
Wayne State University
and University of Augsburg

Wadsworth Publishing Company
Belmont, California

No man is an island, entire of itself; every man is a piece of the continent, a part of the main; if a clod be washed away by the sea, Europe is the less, as well as if a promontory were, as well as if a manor of thy friends or of thine own were; any man's death diminishes me, because I am involved in mankind; and therefore never send to know for whom the bell tolls; it tolls for thee.

John Donne

Devotions XVII

Whosoever hath, to him shall be given, and he shall have more abundance: but whosoever hath not, from him shall be taken away even that he hath.

New Testament:

Matthew, xiii, 12.

Technical Illustrator: Carl Brown

ISBN: 0-534-00169-6

L. C. Cat. Card No: 72-79497

Printed in the United States of America

1 2 3 4 5 6 7 8 9 10—76 75 74 73 72

Introduction to the Series on Grants Economics

This series of volumes might almost be described as radical economics by regular economists. Most of the contributors are members of the Association for the Study of the Grants Economy, and some may indeed be members of the Union for Radical Political Economy too, although most of them are not, we are sure. Nevertheless, the significance of grants economics may well be that it contains the most important clues to the questions the radicals are asking but, alas, are not often answering.

The central idea of grants economics is that exchange economics is not enough. From the days of Adam Smith economics has been dominated on the whole by the analysis of how society is organized by exchange. This is a necessary, but not sufficient, idea on which to base an understanding of the economic system. Exchange, that is, two-way transfer (A gives something to B and B gives something to A), is a powerful organizer of economic life, but it is not the *only* organizer. The *grant*, or one-way transfer (A gives something exchangeable to B, B gives nothing exchangeable to A), is becoming an increasingly common instrument of economic and political organization. Grants economics contends that grants must not be regarded as something exotic, outside the economic system proper, but must be integrated into both the theory and the empirical study of the economy.

The failure to do this has, in part at least, produced radical economics. Pure exchange economics cannot come to grips with some of the most important problems of our day — for instance, those involving the distribution of power, income, and wealth, which exchange economics takes for granted. The dissatisfaction with exchange economics is one of the most important sources of radical dissent. However, radical economists often destroy their own case by throwing exchange economics out the window altogether, thereby "turning off" the "straight" economists to the point where no communication takes place. Grants economics insists that *both* grants and exchange are necessary to the organization of a modern economic system and that any intelligent reform must be based on an integrated view of the system, which includes both grants and exchange as interacting mechanisms.

These volumes are addressed to serious students of economics and the social sciences. We believe that they will fill a crucially important gap in the present state of knowledge and that their influence will be felt far beyond the particular problems to which they are addressed.

Kenneth E. Boulding and Martin Pfaff
Series Editors

Contents

3 Implicit Public Grants and Taxes   169

Distributive Effects of the Grants Economy: An Introduction

Redistribution to the Rich and the Poor is a volume of papers, most of which were given in December 1969 and 1970 at the meetings held jointly by the Association for the Study of the Grants Economy with the American Economic Association, the American Association for the Advancement of Science, or the Public Choice Society. This collection represents the first substantial foray into the interior of what is a surprisingly unknown intellectual continent. We have known for a long time that the continent, problems of nonmarket income distribution, exists. Although we have known something about its main outlines, we have made little serious attempt to explore it thoroughly, with adequate conceptual frameworks and quantitative information.

This book is little more than a first step in this direction, although, we think, an important one. It emerges first of all out of a considerable improvement in basic information, especially as a result of sample surveys, and it represents also the beginning of theoretical and conceptual approaches to the problem, which are more satisfactory than what we had before. Nevertheless we have a long way to go. Anybody who thinks that either the conceptual problem of dealing with poverty by redistribution of income to the poor or the practical steps that have to be taken is easy will certainly miss the message of this volume. The more we get into the problem, indeed, the more difficult it seems to become. However, the problem is most crucial and demands a high priority for intellectual effort.

The emphasis in this volume is on the changes in the distribution of income, especially in regard to the poor, which take place as a result of the grants economy, or the system of one-way transfers.[1] We have confined the cases to the United States and largely to the effect of explicit and implicit public grants on personal and interstate income distribution as subsequent volumes explore the effects of transfers in an urbanized economy as well as the international

---

1 For a statement of the theory and effects of the grants economy as well as a discussion of the conceptual underpinnings, see M. Pfaff and A. B. Pfaff, with an introduction by K. E. Boulding, *The Grants Economy* (Belmont, Calif.: Wadsworth Publishing Company, 1972).

issues.[2] The basic conclusion of these papers is that redistribution toward the poor has increased through the effect of some components of the *explicit* grants economy, but despite this increase the actual distribution of income seems to have changed little, even though the number of poor has diminished, as we have all gotten richer together. On the other hand the "perverse effects" of *implicit* public grants, conveyed either through special provisions of the tax laws, public policy, or administrative practices, tend toward *greater inequality*: They help the rich and propertied more than the poor. Furthermore many public expenditures aimed at improving economic and social well-being in a particular area -- for example, education or agriculture -- tend to reinforce income disparities or even to augment them. In addition to this problem is the effect of grants on the exchange sector of the economy and on that portion of the distribution of income accounted for by the exchange economy, which we still do not understand very well.

In the area of implicit public grants the need for explicit value axioms becomes obvious: If our aspirations and expectations have risen in tandem with the standards of economic and social welfare that we judge fair or equitable, then our evaluation of the role of "poverty amid plenty" must necessarily have changed. We can barely surmise the welfare implications of changes in popularly held values and equity norms. Similarly, if we admit to a wider function of the grants economy and to its task of achieving social and economic goals precisely in the areas where the exchange economy fails to function satisfactorily, we must fashion a much broadened frame to hold the socioeconomic canvas. Just as poverty is both an economic and a social issue, transfers are a medicine for both an economic and a social malaise: Income maintenance policy is geared to a wider set of social goals -- the integration of the individual and of minority groups in society, the maintenance of a viable system of social relations, not to speak of economic freedom and "social security."

The study of the distributive effects of public grants challenges some notions we may have imbibed in the process of accepting prevailing dogma: "Public" goods, or at least a sizable share thereof, convey substantial private benefits to some individuals but not to others. As the papers in the volume indicate, the public hand that wields the allocative levers also distributes benefits and allocates costs. In most cases, using an educated judgment, we can estimate the costs and benefits of these allocations. Public policy-making must take note of this fact. We must examine allocative decisions not only for their stability implications but also for their distributive, integrative (or disintegrative) freedom and security-enhancing and other social welfare effects. Social indicators designed to measure the well-being of society are surely called for to help us gauge the effects of the public grants economy.

---

2 K. E. Boulding, M. Pfaff, and A. B. Pfaff, eds., *Transfers in an Urbanized Economy: Theories and Effects of a Grants Economy* (Belmont, Calif.: Wadsworth Publishing Company, 1972), and K. E. Boulding, J. Horvath, and M. Pfaff, eds., *The Grants Economy in International Perspective* (Belmont, Calif.: Wadsworth Publishing Company, forthcoming).

The empirically oriented expert in public finance and the scholar concerned with general economic analysis should be familiar with the concepts and the language employed in these papers. When we talk of transfer payments, subsidies, and taxes, we generally use terms common to the discipline; however, to interpret the sequence of papers we should develop taxonomy or frame of reference.

We have not attempted in this context to provide an exhaustive and elaborate frame of reference beyond that required to integrate the various papers into an overall concept and thus to facilitate the message of the volume. (A separate volume that sets the tone for the entire series provides an integration that would go beyond this goal.[3]) Here we outline only the main points of the grants economy theory – termed *grants economics*.

Grants result in a variety of offsets from the operation of the market system. Grants affect the input aspect of the economic process in their influence on labor force participation, in their impact on interest rates in the capital market through their provision of capital, and in the provision of material goods. Furthermore they influence technology itself: Government finances a good part of the research and development effort in the form of contracts with large corporations. Grants influence the output aspect of the economic process in the form of public demand for goods and services produced by the economy. Perhaps the most profound influence, however, results from the impact of transfers on the structure of prices. Prices are the regulators par excellence of the traditional exchange system; they aim at the coordination of supply and demand forces in product and factor markets. Even if the invisible hand of market automaticity did ever exist in the course of the last century, when reality came closest to this economic construct, it certainly cannot operate unfettered today or uninfluenced by the forces of transfers. Our economy is far different from the idealized economy that the traditional textbooks of exchange economics discuss. Overriding governmental pressures influence or control exchange processes in many ways. Accordingly the anonymity of prices has been replaced by the bureaucrat and the administrator, who in turn are guided by political leadership or whatever forces fashion political processes. Therefore, we must go from an economic theory of transfers to a political economic theory of the grants economy by identifying the impact that the political, social, and cultural systems have on the nature of the mixed grants–exchange economy.

The ideal function of the grants economy would be to act as a higher level regulator of the exchange economy whenever exchange or market processes fail to achieve economic and social ends. We recognize economic market failures in the form of monopoly, indivisibilities, in situations of increasing returns to scale, and in situations characterized by external benefits and costs. Under these circumstances we cannot expect market prices to lead to a most efficient allocation of resources; in this respect transfers are necessary to offset the

---

3 M. Pfaff and A. B. Pfaff, with an introduction by K. E. Boulding, *The Grants Economy* (Belmont, Calif.: Wadsworth Publishing Company, forthcoming).

deficiencies of the market system. Furthermore we may view the market as a means to achieve social ends – such as stability, growth, freedom, equity, integration – and to maintain the relationships within the system. A host of interferences in the market system may be necessary whenever complex trade-offs between these conflicting goals warrant a result that does not conform to the uncontrolled market result. Thus an ideal political-economic theory of the grants economy would postulate the ideal regulation of the market processes by a set of transfers. Other things being equal, we could, for example, presume that grants would help ameliorate the inequality in income distribution wrought by market forces; that is, we would expect the pattern of redistribution brought about by the grants economy to be highly progressive in order to compensate for the regressive pattern of market distribution of income. That we reject this hypothesis on the basis of the empirical evidence presented in this volume is evident at almost every turn. We then need a more comprehensive political economic theory of grants, which recognize benevolent motives operating to redistribute income from the rich to the poor, or from the middle class to the poor. We also must recognize a vital area of processes of involuntary redistribution, which benefits the rich or the middle class at the expense of the low-income classes. In other words we could postulate two types of redistribution:

1. *Voluntary redistribution* generally takes place from the rich to the middle class or to the poor, or from the middle class to the poor. A theory of voluntary redistribution emphasizes two motives. The first is a recognition of the interdependence of the well-being of all members of the community. This motive is reflected at the micro level through the interdependence of the utility functions of various actors. Based on such an assumption, an individual with a higher level of income will, in fact, be motivated to engage in voluntary transfers to those with lower incomes. He will do so because he can maximize his total utility, consisting of the sum of his consumption (his "selfishness-component") and his contemplation of other people's well-being (his "selflessness-component"), only by making transfers to others.[4] No doubt voluntary redistribution will be a significant factor only in closely integrated groups where one individual perceives his well-being as being intimately tied in with the well-being of others and where one individual is, in fact, aware of the well-being or of the sadder state of other individuals. With a larger group, voluntary redistribution is likely to become less efficient or effective because individuals may not have information about the well-being of others. Accordingly we can proceed from a theory of individual interdependence to a theory of systemic interdependence. An individual associates certain values with his community, his city, and his nation-state. Under the impact of nationalism, for example, an

---

4 The formal theorem postulating this result was named the Boulding Optimum in view of Kenneth Boulding's early formulation of the mixed motive behavior. K. E. Boulding, "Notes on a Theory of Philanthropy," in F. G. Dickenson, ed., *Philanthropy and Public Policy* (New York: National Bureau of Economic Research, 1962), pp. 57–72.

individual may be willing to undertake considerable sacrifices to achieve a collective good. One type of sacrifice is the transfer of income to others who are considered by the collective authority to be worse off than this particular individual. But essentially we could view systemic interdependence as an extension of individual interdependence; we could argue that the willingness to transfer, either privately or publicly through the tax-transfer system, is a function of the degree of integration of a particular society.[5]

The second motive of voluntary redistribution presumes *selfish* behavior as the motivator of transfers. Individuals may be willing to forgo income to insure against drastic losses of income in the future, which might result from social pressure, upheaval, revolution, and so on. Accordingly we may view transfers from high-income individuals to low-income individuals as a form of insurance premium. Such a premium is not necessarily a forced transfer paid by the higher income individual because of his perception of the pressure exerted against him at the present time. It is simply a precautionary move to forestall possible changes in the future.

2. From the concept of transfers as insurance payments to the concept of outright *involuntary* or *forced transfers* is only a small step. Involuntary redistribution generally takes place from the poor to the rich or to the middle class, or from the middle class to the rich; but it could also take place from the wealthy to the poor, in which case it would represent the pressure of the many against the few or of the have-nots against the haves. Several theories of voting behavior suggest that insofar as the majority of voters in the system are likely to be poorer than the rich minority, they probably will use political power to extract economic benefits.

The political economy of redistribution, however, comes fully into its own in those areas that use *political power* not only as an *ameliorative* device equalizing income between the rich and the poor but, on the contrary, as an *exploitative* device leading to the transfer of income from the poor to the middle class, or from the middle class to the wealthy.

Depending upon the degree to which we are willing to associate the power to compel or to exploit with a particular group, clique, or entire class, we could postulate different sociological theories of the political economy as related to the distribution of income and property. Perhaps it suffices to identify three points on this continuum:

a. The *interest group theory* relates changes in the distribution of property or income to a structural change in the government. This modern theory dates from the work of James Harrington,[6] although it proceeds from the American Founding Fathers, particularly from James Madison, to some of the modern

---

5 Empirical evidence in support of this thesis may be found in the work of Günter Schmölders, *Finanz und Steurpsychologie* (Reinbeck bei Hamburg: Rowohlt Taschenbuch-verlag Gmbh., 1970), pp. 54–55.

6 J. Harrington, *Oceana*, ed. S. B. Liljergren (Heidelberg: Carl Winters Universitaets Buchhandlung, 1924).

group process theories of government.[7] The group process approach is often cited as the basis of American political reality. Even though Americans did not have the traditional cleavage between nobility and commons, Madison noted other separating factors, specifically property.

> The most common and endurable source of factions has been the various and unequal distribution of property. Those who hold and those who are without property have ever formed distinct interests in society. Those who are creditors and those who are debtors fall under a like discrimination. A landed interest, a manufacturing interest, and many lesser interests grow out of necessity in civilized nations and divide them into different classes, actuated by different sentiments and views.[8]

Madison concluded that none of the interest groups in America held the dominant power. He believed that a "coalition of a majority of the whole society could seldom take place on any other principles than those of justice and the general good."[9]

Alternatively we could postulate that the pattern of transfers and redistribution that characterizes the American economy of today consists of the patchwork of transfers made in response to the pressures exerted by particular interest groups. At some stage in history one group was stronger than another, and therefore the stronger group managed to subvert the public good for its particular interests. The tax laws, for example, represent this kind of subverted interest. Similarly we can view the whole gamut of exemptions and deductions, which partly make a mockery out of the progressivity of the tax rate schedule, as a product of the push and pull of various interest groups striving for a place in the power structure and using their influence on governmental power to achieve it. In a pluralistic setting groups may exercise a check on the striving of others, yet they may not be entirely successful in securing the public interest at the cost of the particular interest of special groups; groups are more likely to cooperate in order to secure for one another advantages out of the common treasure.

b. C. Wright Mills has challenged the pluralist interpretation of the American power system, which is postulated as a decentralized system of decision making whereby the self-interest of opposing processes leads to a check and balance.[10] Mills postulates that a power elite is in charge of the "command posts" of the three institutional complexes that determine the affairs of America – the national government, the national military apparatus, and the national economy. He defines the power elite as "those political, economic, and

---

7 See, for example, D. Truman, *The Governmental Process* (New York: Alfred A. Knopf, 1951).

8 *The Federalist*, no. 51.

9 *The Federalist*, no. 51.

10 C. W. Mills, *The Power Elite* (New York: Oxford University Press), 1956.

military circles which as an intricate set of overlapping cliques share decisions having at least national consequences."[11] He further notes that:

> . . . there is no longer, on the one hand, an economic, and, on the other hand, a political order containing a military establishment unimportant to politics and to money making. There is a political economy linked, in a thousand ways, with military institutions and decisions. On each side of the world-split running through Central Europe and around the Asiatic rimlands, there is an ever-increasing interlocking of economic, military, and political structures. If there is government intervention in the corporate economy, so is there corporate intervention in the governmental process. . . . In the 19th century, when the scale of all institutions was smaller, the liberal integration was achieved in the automatic economy, by an autonomous play of market forces, and in the automatic political domain by the bargain and the vote. It was then assumed that out of the imbalance and friction that followed the limited decisions then possible a new equilibrium could in due course emerge. It can no longer be assumed, and it is not assumed by the men at the top of each of the three dominant hierarchies.[12]

Mills also postulates that income and wealth and a man's position in society are determined by his position in this political economy. This power elite can become the visible substitute for the invisible hand, which Adam Smith postulates as the automatic regulator of the pure market economy. In terms of the effect of income distribution, Mills states that "the very rich have used existing laws, they [have] circumvented and violated existing laws, they have had laws created and enforced for their direct benefit,"[13] and "a combination of 'tax write-offs' and capital gains has helped the accumulation of private fortunes."[14]

In terms of Mills' theory of the power elite, then, we can explain the allocation of grants, and particularly their regressive characteristics, by the power elites' abuse of power. This abuse is more flagrant in the case of the very rich. We will see that grants or benefits are implicit in the policy of the government, which keeps hands off from the wide variety of practices that result in enormous incomes to the rich. Furthermore the wealthy derive benefits also in the form of explicit transfers.

> In understanding the private appropriations of the rich, we must also bear in mind that the private industrial development of the United States has been much underwritten by outright gifts out of the public domain. State, local, and federal governments have given land free to railroads, paid for the cost of ship building and for the transportation

---

11 *Ibid.*, p. 18.
12 *Ibid.*, pp. 7–8.
13 *Ibid.*, p. 99.
14 *Ibid.*, p. 100.

of important mail. Much more free land has been given to businesses than to small, independent homesteaders. Coal and iron have been legally determined not to be covered by the "mineral" rights held by the government on the land it leased. The government has subsidized private industries by maintaining high tariff rates, and if the taxpayers of the United States had not paid, out of their own labor, for a paved road system, Henry Ford's astuteness and thrift would not have enabled him to become a billionaire out of the automobile industry.[15]

Ferdinand Lundberg holds a similar theory of the power abuses by the rich and the "super-rich," particularly through their ability to manipulate the public grants economy.[16]

c. At the other end of the continuum are Karl Marx's and Friedrich Engels' classical class theories of exploitation. A Marxist theory of the grants economy would postulate that the bourgeois capitalist state is simply an instrument of the ruling class, aiming at the repression of the exploited segments of society. Just as the capitalist exploits the worker by appropriating his surplus — that is, by paying him subsistence level wages and not the full value of his productive effort — the capitalist state expropriates part of the surplus in the form of taxes and uses the expenditure powers of the state to redistribute the surplus to the capitalist class. Marx's concept of the ruling class certainly is a step removed from Mills' power elite. Mills does not believe that only an economic group constitutes the ruling class, and he does not accept the view that "high economic men, unilaterally, make all decisions of national consequence."[17] Furthermore, a Marxist theory is a great step removed from the more modern interest group theories whereby all groups in society exercise power.

Whether we recognize a relative autonomy of political and military institutions from the economic institutions or whether we postulate a more complex intertwining with either economic or any other institution as the dominant group in society, we could postulate nonetheless a pattern of redistribution that does not necessarily go from the rich to the middle class, or from the middle class to the poor.

What then is the political economic message and the overall implication of this volume? If we analyze the role of the public grants economy in terms of its contributions to income redistribution and equity, we must no doubt recognize many perverse patterns. Results that are not generally believed to hold true appear to exist. But in fact the investigator's philosophical point of view determines how he views this perverse pattern of redistribution. He may consider it a result of unchecked maneuvering of interest groups, which at some stage or other appear to cut themselves a large share of the public pie. Or he may view the regressivity of many observed patterns as a result of the power elite's exercise of social power that might be constituted of economic, military, or

---

15 *Ibid.*

16 F. Lundberg, *The Rich and the Super-Rich* (New York: Bantam Books), 1968.

17 Mills, *op. cit.*, p. 277.

governmental institutions. Or, finally, if he accepts the class theory of society, he may explain the regressivity by the unequal distribution of property, which, by its implication of unequal distribution of power, leads also to an inequitable distribution of public transfers. In this sense, then, not only is inequality of power expressed through monopoly relations that disturb the income distribution wrought by market forces, but it also succeeds in using the very corrective instruments fashioned to produce presumably more desirable — that is, more equitable — results.

Whatever one's preference for a social theory, the analysis in any case is bound to be damning for a society that prides itself to be "the land of the free and the home of the brave."

We make no attempt to pursue this theme at any great length at every instant of the analysis. Our focal point centers rather on a definitional scheme based on several conceptual distinctions that identify the various components of the grants economy.

The private versus the public grants economy focuses on the traditional distinction between individuals and families, corporations, foundations, and other nonprofit institutions on the one hand and the government sector on the other. The nonprofit institutions are "private" only in the sense that they are not explicitly within the realm of government. Most transfer payments have significant "public" consequences. For example, a foundation grant is either a private or a public financial transaction. In the domain of the public grants economy again we may use several definitions. Narrow definitions focus on explicit transfers, whereas broader definitions recognize the existence of implicit transfers and consider general public expenditures as transfers in kind. However, not only is this spectrum of definitions contingent on the investigator's breadth of view in distinguishing phenomena that lie between transfer and exchange, but it also depends on the degree of disaggregation employed to view the nonexchange or the nonmarket relations between economic and social actors. For example, if we were to adopt the framework underlying the national income accounts, the personal sector would hide many transfer relationships between families and nonprofit institutions, including foundations. Similarly we could break down other aggregates further to identify internal nonexchange relations among their component individuals or groups. In this volume we attempt to provide broad outlines of public explicit transfers in cash and kind as well as implicit transfers, which generally assume the character of tax reductions or of some benefit expressed in economic terms. The primary focus is on the expenditure side of the public budget. Many studies in the area of public finance and taxation stress the distributive effect of taxation itself. Hence we can place greater weight on the expenditure side. (On the other hand one paper we have included relates also to taxation in kind.)

In covering the range of public transfers we generally abstain from including economic rents within the scope of the grants economy. Thus we have not counted monopoly rents accruing to private enterprises as being part of the grants economy, although they might very well be treated as "forced transfers."

We followed this approach simply because of the difficulty in assessing empirically the sum total of deviations from an abstract competitive market norm. (On the other hand the paper relating to the distributive effect of the conscription tax discusses both the narrow definition, which reflects the implicit assumption that the confiscation of economic rent does not constitute taxation, and the broad definition, which takes the opposite point of view.)

Given these conceptual premises we have arranged the material in the following fashion: The introductory Part 1 provides two overviews of the explicit grants economy. Robert Lampman focuses on one large subset that consists of public transfer payments and public subsidies together with private inter- and intrafamily transfers. He omits consideration of general expenditures, which, no doubt, contain grant and exchange equivalents. Henry Aaron and Martin McGuire's challenge to traditional techniques of allocation rests on the explicit use of utility functions for income. Their results cast doubt on the validity of previous studies and set the tone for other papers concerned with equity implications of public expenditures.

Part 2 investigates explicit public grants in further detail. Benjamin Okner focuses on public transfer payments of various types; he is specifically concerned with the poverty-reducing effect of these transfers. A series of papers investigate in further detail the distributive effects of public expenditures. Lee Hansen and Burton Weisbrod (with Robert Hartman's comment) and Charles Schultze deal with the effects of transfers on certain key processes – welfare policy, higher education, and farm subsidies. Among the last three papers Roy Bahl and Jeremy Warford employ the geographic dimension for a study of distributive effects; they study the effect of federal aid on rich and poor states. Similarly Patricia Horvath and John Burke estimate the distributive effect of research and development funding across states. Finally Bruce Stuart examines the impact of Medicaid on interstate income differentials.

Part 3 is concerned with the relatively neglected area of implicit public grants and implicit taxes. Implicit public grants arise through the tax system, through public fiscal and monetary policies, through taxation in kind, and through administrative procedures. In the area of taxes Gabriel Rudney introduces the overall magnitude of these implicit public grants called *federal tax aids* by various budget items. Martin and Anita Pfaff, in turn, look at the distributive effects of implicit public grants as resulting from the federal individual income tax system. The next two papers center on particular aspects of a market society – home ownership and property ownership. Henry Aaron looks at the distributive effects of implicit public grants under the federal law favoring home ownership, and Thomas Muller treats explicit public grants that arise from the provisions of the local tax law as well as from their administration in a specific instance. Robinson Hollister and John Palmer view the distributive consequences of public policies, specifically of the fiscal and monetary policies employed as anti-inflationary measures. They are concerned with the effect that inflation – or its complement, unemployment resulting from recessions – has on the income shares of the poor. Lestor Thurow, in turn, traces the effects of a variety of public policy instruments on black and white income equalization. As an example of taxation in kind, Larry Sjaastad and Ronald Hansen view the distributive consequences of the draft system.

Part 4 draws certain conclusions for general redistribution policy. Empirically founded explicit equity norms provide the main instrument for rational redistribution. These may be break-even income levels or poverty standards below which an individual or family is qualified for public support as a matter of right, as in the various income maintenance plans. Or they may be equity rules that modify the allocation of private and public resources.

Martin David and Jane Leuthold describe the basic concepts and the distributional impact of several income maintenance proposals. Lampman and Okner both discuss newer transfer plans. Martin McGuire and Harvey Garn demonstrate, in turn, how equity criteria can be traded off against efficiency criteria in the selection of public projects. Finally Hollister and Palmer point out some consequences of the implicit tax levied on various groups by inflation and unemployment.

In the concluding Part 5 Michael Taussig takes the long-run view and paints a broad picture of the economic and social consequences of the public grants economy. Based on some of the preliminary results of the New Jersey experiments, which, among other considerations, examine the effects of transfers on work behavior, Taussig dispels some fears while pointing out some of the dangers that arise from other aspects of the present grants economy or from some of the alternatives for income maintenance discussed in this volume. Kenneth Boulding and Martin Pfaff sound the concluding note by sketching some further routes and future directions in the exploration of the domain of income redistribution.

1

An Overview

Treatises on public finance traditionally maintain that the public economy has as a major function the modification of income inequality brought about by the market economy and that the system of taxes and public expenditures serves to bring about, at least to a significant degree, such a reduction of inequality. Henry Aaron and Martin McGuire challenge this image, and the writers of many subsequent papers cast doubt on the validity of previous studies. Even for those parts of the public transfers system that are heavily redistributive toward the poor, Robert Lampman observes several "biases" that may not conform to the prevailing images.

A concern with alternative views and definitions of the quantitative significance of nonmarket flows or unilateral transfers – termed *the grants economy* – sets the tone for the general overview. The empirical scope of the grants economy is dependent on the *breadth of view* of the investigator or on his willingness to include some transactions under the rubric "grants,"[1] which also have a significant exchange character. In this vein we can classify some public expenditures as either grants or exchange transactions. Ideally we should analyze flows of economic exchangeables and isolate their exchange and grants components. In practice this undertaking proves difficult, although not impossible. Robert Lampman treats only social welfare expenditures and subsidies as transfers. Alternatively we could treat the role of the whole government budget – the tax burdens and the benefits conveyed by public expenditures – as being outside the market economy.

A second dimension for the assessment of the size of the public grants economy rests on the *depth of the definition* – that is, the level of disaggregation employed to assess transfer relations between institutional actors. The more disaggregated a view we take the larger the magnitude of transfer relations will be. They "cancel out" in the process of aggregation, simply because A's receipt of a positive transfer (= grant), equals B's loss (= tax). Part 1 is concerned, however, with relatively highly aggregated patterns, whereas Parts 2 and 3 delve into the relationships between institutional actors or programs, at less aggregated levels.

---

1 We shall use the terms *grants* and *transfer* interchangeably in this book.

Within these definitional differences, Lampman's main focus is on the poverty-reducing effect of the private and public grants economy. He notes that "the increases in money transfers have largely been directed at the pretransfer nonpoor. Of course, the number of people counted as poor has declined dramatically — from 23 percent of the population in 1959 to 12 percent in 1968 — apparently because of the rising wage rates and improved employment opportunities for low-income people." He notes further that of the 16.1 million pretransfer poor families in 1966, 6.1 million were taken out of poverty. Of the 10.0 million families that remained poor even after the receipt of transfers, the mean poverty-income gap had been reduced to $970 (compared to a similar gap of $1,500 for the entire population of 16.1 million pretransfer poor families). He goes on to point out several "biases" of transfers: The aged and family heads who worked very little are among the groups most favored, whereas nonwhites, families headed by women, families of three or more persons, and families in the South are among the groups least favored by the transfer system. On the whole, Lampman concludes, however, that "money transfers . . . added substantially to the income of the poor in 1967." Benjamin Okner takes up this idea in Part Two.

Previous estimates of the distributive role of the government contain an implicit utility function for evaluating the benefits of government expenditures across income classes: The tacit assumption is that marginal utility of income is constant across income levels. Henry Aaron and Martin McGuire question the validity of such an assumption. By making benefit distributions on the basis of two admittedly arbitrary utility functions and on the basis of alternative assumptions on the allocation of specific goods, they conclude:

1. "The results cast doubts on the findings of previous studies that the combined incidence of taxes and expenditures on income distribution is progressive — that is, tending to reduce inequality."

2. "[The analysis] shows an extreme sensitivity in the distribution of public goods benefits to the rationale underlying that distribution. Benefits for the lowest income brackets, for example, range from negligible to substantial, and benefits for upper income brackets may also vary by large amounts, depending on the choice of utility function. In the middle brackets there is less, but still considerable, sensitivity."

3. "Many households with money incomes less than $3,000 are receiving much smaller subsidies than aggregate estimates suggest, and . . . they may even be paying a substantial implicit tax — that is, paying taxes, direct and imputed, greater than the value of government goods and services received."

4. A similar pattern arises in the case of education "with respect to middle and upper income groups and to a lesser extent, along different patterns in each case, for other outlays."

Even at the highly aggregative level of the overview in Part One the image of the redistributive role of the grants economy is thus challenged: Far from being a major force tending to modify substantially the inequalities of income generated by the market economy, the public grants economy may in fact act as a palliative at best or exacerbate inequalities at worst. We pursue this theme at a lower level of aggregation in Part Two.

1

Robert Lampman: Public and Private Transfers As Social Process

There are two ways to alter the pattern of economic inequality among persons. One is to modify the distribution of factor income by changing the underlying distribution of factors or the prices of employment of those factors. The second is to modify the process by which factor income is redistributed away from its recipients. This paper is about the second way. We ask how the distribution to factor owners is and can be modified as income moves from its market origins to its disposition on goods and services. At the outset we sketch an accounting framework within which to envision this process whereby "producer incomes" are transformed into "user incomes."

The Process of Redistribution

The redistributive process involves receipts and payments of both a money and a nonmoney character. It occurs through private as well as public institutions, including the employer, the government agency, the private insurance carrier, the private philanthrophic agency, and the family. Two types of redistributional transaction are involved: *transfer* and what we may call *distributive allocation*. Table 1 (see list of items and column 1; ignore columns 2 and 3 for the moment) sketches out the elements of and offers rough estimates of the amounts involved in this process, which may be said to start with subsidy to factor incomes. It continues with public subsidies to consumers, money transfers, and distributive allocations, and with private gifts, transfers, and distributive allocations. Our accounting includes the payments for pure public goods but, in effect, excludes the benefits of those goods on the grounds that such benefits are indivisible and hence not redistributive. It also excludes those merit-want goods, which are produced in the public sector but are purchased on a user-charge or benefits-received basis and hence, like most private purchases, have no important redistributive effect.

Table 1. Public and Private Transfers and Distributional Allocations Received and Paid by All Households and by Pretransfer Poor Households, 1967

	All Households (Billions of Dollars) (1)	Pretransfer Poor Families	
		Percent of Column 1 (2)	Billions of Dollars (3)
1. Preredistribution income (factor income net of 2 and employer financed part of 9)	644	3	19.3
2. Increase in factor income due to direct subsidy	1	10	0.1
3. Reduction in market price due to direct consumer subsidy	1	10	0.1
4. Benefits of social welfare expenditures under public programs	100	40	40.1
a. Social insurance	37	50	16.5
b. Public aid	9	93	8.4
c. Veterans	7	46	3.2
d. Other welfare services and public housing	3	50	1.5
e. Health	8	50	4.0
f. Education	36	18	6.5
5. Total of 2–4	102	39	40.3
6. Taxes, user charges, fees, and public prices used to finance 5	102	9	9.2
7. Public transfers and distributional allocations net of 6	0	—	31.1
8. Income after public transfer and distributional allocation (1 + 7)	644	8	50.8
9. Privately insured benefits related to health and income maintenance	17	5	0.9
10. Direct interfamily gifts	10	50	5.0
11. Gifts via philanthropic institutions	3	33	1.0
12. Total of 9–11	30	23	6.9
13. Family and employer payments for insurance, gifts by family	30	5	1.5
14. Private transfers and distributional allocations less 13	0	—	5.4
15. Income after public and private transfer and distributional allocation (1 + 7 + 14)	644	9	55.8
16. Benefits of general government activity	100	8–9*	8–9*
17. Taxes to pay for 16	100	7	7
18. Benefits of 16 less taxes of 17	0	—	1–2
19. Postredistribution income (1 + 7 + 14 + 18)	644	9	56.8–57.8
20. Allocations other than 4 or 16 through government having no redistributive impact†	—	—	—
21. Allocations through private sector other than 12 having no redistributive impact			

    * Distributed so as to not alter distribution of income. Note pretransfer poor have 8 percent of item 8 and 9 percent of 15.

    † Omitted on grounds that these are like private nonredistributional allocations.

As seen in Table 1, the items that intervene between preredistribution income and postredistribution income all have a positive and a negative side. Receipts by one family are canceled out by payments made by others. Hence, items 7, 14, and 18 will be zero in value for the nation as a whole. However, an individual family may have either a positive or a negative balance in any one of these items and may gain or lose in the conversion from pre- to postredistribution income. The ranking of families and the overall inequality may be markedly different in the two distributions.

The intermediate income concepts shown in the table are of interest. For example, we might want to know how the public policies reflected in items 5 and 6 alters the preredistribution income, and we therefore might look to item 8. Or we might want to investigate the effect of private activities as indicated by items 14 and 15.

Several conceptual issues surround this accounting scheme. One issue has to do with the inclusion of nonmoney items. Can we say that the purchase by a public agency of health care for a citizen is not only an allocation but also a "distributive allocation" or "transfer-in-kind"? Does it constitute an addition to "income" for the recipient rather than (or as well as) an investment in his future productivity? My answer to these questions is yes, but I must admit that drawing the line between what is and what is not an in-kind transfer to persons is hard. The line has to do with the distinction between merit wants and social wants, which, as Richard Musgrave puts it, depends on whether the want can be satisfied for one person exclusively. It has to do with Ida C. Merriam's definition of "social welfare expenditures" as those that are directly concerned with income security and the health, education, and welfare of individuals and families but exclusive of communitywide utilities and services — such as water and sewer works, urban transportation, or public recreational facilities.[1]

Another conceptual issue has to do with insurance. Should private and social insurance for health care and income maintenance be included? Is the purchase of insurance something that should be accounted for as a simple allocation, like the purchase of postage stamps or automobiles and hence excluded from Table 1? In one view the benefit is realized at the time that pure insurance (disregarding cash values) is purchased. One buys protection against risk and gets his money's worth even though he never has a claim. Transfer or subsidy might be said to arise only if premiums are not correctly adjusted to variations in risk or to size of potential benefits. However, insurance is distinguishable from family saving, which we include here only if it is transferred from one family to another by gift. The insurance intermediary, whether it be a private company or a government agency, does something a family cannot do in pooling risk and thereby converting factor income into payments that respond to stated contingencies rather than to accumulated contributions. Moreover,

---

1 I. C. Merriam and A. M. Skolnik, *Social Welfare Expenditures under Public Programs in the United States (1929-66)*, Research Report No. 25 (Washington, D.C.: Office of Research and Statistics, Social Security Administration, 1968), p. iii.

insurance benefits often flow to persons quite remote from the purchasers, who may be employers or general revenue taxpayers. For these reasons, insurance benefits and contributions paid in the last year are included in the accounting of distributive allocations of that year.

To answer key questions we must have some limits for the terms *transfer* and *redistribution*. We propose to limit those terms to changes in the distribution of income among families, assuming that factor income as it arises in the market is given. Further, we propose to define income to include certain in-kind items that relate directly to family health, education, and welfare and to account for gifts, contributions, and taxes paid out by families for such transfers. We would isolate transfer for purposes of health, education, and welfare from the much broader concepts of Boulding and Martin Pfaff,[2] who suggest that all one-way transactions, including those for all functions of government, fall under the heading of transfer. Our concept stems from a view of a necessary minimum of interpersonal transfer. To perpetuate itself each society must invent ways to shift a substantial part of its yearly output away from those who may be said to have produced it, to others. In simple societies the family manages the defense against want, insecurity, ignorance, and illness. In more advanced societies other, intermediating institutions, including the voluntary association, the employer, the insurance intermediary, and the state assist the family in carrying out these defenses. The relocation of responsibility for these defenses does not necessarily connote social progress. Our accounting of the system of transfers should, ideally, be broad enough to encompass the simultaneous decline of one mode of transfer and the rise of another. Conceivably no more transferring goes on in the United States now than did fifty years ago, even though the transfers that enter the national income are a rising proportion of national income. Increase of transfers may reflect greater concern for what Boulding calls integrative processes and a growing sense of community. Alternatively this increase may indicate a conversion from thinking of transfers as inherently defensive and parasitic and likely to diminish in relative importance as a society gets richer, to something more affirmative. Goals in the health, education, and welfare fields have evolved from relief of suffering, rescue from illiteracy, and shielding against poverty to the promotion of positive health and longevity, the cultivation of talent, skill and new knowledge, and the attainment of income security and constant growth in average income.[3]

This statement of goals would indicate that a student of the subdiscipline of the economics of health, education, and welfare is interested in the allocation of

2 K. E. Boulding, "An Invitation to Join a New Association for the Study of the Grants Economy," *ASGE Newsletter No. 1* (mimeographed, October 15, 1969); also Boulding, "The Grants Economy," Presidential address to the Michigan Economic Association, March 22, 1968.

M. Pfaff, "The Grants Economy and the Transfer Economy: Some Basic Concepts," *ASGE Newsletter No. 1* (mimeographed, October 15, 1969).

3 R. J. Lampman, "Toward an Economics of Health, Education, and Welfare," *The Journal of Human Resources* (Summer 1966), pp. 43–53.

resources to achieve aggregative purposes. That is true, but in the present context we want to emphasize the redistributive aspect of that subdiscipline as shown in a one-year accounting of changes in "income" sharing.

Benefits and Losses from Redistribution

Having resolved the issue of what is being redistributed and how, we turn now to the matter of who receives how much benefit and who loses how much, from redistribution. One may rank families by total monthly income and measure how the share of income received by income-bracket groups changes as we move from one concept of income to another. W. Irwin Gillespie (see Table 2) moves from factor income (roughly the same as item 1 in Table 1) to a postredistributional income, which takes no account of private transfers and distributional allocations.[4] (this income is approximately the same as the sum of items 1, 7, and 18.) Note that Gillespie finds that the share going to those with money incomes under $3,000 is converted from 5 percent to 8 percent in the redistributive process.

Table 2. Distribution of Families and Income, before and after Fiscal Incidence of Federal, State, and Local Government Taxes and Expenditures, by Money Income, 1960

Item	Family Money Income Brackets							
	Under $2,000	$2,000– 2,999	$3,000– 3,999	$4,000– 4,999	$5,000– 7,499	$7,500– 9,999	$10,000 and Over	Total
	(percent)							
1. Families	14	9	9	11	28	15	14	100
2. "Broad income"	2	3	4	7	27	19	39	100
3. "Adjusted broad income"	3	5	5	7	26	20	33	100

Source: W. I. Gillespie, "Effects of Public Expenditures on the Distribution of Income," in R. A. Musgrave, ed., *Essays in Fiscal Federalism* (Washington, D.C.: The Brookings Institution, 1965). Line 1 derived from Table 11; lines 2 and 3 derived from Table 13.

James Morgan, Martin David, Wilbur Cohen and Harvey Brazer document a similar pattern of change (see Table 3).[5] They rerank families each time they change income concept. They show that the degree of inequality is reduced one fifth of the way to zero, by moving from gross factor income (about the same as

---

4 W. I. Gillespie, "Effects of Public Expenditures on the Distribution of Income," in R. A. Musgrave, ed., *Essays in Fiscal Federalism* (Washington, D.C.: The Brookings Institution, 1965), pp. 122–86.

5 J. N. Morgan, M. H. David, W. J. Cohen, and H. E. Brazer, *Income and Welfare in the United States* (New York: McGraw-Hill Book Co., 1962).

item 1 in Table 1) to gross disposable income (similar to item 19). They also portray a significant shift of another one tenth of the way to zero inequality, which is associated with a reranking of families by welfare-ratio – that is, by ` adjusting for family size. A welfare-ratio of unity means that a family is at the poverty line. Similarly Morgan et al. show that the inequality we measure is partly a function of whether we count families "doubled-up" in one household as one or two families. Apparently relatives tend to group together in such a way as to reduce inequality below what we would observe if each adult unit were separately accounted for. Of course, in the study of income redistribution we should know how separate factor incomes are combined into a family-unit-income and how persons who do not receive factor income relate themselves to others who do.

Table 3. Lorenz Coefficients of Inequality for Various Units of Analysis and Measures of Income, 1959

	Families	Adult Units
Gross factor income	.419	
Less: Imputed rent of homeowners		
Less: Home production		
Plus: Regular money transfers		
=Money income	.385	
Less: Federal income taxes		
=Disposable money income	.355	
Plus: Imputed rent of homeowners		
Plus: Home production		
Plus: Nonmoney and irregular transfers including food and housing provided by relatives		
=Gross disposable income	.346	
Divided by budget standard		
=Welfare ratio	.309	.346

Source: J. N. Morgan, M. H. David, W. J. Cohen, and H. E. Brazer, *Income and Welfare in the United States* (New York: McGraw-Hill, 1962). Derived from Table 20–2, p. 315.

Table 4 shows Morgan and his colleagues' finding that what they call "net transfer," which takes account of only some items in Table 1 – nonfamily transfers plus public school benefits, les income and property taxes (note that they find the latter to be nonredistributive) and nonfamily contributions - amounted in 1959 to 26 percent of the gross disposable income of families below the poverty line.

By making use of the findings presented in the Morgan book and in the studies by Irwin Gillespie, Mollie Orshansky, Nelson McClung, Irene Lurie, Benjamin Bridges, and others and by reference to some preliminary findings from the Survey of Economic Opportunity, we can put together rough estimates

Table 4. Specific Transfers as Percentage of Gross Disposable
Income of Adult Units and Families Classified by Welfare-Ratio, 1969

Transfer Items	.0–0.8	0.9–1.2	1.3–1.6	1.7–2.2	2.3 and Over	All Units
			Welfare-Ratio			
A Adult units						
Nonfamily transfers	26	12	9	6	5	8
Income tax	−1	−5	-9	−11	−19	−12
Nonfamily contributions	−4	−4	−4	−4	−7	−5
B Families						
Property tax	−2	−2	−2	−2	−2	−2
Public school benefits	13	7	4	3	1	4
Net transfer	26	7	−2	−7	−18	-6

Source: Morgan et al., *Income and Welfare in the United States, op. cit.* Panel A
derived from Table 16–23, panel B   derived from Tables 19–5 and 19–13.

of the amount of redistribution to the pretransfer poor in 1967.[6] These
estimates are reported in the right-hand columns of Table 1. The figures show
that the whole array of public and private givings and takings raised the share of
pretransfer poor families from 3 percent of preredistribution income to 9
percent of postredistribution income (see items 1 and 19). Public transfers
(positive and negative) and distributional allocations raised the share from 3
percent to 8 percent (item 8); private transfers and allocations raised it to
9 percent (item 15); and taxes for pure public goods raised it by less than 1
percent, so the share remains at about 9 percent (item 19). This gain in share was
accomplished by an offsetting decline in share of income on the part of the
pretransfer nonpoor families.

Instead of showing how income distribution is modified by redistributive
institutions with respect to those in income brackets or welfare-ratio groupings
(of which poor-nonpoor is a variant), one could show income redistribution with
respect to age, sex, color, region, occupation, family size, home ownership
status, health status, labor force status, educational level, or other characteristics
of income recipients. Another method of presentation is to show how a
particular item – for example, income tax – alters distribution among successive
groupings of the population. The Treasury Department recently advocated this
method.[7]

Table 1 suggests the range of approaches for redistributing income to any of
the aforementioned groupings. These approaches include subsidies at the factor

6 This term refers to those persons who have money incomes below the Social
Security Administration poverty guidelines before the receipt of money transfers.

7 J. W. Barr, Secretary of the Treasury, Statement before Joint Economic Committee
of the Congress (January 17, 1969). See especially supplementary statement on "Tax
Expenditure: Government Expenditures Made Through the Income Tax System."

income level and in consumer markets, public and private transfers and distributional allocations, and, on the other side of the ledger, taxes, insurance premiums, and gifts.

Most of these methods have been increasing in quantitative importance over the years.[8] Social welfare expenditures under public programs (item 4 in Table 1) have been rising 10 percent or more per year and now amount to 14 percent of gross national product. The increase in the national redistributional effort as indicated by this rise is not having a maximum impact on the number of people counted in poverty or on the size of the poverty-income gap, because many of the greatest rises have been in such nonmoney items as schooling and health care.

However, the cash benefits in this series (see the right-hand section of Table 5) have been rising in step with the total; in 1968 they added up to almost $50 billion. Since these cash benefits are the only public expenditures, other than "direct subsidies to increase factor incomes," which immediately enter into total money income, and because the poverty line is stated in terms of pre-income tax total money income adjusted for family size, they would seem to have unique relevance out of all the items in Table 1 to the question of poverty reduction. It does seem ironic that cash benefits went up from under $25 billion

Table 5. Social Welfare Expenditures Under Public Programs
(Total, and Cash Benefits Under Public Income Maintenance Programs),
for Selected Years, 1940—68

		Cash Benefits Under Public Income Maintenance Programs (In Billions of Dollars)					
Year	Total (In Billions of Dollars)	Total	Retirement, Disability and Survivors	Unemployment	Temporary Disability	Workmen's Compensation	Public Assistance
1940	8.8	4.2	0.8	0.5	—	0.2	1.0
1950	23.5	8.7	4.3	1.5	0.1	0.4	2.4
1960	52.3	25.9	8.2	3.0	0.4	0.9	3.3
1963	66.8	32.4	24.1	2.9	0.4	1.1	3.6
1967	99.7	42.6	33.4	2.4	0.5	1.4	4.9
1968	112.0	48.2	38.0	2.4	0.5	1.6	5.7
1969	126.8						

Sources: Column 1, I. C. Merriam and Alfred M. Skolnik, *Social Welfare Expenditures under Public Programs in the United States (1929—66)*, Research Report No. 25 (Washington, D.C.: Office of Research and Statistics, Social Security Administration, (1968). For 1969, *Research and Statistics Note* (Washington, D.C.: Office of Research and Statistics, Social Security Administration, November 12, 1962). All other columns, *Social Security Bulletin*, September 1969, Table M—1, p. 33.

8 Solomon Fabricant discusses reasons for this trend in "Philanthropy in the American Economy," *Foundation News*, September—October 1969, pp. 173–86.

in 1959 to $43 billion in 1967, while the poverty-income gap fell only from $13.7 billion to $9.7 billion.

Thirty-two percent of all households received a cash transfer in 1965; yet only about 8 percent of all households were kept out of or taken out of poverty status thereby (see Table 6). We do not have a good series on the number of pretransfer poor, but transfers have apparently been taking gradually increasing numbers of households to posttransfer incomes above the poverty line. Using the 1961 Consumer Expenditure Survey data of the Bureau of Labor Statistics, we found that transfers took 4.7 million households out of poverty in that year.[9] Mollie Orshansky arrived at this same number, only for government transfers in 1965 (see Table 6). Irene Lurie found that transfers took 6.1 million households out of poverty in 1966,[10] and we confirm that number by an independent computation based on Survey of Economic Opportunity data.

Table 6. Percent of Households Receiving Selected Transfers and Number of Households Who Would Be Counted Poor but for Transfer, 1965

Transfer Item	Percent of Families Receiving	Number (In Millions of Families) Who Would Be Counted Poor but for Transfer Payments, Out of a Total of 60.4 Million Households
Any payment	32.3	4.7
Social Security	21.5	3.6
Public assistance	4.8	.4
Other	11.2	1.1

Source: M. Orshansky, "The Shape of Poverty in 1966," *Social Security Bulletin*, March 1968, pp. 7–32.

The increases in money transfers have largely been directed at the pretransfer nonpoor. Of course, the number of people counted as poor has declined dramatically -- from 23 percent of the population in 1959 to 12 percent in 1968 – apparently because of rising wage rates and improved employment opportunities for low-income people. The unemployment rate fell from a postwar high of 6.8 percent in 1959 to below 4 percent in 1966 and has stayed there since that time.

The previous discussion is not meant to minimize the importance of money

---

9 R. J. Lampman, "How Much Does the American System of Transfers Benefit the Poor?," in L. H. Goodman, ed., *Economic Progress and Social Welfare* (New York: Columbia University Press, 1966), pp. 125–57. Also available as *Reprint No. 6*, Institute for Research on Poverty.

10 I. Lurie, "Transfer Payments and Income Maintenance," mimeographed Staff Paper for the President's Commission on Income Maintenance Programs, 1969.

transfer in reducing poverty. Money transfers, public and private, added substantially to the incomes of the poor in 1967 (see Table 7). We estimate that about half the total of $59.1 billion of such transfers went to the pretransfer poor. These transfers cut the pretransfer poverty-income gap almost in half,[11] and provided over half the income of the posttransfer poor.

Table 7. Distribution of Pretransfer Income, Money Transfer Benefits and Posttransfer Money Income, by Household Poverty Status, 1967*

	Total Population (Billions of Dollars)	Pretransfer Poor		Posttransfer Poor (Billions of Dollars)
		Percent of Total	Billions of Dollars	
Pretransfer money income	520	3	15.6	7.8
2. Increase in factor income due to subsidy	1.0	10	0.1	–
4. Benefits under social welfare expenditure programs (money only)	42.6	57	24.3	8.1
a. Social insurance	33.2	53	17.7	4.4
b. Public aid	4.9	93	4.5	3.0
c. Veterans	4.5	46	2.1	0.7
9. Private insurance (money only)	10.0	5	0.5	0.2
10. Direct interfamily gifts (money only)	6.0	33	2.0	1.0
11. Gifts via philanthropic institutions (money only)	0.5	33	0.1	0.1
Subtotal of 2, 4, 9, 10, 11	59.1	46	27.0	9.4
Posttransfer money income (pretransfer money income plus subtotal above)	579.1	7	42.6	17.2
Distribution of households (percent)	100	25		15

* Item numbers correspond to items in Table 1.

However, money transfers tend to do more for the better-off poor than for the poorest poor. They also tend to favor small families as opposed to larger families among the poor.[12] This insight into the bias of the existing set of transfer payments has led many people to advocate new kinds of transfers aimed at children in intact families or "the working poor."

---

11 Note that no accounting is made for the possibility that transfers may have induced a reduction in the pretransfer income of some households.

12 To be fair we need to mention that public school benefits and the income tax exemption system modify this bias in money transfers. Lampman, "How Much Does the American System of Transfers Benefit the Poor?," *op. cit.*, pp. 125–57.

Money Transfers, 1966

The most generally understood type of income redistribution is money transfer. Recently available data collected by the Survey of Economic Opportunity enable us to know more than ever before about who receives the several types of public and private transfers listed in Table 8.[13] The total amount of these transfers recorded for 1966 was $39.2 billion, which was 8.5 percent of the total family money income there recorded of $462.1 billion. Out of all the families and unrelated individuals in the nation, 24.9 million, or 40 percent of the total, received a transfer (see Table 9). (Hereafter, the term *families* includes unrelated individuals. This definition corresponds to the "Interview unit" on the SEO files.)

These transfers have great impact on the pretransfer poor families,[14] who numbered 16.1 million in 1966. This group had a mean pretransfer poverty-income gap[15] of $1,500; 12.3 million of these families received a transfer, the

Table 8. Number of Families Receiving Transfers and the Mean Amount of Those Transfers

Item	Pretransfer Poor		Pretransfer Nonpoor		All Families Receiving Transfers	
	Number (In Thousands)	Mean ($)	Number (In Thousands)	Mean ($)	Number (In Thousands)	Mean ($)
All transfers	12,260	1,840	12,651	1,310	24,911	1,570
Social Security	8,846	1,280	5,248	1,170	14,094	1,240
Government pensions	1,382	1,790	1,236	2,250	2,619	2,010
Veterans' pensions	1,518	1,040	1,842	820	3,360	920
Private pensions	1,195	1,300	793	1,400	1,988	1,340
Workmen's compensation	315	1,050	1,713	410	2,028	510
Unemployment insurance	459	510	2,408	380	2,867	400
Public assistance	2,660	1,170	567	760	3,228	1,100
Other transfers	1,329	1,510	1,899	1,600	3,228	1,570

13 U.S. Bureau of the Census, Survey of Economic Opportunity, 1966 and 1967. This survey, sponsored by the Office of Economic Opportunity, was carried out by the Bureau of the Census. A tape, prepared by the Brookings Institution, was released to research agencies, including the Institute for Research on Poverty, in August 1969. The results reported here are the first computed from that tape by the staff of the Institute with the assistance of the Data and Computation Center of the Social Systems Research Institute of the University of Wisconsin. No attempts have been made to correct for under-reporting. Further, the author has made no further study of possible inconsistencies between these data and those from other sources.

14 Throughout this paper, the word *poor* refers to families with incomes below the Social Security Administration guidelines. *Pretransfer poor* families are those that would be counted as poor in the absence of transfer payments.

15 This term is the difference between the poverty-line income for each family size and the actual pretransfer income.

Table 9. Total Money Transfers Received by Families and the Effects of These Transfers on Family Poverty Status, 1966

	No. Families (Millions)	Transfers Received, Total		Poverty-Income Gap, Total	
		No. Families Receiving (Millions)	Total Received ($ Billions)	Pretransfer ($ Billions)	Posttransfer ($ Billions)
All families	61.7	24.9	39.2	–	–
Pretransfer nonpoor	45.6	12.6	16.6	–	–
Pretransfer poor	16.1	12.3	22.6	24.3	1.7
Taken out of poverty by transfers	6.1	6.1	15.8	7.8	–8.0
Posttransfer poor	10.0	6.2	6.8	16.5	9.7

	No. Families (Millions)	Transfers Received, Mean		Poverty-Income Gap, Mean		Income, Mean	
		Families Receiving ($)	All families ($)	Pretransfer ($)	Posttransfer ($)	Pretransfer ($)	Posttransfer ($)
All families	61.7	1,570	640	–	–	6,850	7,490
Pretransfer nonpoor	45.6	1,310	360	–	–	8,980	9,350
Pretransfer poor	16.1	1,840	1,400	1,500	106	850	2,250
Taken out of poverty by transfers	6.1	2,590	2,590	1,280	–1,310	825	3,410
Posttransfer poor	10.0	1,100	680	1,650	970	870	1,550

mean amount of which was $1,840 per recipient; 6.1 million families were taken out of poverty by transfers; and 10.0 million remained poor after transfers, but after transfers the latter group had a mean poverty-income gap of only $970.

The pretransfer poverty-income gap total was $24.3 billion; after transfers the gap was $9.7 billion. Of the total $39.2 billion of transfers, $22.6 billion, or 58 percent, went to the pretransfer poor. This amount, in turn, was divided between those taken out of poverty, who received $15.8 billion by receipt of transfer, and those left in poverty, who received $6.8 billion.

Table 10 gives an insight into the shifting of families by welfare-ratio,[16] which is accomplished by transfers. For example, the number of families having welfare-ratios under 0.5 is reduced from 11,105,000 to 3,224,000. For another example, about 1.8 million families are added to the top welfare-ratio group. Transfers cannot, by definition, raise everyone's income; someone must pay for them, so the welfare-ratio of some families will be reduced. We shall return to this point later in a discussion of taxes and other means of paying for transfers.

Table 10. All Families Ranked by Pretransfer and Posttransfer Welfare-Ratio and Number of Families Receiving Transfers by Pretransfer Welfare-Ratio, 1966

Welfare-Ratio	Families Ranked by Pretransfer Welfare-Ratio (Thousands)	Number of Families Receiving a Transfer (Thousands)	Families Ranked by Posttransfer Welfare-Ratio (Thousands)
Negative	212	110	138
0	4,266	3,907	402
0–.25	4,021	3,514	762
.25–.50	2,666	1,933	1,922
.50–.75	2,472	1,503	3,216
.75–1.0	2,517	1,293	3,573
1.0–1.25	2,809	1,275	3,738
1.25–1.50	2,866	1,145	3,744
1.5–2.0	6,998	2,117	8,297
2.0–3.0	12,755	3,489	13,977
Over 3.0	20,136	4,625	21,948
Total	61,717	24,911	61,717

Table 11 shows how transfers change the mean incomes of those in the several pretransfer welfare-ratio groupings. While the mean income was raised by $640 for all families, it was raised by successively larger amounts for those in the lower welfare-ratio groupings above the zero group. Undoubtedly this pronouncedly propoor effect is the most striking effect observed relative to these transfers.

---

16 A family with income at the poverty line has a welfare-ratio of 1.0. A welfare-ratio of 0.5 means that the family has an income one-half the poverty line for its family size.

Table 11. Mean Pretransfer Income, Mean Amount of Transfer and
Mean Posttransfer Income of All Families, by Pretransfer
Welfare-Ratio, 1966

Pretransfer Welfare-Ratio	Mean Pretransfer Income	Mean Transfer	Mean Posttransfer Income
Negative	$-1,390	$ 750	$- 650
0	30	1,620	1,650
0–25	240	1,840	2,080
.25–.50	900	1,330	2,230
.50–.75	1,660	1,070	2,740
.75–1.0	2,530	760	3,290
1.0–1.25	3,570	700	4,270
1.25–1.50	4,460	560	5,020
1.5–2.0	5,620	370	5,990
2.0–3.0	7,430	340	7,770
Over 3.0	12,530	300	12,840
Total	6,850	640	7,490

Table 12. Pretransfer Poor Families Taken Out of
Poverty by Transfer Having Selected Characteristics,
by Percentage, 1966

Characteristic	Pretransfer Poor Families	Families Taken Out of Poverty by Transfer
Family head 65 or over	50%	70%
Principal earner worked nor more than thirteen weeks during the year	61	69
Family resides in central city or urban fringe of SMSA	55	61
Family head has completed no more than eight grades of schooling	58	56
Family head female	44	35
Family resides in South	36	27
Family head nonwhite	18	8
Family has three or more members	31	19

As previously mentioned, in 1966, 6.1 million families were taken out of poverty by transfers. However, it is interesting to note that the group thus taken out is not representative of the poor before transfer (see Table 12). The groups that appear to be most favored include the aged and the family heads who worked little. By contrast, the groups that are least favored include nonwhites, who make up 18 percent of pretransfer poor families but only 8 percent of those taken out of poverty, families headed by women, families of three or more persons, and families in the South.

We can pursue the extent of these biases of the transfers, first, by looking at the frequency of receipt of transfer and the mean amount of transfer by color and by sex of family head. Table 13 shows that whites have a higher mean

Table 13. Number of Families and Types of Income Received by Color and Sex of Family Head, 1966

Item	Color of Family Head		Sex of Family Head	
	White	Nonwhite	Male	Female
Number of families (in thousands)	55,174	6,543	48,945	12,829
Pretransfer income, mean	7,160	4,280	7,930	2,730
Poverty-income gap, mean (Poverty cutoff level minus pretransfer income)	$−4,430	−1,370	−5,000	−690
Transfer, mean, for those receiving and not receiving transfer	$ 640	560	550	960
Posttransfer income, mean	$7,800	4,840	8,480	3,680

transfer than nonwhites but that women heads have a higher mean transfer than do men. Table 14 shows that nonwhites receive lower mean amounts than do whites of most, but not all, of the several types of transfers. They received a total amount of transfer of $3.7 billion, or a little less than 10 percent of the total. Women heads received a total amount of transfer of $12.3 billion, or about 31 percent of the total.

We get more detail on the differential treatment of nonwhites from Table 15, which shows that transfers fill a smaller share of the poverty-income gap for nonwhites than for whites within welfare-ratio groups. (Compare the numbers in column 5 for whites and nonwhites.)

Families headed by women have a larger share of the poverty-income gap filled by transfers, on the average, than do families headed by men. However,

---

17 We were able to derive considerable information on this relationship from the Survey of Consumer Expenditures of 1961. Those findings are reported in Lampman, "How Much Does the American System of Transfers Benefit the Poor?," *op. cit.*, pp. 125–157.

Table 14. Types of Transfers Received, by Color and Sex of Family Head, 1966

	Color of Family Head				Sex of Family Head			
	White		Nonwhite		Male		Female	
	Number (Thousands)	Mean	Number (Thousands)	Mean	Number (Thousands)	Mean	Number (Thousands)	Mean
All transfers	22,053	$1,610	2,858	$1,280	16,741	$1,610	8,170	$1,500
Social Security	12,850	1,260	1,244	1,010	8,689	1,360	5,405	1,030
Government pensions	2,465	2,040	153	1,490	1,806	2,270	812	1,430
Veterans' pensions	3,098	920	262	920	2,712	930	648	860
Private pensions	1,894	1,360	93	960	1,605	1,410	383	1,050
Workmen's compensation	1,833	510	195	490	1,810	500	218	590
Unemployment insurance	2,484	400	382	390	2,467	390	400	450
Public assistance	2,171	1,060	1,057	1,170	1,466	1,000	1,762	1,180
Other transfers	2,875	1,630	353	1,050	1,840	1,550	1,388	1,590
Amount of Total Transfers Received	$35.5 Billion (91%)		$3.7 Billion (9%)		$26.9 Billion (69%)		$12.3 Billion (31%)	

Table 15. Mean Pretransfer Poverty-Income Gap, Pretransfer Income, Transfer, and Posttransfer Income of All Families, by Pretransfer Welfare-Ratio and by Race, 1966

Pretransfer Welfare-Ratio	(1) Mean Pretransfer Poverty-Income Gap		(2) Mean Pretransfer Income		(3) Mean Transfer		(4) Mean Posttransfer Income		(5) Col. 3 As a Percent of Col. 1	
	W	N	W	N	W	N	W	N	W	N
Negative	$4,030	$4,100	$−1,390	$−1,380	$750	$660	$−640	$−710	19%	16%
0	1,940	2,160	10	100	1,650	1,510	1,660	1,610	85	70
0–.25	1,790	2,480	230	340	1,960	1,190	2,190	1,520	109	48
.25–.50	1,420	1,950	840	1,170	1,480	620	2,320	1,790	104	32
.50–.75	900	1,210	1,560	2,110	1,190	520	2,760	2,630	132	43
.75–1.0	330	430	2,410	3,030	860	320	3,270	3,350	261	74
1.00–1.25	−420	−430	3,520	3,790	770	400	4,280	4,190	−183	−93
1.25–1.50	−1,220	−1,220	4,450	4,510	620	230	5,070	4,740	−51	−19
1.50–2.00	−2,440	−2,290	5,650	5,360	390	240	6,040	5,600	−16	−10
2.00–3.00	−4,450	−4,060	7,470	6,880	350	250	7,820	7,130	−8	−6
Over 3.00	−9,990	−8,450	12,610	11,010	310	160	12,910	11,170	−3	−2
Total	−4,430	−1,370	7,160	4,280	640	560	7,800	4,840	−14	−41

W = White
N = Nonwhite

Table 16. Mean Pretransfer Poverty-Income Gap, Pretransfer Income, Transfer, and Posttransfer Income of All Families, by Pretransfer Welfare-Ratio and by Sex of Family Head, 1966

Pretransfer Welfare-Ratio	(1) Mean Pretransfer Poverty-Income Gap		(2) Mean Pretransfer Income		(3) Mean Transfer		(4) Mean Post-transfer Income		(5) Col. 3 As a Percent of Col. 1	
	M	F	M	F	M	F	M	F	M	F
Negative	$4,310	$2,390	$−1,510	$−650	$710	$930	$ − 800	$ 280	16%	39%
0	2,080	1,910	10	60	1,930	1,370	1,940	1,430	93	72
0−.25	1,980	1,810	260	220	2,100	1,560	2,370	1,780	106	86
.25−.50	1,630	1,360	980	790	1,490	1,140	2,470	1,930	91	84
.50−.75	1,060	760	1,830	1,340	1,080	1,050	2,910	2,390	102	138
.75−1.0	370	270	2,750	1,920	710	890	3,470	2,800	192	33
1.00−1.25	−460	−280	3,860	2,510	640	910	4,500	3,410	−139	−325
1.25−1.50	−1,320	−820	4,790	3,010	510	780	5,300	3,790	−39	−95
1.50−2.00	−2,580	−1,490	5,970	3,520	340	520	6,320	4,040	−13	−35
2.00−3.00	−4,630	−2,900	7,780	4,880	310	560	8,090	5,440	−7	−19
Over 3.00	−10,320	−6,300	13,020	8,160	290	380	13,320	8,550	−3	−6
Total	−5,000	−690	7,930	2,720	550	960	8,480	3,680	11	−139

M = Male
F = Female

Table 17. Number of Families Pretransfer Poor, Posttransfer Poor, and Taken Out of Poverty by Transfers and Mean Pretransfer Income of Pretransfer Poor Families, by Family Size, 1966

Family Size	Number of Pretransfer Poor Families (Thousands)	Number of Posttransfer Poor Families (Thousands)	Number of Families Taken Out of Poverty (Thousands)	Mean Pretransfer Income of Pretransfer Poor Families
1	6,340 (39%)	4,253	2,087 (34%)	$ 390
2	4,847 (30)	1,983	2,864 (47)	570
3	1,487 (9)	898	589 (10)	930
4	998 (6)	746	252 (4)	1,490
5	795 (5)	624	171 (3)	1,720
6	526 (3)	451	75 (1)	2,190
7	507 (3)	475	32 (.5)	2,780
8 or more	652 (4)	583	69 (1)	2,590
Total	16,154 (100)	10,013	6,141 (100)	850

this statement is not true for many of the lowest welfare-ratio groups (see Table 16).

We turn next to the important question of how transfers relate to family size (see Tables 17, 18, and 19).[17] Table 17 shows that relatively few large families are taken out of poverty by transfers. Although families of four or more persons made up 21 percent of the pretransfer poor, they were only 10 percent of the families taken out of poverty.

Table 18 shows that on the average except for families of one person, the share of the poverty-income gap filled by transfers declines as family size increases. For the families with eight or more persons, only 42 percent of the poverty-income gap was filled by transfer. Table 19 shows that transfers vary by family size within welfare-ratio groups but do not appear to be responsive to the needs of the larger families.

The amounts transferred increase with age from a low of $190 for families headed by persons under 25 years to a high average of $1,680 for those headed by persons 65 years or older (see Table 20). Those family heads in the extremes of the age distribution have the greatest poverty-income gaps, or least negative gaps.

Table 21 indicates that transfers to poor families do not vary significantly by years of educational attainment of the family head. However, in the case of the nonpoor, mean transfers rise sharply for the college educated.

Table 18. Mean Pretransfer Poverty-Income Gap, Pretransfer Income, Transfer, and Posttransfer Income of All Families, by Family Size and Pretransfer Poverty Status, 1966

Family Size	(1) Mean Pretransfer Poverty-Income Gap		(2) Mean Pretransfer Income		(3) Mean Transfer		(4) Mean Posttransfer Income		(5) Col. 3 As a Percent of Col. 1	
	P	NP	P	NP	P	NP	P	NP	P	NP
1	$1,200	$−3,790	$ 390	$ 5,450	$1,020	$230	$1,410	$ 5,680	85%	
2	1,440	−6,220	570	8,350	1,940	580	2,510	8,930	135	
3	1,600	−6,710	930	9,280	1,620	390	2,550	9,670	101	
4	1,770	−6,850	1,490	10,140	1,610	260	3,100	10,410	91	
5	2,100	−6,440	1,720	10,320	1,280	230	3,000	10,550	61	
6	2,110	−5,980	2,190	10,340	1,080	290	3,280	10,620	51	
7	2,240	−6,110	2,780	11,530	820	350	3,600	11,880	37	
8 or more	2,390	−5,300	2,590	10,610	1,010	340	3,600	10,950	42	
Total	1,500	−6,100	850	8,980	1,400	360	2,250	9,350	93	

P = Pretransfer Poor
NP = Pretransfer Nonpoor

Table 19. Mean Transfer Received by All Families,
by Pretransfer Welfare-Ratio and by Family Size, 1966

Pretransfer Welfare-Ratio	Family Size							8 or More	All Families
	1	2	3	4	5	6	7		
Negative	$ 650	$1,200	$ 910	$ 760	$ 90	$ 690	$ 70	$ 10	$ 750
0	1,140	2,000	2,250	1,880	2,620	2,370	2,560	2,970	1,620
0–.25	1,210	2,250	2,150	4,700	1,270	1,930	1,050	1,580	1,840
.25–.50	930	1,920	1,580	1,350	1,640	1,210	510	880	1,330
.50–.75	700	1,750	1,430	680	920	720	480	580	1,070
.75–1.0	660	1,340	710	600	650	450	280	310	760
1.0–1.25	460	1,350	920	740	320	320	510	470	700
1.25–1.50	430	1,050	790	390	370	390	230	510	560
1.5–2.0	230	890	410	250	270	160	260	240	370
2.0–3.0	190	550	510	240	180	340	380	220	340
Over 3.0	190	440	260	220	190	300	410	350	300
Total	640	990	560	400	360	410	490	590	640

Weeks worked by the principal earner vary inversely with the share of the poverty-income gap filled by transfers (see Table 22). Over 100 percent of the gap is filled, on the average, for those poor families whose principal earners work no more than 13 weeks in the year; but only 60 percent of the gap is filled for poor families whose principal earners work 40 or more weeks.

Transfers are not responsive to the greater poverty-income gap of the rural areas (see Table 23) and the Southern region (see Table 24).

Table 20. Mean Pretransfer Poverty-Income Gap, Pretransfer Income,
Transfer, and Posttransfer Income of All Families, by Age of
Family Head, 1966

Age of Family Head	Mean Pretransfer Poverty-Income Gap	Mean Pretransfer Income	Mean Transfer	Mean Posttransfer Income
Less than 20	$ −100	$2,080	$ 190	$2,260
20–24	−2,760	5,190	190	5,370
25–34	−4,170	7,340	270	7,610
35–44	−5,130	8,560	320	8,880
45–54	−6,330	9,250	410	9,660
55–59	−5,610	8,050	420	8,480
60–64	−4,230	6,500	920	7,410
65 and over	−530	2,470	1,680	4,140
Total	−4,110	6,850	640	7,490

Table 21. Mean Pretransfer Poverty-Income Gap, Pretransfer Income, Transfer, and Posttransfer Income of All Families, by Years of Schooling Completed by Family Head and by Pretransfer Poverty Status, 1966

Years of Schooling Completed by Family Head	(1) Mean Pretransfer Poverty-Income Gap		(2) Mean Pretransfer Income		(3) Mean Transfer		(4) Mean Post-transfer Income		(5) Col. 3 As a Percent of Col. 1	
	P	NP	P	NP	P	NP	P	NP	P	NP
0–7	$1,600		$ 780	$ 6,640	$1,270	$440	$2,050	$ 7,080	79%	
8	1,460		790	7,470	1,440	450	2,220	7,930	99	
9–11	1,600		900	8,150	1,350	310	2,240	8,460	84	
12	1,420		1,000	8,630	1,580	290	2,580	8,920	111	
13–15	1,170		900	10,270	1,460	310	2,360	10,570	125	
16	1,180		760	12,070	1,950	340	2,710	12,420	165	
Over 16	950		1,100	13,600	1,820	750	2,920	14,350	192	
Total	1,500		850	8,980	1,400	360	2,250	9,350	93	

P = Pretransfer Poor
NP = Pretransfer Nonpoor

Table 22. Mean Pretransfer Poverty-Income Gap, Pretransfer Income, Transfer, and Posttransfer Income of All Families, by Number of Weeks Worked in Past Year by Principal Earner of Family and by Pretransfer Poverty Status, 1966

Weeks Worked by Principal Earner	(1) Mean Pretransfer Poverty-Income Gap		(2) Mean Pretransfer Income		(3) Mean Transfer		(4) Mean Posttransfer Income		(5) Col. 3 As a Percent of Col. 1	
	P	NP	P	NP	P	NP	P	NP	P	NP
None	$1,680		$ 230	$5,230	$1,860	$2,910	$2,090	$8,130	111%	
1–13	1,770		600	5,700	1,390	1,610	1,990	7,310	79	
14–26	1,250		1,210	5,220	1,010	1,080	2,220	6,300	81	
27–39	1,190		1,720	6,220	1,000	680	2,720	6,900	84	
40–49	1,140		2,000	7,450	780	410	2,780	7,850	68	
50–52	1,210		1,840	9,550	650	270	2,500	9,820	54	
In armed forces	700		2,380	7,320	600	270	2,980	7,590	86	
Total	1,500		850	8,980	1,400	360	2,250	9,350	93	

P = Pretransfer Poor
NP = Pretransfer Nonpoor

Table 23. Mean Pretransfer Poverty-Income Gap, Pretransfer
Income, Transfer and Posttransfer Income of All Families,
by Extent of Urbanization of Family Residence

	Mean Pretransfer Poverty-Income Gap	Mean Pretransfer Income	Mean Transfer	Mean Posttransfer Income
Central City, in SMSA	−3,860	6,490	660	7,150
Residence Urban Fringe in SMSA	−5,640	8,520	550	9,070
Urban, Outside SMSA *	−3,540	6,210	770	6,980
Rural, Outside SMSA	−2,440	5,200	640	5,840

Table 24. Mean Pretransfer Poverty-Income Gap, Pretransfer
Income, Transfer and Posttransfer Income of All Families,
by Region of Residence

Region	Mean Pretransfer Poverty-Income Gap	Mean Pretransfer Income	Mean Transfer	Mean Posttransfer Income
Northeast	−4,540	7,260	720	7,980
North Central	−4,250	6,980	580	7,570
South	−3,170	5,960	620	6,580
West	−4,330	7,560	630	8,190

Mentalities That Guide Decision on Money and Nonmoney Transfers

The amounts transferred for health, education, and welfare are substantial. Items 5 and 12 in Table 1 total $132 billion, which was over one fifth of the national income in that year. These amounts have been increasing both absolutely and relatively, and they indicate that the United States is approaching maturity as a welfare state. Decisions have been made in a decentralized fashion as to how the transfer "growth dividend" for each year is to be distributed among the several items in Table 25 and among possible groups of beneficiaries.

There are several ways to describe this process of decision making, but one way is a contest of four competing mentalities, which we can identify as the minimum-provision mentality, the replacement of loss mentality, the horizontal and vertical equity mentality, and the efficiency of investment mentality. The first mentality has traditionally guided public assistance, public housing, and special services for the poor. Here the emphasis is upon the adequacy of the benefit for those individuals unable to provide any part of the necessary item.

Table 25. Public and Private Transfers and Distributional
Allocations Received and Paid by All Families and by
Pretransfer Poor Families, 1967

Items	Money	All Families (In Billions of Dollars) Money and In-kind	Pretransfer Poor Families (% of Col. 2)	(Billions of Dollars)
1. Preredistribution income (factor income net of 2 and employer financed part of 9)		$644	3%	$19.3
2. Increase in factor income due to direct subsidy	1	1	10	0.1
3. Reduction in market price due to direct consumer subsidy		1	10	0.1
4. Benefits of social welfare expenditures under public programs	43	100	40	40.1
a. Social Insurance	33	37	55	16.5
b. Public Aid	5	9	93	8.4
c. Veterans'	5	7	46	3.2
d. Other welfare services and public housing		3	50	1.5
e. Health		8	50	4.0
f. Education		36	18	6.5
5. Total of 2—4		102	39	40.3
6. Taxes, user charges, fees and public prices used to finance 5		102	9	9.2
7. Public transfers and distributional allocations net of 6		0		31.1
8. Income after public transfer and distributional allocation (1 + 7)		644	8	50.8
9. Privately insured benefits related to health and income maintenance	10	17	5	0.9
10. Direct interfamily gifts	6	10	50	5.0
11. Gifts via philanthropic institutions	1	3	33	1.0
12. Total of 9—11		30	23	6.9
13. Family and employer payments for insurance, gifts by family		30	5	1.5
14. Private transfers and distributional allocations less 13		0		5.4
15. Income after public and private transfer and distributional allocation (1 + 7 + 14)		644	9	55.8
16. Benefits of general government activity		100	8–9[a]	8–9[a]
17. Taxes to pay for 16		100	7	7
18. Benefits of 16 less taxes of 17		0		1–2
19. Postredistribution income (1 + 7 + 14 + 18)		644	9	56.8–57.8
20. Allocations other than 4 or 16 through government having no redistributive impact[b]	—	—	—
21. Allocations through private sector other than 12 having no redistributive impact				

[a]Distributed so as not to alter distribution of income. Note pretransfer poor have 6% of item 8 and 9% of 15.

[b]Omitted on grounds that these allocations are like private nonredistributional allocations.

Little attention is paid to the equities vis-à-vis those persons able to pay part of the cost of a minimum provision. The purpose is essentially defensive and crisis oriented.

The replacement of loss mentality finds expression in insurance, both private and social. Here the emphasis is on the sharing of loss without reference to need, but with reference to the several parties' ability to pay and ability to prevent the loss. This mentality traditionally has little concern for the maximum need requiring public assistance but concentrates on irregularities of income or expenditure (as for health) experienced by regular members of the labor force.

The horizontal and vertical equity mentality is most fully developed in the individual income tax. The emphasis is on treating equally individuals at similar stations and narrowing inequality among the groups ranked in a superior to inferior relationship. This mentality comes into direct conflict with the two previously discussed mentalities when a negative income tax is proposed to replace some or all public assistance and social insurance benefits. The advocate of the negative income tax tends to view with horror the categorical exclusions, the abrupt withdrawal of benefits, the high marginal tax rates, and the capricious changes of rank order of families observed in both public assistance and social insurance. On the other hand, advocates of the latter charge that the income tax mentality has no motive power to expand because its goal of narrowing inequality is vague and formless and, to some, alarming.

The fourth mentality is that of efficiency of investment, wherein the goal is not equity but improvement of the quantity or quality of final output. The recipient of the transfer or distributive allocation (for example, a higher education subsidy) is seen as a means to an end (for example, a higher national product in some future year). The issue is not equity in the distribution of the benefits but the relationship between the costs to the society and the benefits that will flow from those costs.

These four mentalities are presently expressed in our system of transfers. None of them speaks to the strong points of any of the others, yet each puts some constraint on the others. Perhaps what we see evolving in this late stage of growth of the national system of transfers is a new balance -- or tension -- among the four mentalities.

2

Henry Aaron and Martin C. McGuire:
Benefits and Burdens of Government
Expenditures

For decades economists have estimated the proportion of the burdens of taxation borne by various income classes or social groups and the proportion of the benefits of government expenditures received by them [see 5 and 7 and references cited therein]. This paper presents a new method for making such estimates in light of recent advances in the theory of public goods. For illustrative purposes, George A. Bishop's estimates, recently published by the Tax Foundation [7], will be used to furnish numerical examples.

Authors of studies of the distributional effects of governmental fiscal operations are driven into countless compromises to obtain any results at all, because comparison of the actual distribution of income with that which would prevail under substantially different government policies is the general equilibrium problem par excellence.

The distributional patterns that such studies reveal are quite similar. First, all such studies estimate what private incomes would be in the absence of both government expenditures and taxes.[1] The basis for such estimates are usually ad hoc and intuitive. For example, the Tax Foundation distributes certain taxes and government expenditures among income classes (the property tax) by housing expenditures, but the connection between housing expenditures and various items in government accounts is loose. The payroll tax in some studies is assumed to be borne by wage earners, in others by employers, in still others by purchasers of commodities. Recent work on the theory of incidence [4] casts considerable doubt on some of the rules of thumb employed in distribution studies, but they will not be treated further here.

Second, none of the studies treat asset-creating expenditures differently from outlays, which provide current goods and services only, even though many governmental expenditures do create assets that yield benefits much beyond the year in which they are purchased. Thus, highway expenditures are assumed to generate benefits in the year of the expenditure, but not later. Although this

From "Public Goods and Income Distribution" by Henry Aaron and Martin C. McGuire, from *Econometrica*, Vol. 38, No. 6, November 1970, pp. 907–20. Reprinted by permission of Econometric Society and the authors. Henry Aaron and Martin McGuire are from the University of Maryland Department of Economics, and Mr. Aaron is also affiliated with The Brookings Institution.

1 The distributional studies referenced do not attempt to solve the general equilibrium problem of closing down governments and reallocating their resources to the private economy. As an approximation, they attempt to estimate for each income class its income before taxes *at the existing equilibrium* and its expenditure equivalent after government disbursement *at the same existing equilibrium.*

problem is serious, no study has attempted to meet it; we shall not deal further with it here.

Third, diverse methods are used to allocate government expenditures, but certain broad patterns emerge.[2] In particular, the necessity arises to distinguish between government expenditures on commonly shared "public goods" and government expenditures on private or specific[3] goods that are apportioned and exhausted among individuals. The benefits of specific goods and transfer payments are allocated on the basis of proxies, which are thought to be distributed among users in the same proportions as specific goods or transfer payments. For example, the benefits of highway expenditures are allocated, as a rule, according to some indicator of highway use, such as personal expenditures on oil or gas. In contrast, the allocation of benefits from those expenditures the government undertakes because the commodities produce major externalities (that is, they are "public goods") entails much greater difficulties. The magnitude of the uncertainty is perhaps best indicated by W. Irwin Gillespie [1], who allocates the benefits from expenditures on national defense, international affairs, space research, and technology alternately by money income, by disposable income, by capital income, and by equal amounts per family. Although his results are acutely sensitive to the choice, Gillespie offers nothing more than a personal preference for disposable income to guide the reader.

This paper presents an alternative approach to the measurement of the benefits and burdens of government expenditures on public goods. To accomplish this end, we need to explore the implications for such estimates of recent work on the theory of public goods [3, 6]. The relevant portions of this work are set forth in sections I and II. In section III the distributional results of applying our approach to Tax Foundation data are compared with the distribution presented by the Tax Foundation itself.

I

How should the value of public goods be imputed to households? Consider a models in which commodities are either pure private goods (goods that are exhaustively apportioned among individuals and produce no external effects) or pure public goods all of which enter the utility function of every person. Assume

---

2 For example, the benefits of education have been allocated on the basis of population, of the number of children, of the income of families with school age children, of education expenses, and of other indicators [7, p. 63]. But because the benefits of education may accrue over several decades, the value of the discount rate implicitly assumed is critical. If savings habits at prevailing rates of return may be taken as prima facie evidence that the time preference of the rich is weaker at the margin than that of the poor, then these methods of allocating the benefits from the public expenditures on education probably overstate the value of benefits accruing to the poor and understate the value of benefits accruing to the rich, at least if the utility functions of the households are taken as indicators of value.

3 We use the term *specific goods* to indicate goods or services produced by governments but are otherwise similar to private goods privately produced – *not* commonly shared but consumed exclusively by their "owner."

that some resources are taxed away from households (thereby diminishing each household's consumption of private goods) and are devoted to the production of public goods. The resulting distribution of public and private goods consumption may be analyzed into two conceptually discrete steps [3, 6]: the first step is an implicit redistribution of private goods or income by taxes and transfers; the second is a purchase of public goods paid for by other taxes levied on each household at a rate equal to its marginal rate of substitution between private and public goods (at the final private-public goods position of the household).

The logic behind this dichotomy is as follows: Assume temporarily that decisions regarding public goods expenditures have been *efficient*, in the usual sense that the sum of the marginal rates of substitution (MRS^i) of all households (i) between the public goods and income (the private goods bundle selected as numeraire) equals the marginal cost of the public goods ($\Sigma MRS^i = MC$). Assume further that each household pays a tax equal to a certain fraction of public expenditures. (Transfer payments are regarded as negative taxes, not as expenditures on public goods.) Let t^i denote the amount that each household pays per unit of public goods. In general, the condition for the efficient allocation of resources to public goods does not require that the tax price or unit tax share of any household equal its marginal rate of substitution ($t^i \neq MRS^i$). All that is required for efficiency is $\Sigma t^i = \Sigma MRS^i = MC$. If, by change, $MRS^i = t^i$ for every household, the situation is called a *Lindahl solution*, named after Erik Lindahl who first described this analogue to market equilibrium in which prices equal marginal rates of substitution. Clearly the Lindahl solution is efficient.

Now, the income value to each household of the public goods equals the product of MRS^i and the amount of public goods. This relation is exactly analogous to the equality between the income value of a private good and the product of quantity times MRS, which each consumer equates to price in the course of maximizing utility. Therefore, if t^i is less (more) than MRS^i the household values the public goods as more (less)[4] than the tax it actually pays out as its share of the cost. This value, of course, does not measure the full *benefits* to each household from public goods production; the full benefits include not only the marginal utility attributable to each unit of public goods but also the consumer surplus on inframarginal units of public goods. Hence, the difference between the household's MRS and the tax it actually pays represents the entire *income redistribution effect* of public goods supply. The decision to produce so much public goods and to levy particular tax rates may be viewed as a decision first to redistribute income by the aforementioned difference and then to levy another set of tax rates such that $t^i = MRS^i$ for every household at the quantity of public goods supplied to all. Once the redistributive transfers are made, no further income redistribution occurs, because each household pays out

---

4 We use the term *value* in its neoclassical sense of exchange value — marginal utility times quantity. This excludes the inframarginal utility gains or consumer surplus included in the "value in use." Of course, in the situation under consideration, individual households cannot exchange the public good.

in taxes an amount equal to the value of the goods received (just as in private markets).

Following this argument a step further, we can see that if too much or too little public goods is supplied, positive and negative transfers will not balance; that is, if too much public goods is supplied, net transfers will be negative. Similarly, if public goods are produced at increasing (decreasing) average cost, the efficiency condition $\Sigma MRS = MC$ obtains while total taxes collected ($\Sigma t^i = MC$) exceed (fall short of) total production costs. In this case, again, the surplus (loss) the government incurs as a result of marginal cost pricing is absorbed as a compensating deficit or surplus in the "redistribution" accounts.

II

The difficulty in measuring the distributional impact of actual taxes and expenditures in practice surpasses that difficulty of the previously described procedure for a variety of reasons. Governments tax citizens not only to produce pure public goods but also to produce and distribute specific goods. The tax bill of each household, however, cannot be separated into identifiable components, one supporting public goods, the other supporting specific goods. Further difficulty arises from the fact that the redistributive element of government budgets can be estimated only as a residual once the income value, to each individual, or public goods, supplied to all, has been estimated.

At this point, we might concede that we do not now possess, and are unlikely to acquire, the knowledge regarding marginal rates of substitution (and, hence, household utility functions) necessary to assign to households the value of public goods. We might, therefore, abandon efforts to measure the distributional effects of public budgets. Or we might make assumptions regarding utility functions and generate estimates, however arbitrary. Past studies have failed to recognize that the estimation of the benefits from government expenditures implies certain implicit utility function applicable at least on the average. Accordingly, we shall make benefit distributions on the basis of two arbitrary utility functions and compare them with the distributions presented in previous studies. To do so, we must make the following assumptions:

1. Each household's marginal rate of substitution between public goods and other goods is known or assumed.
2. The total and marginal cost of public and specific goods is known for all relevant outputs of these goods.

None of the following assumptions is necessary, but we will use them to simplify exposition:

3. All utility functions are identical.
4. All of each public good enters every household's utility function.
5. All households in each income bracket can be represented by the average income level and expenditure mix in that bracket.

6. The marginal cost of public goods equals the average cost at the amount supplied.
7. The actual output of public and specific goods is allocatively efficient so that marginal cost equals the sum of marginal rates of substitution ($MC = \Sigma MRS$).
8. The utilities of public goods and of other goods are independent.

A few comments about some of these assumptions are in order. We could drop any one or all of assumptions 3 through 8 if information that supported some other relation were available or if some other assumption seemed preferable. For example, if assumption 8 were dropped, we would need to specify how private income affects the marginal utility of public goods. To the extent that the utility of public goods rises with private income (defense outlays protect property as well as people), we should impute to the wealthy a larger proportion of public goods benefits. To the extent that the utility of public goods declines with income (public swimming pools mean less to the man who owns a pool than to the man who does not), the reverse is true. On balance, the assumption of independence does not seem unreasonable. Similarly, although assumption 7 keeps computations relatively simple we could drop it, but we would encounter a problem familiar to students of national income: Should we value output at factor cost or at the (different) valuation placed on commodities by households? At this point we shall retain the assumption that all commodities fall neatly into the category of (a) pure private or specific goods or (b) public goods all of which enter everyone's utility function. (We shall relax this assumption later.)

If we employ the preceding assumptions, we may show that *to each household should be imputed a fraction of the total value of the public goods proportional to the reciprocal of its marginal utility of income.* To demonstrate, we use the following symbols:

Y_T^i = total income of household i.

Y_D^i = disposable money income of household i.

Y_S^i, T_S^i = government supplied specific goods income of household i, taxes paid by household i for specific goods.

Y_P^i = public goods income of household i.

Y_M^i = money income of household i in the absence of taxes (including imputed items such as corporate profits and indirect taxes).

T_A^i = actual tax payments of household i (including imputed items).

T_P^i, T_S^i = effective taxes levied on household i for public goods and specific goods respectively. These do not represent observable data.

T_{RE}^i = explicit transfer payments to household i.

T_{RI}^i = implicit transfers to household i. This is the redistributive element in public budgets. T_{RI}^i has the sign of a tax, a receipt being negative, and a payment positive.

C_S^i = the unit cost (assumed constant) of producing specific goods i.

Y_{PG} = total expenditures on pure public goods, which, in turn, equals the physical quantity of public goods (denoted P) multiplied by the average cost of public goods.

These quantities are related to one another by the following identities:

$$Y_T{}^i \equiv Y_D{}^i + Y_S{}^i + Y_P{}^i. \tag{1}$$

This identity states that total income of each household consists of its disposable money income plus the value of the government goods and services that accrue specifically to the household itself and the value to the household of pure public goods.

$$Y_D{}^i \equiv Y_M{}^i - T_A{}^i + T_{RE}{}^i. \tag{2}$$

Disposable income is equal to the difference between pretax income and taxes paid less explicit transfer payments. Both Y_M and T_A include imputed items, such as corporate profits and indirect taxes [1,7].

$$T_S{}^i \equiv Y_S{}^i. \tag{3}$$

$$T_P{}^i \equiv Y_P{}^i. \tag{4}$$

Both T_P and T_S are defined (on the benefit principle) to match exactly the value to the household of public and specific goods received. Therefore, there is no reason to expect actual taxes less transfer payments to equal $T_P{}^i + T_S{}^i$. The difference, $T_{RI}{}^i$, measures the size of income redistribution due to the public goods budget. ($T_{RE}{}^i$ and $T_{RI}{}^i$ properly have different signs because T_{RE} represents an offset to taxes, whereas T_{RI} measures the degree to which net tax payments exceed or fall short of the value of goods and services provided by government to a particular household.)

$$T_A{}^i + T_{RI}{}^i = T_{RE}{}^i + Y_P{}^i + Y_S{}^i \tag{5}$$

$$(T_A{}^i - T_{RE}{}^i) - (Y_P{}^i + Y_S{}^i) + T_{RI}{}^i = 0. \tag{6}$$

By equations (4) and (5) and assumption 7, $\Sigma_i T_{RI}{}^i = 0$ if and only if the budget is balanced.

Certain commodities provided through government generate disproportionate benefits for particular groups, although externalities may affect other citizens. Here we assume that some fraction, a, of the expenditure on the relevant activity accrues to individuals as a specific good, whereas the remainder accrues to the public at large.

$$Y_S{}^{ij} \equiv a^j C_S{}^{ij} \quad 1 \geqslant a \geqslant 0 \tag{7}$$

$$Y_S{}^i \equiv \Sigma_j a^j C_S{}^{ij}, \tag{8}$$

where j indicates the jth specific good. As a result of (7) the category of public goods attributable to household i may include not only the value of pure public goods, $Y_{PG}{}^i$, but also the external benefits of specific goods, $\Sigma_j(1 - a^j) C_S{}^{ij}$

$$Y_P{}^i \equiv Y_{PG}{}^i + \Sigma_j(1 - a^j) C_S{}^{ij} \tag{9}$$

$$Y_P \equiv \Sigma_i Y_P{}^i, \tag{10}$$

where Y_P is the total expenditure on pure public goods plus that portion of total specific goods outlays that generates diffused external benefits. We must now show how $Y_P{}^i$ should be estimated for each household.

By assumption 8,

$$U^i = f[(Y_D{}^i + Y_S{}^i), P] = g_{PVIV}(Y^i) + g_{PUB}(P), \tag{11}$$

where $Y^i = Y_D{}^i + Y_S{}^i$ is the value of commodities consumed by household i alone and, as previously noted, P is the physical quantity of public goods. The right-hand side of equation (11) illustrates that assumption 8 allows the household's total utility to be written as the sum of two utilities independently generated by the consumption of public and private goods. For any two households, α and β, we know, by assumptions 3 and 4, $f_P{}^\alpha = f_P{}^\beta$, where $f_P{}^\alpha$ is the first partial derivative of U^α with respect to P. Hence,

$$\frac{MRS^\alpha}{MRS^\beta} = \frac{dY^\alpha/dP}{dY^\beta/dP} = \frac{f_P{}^\alpha/f_Y{}^\alpha}{f_P{}^\beta/f_Y{}^\beta} = \frac{f_Y{}^\beta}{f_Y{}^\alpha}$$

or

$$MRS^\alpha f_Y{}^\alpha = MRS^\beta f_Y{}^\beta \cdots = MRS^i f_Y{}^i = K, \text{ a constant.}$$

By assumptions 6 and 7, we know that $\Sigma_i MRS^i = MC = \Sigma t^i = t$, the total tax imposed per unit of P.

To evaluate each household's consumption of public goods P, according to the benefit principle, we construct a tax rate imposed on each household equal to its marginal rate of substitution ($t^i = MRS^i$). Hence, the proportion of the value of public goods accruing to each household is

$$t^i P^* = Y_P{}^i = tP * \frac{MRS^i}{\Sigma_i MRS^i} = tP * \frac{k/f_Y{}^i}{\Sigma_i k/f_Y{}^i} = tP * \frac{1/f_Y{}^i}{\Sigma_i 1/f_Y{}^i}, \tag{12}$$

where P^* is the particular physical amount of P observed to be supplied by the government and tP^* is the total tax collections, equal to Y_P total expenditures on public goods. It follows from equation (12) that, for determining the proportions $Y_P{}^\alpha/Y_P{}^\beta$, and so forth, only the ratios of the *MRS*s matter; therefore, $\Sigma_i l/f_Y{}^i$ may arbitrarily be set equal to 1 so that $Y_P{}^i = tP^*(1/f_Y{}^i)$. Thus, to estimate the income value to each household of public goods, $Y_P{}^i$, we must specify the marginal utility schedule for each household, $f_Y{}^i$. Then,

$$T_P{}^i \equiv Y_P{}^i = Y_P \frac{1}{f_Y{}^i} . \tag{13}$$

By assumption, utilities of private goods and of public goods are independent. Therefore, we may specify $f_Y{}^i$ on the basis of disposable cash income plus the estimated value of specific goods received $(Y_D{}^i + Y_S{}^i)$. In turn, we can evaluate equation (13).

In summary, to estimate income redistribution, the analyst may proceed as follows:

1. For each income class calculate the final disposable income, after payment of all taxes (actual or imputed).

2. Add to the figure so calculated for each income class the specific (private goods type) benefits of government expenditures received by each class. Transfer receipts are included here.

3. The foregoing procedure will produce a private (or "private-type") income or "product received" estimate for the representative individual (or family) of each class. The procedure will also result in an unallocated total expenditure for public goods. Hypothesize any marginal utility of *private income* schedule and, with that utility schedule, distribute the residual expenditure on public goods so that for all representative families the product of *MU* of private income times the family's share of public goods expenditure is the same. Naturally, the sum of these allocations weighted by the number of families in each income class must add to the total public goods expenditure.

4. Add the private or specific incomes of each family to its allocation of public goods expenditures to give a total final income, or more accurately, "product received." Compare this final product received with the reconstructed pretax prebenefit income of families to determine the net distributional impact of taxation and expenditure.

III

The preceding sections have shown that we cannot evaluate the impact of the budget on income distribution unless we employ a utility function, explicitly or implicitly, to estimate public goods income. However, the assumption that government taxes and expenditure implement a welfare maximization policy in no way limits or determines any particular utility function as being necessary for consistency with the supposed welfare policy. In this section, therefore, we assume arbitrary, but nevertheless plausible, explicit utility functions for purposes of distributing benefits of public good expenditures. We make alternative assumptions and show the sensitivity of the results with respect to the utility function chosen and to various other assumptions.

The distributive impact of taxes and government expenditures presented by the Tax Foundation is reestimated using two utility functions. In the first

$$U^i = A \log (Y_D{}^i + Y_S{}^i) + B,$$

where A and B are arbitrary constants and other symbols are defined as previously. In this case, marginal utility,

$$dU^i/d(Y_D{}^i + Y_S{}^i) = A/(Y_D{}^i + Y_S{}^i),$$

is always positive, and total utility rises without limit as income rises. Because only the ratios of marginal utilities enter the calculations, the values of A and B are irrelevant.

In the second utility function,

$$U^i = E - C/(Y_D{}^i + Y_S{}^i),$$

C and E being arbitrary constants. The marginal utility of private goods income,

$$dU^i/d(Y_D{}^i + Y_S{}^i) = C/(Y_D{}^i + Y_S{}^i)^2,$$

is always positive but tends to zero as income increases. Hence, total utility converges to E. Once again, the values of E and C are irrelevant.

Tables 1 through 4 compare results based on these two utility functions and those obtained by the Tax Foundation. The results cast doubt on the findings of previous studies that the combined incidence of taxes and expenditures on income distribution is highly progressive – that is, tending to reduce inequality.

Not having access to the underlying data in Table 1 [7], we avoid any recomputations to retain comparability.

Table 2 presents the allocations of benefits of government expenditures. As we noted in section II, some commodities supplied by government are consumed by identifiable households or groups of households, although these commodities may generate some externalities. Lines 1 and 2 of Table 2 show the allocation of such specific goods under alternative assumptions -- that they generate no major externalities (allocation *NE*) and that they do generate externalities (allocation *E*). In the former case, the distribution of specific goods benefits is taken directly from the Tax Foundation. In the latter case, only a fraction of the value (or cost) of the specific goods is assumed to generate benefits for the identifiable households, with the remainder assumed to fall into the public goods category. As Table 2 shows, out of total government expenditures of $149 billion, allocation *E* assumes $42.3 billion to be for specific goods, whereas allocation *NE* assumes $78.4 billion to be for specific goods. Note b of Table 2 indicates

Table 1. Family Population, Factor Income, Taxes, and Disposable Income by Money Income Class, as Reported by Tax Foundation

	Under $2,000	$2,000– 2,999	$3,000– 3,999	$4,000– 4,999	$5,000– 5,999	$6,000– 7,499	$7,500– 9,999	$10,000– 14,999	$15,000 and Over	National Total
1. Number of families (000)	7,860	6,077	6,334	6,972	7,018	8,399	7,585	3,962	1,100	55,307
2. Factor income before taxes[a] per family	$1,046	$2,801	$4,674	$6,561	$8,328	$10,148	$13,482	$19,453	$44,520	$474.8 billion
3. Taxes per family	476	930	1,471	1,923	2,407	2,948	3,822	5,748	17,330	144.6 billion
4. Disposable income excluding transfer payments per family	570	1,871	3,203	4,638	5,921	7,200	9,660	13,705	27,190	330.2 billion

[a] "Factor income before taxes" exceeds "money income" because "before tax income" includes various imputations, whereas "money income" includes only cash receipts of the family. Factor income distribution figures were taken directly from the Tax Foundation study.

Table 2. Benefits of Government Expenditures

	Under $2,000	$2,000– 2,999	$3,000– 3,999	$4,000– 4,999	$5,000– 5,999	$6,000– 7,499	$7,500– 9,999	$10,000– 14,999	$15,000 and Over	National Total
Specific Goods Benefits										
1. Allocation NE[a]	$1,115	$1,414	$1,315	$1,085	$1,143	$1,190	$1,274	$1,652	$2,801	$70.6 billion
2. Allocation E[b]	741	918	819	614	632	643	721	997	1,967	42.3 billion
Public Goods Benefits Allocation NE										
3. Tax Foundation	$854	$1,004	$1,128	$1,262	$1,389	$1,553	$1,801	$2,239	$3,906	$78.4 billion
4. $U = A \log Y$	392	641	887	1,116	1,377	1,689	2,132	2,995	5,848	
5. $U = E - C/Y$	52	196	370	594	905	1,361	2,169	4,279	16,320	
Public Goods Benefits Allocation E										
6. Tax Foundation	$1,162	$1,366	$1,535	$1,717	$1,890	$2,113	$2,451	$3,047	$5,315	$106.6 billion
7. $U = A \log Y$	375	798	1,151	1,503	1,875	2,321	2,971	4,207	8,344	
8. $U = E - C/Y$	48	217	451	770	1,199	1,838	3,009	6,035	23,736	

[a] Assumes that specific goods – elementary and secondary and higher education, public assistance and other welfare, labor, veterans' benefits, streets and highways, agriculture, net interest, and social insurance benefits – produce no external benefits.

[b] Assumes the following proportions of the cost of specific goods are allocable as public goods – elementary and secondary education (.7), higher education (.5), public assistance and other welfare (.3), labor (.3), veterans' benefits (.3), streets and highways (.5), agriculture (.5), net interest (0), social insurance (.3).

the proportions of specific goods reallocated to the public goods category. These fractions are arbitrary and were chosen for illustrative purposes.

Next, for allocation *NE,* lines 3, 4, and 5 show the distribution of the total of $78.4 billion of public goods benefits, using, respectively, the Tax Foundation weights and the indicated utility functions inserted in equation (11). Lastly, lines 6, 7, and 8 show the corresponding results if specific goods generate externalities (to the extent indicated in note b), with $106.6 billion in public goods to be distributed.

Table 2 shows an extreme sensitivity in the distribution of public goods benefits to the rationale underlying that distribution. Benefits for the lowest income brackets, for example, range from negligible to substantial, and benefits for upper income brackets may also vary by large amounts, depending on the choice of utility function. In the middle brackets there is less, but still considerable, sensitivity.[5]

Next, Table 3 shows the total net tax and benefit impacts on income by income class under the six alternative assumptions. The results, as explained in note a of Table 3, are simply the algebraic sum of taxes, specific goods benefits, and public goods benefits of government expenditures. The estimates of total net income redistribution are so sensitive to underlying assumptions that all but three income brackets may switch from net gains to net losses. The variability of the top bracket, which may pay net taxes of over $10,000 per family or enjoy net benefits of over $8,000, is particularly striking. The two bottom brackets gain under all assumptions but by widely differing amounts. The $7,500--$9,999 bracket loses under all assumptions but again by widely different amounts.[6]

Interpretation of the distributional patterns of Table 3 must be qualified. Most benefits of specific goods accrue to particular spending units who have the set of characteristics that qualify them for the service. For example, the *direct* benefits of education accrue only to spending units, some member of which is in school; the direct gains from veterans' benefits of public assistance accrue only to spending units at least one member of which is a veteran or "on welfare." The significance of the results in Table 3 and the interpretation to be placed on them depend critically, therefore, on whether the characteristics that make spending

---

5 If we were asked to impute the benefit to purchaser of ten shirts, for example, we would have two choices. We could value the shirts at their price, p, and attribute the benefit of $10p$ to the purchaser. The price presumably equals the marginal rate of substitution between shirts and money, because otherwise the purchaser would have bought more or fewer shirts. Alternatively we could take note that the purchaser probably enjoys some consumer surplus on all inframarginal shirts. Customarily we use the former measure in valuing benefits of private goods to individuals because the latter would result in a sum of benefits greater than the value of production. Just as with shirts, government services produce consumer surplus, but again as with shirts, this surplus should be ignored in computing the income value of government services in the total income of each person.

6 Note that Tables 1 and 2 indicate total tax receipts of $144.6 billion and total government expenditures of $149.0 billion in 1961. This budget deficit of $4.4 billion was 0.9 percent of net national product. Therefore, to obtain a "product received" distribution comparable to the factor income distribution of Table 1, add the factor incomes to the net redistribution row of Table 3 and deflate the resulting sums by 0.9 percent.

Table 3. Net Income Redistribution

	Under $2,000	$2,000 – 2,999	$3,000 – 3,999	$4,000 – 4,999	$5,000 – 5,999	$6,000 – 7,499	$7,500 – 9,999	$10,000 – 14,999	$15,000 and Over
Effective Transfers[a] Allocation *NE*									
1. Tax Foundation	$1,493	$1,488	$972	$424	$125	$-205	$-747	$-1,857	$-10,623
2. $U = A \log Y$	968	1,125	725	278	113	-69	-416	-1,101	-8,682
3. $U = E - C/Y$	691	680	214	-244	-359	-397	-379	183	1,790
Effective Transfers[b] Allocation *E*									
4. Tax Foundation	$1,427	$1,354	$883	$408	$115	$-192	$-650	$-1,704	$-10,048
5. $U = A \log Y$	640	786	499	194	100	16	-130	-544	-7,019
6. $U = E - C/Y$	313	205	-201	-539	-567	-467	-92	1,284	8,373

[a]Lines 1, 2, and 3 are obtained by adding line 3, Table 1; line 1, Table 2; and, respectively, lines 3, 4, 5, Table 2.
[b]Lines 4, 5, and 6 are obtained by adding line 3, Table 1; line 2, Table 2; and, respectively, lines 6, 7, and 8, Table 2.

Table 4. Particular Specific Goods Benefits as a Percent of
Total Specific Goods Benefits

	Under $2,000	$2,000 – 2,999	$3,000 – 3,999	$4,000 – 4,999	$5,000 – 5,999	$6,000 – 7,499	$7,500 – 9,999	$10,000 – 14,999	$15,000 and Over
1. Direct Transfers	55.5	44.2	28.8	13.9	12.1	8.6	6.9	6.7	1.6
2. Education	10.1	16.2	21.5	34.1	36.2	40.8	36.1	32.8	25.6

units eligible for specific goods are widely diffused within the income class or are highly concentrated. In the former case, we may conclude that the bulk of the spending units in the group are affected approximately as indicated in Table **3** (given our choice of a utility function); in the latter case, we may conclude that some spending units within a class experience substantially larger subsidies or smaller taxes than do others.[7]

For example, as shown in Table 4, transfer payments are the largest specific goods benefits accruing to the two bottom income brackets. Moreover, transfer payments are concentrated on certain recipients within particular income brackets. Households classified as poor by federal poverty standards are concentrated in the two lowest money income classes. Public assistance accrues only to poor households roughly 25 percent of whom receive public assistance. Because some households in the two lowest income classes would not be classified as poor, probably not more than 25 percent of the two lowest brackets receive public assistance. Similarly, the aged, who receive 70 percent of Social Security benefits, constitute approximately 30 percent of all poor households. If the aged poor also comprise 30 percent of the two lowest money income brackets, then a substantial fraction of the bottom two brackets receive neither public assistance nor Social Security benefits. Actually, some overlap exists between public assistance recipients and Social Security beneficiaries, because a substantial number of old-age assistance recipients also receive Social Security. On the other hand, such transfers as unemployment insurance and veterans' disability pensions would reduce the fraction. Although the data do not support any firm conclusion, it seems unlikely that substantially more than half of the households with money incomes below $3,000 receive any direct cash transfers. Because about half the specific good benefits to the two bottom money income classes consists of transfer payments, the concentration of these benefits on roughly half those spending units implies that many households with money incomes of less than $3,000 are receiving much smaller subsidies than aggregate estimates suggest and that they may even be paying a substantial implicit tax – that is, paying taxes, direct and imputed, greater than the value of government goods and services received.

A similar problem arises in the case of education (see Table 4), with respect to middle and upper income groups, and to a lesser extent, along different patterns in each case, for other outlays. Moreover, the direct benefits of education are the largest fraction of specific goods benefits among those income brackets that receive only modest net benefits or suffer net losses under most assumptions in Table 3 – those with incomes of $5,000 to $9,999. Families in these brackets without school-age children are probably heavy net taxpayers.

---

7 The same issue arises in the case of taxes because liabilities depend on spending patterns, for which income may be a bad proxy.

IV

Previous studies of the distributional effects of public budgets have not acknowledged that allocation of the benefits of public goods depends, explicitly or implicitly, on an assumed utility function. For example, allocation of public goods benefits by the number of families amounts to the assumption that the marginal utility of income is constant as income rises. This study has shown that the selection of a utility function critically influences results. This conclusion is reinforced if we recognize that many publicly provided goods and services, the benefits of which accrue to identifiable households, also generate widely diffused externalities, as do public goods. Finally, there is strong reason to suspect that studies focusing on income brackets alone obscure some of the more significant distributional questions, such as the difference between the impact of public budgets on the working poor and that on the dependent population. More fruitful studies should take into account the distributional impact of public budgets among groups defined not only on the basis of income but also on other economic, social, and demographic characteristics that affect tax liabilities and eligibility for benefits of government expenditures.

References

1. Gillespie, W. I. "The Effect of Public Expenditures on the Distribution of Income. An Empirical Investigation." In R. A. Musgrave, ed., *Essays in Fiscal Federalism*. Washington, D.C.: The Brookings Institution, 1965.
2. Margolis, J. "A Comment on the Pure Theory of Public Expenditure." *Review of Economics and Statistics* 37 (November 1955): 347–49.
3. McGuire, M. and H. Aaron. "Efficiency and Equity in the Optimal Supply of a Public Good." *Review of Economics and Statistics* 51 (February 1969).
4. Mieszkowski, P. "On the Theory of Tax Incidence." *Journal of Political Economy* 75 (June 1967): 250–62.
5. Peacock, A., ed. *Income Redistribution and Social Policy*. London: Jonathan Cape, 1954.
6. Samuelson, P. "Pure Theory of Public Expenditure and Taxation." Paper presented at meetings of the International Economic Association at Biarritz, 1966.
7. Tax Foundation, Inc. *Tax Burdens and Benefits of Government Expenditures by Income Class, 1961 and 1965*. New York: Tax Foundation, Inc., 1967.

2   Explicit Public Grants

Part 2 focuses more narrowly on components of the public grants economy. Our specific concern is with public activities that involve explicit public transfers in cash – for example, transfer payments made under the social welfare system, subsidies paid to farmers, federal funds paid to state and local governments and to private organizations and individuals, and federal research and development funding – or transfers in kind made by the government to the population through the education system. (Several of these programs also contain implicit public grants – for example, farm subsidies.)

We generally expect that these and other programs would tend to narrow income inequality. This would particularly be the case with programs designed to promote economic and social welfare, to enhance education and upward mobility, or to improve the position of a group affected by technological change (such as the farm population). No doubt many programs do achieve redistributive results that ameliorate the position of the poor. However, as the papers in Part 2 indicate, some surprising patterns emerge.

Benjamin Okner notes that the net effect of taxes and transfers "is to raise the poor's share of income from 3 percent before taxes and transfers to 10 percent and to lower the share of the nonpoor from 97 percent before to 90 percent after taxes and transfers." On the other hand he observes that "although it is widely believed that social welfare expenditures mainly benefit the poor, in fact, the estimates ... indicate that the distribution is fairly close to 50–50 between the poor and nonpoor. The programs that chiefly involve cash transfers do favor the poor, but the effect of these is overwhelmed by their disproportionately low share of benefit from education expenditures (the 25 percent of poor families are estimated to receive only 18 percent of the benefits), so the overall distribution of public social welfare expenditures is quite evenly divided." Further, government pensions, veterans' benefits and Social Security "benefits are concentrated among families removed from poverty rather than among the poorest of the poor." And finally, "Social Security alone completely fills the poverty gap for only about half the 1.5 million families under age 65 who are moved across the poverty line."

Although the Social Security system was never intended as an antipoverty program per se, its de facto impact is nonetheless less favorable to the poor than what may be expected.

Based on an examination of California's higher education system, W. Lee Hansen and Burton A. Weisbrod conclude that public subsidization of higher education in effect promotes "greater rather than less inequality among people of various social and economic backgrounds, by making available substantial subsidies that lower-income families either are not eligible for or cannot make use of because of other conditions and constraints associated with their income position." And, "for families with a child at one of the state colleges or at one of the university campuses, the net transfers range from $630 to $790 per year. Meanwhile, families without children or with children not enrolled in public institutions of higher education receive no subsidy whatsoever, although they pay an average of $650 in state and local taxes. . . . [It is evident that] the current method of financing public higher education leads to a redistribution of income from lower- to higher-income families." Moreover, the authors observe that "there is little reason to believe that the distribution of public subsidies through the higher education system is less unequal in other states than it is in California."

Joseph Pechman provided the antithesis to the Hansen—Weisbrod thesis of the regressivity of California's system of public higher education. Even if we were to use their figures to distribute the benefits and costs of the public education system by income levels, Pechman argued, we would conclude that the system is indeed progressive.[1]

As Pechman's antithesis is summarized, and to some extent synthesized with the Hansen--Weisbrod thesis, only Robert Hartman's synthesis is offered as further reading for the sake of learning both sides of an inspiring argument.[2] Hartman concludes that a debate over higher education finance must start with two principles and an empirical question: "The basic principles are that public higher education should be seeking to achieve two goals: (1) Equalization of opportunity. This goal clearly implies that subsidies be targeted on lower-income students. (2) The provision of below-cost higher education to ensure that both public and private benefits are accounted for in the enrollment decision. This goal need not imply that subsidies be targeted on children from low-income families. Indeed, it seems to me that a good starting point for developing criteria for the appropriate distribution of subsidies to ensure that public benefits are preserved is that all students in postsecondary education should receive approximately equal subsidies. . . . Finally, the empirical question raised by Pechman, and skirted by Hansen and Weisbrod, is: How serious is the trade-off between efficient support for equalization and the partial support of higher education from public treasuries? Policy analysts should ask whether programs of support for higher education at the federal and state levels can be articulated

---

1 J. A. Pechman, "The Distributional Effects of Public Higher Education in California," *Journal of Human Resources* 5, no. 3 (Summer 1970): 361–70.

2 R. W. Hartman, "A Comment on the Pechman–Hansen–Weisbrod Controversy," *Journal of Human Resources* 5, no. 4 (Fall 1970): 519–23.

in such a way as to preserve and broaden the social benefits of higher education and eliminate the disgraceful lack of equality of opportunity in the United States."

Charles Schultze evaluates the distributive results of farm subsidies. He includes explicit federal budget outlays for farm price support programs and related direct payments (of about $3.1 billion per year for the period 1956 through 1968 and of about $5 billion for the period 1968 through 1970), as well as the implicit subsidy conveyed by nonfarm consumers through the purchase of farm products at prices that, in his estimation, would have been 15 to 20 percent lower had federal price support programs not been in effect.

Although farm marketings amounted to over $47 billion in 1969, they could have been purchased for about $7 billion less if prices had been 15 percent lower: "Some $1.5 billion of this reduction would represent lower prices paid by farmers themselves in buying feed, seed, and livestock. Lower prices for export would represent another $1 billion. Nonfarm consumers, therefore, paid in recent years about $4.5 billion more for the farm products they purchased than they would have had there been no federal price support programs.... Farm price support and related programs thus cost the taxpayer some $5 billion per year in budgetary outlays and consumers of food and fiber some $4.5 billion in higher food prices ... The total transfer from consumers and taxpayers, in the range of $9 to $10 billion, compares with a total federal, state, and local cost of various ... public assistance (welfare) programs, including Medicaid, of slightly over $10 billion in 1969."

Turning to the distributive consequences of these programs. Schultze concludes, "Whatever the advantages or disadvantages of the farm subsidy program, it is not a welfare program in the sense of transferring income to low-income farm families. The bulk of the subsidies accrue to that small group of farmers with net incomes averaging $20,000. And because the value of the subsidy tends to get reflected in farmland prices, the subsidies are gradually translated into capital gains for long-term holders of land, while recent purchasers and renters receive a much smaller benefit, losing at least part of the subsidy in higher carrying costs or rents.... Because the increase in land rents brought about by price support programs is capitalized into higher land prices, many of the benefits of the farm price support programs are not felt in farm income itself, as farmland gradually changes hands (at about 3 percent per year) and as farm landlords raise cash rents to their tenant farmers.... A removal or reduction in price supports would cause substantial capital losses to second generation landowners who purchased land at the higher prices and typically are paying sizable carrying costs in the form of mortgage interest.... Viewed in this light, the concept of parity income as a possible goal for agricultural policy becomes a dubious objective."

Roy Bahl and Jeremy Warford study and explain the interstate variation in federal aids to states — including grants-in-aid to state and local governments and to private organizations and individuals, as well as a part of federal expenditures. A major concern is with the redistribution of real income among states. They note a significant negative relationship between per capita income and a positive association between per capita direct federal expenditures, which leads to an overall neutral pattern of relationship between total federal assistance and income. "However, when per capita total federal assistance is adjusted for interstate variations in the level of idle resources, an overall pattern of income equalization is revealed. The state-to-state variance in the real benefits of federal grants is sufficiently equalizing to offset the neutral real income effect of direct federal expenditures." However, after considering political explanators, which they assume to be reflected in a negative and statistically significant partial relation between population and per capita assistance, Bahl and Warford conclude that "the political process influences the interstate distribution of real grant benefits to a significantly greater extent than it does the distribution of real expenditure benefits. Alternatively, the division of direct federal expenditure benefits among states is more responsive to high levels of unemployment than is the division of grants-in-aid." They also conclude that "the federal allocation process tends to work in favor of states with small populations. In fact, we would argue that the bias in the federal fund distribution process is even greater than is usually thought; it is more pronounced in the case of real benefit distribution than in the case of monetary distribution. It also appears that expenditure-aid is relatively less responsive to population differences (political influence) than is grant-aid. . . . Finally, our results indicate that the real interstate progressivity of the budgetary process is substantially greater than the progressivity observed when we consider only dollar flows."

Based on the size of external economies relative to direct benefits, John Burke and Patricia Horvath attribute a greater or lesser degree of grants character to knowledge anticipated from research and development (R & D) expenses. The expectational measure -- termed "the degree of expected embodiment" -- becomes the basis for the measurement of the grants component of federal R & D funding. Burke and Horvath note that this grants component has steadily increased, from 5.1 percent between 1957 and 1959 to 9.2 percent between 1966 and 1968; "The low level of the grants component . . . results from the unequal distribution of total outlays. Agencies that absorb the largest proportion of R & D funding -- Defense and NASA -- show the lowest grants component; agencies for which high grants components have been calculated -- HEW, NSF, and Agriculture -- make under 10 percent of all R & D expenditures." They also note a "high" grants orientation for universities and a "low" grants orientation for government (intramural) laboratories and industrial firms. Turning to the distributional or equity benefits of federal R & D grants policy by states, Burke and Horvath note that "the bulk of the *lowest* per capita R & D figures are found among the *lowest* income states." They conclude that grants funding of R & D is no more equitably distributed across states than exchange funding. Furthermore, "among low grantors [agencies] and grantees [states], especially Defense and NASA, extraordinarily small amounts of R & D funds are awarded to a number of the poorest states. . . . An overall tendency to direct larger per capita allocations to high-income states, therefore, becomes more evident.

In the final paper of Part 2 Bruce Stuart examines the impact that the Medical Assistance (Medicaid) program has had on interstate income differentials in 1967-68. Medicaid is one of the most recent and the largest welfare programs. In 1969, this program accounted for over 41.9 percent of all public assistance.

Medicaid was designed in part to eliminate the inequity resulting from the matching requirement of federal funds released to states: Generally the federal government made larger welfare expenditures in richer than in poorer states. Although the federal government has overtly aimed at the reduction of regional and interstate differences in income, Stuart notes that the program "has widened an existing gap in assistance levels. Prior to the enactment of Medical Assistance, poor households in the rich industrial states of the North received far higher welfare grants than their counterparts in less affluent regions. After two and a half years of Medicaid these differences have become more, not less, pronounced. At the same time the Medicaid program has in many cases redistributed real income from the poor to the wealthy states. In so doing it has violated even the weakest standards of horizontal and vertical equity."

The study concludes that federal incentives for the development of comprehensive state Medicaid programs are inadequate to ensure an equitable system for the distribution of benefits and costs. If such a system is considered desirable, it must be developed and financed on a national rather than a state basis.

As the papers of Part 2 demonstrate, explicit transfers do by no means provide a drastic modification of income inequities brought about by different factor incomes generated by market or exchange processes. Study of the distributive effects of implicit public grants in Part 3 conveys an even more striking result.

3

Benjamin A. Okner: Transfer Payments:
Their Distribution and Role in
Reducing Poverty

Federal, state, and local spending on social welfare programs amounted to $127 billion in fiscal year 1969, or 14 percent of the gross national product and almost 45 percent of total government spending for all purposes.[1] Federal expenditures of $69 billion accounted for just over half the total, and state and local government spending made up the remaining $58 billion. Welfare expenditures have risen steadily for many years; in the 1960s alone, they increased by almost $75 billion – close to 140 percent.

In fiscal year 1969, $51 billion (40 percent of the total) was in the form of cash transfers and the remaining $76 billion was for goods and services (see Table 1). Most cash transfers are made under programs in the social insurance category – Social Security, railroad and public employee retirement, unemployment insurance, and workmen's compensation. In addition, some cash payments are made under programs in the public aid category (public assistance) and under the veterans' disability and pension programs. Direct provision of hospital and

Table 1. Social Welfare Expenditures under Public Programs, Fiscal Year 1969 (In Billions)

Program	Money	Nonmoney	Total
Social insurance	$40	$ 9	$49
Public aid	6	7	13
Health and medical	–	9	9
Veterans'	5	3	8
Education	–	43	43
Housing and other social welfare	–	5	5
All social welfare programs	51	76	127

Source: A. M. Skolnik and S. R. Dales, "Social Welfare Expenditures, 1968–69." *Social Security Bulletin*, 32 (December 1969), Table 9, p. 16.

Presented at the Symposium on the Grants Economy held between the Association for the Study of the Grants Economy and the American Association for the Advancement of Science in December, 1969, in Boston, Mass. All rights reserved. Used by permission of the author. Mr. Okner is a member of the Economic Studies staff of the Brookings Institution. The views expressed are his own and do not purport to represent the views of the other staff members, officers, or trustees of the Brookings Institution. The study was financed under a research grant to the Brookings Institution from the U.S. Office of Economic Opportunity.

1 A. M. Skolnik and S. R. Dales, "Social Welfare Expenditures, 1968–69," *Social Security Bulletin*, 32 (December 1969).

other health services for veterans, expenditures for schools and teachers, and housing programs are illustrative of nonmoney goods and service expenditures under social welfare programs. Almost three quarters of all such spending is for social insurance and education programs. Public aid, health and medical programs, and veterans' programs account for almost all of the remaining 25 percent.

Like all government spending, social welfare expenditures influence the allocation of economic resources, the distribution of income, and the total level of national production and employment.[2] However, in this study we are concerned only with the effect of social welfare expenditures on the distribution of income. And because poverty and the various means for its alleviation are such important areas of domestic economic policy, we concentrate on how transfers affect the incomes of the poor.[3]

The first section of the paper summarizes the overall U.S. tax and transfer system. We then examine the current role of money transfers in altering the pretransfer income distribution and helping to reduce poverty.[4] Because the most up-to-date figures available are those for 1966, the study is confined to that year.

U.S. Taxes and Transfers

Overall, families classified as poor[5] before receiving transfer payments comprise 25 percent of the population. They earn 3 percent of income before transfers and receive 43 percent of the benefits from public social welfare

---

2 See R. A. Musgrave, *The Theory of Public Finance* (New York: McGraw-Hill Book Co., 1959).

3 Readers familiar with the literature in this area will recognize that in several sections of this paper my analysis closely parallels an earlier study by R. J. Lampman, "How Much Does the American System of Transfers Benefit the Poor?," in L. H. Goodman, ed., *Economic Progress and Social Welfare*, 93rd Annual Forum, National Conference on Social Welfare (New York: Columbia University Press, 1966), pp. 125--57. I am pleased to acknowledge the many valuable insights derived from Lampman's work.

4 Unless noted otherwise, all distributional data presented in the remainder of the paper were derived from the Survey of Economic Opportunity (SEO) conducted in 1967 by the U.S. Bureau of Census for the Office of Economic Opportunity (this is more fully described in the appendix). All programming and tabulations for the study were prepared at the Brookings Computer Center. Jon K. Peck was primarily responsible for the programming, without which the study would have been impossible. Grateful acknowledgment is given for his efforts in my behalf.

5 Families (including one-person families) are classified as "poor" or "nonpoor" on the basis of the economy poverty-income levels developed by the Social Security Administration. The original 1966 cutoffs were slightly modified in the spring of 1969 to reflect a change in the price index used to derive the poverty levels and a different method of computing farm-income cutoffs. The new poverty-income levels are still based on family size, composition, and farm-nonfarm place of residence. For a description of how the levels were developed, see M. Orshansky, "Counting the Poor: Another Look at the Poverty Profile," *Social Security Bulletin*, 28 (January 1965).

Table 2. Estimated Distribution of Pretax Income, Transfers, and Taxes among the Pretransfer Poor and Nonpoor, 1966 (In Billions)

Item	Total Amount	Pretransfer Poor Share (Percent)	Pretransfer Poor Amount	Nonpoor Share (Percent)	Nonpoor Amount
1. *Total Income before Transfers*	$548	3	$22.7	97	$525.3
2. Wages and other labor income	410	3	12.3	97	397.7
3. Business and farm proprietorship	61	2	1.2	98	59.8
4. Property and other income	77	12	9.2	88	67.8
5. *Total Public Transfers*	$ 94	43	$40.5	57	$ 53.5
6. Social insurance	35	54	18.9	46	16.1
7. Public aid	8	87	7.0	13	1.0
8. Health and medical programs	7	50	3.5	50	3.5
9. Veterans' programs	7	50	3.5	50	3.5
10. Education	34	18	6.1	82	27.9
11. Housing and other social welfares	3	50	1.5	50	1.5
12. *Total Taxes*	$ 94	6	$ 5.8	94	$ 88.2
13. *Income after Taxes and Transfers*	$548	10	$57.4	90	$490.6
14. *Net Transfer*	0	—	$34.7	—	$−34.7

Sources: Line 1 is derived from U.S. Department of Commerce data for 1966. Property and other income include rental income of persons, dividends, and personal interest receipts. The published figures were adjusted to exclude income accruing to fiduciaries and other institutions, which is part of personal income but is not distributed to individuals. Basic data are from *Survey of Current Business*, 49 (July 1969), Table 2.1, p. 26.

Lines 2, 3, 4, 6, 7, and 9 are estimated from U.S. Bureau of the Census, 1967, Survey of Economic Opportunity (SEO) data.

Lines 8 and 11 are distributed by the author.

Line 10 is distributed on the basis of school enrollment as reported in the SEO. Twenty percent of all persons attending elementary and secondary grades and 9 percent of those in college were members of poor families. No adjustment was made to take account of lower per capita expenditures (especially in the elementary and secondary grades) for the poor. Thus, the total education benefit accruing to the poor is probably overstated in Table 2.

Line 12 is based on unpublished background data for the discussion and chart in *Economic Report of the President, 1969*, pp. 160–61.

Line 13 is equal to line 1 plus line 5, less line 12.

expenditures (see Table 2). Thus, to their income of $22.7 billion, an estimated $40.5 billion of public transfers is added, to yield $63.2 billion of total income. However, taxes to finance social welfare programs are collected from both poor and nonpoor families. Although the nonpoor contribute most revenue, an estimated $5.8 billion, or 6 percent of all taxes — federal, state, and local — are collected from the poor, leaving them $57.4 billion of income after taxes and transfers. Including both transfers and taxes, then, the poor receive net benefits of $34.7 billion, which, of course, comes from the nonpoor. The net effect is to raise the poor's share of income from 3 percent before taxes and transfers to 10 percent and to lower the share of the nonpoor from 97 percent before to 90 percent after taxes and transfers.

Although it is widely believed that social welfare expenditures mainly benefit the poor, in fact, the estimates in Table 2 indicate that the distribution is fairly close to 50–50 between the poor and nonpoor. The programs that chiefly involve cash transfers do favor the poor, but the effect of these is overwhelmed by their disproportionately low share of benefit from education expenditures (the 25 percent of poor families are estimated to receive only 18 percent of the benefits), so the overall distribution of public social welfare expenditures is quite evenly divided.[6]

Unfortunately, such a global view of the tax and transfer system tends to obscure some of the most significant aspects of the present system of transfer payments. Some segments of the poor population benefit greatly and many others little (or not at all) from the receipt of transfer income. In the following section[7] we examine more closely how *money* transfers are distributed among various subgroups of the population.

---

6 In examining Table 2, the reader may be surprised to see that 13 percent of the $8 billion of public aid expenditures is allocated to the nonpoor. There is little doubt that these programs really benefit mainly the poor, and the figures shown are a "statistical artifact" due to the difference between the SEO reporting unit and the program "dispensing unit" (see appendix). Even if the data were adjusted to allocate all the public aid expenditures to the pretransfer poor, the results would not be appreciably changed; public transfers received by the poor would increase by $1 billion, and their share of the total would be raised from 43 percent to 44 percent.

7 Because the SEO contains data only on money transfers, the following sections exclude any consideration of the distribution of the nonmoney items included in the total social welfare expenditure series. The transfers included in the SEO figures are Social Security, unemployment insurance, workmen's compensation, government pensions, veterans' benefits, and public assistance (see Table 4).

In addition to the exclusion of nonmoney transfers, no attempt has been made to estimate taxes paid by individual families, and only estimates of the distribution of gross transfer benefits are presented. Although information on net benefits (gross transfers less tax payments) would be desirable, an estimation of total taxes paid by individual families would be extremely difficult and time-consuming. Although average overall effective tax rates by income class are available, such figures cannot be applied to family units in the various subgroups of the population dealt with in this paper, and the analysis is therefore confined to gross benefits.

Distribution of Money Transfers among the Poor and the Nonpoor

Because transfer receipts will alter the relative ranking of families who are poor before receiving such income, the poor are divided into those who are poor both before and after transfers and those who are poor before transfers but nonpoor after them. Later, the first group is further divided into those who remain poor even though they receive some transfer income and those who are poor and receive no transfers.

Poor families receive 57 percent of all money transfers, whereas the nonpoor receive 43 percent (see Table 3). About two thirds of the transfers to the poor are received by those who would be considered poor if classified only

Table 3. Distribution of Pretransfer Income and Income after Money Transfers among the Poor and the Nonpoor, 1966

Item	Poor before and after Transfers	Poor before But Nonpoor after Transfers	Nonpoor before Transfers	Total Population
Pretransfer income (percent)	2	1	97	100
Transfer income (percent)	20	37	43	100
Posttransfer income (percent)	3	4	93	100
Transfer per capita	$223	$1,054	$ 87	$163
Transfer per family	$627	$2,214	$290	$510
Transfers as percent of posttransfer income	41	70	3	7
Families and persons				
Number of families (thousands)	9,887	5,318	46,510	61,715
Percent of families	16.0	8.6	75.4	100.0
Number of persons	27,752	11,168	154,695	193,615
Percent of persons	14.3	5.8	79.9	100.0

on the basis of their nontransfer income but are nonpoor after transfers. These 5.3 million families comprise 8.6 percent of the total population and receive 37 percent of all transfer income. The importance of transfer income for families who are either taken out or kept out of poverty by transfer payments can be seen by the extremely high average amount they receive – $2,200 – as compared with an average of only $600 received by the poor not removed from poverty. In addition, transfers comprise 70 percent of their posttransfer income as compared with only 41 percent for the poor who remain impoverished. Because the average transfer received by poor families is much larger than that received by nonpoor families, the share of posttransfer income accruing to the nonpoor is reduced to 93 percent (from 97 percent of pretransfer income), and the share of income after transfers received by poor families is increased to 7 percent from their pretransfer share of 3 percent.

In addition to all families who are poor before but nonpoor afterward, about 58 percent of the 9.9 million families who remain poor also receive some transfer income. As we might expect, public assistance paid on the basis of extreme financial need is concentrated among poor families who remain impoverished (see Table 4). On the other hand, the primarily the nonpoor receive unemployment insurance and workmen's compensation benefits, eligibility for which is based on recent membership in the labor force. Government pensions and veterans' benefits are divided about 50–50 between the poor and nonpoor, whereas the distribution of social security benefits tends to favor slightly the poor (60 percent to the pretransfer poor). For all three of the latter types of transfers, benefits are concentrated among families removed from poverty rather than among the poorest of the poor.

Table 4. Distribution of Transfer Income, by Type,
among Poor and Nonpoor Families, 1966 (In Percentages)

Type of Transfer	Poor before and after Transfers	Poor before But Nonpoor after Transfers	Nonpoor before Transfers	Total Population
All transfers	20	37	43	100
Social Security	19	41	40	100
Unemployment insurance and workmen's compensation	8	17	75	100
Government pensions	3	43	54	100
Veterans' benefits	11	39	50	100
Public assistance	63	24	13	100

Money Transfers and Poverty Reduction

Overall, transfer payments are responsible for keeping or taking out of poverty 35 percent of the 15.2 million families who would otherwise be counted poor. One way to summarize the poverty-reducing effect of such explicit grants is to compare them with the gap that exists between income and the poverty line before the transfers are made — that is, the total amount by which the income of the poor falls below their poverty-line income. For 1966, we estimate a pretransfer poverty gap of $22 billion and total transfers to the poor of $18 billion. Thus, transfer receipts are equal to 81 percent of the pretransfer poverty gap.[8]

8 The poverty gaps measured on the basis of SEO data are probably overstated because respondents tend to underreport their income in surveys. It is estimated that pretransfer income of the poor may be understated by as much as $4 billion, which would reduce the pretransfer poverty gap to $18 billion. And there may be as much as a $4 billion understatement in the amount of transfer income reported by the poor. Taking these figures into account, the "true" posttransfer poverty gap in 1966 would be substantially below $10 billion. These are rough estimates based on aggregate data, and it is impossible to use them in the detailed analysis in the study.

Table 5. Poverty Reduction among Poor Families through
Money Transfers by Pretransfer Status, 1966

Item	Poor before and after Transfers		Poor before But Nonpoor after Transfers	Total
	Nonrecipients of Transfers	Recipients of Transfers		
Pretransfer poverty gap (millions)	$5,279	$10,773	$ 6,149	$22,201
Transfers (millions)	0	$ 6,198	$11,773	$17,971
Posttransfer poverty gap (millions)	$5,279	$ 4,575	$-5,624	$ 4,230
Transfers as percent of pretransfer poverty gap	0	58	191	81
Number of families (thousands)	4,174	5,713	5,318	15,205
Percent of families	27	38	35	100

However, the posttransfer poverty gap is equal to $9.9 billion – *not* the $4 billion implied by subtracting transfers of $18 billion from the pretransfer poverty gap of $22 billion. The figures in Table 5 clarify this seeming anomaly. For some 4.2 million poor families who receive no transfers, the poverty gap is not filled at all; for the 5.3 million families removed from poverty, the gap is "overfilled" by about $5.6 billion. Transfer income amounts to 58 percent of the pretransfer poverty gap for the 5.7 million families who remain poor, whereas transfers to those removed from poverty are close to double their pretransfer poverty gap.[9]

Although an efficiently designed new program providing $10 billion of aid to the poor might seem adequate to fill the posttransfer poverty gap, this is not true. It is not possible to design an acceptable transfer program without some spillover of benefits to the nonpoor. The best alternative is minimization of the spillover so that most benefits accrue to the most needy group.

Transfers to the Poor by Age, Race,
and Family Composition

The extent to which transfers benefit any subgroup of the population depends on the proportion of families in the group who receive any transfer income, the average amount of payment, and the relationship between the amount received and the financial need. Under existing programs, the transfer recipient rate varies substantially among different subgroups of the poor (see

9 The reader should not infer from these figures that those removed from poverty because of transfers make a "killing." The average pretransfer income for families in this group is $926, and the average income after transfers is $3,140. Although clearly better off financially than other poor families, the families removed from poverty could hardly be described as "affluent."

Table 6). Ninety-five percent of all families with family head aged 65 or over who are poor before transfers receive some transfer income, and aged-couple families are virtually certain to receive such income. Thus, judged only by this criterion, the present transfer system serves quite well poor families with family head aged 65 or over (who comprise half of the pretransfer poor).

The other 50 percent of the pretransfer poor — with family head under age 65 -- do not fare nearly so well in terms of transfer receipts; only 50 percent of all these families receive any transfer. At the bottom of the receiving ladder are nonwhite families with children (32 percent recipient rate), and only slightly higher are white families with children (38 percent). Continuing up the ladder are unmarried individuals, married couples with no children, and families headed by females. For all these groups, the recipient rate for nonwhite families is below the rate for white families of similar composition.

Under the present categorical system of money transfers, such results are not surprising. The largest program, OASDI, distributes benefits mostly to aged retirees.[10] Public assistance, the second largest program of money transfers, is paid to tightly defined categories of the "deserving poor." If an individual is poor but does not fall into one of the eligible categories, his chances of receiving financial aid are meager. Even if he does qualify for help under one of the categorical programs, his chances of receiving an "adequate" amount of financial aid still are slight.[11]

The dual conditions for poverty reduction by means of transfer payments — the recipient rate and the relation between the amount received and financial need — are well illustrated by comparison of poor families headed by an aged person with families headed by a nonaged person. Because families with aged heads are generally small, these families require less total income to be considered nonpoor. Thus, for two families with equal pretransfer income, a transfer payment of any given amount will fill a larger proportion of the aged family's smaller poverty gap than it will for the nonaged family. In fact, the average transfer amount received by poor aged families is somewhat lower than the average for the nonaged. But because of the differential sizes of the poverty gaps for the two groups, transfers to the aged poor average 116 percent of their pretransfer poverty gap, whereas transfers to the nonaged poor average only 52 percent of the poverty gap (see Table 7).

The recipient rate affects the overall poverty-reducing results through the

10 Of the 21.7 million Social Security beneficiaries in 1966, 67 percent received benefits because they or their spouses were retired workers aged 65 or over. Disabled-worker and survivor beneficiaries amounted to only 33 percent of the total. U.S. Department of Health, Education and Welfare, Social Security Administration, *Social Security Bulletin, Annual Statistical Supplement,* 1967, Table 9, p. 18.

11 For example, in December 1966 the average monthly payment per family under the aid to families with dependent children program ranged from a low of $38 in Mississippi to a high of $227 in New York. Old-age assistance benefits are generally higher than payments under the other categorical programs. They ranged between $39 per person monthly in Mississippi and $104 per month in California. *Welfare in Review,* 5, no. 4 (April 1967), Tables 4 and 7, pp. 25 and 28.

Table 6. Proportion of Poor Families Receiving Any
Transfer Income, by Age, Race, and Family Composition, 1966

Family Characteristic	Total Families Poor before Transfers (Thousands)	(Percent)	Transfer Recipients (Percent)	Nonrecipients (Percent)
Head aged 65 and over	7,578	49.8	95	5
Single individuals	3,545	23.3	93	7
Head and spouse only	2,638	17.3	99	1
All other families	1,395	9.2	95	5
Head under age 65	7,628	50.2	50	50
Single individuals				
White	1,759	11.6	43	57
Nonwhite	472	3.1	42	58
Families				
Male head and spouse only				
White	628	4.1	58	42
Nonwhite	115	0.8	53	47
Female head with children				
White	1,033	6.8	71	29
Nonwhite	684	4.5	69	31
Male head, spouse, and children				
White	1,882	12.4	38	62
Nonwhite	618	4.1	32	68
All other families				
White	270	1.8	69	31
Nonwhite	167	1.1	63	37
Total	15,205	100.0	73	27

Table 7. Percent of Pretransfer Poverty Gap Filled by Transfers, by Age, Family Composition, and Race, 1966

Family Characteristic	Poor before and after Transfers		Poor before but Nonpoor after Transfers	Total Poor before Transfers
	Nonrecipients	Recipients		
Head aged 65 and over	0	63	193	116
Single individuals	0	63	178	91
Head and spouse only	0	69	202	156
All other families	0	58	187	99
Head under age 65	0	52	189	52
Single individuals				
White	0	56	162	48
Nonwhite	0	55	154	38
Families				
Male head and spouse only				
White	0	59	208	76
Nonwhite	0	55	140	48
Female head with children				
White	0	57	204	75
Nonwhite	0	52	161	48
Male head, spouse, and children				
White	0	47	196	44
Nonwhite	0	39	176	23
All other families				
White	0	58	219	88
Nonwhite	0	44	158	41
Total	0	58	191	81

relative weight of those in the group who receive no transfers. With 95 percent of the aged poor receiving some transfer income, the overall ratio of transfers to the pretransfer poverty gap is primarily determined by the extent of "gap-filling" for recipients. For the nonaged poor, on the other hand, even though the gap-filling ratios for recipients are only slightly lower, half the younger families receive no transfers — that is, the ratio is zero. The overall proportion by which transfers close the pretransfer poverty gap for the nonaged is therefore substantially lower.

When we rank the nonaged poor according to the proportion of poverty gap filled, we find that for all nonwhite families — regardless of family composition — transfers close less than the 52 percent overall average for the nonaged. These nonwhite families comprise 27 percent of the nonaged pretransfer poor. More surprisingly, twice as many poor white families — single individuals and families with children headed by a male — also receive transfers amounting to less than half their pretransfer poverty gap. The remaining 25 percent of the nonaged poor, who receive transfers that close more than half their poverty gap, are primarily white couples with no children and white families headed by a female.

Patterns of Transfer Receipts

A great diversity exists in the kinds of transfers received by different subgroups of the poor. Benefits paid under the Social Security programs — including survivor and disability payments to the nonaged as well as retirement payments to the aged — are by far the most prevalent form (see Table 8). Only among nonaged families who remain poor after transfers is the prevalence of Social Security recipients surpassed — although only slightly — by those families receiving public assistance.

Substantial differences exist in the pattern of payments other than Social Security benefits received by the aged and nonaged. Differences in the pattern also exist between families who remain poor and those removed from poverty by transfers. Among aged families removed from poverty, for example, the most prevalent forms of transfers received (other than Social Security) are veterans' and government pensions. Among the nonaged removed from poverty, a much larger proportion of families receive some payments under public assistance, unemployment insurance, and workmen's compensation programs.

We would not expect many families who remain in poverty to receive payments under a large number of different programs. Yet 91 percent of such aged families receive some transfer income, and 78 percent are Social Security recipients. The younger families who remain poor are least likely to receive any transfer payments. For those who do receive some help, the most prevalent form is public assistance. Few nonaged remaining in poverty receive any payments from veterans' programs, government pensions, unemployment insurance, or workmen's compensation.

Table 8. Proportion of Poor Families Receiving Transfers,
by Type of Transfer and by Age of Family Head, 1966
(In Percentages)

Types of Transfer	Families Poor before and after Transfers			Families Poor before but Nonpoor after Transfers		
	Head 65 Years and Over	Head under 65 Years	Total	Head 65 Years and Over	Head under 65 Years	Total
Social Security	78	13	38	94	66	86
Unemployment insurance or workmen's compensation	a	6	4	b	19	6
Public assistance	23	19	20	8	20	11
Veterans' benefits	4	4	4	19	23	20
Government pensions	3	1	2	23	17	21
Any transfer[c]	91	38	58	100	100	100

[a] Less than half of 1 percent.
[b] Insufficient number of cases to show separately.
[c] Details will not add because some families receive more than one type of transfer.

Do many families removed from poverty receive sufficient income from any one program to fill completely their pretransfer poverty gap, or do they more typically require receipts from multiple sources to cross the poverty-income threshold? We find that 92 percent of these families receive transfer payments from only one source (see Table 9). For two thirds of these families, Social Security benefits alone are responsible for keeping or taking them out of poverty. This is a significant accomplishment for a program whose primary objective is not poverty reduction. For all families, the next most important source of aid is government pensions, and this is also the case for the aged.

Table 9. Poor Families Removed from Poverty by Transfers,
by Type and by Age of Family Head, 1966 (In Percentages)

Type of Transfer	Head 65 Years or Over	Head under 65 Years	Total
One type only			
Social Security	71	47	64
Unemployment insurance or workmen's compensation	a	13	4
Government pensions	12	11	12
Veterans' benefits	5	9	6
Public assistance	2	15	6
Two or more types	9	5	8
Total	100	100	100
Number of families (thousands)	3,848	1,472	5,318

[a] Insufficient number of cases to show separately.

However, 10 to 15 percent of the nonaged families removed from poverty receive sufficient benefits to move out of poverty solely from veterans' programs, unemployment insurance, workmen's compensation, or public assistance. Social Security alone completely fills the poverty gap for only about half the 1.5 million families under age 65 who are moved across the poverty line.

Summary and Conclusion

The overall effect of transfer payments in reducing poverty is most pronounced for the aged. Over half the aged poor are taken or kept out of poverty by transfers; this is the case for less than a fifth of nonaged families (see Table 10). But despite this larger percentage reduction, the posttransfer incidence of poverty among the aged is still close to three times the overall rate for nonaged families. Only among aged husband—wife couples is the posttransfer incidence of poverty (16 percent) even close to the 12 percent nonaged rate.

Table 10. Poverty Reduction through Transfers, by Age, Family Composition, and Race, 1966

Family Characteristic	Percent of Families Removed from Poverty by Transfers	Percent Poor before Transfers	Percent Poor after Transfers
Head aged 65 and over	51	64	31
Single individuals	36	78	50
Head and spouse only	74	60	16
All other families	45	46	26
Head under age 65	19	15	12
Single individuals			
White	20	27	22
Nonwhite	9	42	38
Families			
Male head and spouse only			
White	29	8	5
Nonwhite	25	18	13
Female head with children			
White	29	42	30
Nonwhite	11	70	62
Male head, spouse, and children			
White	17	7	6
Nonwhite	8	27	25
All other families			
White	36	15	10
Nonwhite	12	35	31
Total	35	25	16

Although a relatively low percentage of all nonaged families remain poor after transfers, the 12 percent average poverty rate obscures the appallingly high incidence of poverty among certain subgroups of the poor even after receipt of such payments. Thirty-three percent of all nonwhite families remain poor after transfers, whereas the incidence of poverty among white families is only 10 percent. The nonwhite poverty rate among the nonaged is higher than the white rate for all types of families; but for nonwhite families headed by a female, the chances of remaining poor are better than 6 out of 10 even after receipt of transfer income.

Our existing social welfare payments have many objectives and, with the exception of categorical public assistance, were not inaugurated as antipoverty measures. Most of the cash transfer programs began in the 1930s and are predicated on the assumption that a vast majority of people can earn an adequate living through steady employment. Although high employment levels and continued economic growth are necessary for continued progress in reducing poverty, our experience during the postwar period demonstrates that they are not sufficient. It is simply not true that all employed persons can earn incomes sufficient to keep them out of poverty. But our social welfare programs continue to ignore this fact.[12]

Yet even though our social insurance programs were not designed to help people simply because they are poor, as a side effect they do have a significant impact in helping to alleviate poverty. However, we now clearly need new income maintenance programs aimed specifically at the poor if we are to aid the millions of poor families currently ineligible for any financial aid.

Appendix

The Survey of Economic
Opportunity Data

This study is based on 1966 data derived from the 1967 Survey of Economic Opportunity (SEO). This survey was conducted for the Office of Economic Opportunity in the spring of 1967; the field work was performed for OEO by the Bureau of the Census. Creation of the machine-readable SEO files was the joint product of OEO, the ASSIST Corporation, and members of the Brookings Economic Studies and Computer Center staffs.[13]

---

12 An individual employed 40 hours a week for a full year at the minimum wage of $1.60 per hour would earn $3,328. This amount is just $39 above the 1966 economy poverty-income level for a four-person nonfarm family. It is $227 below the 1968 poverty-income threshold of $3,555.

13 Also in existence is a 1966 Survey of Economic Opportunity, which contains a large amount of information comparable to that collected in 1967. A full description of the surveys, including codebooks, sample design and other technical information, may be obtained from the Planning, Research and Evaluation Section, Office of Economic Opportunity, Washington, D.C.

The Surveys of Economic Opportunity include much information routinely collected in the annual February–March Current Population Surveys (CPS). In addition, they contain supplemental financial and demographic information not usually obtained between decennial Census years. CPS items contained in the SEO files include personal characteristics such as age, race, sex, education, family relationship and marital status, as well as work experience and income for the previous year. In addition, in both years information was obtained regarding family assets and liabilities, housing, and migration of individuals.

The SEO sample of 30,000 households, or addresses, consists of two parts. The first part is a national self-weighting sample of approximately 18,000 households, drawn in the same way as the Current Population Survey sample. To obtain better information concerning the poor – particularly the nonwhite poor – the survey also included 12,000 additional households from areas with large nonwhite populations.

Of particular importance for this study is the detailed information collected concerning the receipt of various types of money transfers. Separate questions were asked about Social Security, public assistance, workmen's compensation, unemployment insurance, veterans' pensions, and other government pensions. In combination, these transfers coincide quite closely with the items classified as public welfare expenditures in the Social Security series.

As is true of all sample surveys, the data collected in the SEO are subject to both sampling error and response error. Because of the relatively large sample, the error due to sampling is probably quite small. However, in certain areas the data are known to contain significant errors caused by the nonreporting or underreporting of information.

The extent of nonreporting of various transfer payments is extremely difficult to estimate because the beneficiary unit reported in program statistics is often different from the Census "family" enumeration unit. For example, for a family where two or more members collected unemployment insurance, the survey would report only that (some member of) the family had received such income. The noncomparability of reporting units is especially troublesome with respect to the public assistance programs whereby individuals may be on and off the program rolls at various times during the year. Another reporting error in these data occurs because of the respondent's confusion in reporting the type of payment received. There are undoubtedly many instances where a person knows that "he gets a check from the government" but is not sure of the program under which he should report the payment.

Overall, the transfer payment data reported in the survey accounts for over 80 percent of the aggregate amounts reported in program statistics. However, as is evident in Table A–1, the extent of agreement varies substantially among the different programs. Work is currently under way to correct the data in those cases where the "proper" response can be inferred from other information on the family.

The original SEO data for this study has not been corrected. The estimates should be interpreted as the best available estimates at this time, but they are

Table A–1 Comparison of Money Transfers Reported in the
Survey of Economic Opportunity with Program Data
(In Millions of Dollars)

Type of Transfer	SEO (1)	Program Data[a] (2)	Percent Reported (1) ÷ (2)
Social Security and railroad retirement	$17,408	$20,774	83.8
Unemployment insurance	1,153	1,836	62.8
Government pensions	5,253	5,135	102.3
Veterans' pensions and disability benefits	3,201	4,873	65.7
Public assistance	3,545	4,291	82.6
Workmen's compensation	1,037	2,067	50.2
All transfers	31,597	38,976	81.1

[a] Program data are derived from U.S. Department of Commerce personal income figures for 1966, *Survey of Current Business*, 49 (July 1969), Tables 2.1 and 3.9, pp. 26 and 32. The published data have been adjusted to exclude estimated payments to persons in institutions, persons living abroad, and people who received benefits for part of the year but died prior to the time of the survey.

definitely *only* estimates. The reader should accept the implicit assumption that although the absolute amounts are known to be different from "truth" as recorded in program statistics, the data used are still valid as the best available estimates of "truth."

4

W. Lee Hansen and Burton A. Weisbrod:
The Distribution of Costs and Direct
Benefits of Public Higher Education:
The Case of California

The public higher education system in the United States provides — or at least offers – a public subsidy to young people of college age. The extent to which the young people actually receive the subsidies depends on whether they can qualify for admission, whether they avail themselves of the opportunity to attend, and, if they do, what quantity and quality of education they receive. As a result, the amount of subsidy received through the public financing of higher

From *Journal of Human Resources*, Vol. IV, Spring 1969. © 1969 by the Regents of the University of Wisconsin. Reprinted by permission of The University of Wisconsin Press and the authors. Mr. Hansen and Mr. Weisbrod are from the University of Wisconsin.

education varies greatly from one person to another. Our objective is to estimate the amounts of subsidies received through higher education, the variation in subsidies received by students depending upon the amount of schooling and the kind of schooling they obtain, and the extent to which these subsidies are received in different amounts by students whose families are at different socioeconomic levels.[1]

Attention is restricted to undergraduate education, and the data used are for public education in California. Although higher educational systems differ among states, the results for California appear to be broadly characteristic of those for a number of other states.

A knowledge of the magnitude and distribution of subsidies or direct benefits provided through public higher education, or indeed, through any public program, is important because of what it suggests as appropriate pricing, tax, and expenditure policy. By "appropriate," we mean policies that will be efficient, in the sense of doing the most to raise output, and at the same time equitable, in the sense of doing the most to achieve society's distribution goals, such as providing greater equality of opportunity for young people. We can illustrate some of the possibilities. For those "eligible" for higher education, uniform subsidies may provide a "windfall" to the more financially able but do little to facilitate college attendance by the less well-off. This point might serve as an argument for some kind of flexible pricing system in higher education, although much the same effect might be achieved less directly through the tax system. For those not eligible for public higher education, the provision of other kinds of subsidies or direct-benefit programs may not only yield substantial benefits to others but also help to achieve greater equality — of both educational opportunity and opportunity in general.

Subsidies Students Can Receive

The amounts of public higher education subsidies that college students can and do receive are the difference between tuition and costs -- instructional and capital -- of providing instruction to them. The size of this difference for any student depends on the number of years of instruction received, and the subsidy per year of schooling. The latter, in turn, depends essentially on the costs of the particular college and on its price (primarily tuition).

In 1965 the public subsidy provided through higher education in California ranged from $720 for a year at a junior college to $1,350 and $1,450 for a year in the lower division (first two years) at a California state college and at the University of California, respectively. But the one-year subsidies tell only a

---

1 Little effort seems to have been given to this subject. For one interesting and perceptive foray, see C. Jencks, "Social Stratification and Mass Higher Education," *Harvard Educational Review*, Spring 1968.

portion of the subsidy story, for whereas some students may attend a public college for only a year or even less, others attend for four years or more. Those who attend for longer periods receive larger subsidies not only for that reason alone but also because the subsidies increase as students progress to the upper division levels. For California, students who complete a two-year junior college program receive an average subsidy totaling $1,440, whereas those completing a baccalaureate program at a state college receive four times as large a subsidy ($5,800) and graduates from a University of California campus receive a four-year subsidy of more than $7,100. The actual amounts of subsidies vary, depending upon patterns of transfer among these three segments of the California public higher education system.

The proportions of entering students completing each segment of higher education vary considerably, from about 60 percent at the university, to 55 percent at the state colleges, and to 30 percent at the junior colleges. But even these figures are deceptive because many students do not avail themselves of any public higher education. Some prefer to enter the work force, others enter the military service, and many females marry and do not continue their schooling. Still others enroll in private institutions of higher education in California, whereas another, although smaller, group seeks higher education outside of California.

Of those who do enroll in public higher education in California, the proportions eligible for each segment who actually enroll in that segment is often low. For example, of the 19 percent of high school students eligible for the University of California in 1965, only 5 percent planned to enroll at the university; another 4 percent planned on going to a state college, 5 percent to a junior college, 3 percent to another institution, and 2 percent planned no further education. Of those 17 percent eligible for state colleges (but not for the university), 2 percent planned to enroll at a state college, 8 percent at a junior college, and 4 percent did not plan to enroll at all. With respect to the junior colleges, for which all students are eligible, only some 30 percent of high school graduates planned to enroll; this portion constituted one half of the 64 percent of high school graduates who were not eligible (on the basis of scholastic performance in high school) for either the university or a state college. Thus, whatever their reasons, many high school students enroll at public institutions of higher education in California that provide subsidies smaller than those for which they are eligible.

Just as the amount of public subsidy varies among the three segments of the California higher education system, so do the attrition rates. Students who enter a junior college not only receive the smallest subsidy per year but are most likely to remain in school for only a short time. By contrast, students who enter the University of California receive a far greater subsidy per year and are most likely to receive that subsidy for four years, until graduation. The high attrition rate at the junior college level reflects in part that a number of junior college programs require only one year of schooling. The rate of attrition at the state colleges is somewhat lower, and attrition at the University of California is the lowest, largely as a result of its greater selectivity in admissions.[2] Its first-year attrition rate (15 percent) seems rather high, but the four-year completion rate of 55 percent is within the range for most other comparable four-year institutions. However, an additional three percent of the initial entrants to the University of California completed their work at a state college, and some others undoubtedly graduated from colleges outside the California system of public higher education.

Distribution of Amounts of Subsidies

Using data on instructional and capital costs, transfer patterns among the three systems, and attrition rates, we have constructed a rough distribution of the percentage of an age cohort of high school graduates who receive different amounts of public subsidies for higher education. The information is summarized in Table 1. The rather startling conclusion is that although a small

Table 1. Estimated Distribution of Public Subsidies for Higher Education Based on Amount Received during Period Enrolled

Amount of Subsidy	Percentage of Persons Receiving
0	41
$1–749	14
$750–1,999	30
$2,000–3,499	3
$3,500–4,999	3
$5,000–6,499	6
$6,500 +	3
	100

Source: Developed from data in Tables 1, 2, and 3.

proportion (9 percent) receives rather large subsidies, exceeding $5,000, more than half of the young people in California receive under $750 in total subsidy from higher education. And a substantial fraction (41 percent) receive no subsidy at all. This group is divided between those who obtain no higher education whatsoever (almost 80 percent) and those who plan to attend private colleges within California or colleges outside the state (about 20 percent).

In short, there is a highly unequal distribution in the amounts of public subsidies actually received, even though California prides itself on the wide access to higher education it provides and the high enrollment ratios that

---

2 For additional details see W. L. Hansen and B. A. Weisbrod, *Benefits, Costs, and Finance of Higher Education* (Chicago: Markham Publishing Co., 1969), ch. 4.

presumably reflect this access. Moreover, there is little reason to believe that the distribution of public subsidies through the higher education system is less unequal in other states than it is in California. No state has as widely accessible a junior college system as does California, thus, other states probably have larger proportions of young people who obtain little or no college education.

Distribution of Subsidies by Family Income

What can we say about the distribution of subsidies provided through higher education when measured against students' family income levels? Although this is a difficult question to answer with the available data, we have tried to shed light on it.

First, it is useful to examine the patterns of college-going by level of family income. These patterns are shown in Table 2, where columns 3 through 6 show the family income distributions for all California public college students in 1964, column 2 shows the income distribution for families without children in California public higher education, and column 1 shows the distribution for all California families.

The distributions by family income clearly differ among the groups shown. Median family incomes (see bottom row of Table 2) are highest for parents of university students, followed by state college student families and junior college student families. Lowest is the median for all families without children in the California system. (This category is heavily weighted with elderly and, on average, low-income families.) These patterns are about what we might expect and, in general, conform to the patterns shown in other surveys.[3] Thus, we conclude that access to subsidies is positively related to levels of family income, with the highest single-year subsidy going to UC students (and their families) who already have the highest median family income ($12,000).[4]

We can present some crude figures to illustrate the association of family income and subsidies received, by comparing median family incomes for the groups shown in Table 2 with the amounts of the subsidies going to each of these groups. Table 3 presents our estimates of these data. Median income of

---

3 For example, see the Wisconsin data in L. J. Lins, A. P. Abell, and D. R. Stucki, *Costs of Attendance and Income of Madison Campus Students, The University of Wisconsin, 1964–1965 Academic Year,* Office of Institutional Studies, January 1967; I. M. Boyak, A. P. Abell, and L. J. Lins, *Costs of Attendance and Income of University of Wisconsin-Milwaukee Students, 1964–1965 Academic Year,* Office of Institutional Studies, March 1967; and L. J. Lins, A. P. Abell, and R. Hammes, *Costs of Attendance and Income of University of Wisconsin Center Students, 1964–1965 Academic Year,* Office of Institutional Studies, May 1966.

4 Were we to relate the data shown in Table 2 to the data on subsidies received over the entire college stay, the differences in the subsidies received would be accentuated. The reason is that University of California students are more likely to complete four years than are state college students, and the latter are more likely to complete four years than the vast bulk of students who begin at junior colleges.

Table 2. Distributions of Families, by Income Level and Type of College or University, California, 1964 (In Percents)

Income Class	All Families	Families with Children in California Public Higher Education	Families with Children in California Public Higher Education			
			Total	JC	SC	UC
	(1)	(2)	(3)	(4)	(5)	(6)
$0- 3,999	16.1	17.0	6.6	8.1	4.1	5.0
$4,000–5,999	14.8	14.9	13.0	15.9	10.2	7.5
$6,000–7,999	18.9	19.0	17.6	19.6	17.0	11.1
$8,000–9,999	18.1	18.3	16.4	16.9	17.2	13.1
$10,000–11,999	12.4	12.1	15.8	14.4	19.9	13.3
$12,000–13,999	7.4	7.3	8.8	17.2	10.8	11.3
$14,000–19,999	7.9	7.5	13.0	11.1	13.0	20.3
$20,000–24,999	1.8	1.6	3.4	2.6	3.3	6.6
$25,000 +	2.6	2.3	5.4	4.2	4.5	11.8
Total	100.0%	100.0%	100.0%	100.0%	100.0%	100.0%
Median income	$8,000	$7,900	$9,560	$8,800	$10,000	$12,000

Source: Col. (1) — Letter from Office of Legislative Analyst, California Legislature, in *Tuition for California's Public Institutions of Higher Education*, Joint Committee on Higher Education Hearings, October 13 and 16, 1967, see Tab T, Table 1.
Col. (2) — Percentage distribution of Col. (2), calculated by authors.
Col. (3) — Weighted average of Cols. (4), (5), and (6).
Cols. (4), (5), (6) — Edward Sanders and Hans Palmer, *The Financial Barrier to Higher Education in California* (Claremont: Pomona College, 1965), Table M, p. 21, which relates to distribution of parent-supported students only.

Table 3. Average Family Incomes and Average Higher Education Subsidies Received by Families, by Type of Institution Children Attend, California, 1964

	All Families	Families without Children in California Public Higher Education	Families with Children in California Public Higher Education			
			Total	JC	SC	UC
	(1)	(2)	(3)	(4)	(5)	(6)
1. Average family income[a]	8,000	7,900	9,560	8,800	10 000	12,000
2. Average higher education subsidy per year[b]						
a. Amount in dollars	—	0	880	720	1,400	1,700
b. Percent of line 1	—	0	9	8	14	13
3. Average number of years of higher education completed[c]	n.a.	n.a.	n.a.	1.2	2.6	2.8
4. Average total higher education subsidy[c]						
a. Amount in dollars	—	0	1,700	1,050	3,810	4,870
b. Percent of line 1	—	0	18	12	31	41

[a] Median incomes from Table 5.

[b] Average subsidies are based on the distribution of enrollment by year of school and on distribution of enrollment by type of institution.

[c] Average number of years and average subsidies are based on the assumption that entering students progress through the various types of institutions shown in Table 2, that students are distributed among the various types of institutions as shown in Table 3, and that the various subsidies are those shown in Table 1. Because students transfer among the three higher education systems, the average subsidy shown in line 4a is not obtained simply by multiplying line 2a by line 3.

families of various types is shown in line 1, the one-year subsidy received is given in line 2a, and the subsidy as a percentage of family income is presented in line 2b. Because students first enrolling at each type of institution do not remain in college equally long, the average number of years they are enrolled is also shown, in line 3. The total subsidy received is shown in line 4a, and the percentage of family income that the subsidy constitutes is in line 4b. Because students transfer among the three higher education systems, the average subsidy is not simply the product of the average subsidy in a particular system and the average number of years of schooling obtained by students who *begin* their schooling in that system. As indicated by line 2b, the values of the single year subsidies vary from zero percent of family income for those without children in public colleges and universities (some of these people may have children in private colleges or in public colleges not in California) to 14 percent of family income for those families with state college students.

The average overall subsidy is equal to 9 percent of current money income for all parents of publicly enrolled college students (line 2b, column 3), but the subsidy climbs to 18 percent of family income when we take into account the number of years the educational subsidy is received (line 4b, column 3). Because, as previously noted, the amount of schooling received differs, the average total subsidies (line 4a) rise far more sharply than the single year subsidies (line 2a), as we contrast the families with children enrolled in California junior colleges, state colleges, and university campuses. These patterns of subsidies raise serious questions about the equity of the current system for financing public higher education in California.

At the same time, however, the distributions of students by parental income (as each column in Table 2 shows) are so wide for each type of system – University of California, state college, and junior college – that we cannot draw any strong conclusions about the "class-serving" nature of the entire system of higher education in California. Although the higher subsidy schools tend to draw a higher-income clientele, the overlap of the distributions is still substantial.

We can throw some added light on the equity issue by restructuring recent data presented by the California Coordinating Council for Higher Education.[5] Data from several tables have been combined to show how eligibility and plans for higher education enrollment vary systematically with income.

We see in Table 4 that under 20 percent of the high school graduates qualify for the substantial university subsidies, a product of the academic entry requirements. Even more striking is that the percentage of all students qualifying for the University of California (column 1) rises quite dramatically by family income level – from about 10 percent in the lowest income bracket (under $4,000) to 40 percent in the highest (over $25,000). Thus, the correlation between high school achievement and family income – and all that it reflects –

---

5 Coordinating Council for Higher Education, State of California, *Financial Assistance Programs*, 67–13 (second revision), October 31, 1967, Table 1–2, p. 1–9; Table 1–3, p. 1–10, and Appendix Table B–3.

Table 4. Distribution of High School Graduates by Eligibility for Public Higher Education in California, by Type of Education and Family Income (In Percents)

| Family Income | Percentage Distribution of High School Graduates by Eligibility for | |
	University of California	University of California and State Colleges
	(1)	(2)
$0–3,999	10.7	28.0
$4,000–5,999	11.5	26.3
$6,000–7,999	11.9	30.5
$8,000–9,999	16.2	33.2
$10,000–12,499	19.4	37.1
$12,500–14,999	22.5	39.8
$15,000–17,499	27.9	45.4
$17,500–19,999	29.5	45.1
$20,000–24,999	33.3	46.1
$25,000 +	40.1	54.3
Not reported	13.3	28.0
All	19.6	36.3

Source: Based on data from CCHE, *Financial Assistance Programs*, 67–13 (Second Revision), October 31, 1967, Table 1-2, p. 1–9; Table 1–3, p. 1–10, and Appendix Table B–3.

Note: Excluded from the sample of 8,162 were 302 students planning vocational training, 38 nonrespondents on enrollment plans, and 20 for whom eligibility was indeterminate.

is startling indeed. This pattern persists as we include those eligible for both the university and those eligible for state colleges (column 2). But a close examination of the differences between the two columns shows that the percentage of those eligible only for the state college system is roughly constant with respect to income level; thus, university eligibility requirements account largely for the unequal distribution of opportunity.

Table 5 indicates the extent to which family income influences the likelihood that a student *eligible* for a high subsidy school will go to such a school. For the university (column 1), a larger fraction of the upper- than lower-income students plan to attend; the same holds for the combined university–state college system group (column 2); and the pattern continues – although to somewhat lesser degree – when we consider all high school graduates (column 3). Actually, these results are somewhat deceptive, because those eligible for a "higher" system can also attend a "lower" system. Indeed, when we compare the percentage of university-eligible students who plan to attend one of the three public systems, we find that the proportion is fairly constant with respect to family income, at about 70–75 percent (these data are

Table 5. College Attendance Plans of California High School
Graduates, by Family Income and Higher Education Segment, 1966

Family Income Level	Percent of UC Eligibles Planning to Attend UC	Percent of UC–SC Eligibles Planning to Attend Either UC or SC	Percent of All California High School Graduates Planning to Enroll in UC, SC, or JC
	(1)	(2)	(3)
$0–3,999	30.4	22.5	53.1
$4,000–5,999	26.1	29.7	56.1
$6,000–7,999	23.4	28.1	56.3
$8,000–9,999	21.5	36.5	60.0
$10,000–12,499	25.3	32.6	62.0
$12,500–14,999	26.2	37.5	64.6
$15,000–17,499	26.9	32.1	63.4
$17,500–19,999	33.3	45.7	64.2
$20,000–24,999	45.4	52.0	68.2
$25,000 +	46.7	47.8	57.8
No response	30.5	30.1	47.9

Source: Same as Table 4.
Note: UC (University of California); SC (State Colleges); JC (Junior Colleges).

not shown in the accompanying tables). Much the same kind of pattern emerges
for both the university and the state college eligibles who plan to undertake
higher education. The point, however, is that enrollment in a lower system --
often dictated by family income considerations -- inplies a reduced level of
subsidies.

Who Pays the Taxes?

Having shown the extent to which families in different income groups are
awarded subsidies through the fiscal system by virtue of the provision of higher
education, we turn now to the question of how these subsidies are financed.
Specifically, we estimate distributions of state and local taxes paid by families at
each income level. The objective is to provide a basis for comparing the subsidies
received with the tax payments made. Such information is essential in assessing
the equity of the current methods of financing higher education in the state of
California.

Our approach is to estimate the incidence of the most important state and
local taxes by family income level, so as to note the absolute amount of taxes
paid at each income level. We can then compare this amount with the subsidy
received and note any differences. But we still have no real way of determining
how much of whatever taxes are paid reflect support for higher education, as
against the many other services provided by state and local governments.

Table 6. Estimated Tax Burdens by Income Class, California, 1965

Adjusted Gross Income Class	State Taxes Only Per Family[a]	Effective State Tax Rate[b]	State and Local Taxes Per Family[c]	Effective State and Local Tax Rate[b]
	(1)	(2)	(3)	(4)
$0–3,999	$ 104	5.2	$ 474	23.7
$4,000–5,999	132	2.6	527	10.5
$6,000–7,999	161	2.3	576	8.2
$8,000–9,999	221	2.4	696	7.7
$10,000–11,999	301	2.7	833	7.6
$12,000–13,999	389	3.0	984	7.6
$14,000–19,999	539	3.2	1,228	7.2
$20,000–24,999	865	3.8	1,758	7.8
$25,000 +	2,767	5.5	4,093	8.2

Sources: Personal income, sales, cigarette and beverage taxes by income level were obtained from Letter from Office of Legislative Analyst, State of California in *Tuition for California's Public Institutions of Higher Education*, Joint Committee on Higher Education, Hearings, October 13 and 16, 1967, see Tab T, Table 1. State gasoline taxes and local property taxes were based on itemized tax deductions reported on state income tax returns, 1965, and summarized in Franchise Tax Board, *Annual Reports, 1965* and *1966*, Table 13. Local sales taxes were assumed to be distributed in the same manner as state sales taxes above. Since local sales tax revenues in 1965 equaled one-third of state sales tax revenues, this factor was applied to the estimated amount of state sales taxes in each income level.

[a]Personal income, state sales, cigarette, and alcoholic beverage taxes only.

[b]Taxes as a percent of estimated mean income of each income class. The mean of the highest income interval was arbitrarily assumed to be $50,000.

[c]State taxes include personal income, sales, cigarette, alcoholic beverage, and gasoline taxes. Local taxes include local sales and property taxes.

The average amount of taxes paid at each income level as well as the effective tax rate, for California state taxes alone and for state and local taxes combined, are shown in Table 6. The most important finding is that although the state tax structure (column 2) seems to be somewhat progressive — that is, the effective tax rate rises with income — except in the lowest income classes, the combined state and local tax structure (column 4) is regressive below $8,000 and is essentially proportional above that level.[6]

Let us return to our comparison of the taxes paid with the subsidies received by families with children enrolled in college so that we can observe the extent to which broad groups of families do or do not receive net subsidies through higher education. Such comparisons involve *all* taxes with benefits received from higher education *alone*. As Table 7 shows, the annual value of higher education subsidies (line 2) received by a family with a single child enrolled in a public college exceeds the total amount of all state and local taxes they pay (line 3), by rather substantial amounts. On an overall basis the average higher education subsidy is $880 per year (line 2, column 3), in contrast to total

---

6 The 1967 changes in the California state income tax structure increased, but only slightly, the overall progressivity of the state tax structure.

Table 7. Average Family Incomes, Average Higher Education
Subsidies Received, and Average State and Local Taxes Paid by
Families, by Type of Institution Children Attend in California, 1964

	All Families	Families without Children in California Public Higher Education	Families with Children in California Public Higher Education			
			Total	JC	SC	UC
	(1)	(2)	(3)	(4)	(5)	(6)
1. Average family income[a]	8,000	7,900	9,560	8,800	10,000	12,000
2. Average higher education subsidy per year[b]	–	0	880	720	1,400	1,700
3. Average total state and local taxes paid[c]	620	650	740	680	770	910
4. Net transfer (Line 2 – Line 3)	--	--650	+140	+40	+630	+790

[a]From Table 5.

[b]From Table 6.

[c]Total state and local tax rates were applied to the median incomes for families in each column.

state and local taxes paid of $740 (line 3, column 3); this result indicates an annual net transfer of $140 from all taxpayers to parents of each college student. But this average conceals wide differences by type of college.

For families with a child at one of the state colleges or at one of the university campuses, the net transfers range from $630 to $790 per year. Meanwhile, families without children or with children not enrolled in public institutions of higher education receive no subsidy whatsoever, although they pay an average of $650 in state and local taxes. This is not to suggest that such families should pay no state and local taxes, for some may have benefited in the past, others may benefit in the future, and still others may have opted for more expensive nonpublic California higher education. Moreover, state and local taxes finance public services other than higher education. In any case, as is evident from a comparison of line 1 and line 4, the current method of financing public higher education leads to a redistribution of income from lower- to higher-income families; indeed, substantial progressivity exists in the resulting pattern of transfers.

Conclusion

Public policy regarding higher education must consider a number of factors, among which the economic efficiency of expenditures on higher education and the distributional equity of the public support for higher education are surely prominent. After a brief analysis of the economic efficiency issue, we turned to the primary objective, an empirical investigation of the distributional effects of public higher education in our most populous state, California.

The general nature of the redistributive effects of the current method of financing public higher education in California is clear. Some low-income persons have benefited handsomely from the availability of publicly subsidized higher education. But on the whole, the effect of these subsidies is to promote greater rather than less inequality among people of various social and economic backgrounds, by making available substantial subsidies that lower-income families either are not eligible for or cannot make use of because of other conditions and constraints associated with their income position.

To overcome the effects of the present system would require a substantial overhaul of the pricing system in public higher education, a realignment of the tax structure, and/or a broadening of the eligibility base for public expenditure programs. With respect to the latter alternative, eligibility for public subsidies to young people might well be expanded so as to embrace all young people – not just those who go on to college but also those who opt for alternative ways of expanding their earning power, such as apprenticeship or on-the-job training. Public subsidies may even be used as investments in businesses. In any case, whatever the degree to which our current higher education programs are rooted in the search for equality of opportunity, the results clearly leave much to be desired.

---

5   Robert W. Hartman: A Comment on the Pechman– Hansen–Weisbrod Controversy

---

The controversy over financing higher education in the pages of the *Journal of Human Resources*[1] has told readers that the system of public higher education is (a) regressive,[2] and (b) progressive,[3] and therefore the system

From *Journal of Human Resources*, Vol. V, No. 4, 1970. © 1970 by the Regents of the University of Wisconsin. Reprinted by permission of The University of Wisconsin Press and the author. Robert Hartman is affiliated with the Brookings Institution.

1 See W. Lee Hansen and Burton A. Weisbrod, "The Distribution of Costs and Benefits of Public Higher Education: The Case of California," *Journal of Human Resources*, 4 (Spring 1969), pp. 176–91; Joseph A. Pechman, "The Distributional Effects of Public Higher Education in California," *Journal of Human Resources*, 5 (Summer 1970), pp. 361–70.

2 Hansen and Weisbrod, "The Distribution . . .," p. 191.

3 Pechman, "The Distributional Effects . . .," p. 361.

should be (c) scrapped, or (d) replicated and broadened. This note discusses why both (a) and (b) are true, but irrelevant to (c) and (d).

Description of the Data

In Table 1 I have tried to capture the essence of both the Hansen–Weisbrod and the Pechman discoveries about the nature of the public higher education system. The numbers are fictitious but easy to deal with, and they are representative of the California system probed by the two articles cited.

Table 1. Illustrative Distribution of Benefits and Taxes For Public Higher Education

Income Levels	Number of Potential Students	Tax Per Family (Dollars)	Benefits Per Family (Dollars)	Net Benefits (Dollars)	Average Net Benefits (Dollars)
$ 2,000	3	100	0	− 100	
		100	0	− 100	
		100	500	+ 400	
Total		300	500	+ 200	+ 67
$10,000	3	400	533	+ 133	
		400	533	+ 133	
		400	533	+ 133	
Total		1,200	1,600	+ 400	+133
$30,000	3	1,200	1,500	+ 300	
		1,200	1,500	+ 300	
		1,200	0	−1,200	
Total		3,600	3,000	− 600	−200

The data illustrate a potential nine-student world; some students are poor (family income of $2,000), some are rich ($30,000), some middling. The middling students make heaviest use of public higher education, and they go to middling-subsidized schools (state colleges in California). The rich participate to a lesser extent, but they go first-class (University of California) when they go. The poor participate least, and when they use the system they take the smallest subsidy home.[4]

Hansen and Weisbrod have sliced the table by the *benefits* column to derive their conclusions, as set out in Table 2, concluding thereby that the system is regressive. It is regressive in the sense that the higher one goes on the benefit scale, the richer are the families. It is even regressive when the taxes paid by

---

4 See entries in the benefit column. Zero signifies nonattendance at any public institution.

Table 2. Income and Taxes by Benefits Received[a]

	Benefits Received			
	$0	*$500*	*$533*	*$1,500*
Median income	$2,000	$2,000	$10,000	$30,000
Median tax	100	100	400	1,200
Net benefit of median family	−100	+400	+133	+300

[a]See Hansen and Weisbrod, "The Distribution of Costs and Benefits of Public Higher Education: The Case of California," *Journal of Human Resources*, 4 (Spring 1969), Table 10, p. 190. Reprinted by permission of the publisher.

those families are taken into account, as can be seen by the fact that the typical "University of California" student, receiving $1,500 in benefits, pays taxes well under the cost of his education, while the non-participating family or the "junior college student," whose family is poor, receives a nonexistent or low subsidy.

Pechman aggregates the same raw data by *income class* to get the figures set out in Table 3, concluding thereby that on the average, at least, public higher education accomplishes about what its advocates expected of it: the rich pay for the education of the middle- and lower-income classes. Even though state-local taxes are regressive (in the formal sense) in this illustration — and in California — they are not as regressive (that is, pro poor) as the distribution of benefits. Thus, high-income classes are net payers and low-income classes are net recipients under the higher education system.

All these manipulations are simply another way of describing the raw facts, which are: (1) Poor people pay taxes and very few of them use public higher education. Those who do, gain thereby; those who don't, don't. (2) Middle income people are heavy users of the system. Their taxes don't cover the costs. (3) A few rich people use the system and gain handsomely thereby. The rest of the rich pay substantial taxes and get no direct return.

Table 3. Net Benefits by Income Class[a]

Income Class	Average Tax	Average Benefit	Net Benefit
$ 2,000	$ 100	$ 167	$ + 67
$10,000	400	533	+ 133
$30,000	1,200	1,000	− 200

[a]See Pechman, "The Distributional Effects of Public Higher Education in California," *Journal of Human Resources*, 5 (Summer 1970), Table 3, p. 366. Reprinted by permission of the publisher.

If there is some way to reduce all these words to a scalar measure, neither author has discovered it. Pechman's method of presenting data would probably condone farm subsidies,[5] while Hansen-Weisbrod would condemn TVA (among all subsidized consumers of high kilowattage will be found a disproportionate share of the rich).

Confusion about Goals

Hansen and Weisbrod put their collective finger over the tax column (in the first table) and, looking at the benefit column, ask: "Is this the best way to spend public funds for redistributive purposes?" Their conclusion is that "it is clear that whatever the degree to which our current higher education programs are rooted in the search for equality of opportunity, the results still leave much to be desired,"[6] which is a restrained way of saying that the distribution of benefits is the reverse of what would be required for equalization. Pechman's response to this is to assert that if all the benefit and tax entries in the first table were to be zero and higher education reverted entirely to the private market, society would be worse off. He offers two reasons for this assertion and, as he indicates, neither has anything much to do with the tax and benefit distributions.

First, Pechman points out that elimination of government subsidies can be optimal only if "the ratio of private benefits to total benefits . . . is as high as 100 percent, as Hansen and Weisbrod and other economists assume."[7] Pechman clearly assumes otherwise.

Second, Pechman concedes that some "grant-loan systems, combined with full-cost tuition fees, may appear to be more 'efficient' in principle," but he is not persuaded that "such systems can be operated with the evenhandedness with which the free tuition system has operated."[8] In a nutshell, what he seems to

---

5 There were 264 producers who received in excess of $100,000 under the major agricultural subsidy programs in calendar 1968. These farms collected "only" $52 million out of the total $3.2 billion in agricultural subsidies under these programs in that year. By contrast there were (in 1967) more than 66,000 taxpayers whose gross income exceeded $100,000, and the aggregate individual income tax revenues of these payers exceeded $5 billion. Assuming that 2 percent of the taxes of the rich went to pay for agricultural subsidies (agricultural subsidies were about 2 percent of federal nontrust fund outlays in fiscal 1968), we should allocate $100 million (0.02 of $5 billion) to farm subsidies. Thus agricultural price support programs result in $52 million in benefits but $100 million in taxes in the highest income classes. Another progressive program! Data from Walter W. Wilcox, "Economic Aspects of Farm Program Payment Limitations," Legislative Reference Service, Library of Congress, November 6, 1969, p. 2; *Statistics of Income, 1967, Individual Income Tax Returns*, Department of the Treasury, Internal Revenue Service, 79 (7–69), p. 8; *The Budget of the United States Government, 1970*, pp. 9, 16.

6 Hansen and Weisbrod, "The Distribution . . .," p. 191.

7 Pechman, "The Distributional Effects . . .," p. 369.

8 *Ibid.*, pp. 369–70. Hansen and Weisbrod have recommended a full-cost tuition cum grant program for Wisconsin. See their "A New Approach to Higher Education Finance," University of Wisconsin Institute for Research on Poverty, Discussion Paper 64–70, mimeo.

fear is that proposals for "efficiency" in distribution of benefits will lead to withdrawal of all public support.

And that brings us back to where we should be in the debate over higher education finance: namely, at basic principles and empirical questions. The basic principles are that public higher education should be seeking to achieve two goals: (1) Equalization of opportunity. This goal clearly implies that subsidies be targeted on lower-income students. (2) The provision of below-cost higher education to ensure that both public and private benefits are accounted for in the enrollment decision. This goal need not imply that subsidies be targeted on children from low-income families. Indeed, it seems to me that a good starting point for developing criteria for the appropriate distribution of subsidies to ensure that public benefits are preserved is that all students in post-secondary education should receive approximately equal subsidies. Advocates of public-supported institutions should tell us why a Berkeley student is more productive of social benefits than a Stanford student or than a junior college student.

The third basic principle is that nature and legislatures are niggardly, and there is a trade-off between the two public policy goals. We cannot avoid asking whether we are willing to risk a little less assurance of public benefits in exchange for a little more equalization of opportunity. And that means that we do have to talk about how much we value such things as the growth of nonauthoritarianism (attitudes that "are characterized by flexibility, tolerance, objectivity, and a lack of dependency upon rules or rituals for dealing with ideas, objects, and people")[9] and other social benefits of higher education as well as debating the value of opportunity equalization.

Finally, the empirical question raised by Pechman, and skirted by Hansen and Weisbrod, is: How serious is the trade-off between efficient support for equalization and the partial support of higher education from public treasuries? Policy analysts should ask whether programs of support for higher education at the federal and state levels can be articulated in such a way as to preserve and broaden the social benefits of higher education and eliminate the disgraceful lack of equality of opportunity in the United States. This problem is not easy. It is serious. And no distribution of taxes and benefits is going to help much in providing the answer.

---

9 See Robert H. Berls, "An Exploration of the Determinants of Effectiveness in Higher Education," in *The Economics and Financing of Higher Education in the United States* (Joint Economic Committee, 1969), p. 221. Berls reports on several studies of the attitudinal change of college students. The possibility that non-authoritarian attitudes may also increase the likelihood of violent antisocial behavior (a social disbenefit) does not allow us to conclude that the social benefits cancel or that they are "vague and general" (Milton Friedman, "The Higher Schooling in America," *The Public Interest* (Spring 1968), pp. 110–11). The debate over the external effects must be value-laden and explicitly so. How do we value the risk of riots versus the risk of repression?

6

Introduction

Between 1956 and 1970, federal budget outlays for farm price support programs and related direct payments to farmers averaged $3.1 billion per year. In the last three years of this period, 1968 through 1970, annual budget outlays averaged $5 billion. These costs of supporting farm prices and incomes were paid by the taxpayer. But consumers also pay, through higher prices, part of the costs of farm price support programs. Federal farm programs are designed — recently through output restrictions, in earlier years through loans and purchases of farm products -- to raise the price of farm products above what a free market would have yielded. While estimates vary, actual farm prices in recent years would have been perhaps 15 percent lower had federal price support programs not been in effect. At supported prices the value of farm marketings in 1969 amounted to over $47 billion. With prices 15 percent lower, the same volume of farm output could have been purchased for about $7 billion less. Some $1.5 billion of this reduction would represent lower prices paid by farmers themselves in buying feed, seed, and livestock. Lower prices for exports would represent another $1 billion. Nonfarm consumers, therefore, paid in recent years about $4.5 billion more for the farm products they purchased than they would have had there been no federal price support programs.[1]

Farm price support and related programs thus cost the taxpayer some $5 billion per year in budgetary outlays, and consumers of food and fiber some $4.5 billion in higher food prices — although the latter figure may overstate somewhat the long-term price-raising effects of farm support programs. The total transfer from consumers and taxpayers, in the range of $9 to $10 billion, compares with a total federal, state, and local cost of various public assistance (welfare) programs, including Medicaid, of slightly over $10 billion in 1969. Procurement, operation, and maintenance of the nation's strategic nuclear forces cost about $9 billion in fiscal 1969.

In terms of their cost, farm subsidies clearly rank among the more important public programs. They have a noticeable effect on many vital factors

From *The Distribution of Farm Subsidies* by Charles Schultze, pp. 1–44. © 1971 by The Brookings Institution, Washington, D.C. Reprinted by permission of The Brookings Institution.

1 With output restrictions removed and prices lower, more food and fiber would be produced and consumed. As a consequence farmers' cash receipts from marketing would not fall by the same percentage as prices.

in the national economy – the allocation of resources, the location of population and industry, the balance of payments, and so on. One of the major impacts of farm subsidies is upon income distribution, which raises the question "Who gets the subsidies?" Specifically, to what extent do farm programs represent a transfer of income from a relatively affluent urban population to a relatively depressed and low-income farm community? While such a transfer would not necessarily in itself justify the programs, it would at least indicate an effort to distribute income in a way that most people would consider equitable.

In 1969 the median family income of the nonfarm population was $9,600, that of farm families $6,400, or some 33 percent lower. The transfer of substantial sums from the nonfarm to the farm population would thus seem likely to distribute income more evenly. This is not the case, however. Farm subsidies are not distributed in accordance with income levels – poor families receiving the most assistance and rich families the least. Rather they tend, at least roughly, to be distributed in proportion to the volume of production on each farm. The more a farm produces, the greater the value of price supports. Moreover, most of the cash payments a farmer receives from the government depend on the size of his acreage allotment or his production, both of which vary directly with the size of his farm.

A relatively small number of large farmers produce the bulk of agricultural goods sold in the United States. Three-fourths of the sales of farm products are made from 568,000 farms with annual sales of $20,000 or more. Those farms comprise only 19 percent of all farms. The average income of their operators, from farm and nonfarm sources, was $19,900 in 1968 and $20,900 in 1969. Since farm subsidies accrue roughly in proportion to sales, it follows that the bulk of subsidies go to that fifth of farmers with the highest average income. At the other end of the scale are 1.5 million small farmers with annual sales of less than $5,000 and annual incomes, from farm and nonfarm sources, averaging about $7,900.[2] They account for only 5 percent of farm sales and a correspondingly small fraction of farm subsidy benefits.

Most farm subsidy programs are vested not in the farmer as an individual but in the land on his farm. The farmer's benefits are based on his acreage allotment or acreage history. This determines how many acres he must refrain from planting, as a condition for participation in the program. Should the farmer leave the farm, he cannot directly take his subsidy with him. The subsidy privileges remain with the land. As a general rule, the land retains its acreage allotment and its acreage history, whoever owns it. Naturally, therefore, the value of the annual subsidy tends to get reflected, at least partially, in the price of the farmland.[3] In combination with a number of other factors, this

---

2 A large number of part-time farmers are included in this total. The average net income of this group from farming is only $1,300.

3 Cotton and tobacco allotments may be sold. Thus the capitalized value of the subsidy program may be separated from the land, and the farmer can realize that value without selling the land itself.

capitalization process has tended to drive the price of farmland up. As a consequence, the chief benefits of farm subsidies have accrued to those who purchased land before subsidies became prevalent. Farmers buying land in later years, however – younger farmers and those expanding their acreage to take advantage of technological advances – have received less advantage from the farm programs. The benefits of higher prices and direct subsidies have at least partly been offset by the added costs incurred because of higher land prices. And farmers who have rented land have found many of the benefits disappearing in higher rental payments to landlords.

Indeed, at the limit, a subsidy attached to land eventually ends up granting no benefits to farmers. To the extent that the value of the subsidy is capitalized into land prices, the higher carrying costs soak up the annual subsidy, as land gradually changes hands over the years. But since subsidy values are frozen into the price of land, any attempt to reduce or remove them would leave recent purchasers of land with incomes below what they would have been before the subsidy program started and confront them with a capital loss. Paradoxically, therefore, after a number of years have passed, such programs end up transferring little net income to the second generation of recipients, but at the same time become so frozen into asset values that their removal would bring substantial hardship.

Whatever the advantages or disadvantages of the farm subsidy program, it is not a welfare program in the sense of transferring income to low-income farm families. The bulk of the subsidies accrue to that small group of farmers with net incomes averaging $20,000. And because the value of the subsidy tends to get reflected in farmland prices, the subsidies are gradually translated into capital gains for long-term holders of land, while recent purchasers and renters receive a much smaller benefit, losing at least part of the subsidy in higher carrying costs or rents.

The Distribution of Benefits from Farm Programs

The benefits of farm price support programs are measured in this study principally in terms of the income farmers receive beyond what they would have received in the absence of the programs. This additional income is composed of both direct payments and price support benefits resulting from the support of farm market prices at levels above what a free market would yield.[4]

---

4 The use of the term "price supports" can sometimes be confusing. In the case of corn, for example, farmers receive a market price for their crop, plus a direct government payment per bushel produced. These direct payments are called "price support payments," and the sum of the two (market price plus price support payments per bushel) is called "the support price." For purposes of clarity, price supports in this study refer to actions taken to hold actual market prices above free market levels. Payments received from the government (including the value of wheat certificates) are called "direct payments."

Distribution of Benefits by Size of Farm

There are several different ways of looking at the question "Who gets the benefits of farm programs?" James Bonnen has made extensive calculations of benefits under the major farms programs, ranking farms by the size of their acreage allotments and then indicating percentages of benefits going to farms in the various size classes. Bonnen uses Department of Agriculture data on acreage allotments distributed by size to compute the distribution of price support benefits; he assumes the benefits are proportional to acreage allotment, increasing as the allotments increase. The distribution of the direct payment benefits for wheat and feed grains he also calculates from Department of Agriculture data on payments to farmers in each allotment size class.

Bonnen's data, summarized in Table 1, show a significant concentration of benefits from price support programs among large farmers. With two exceptions sugar beets and feed grain diversion payments — both price support and direct payment benefits of the farm commodity programs are more highly concentrated among large farmers than is farm income itself.[5] In almost every case, the top 20 percent of farmers got more than half the benefits. Conversely, the smallest 40 percent of farmers received only a very modest fraction of the benefits, usually less than 10 percent. The difference in the degree of concentration of benefits among different programs (sugar, rice, wheat, and so forth) appears to depend primarily on the degree of concentration of their production and sales among larger producers. Analysis of census of agriculture data indicates that the ranking of crops by benefits concentration, as in the Bonnen table, would match a ranking by sales concentration. Production of sugar cane, cotton, and rice is far more concentrated among large producers than is production of wheat, feed grains, peanuts, tobacco, and sugar beets.

The very nature of current price support programs guarantees that benefits will be more heavily concentrated among large farmers than is total farm income. On small farms, net income is a high percentage of cash receipts. Much of the small farmer's input is his own labor, the return to which is treated not as an expense but as part of income. While large farmers' cash receipts are much higher, their expenses — for fertilizer, machinery, and hired labor — are also much greater. Their own labor is a smaller fraction of total inputs and their net income a smaller fraction of cash receipts than are those of small farmers. Price supports raise prices and cash receipts above free market levels by about the same percentage for large and small farmers, but raise net income proportionately more for large farmers than for small ones. And the large farmers' share of total price support benefits will be proportionally larger than their share of net income.

An example will help. Assume a situation with two farm classes, each with

---

5 The agricultural conservation program, which shows the least concentration, is not a commodity support program and therefore is not tied to production volume. Moreover, it has certain built-in features effectively limiting the payment large farmers can receive.

Table 1. Distribution of Farm Income and Commodity Program Benefits by Farm Size, Mid-1960s (Percent of Total Income or Benefits)

Source and Year	Lower 20 Percent	Lower 40 Percent	Lower 60 Percent	Top 40 Percent	Top 20 Percent	Top 5 Percent	Gini Concentration Ratio[a]
Farm and farm manager total money income, 1963	3.2	11.7	26.4	73.6	50.5	20.8	0.468
Program benefits							
Sugarcane, 1965	1.0	2.9	6.3	93.7	83.1	63.2	0.799
Cotton, 1964	1.8	6.6	15.1	84.9	69.2	41.2	0.653
Rice, 1963	1.0	5.5	15.1	84.9	65.3	34.6	0.632
Wheat, 1964							
Price supports	3.4	8.3	20.7	79.3	62.3	30.5	0.566
Direct payments	6.9	14.2	26.4	73.6	57.3	27.9	0.480
Total	3.3	8.1	20.4	79.6	62.4	30.5	0.569
Feed grains, 1964							
Price supports	0.5	3.2	15.3	84.7	57.3	24.4	0.588
Direct payments	4.4	16.1	31.8	68.2	46.8	20.7	0.405
Total	1.0	4.9	17.3	82.7	56.1	23.9	0.565
Peanuts, 1964	3.8	10.9	23.7	76.3	57.2	28.5	0.522
Tobacco, 1965	3.9	13.2	26.5	73.5	52.8	24.9	0.476
Sugar beets, 1965	5.0	14.3	27.0	73.0	50.5	24.4	0.456
Agricultural conservation program, 1964							
All eligibles	7.9	15.8	34.7	65.3	39.2	n.a.	0.343
Recipients	10.5	22.8	40.3	59.7	36.6	13.8	0.271

Source: James T. Bonnen, "The Absence of Knowledge of Distributional Impacts: An Obstacle to Effective Public Program Analysis and Decisions," in *The Analysis and Evaluation of Public Expenditures: The PPB System*, A Compendium of Papers Submitted to the Subcommittee on Economy in Government of the Joint Economic Committee, 91 Cong. 1 sess. (1969), Vol. 1, Table 7, p. 440.

n.a. = not available.

[a]The more closely the Gini concentration ratio approaches 1, the more unequal is the distribution; 0 represents a completely equal distribution.

the following characteristics (remembering that the return to the farmer's own labor is included in the net income figure):

Item	Total	One Large Farm	Five Small Farms
Cash receipts	$110,000	$60,000	$50,000
Expenses	75,000	45,000	30,000
Net income	$ 35,000	$15,000	$20,000

Now assume a price support program that raises prices and cash receipts by 20 percent. The result will be as follows:

Item	Total	One Large Farm	Five Small Farms
Original cash receipts	$110,000	$60,000	$50,000
Addition from price supports			
(20 percent of cash receipts)	22,000	12,000	10,000
Less: expenses	75,000	45,000	30,000
Net income	$ 57,000	$27,000	$30,000
Percent of net income before			
price supports	100	43	57
Percent of total price support			
benefits	100	55	45

The Bonnen approach to measuring the distribution of benefits from farm programs has one major advantage. It does not require the very difficult and controversial estimate of the dollar value of price support benefits, which involves a calculation of what free market prices and incomes would be. Since it only seeks to determine the relative distribution of benefits, the Bonnen approach avoids the necessity of calculating absolute benefits.

But one of the shortcomings of Bonnen's measurements is their failure to provide information on the income level of the farmers receiving the benefits. A concentration of 57 percent of price support benefits among the top 20 percent of feed grain producers, ranked by size of acreage, is indeed significant. But in terms of income distribution, it makes all the difference in the world whether their net income averages $4,000 per year or $20,000. If their average income were $4,000, those producers by most standards would be judged far from affluent. The opposite judgment would seem reasonable in the $20,000 case. The income distribution effects of farm programs can best be judged by the distribution of benefits by income size class and the absolute magnitude of the income support provided each farm income group.

Even for judging the relative distribution of benefits, it is improper to assume a one-to-one correlation between acreage size class and economic size class. Not all large farms have large sales and income; and not all farms with high sales and income are large acreage farms. The 1964 census of agriculture showed, for example, that there were 19,300 feed grain farms with annual sales of over $40,000. The average size of these farms was 1,540 acres. But 2,800 of them were of less than 500 acres, and 7,000 less than 700 acres. Conversely, 106,000 feed grain farms had annual sales in the $5,000–$10,000 range, and an average size of 347 acres. Yet, 19,000 of these farms had more than 500 acres. There were almost as many farms in this $5,000–$10,000 sales class, with acreages in the 1,000 to 2,000 range, as there were in the $40,000-and-over sales class.

Another problem in distributing benefits by acreage classes is the large number of farms that produce significant amounts of more than one product. A farm with a small acreage of cotton may have a large acreage devoted to soybeans. Feed grain producers may also grow wheat, and vice versa. In 1968, for example, of the farmers who received total payments exceeding $10,000, 21,000 received cotton payments in combination with direct payments under other programs such as feed grain, wool, and wheat. Only 7,768 farmers received cotton payments exclusively. Distributing benefits by farm size group on a crop-by-crop basis does not reveal the distributive effects of multiple cropping.

Distribution of Benefits by Income Groups

Determining how the benefits from U.S. farm programs are distributed among farmers of different income levels presents three major problems: measuring the magnitude of the benefits; estimating the distribution of benefits to farms grouped according to economic class; and relating the economic class grouping to a net income grouping.

Measuring the Magnitude of the Benefits   Data are readily available on the magnitude of direct payment benefits. Table 2 summarizes those payments annually from 1955 to 1969. Except for a sharp peak in 1957 and 1958, as the soil bank contracts were inaugurated, payments have grown steadily over the period, from $229 million in 1955 to $3.8 billion in 1969.[6] This increase is partly due to the more ambitious income and price support objectives adopted in the early 1960s. Beginning in 1961, direct payments were made to feed grain producers as a means of purchasing acreage restrictions. In 1963, direct payments were partially substituted for high market price supports and mandatory controls in the feed grains program, in 1964 in the wheat program, and in 1965 in the cotton program. Continued large increases in yields raised the cost of achieving supply controls for feed grains, and to a lesser extent wheat. At any given support price level, increases in yields raise the potential return on planted acres and, therefore, the cost of inducing farmers to forgo planting.

---

6 The total budgetary costs of farm programs exceed this amount because they include administrative expenses, storage and interest costs, inventory transactions, and similar items.

Table 2. Direct Payments under Various Farm Programs, 1955 through 1969 (In Millions of Dollars)

Year	Conservation[a]	Soil Bank	Farm Program Sugar	Wool	Feed Grain	Wheat	Cotton	Cropland Adjustment	Total
1955	188	—	41	—	—	—	—	—	229
1956	220	243	37	54	—	—	—	—	554
1957	230	700	32	53	—	—	—	—	1,016
1958	215	815	44	14	—	—	—	—	1,089
1959	233	323	44	82	—	—	—	—	682
1960	223	370	59	51	—	—	—	—	702
1961	236	334	53	56	772	42	—	—	1,493
1962	230	304	64	54	841	253	—	—	1,747
1963	231	304	67	37	843	215	—	—	1,696
1964	236	199	79	25	1,163	438	39	—	2,181
1965	224	160	75	18	1,139	525	70	—	2,463
1966	231	145	71	34	1,293	679	773	51	3,277
1967	237	129	70	29	865	731	932	85	3,079
1968	227	114	75	66	1,366	747	787	81	3,462
1969	201	46	78	61	1,643	858	828	78	3,794

Source: USDA, Economic Research Service (ERS), *Farm Income Situation*, FIS-216 (July 1970), p. 64

[a]Includes payments under the agricultural conservation program (ACP) and the Great Plains conservation program.

Table 3. Net Farm Income, with and without Direct Payments,
1955 through 1969

Period	Realized Net Income, Excluding Payments	Direct Payments[a]	Realized Net Income, Including Payments
	Average Annual Total Income (Millions of Dollars)		
1956–60	11,666	10	11,676
1961–65	11,755	1,230	12,985
1966–69	12,774	2,660	15,434
1967–69[b]	12,430	1,704	15,134
	Average Annual Income Per Farm (Dollars)		
1956–60	2,761	2	2,763
1961· 65	3,307	345	3,652
1966--69	4,123	857	4,980
1967–69[b]	4,074	885	4,959

Source: *Farm Income Situation,* July 1970, pp. 44, 46, 57, 64.

[a]Direct payments for wheat (including value of certificates paid by processors), feed grains, cotton, sugar, and wool; excludes portion going to nonfarm landlords.

[b]These figures show the final period excluding 1966, a year of exceptionally short crops and high income.

Farm income exclusive of direct payments has remained remarkably constant since the late 1950s. The continuing rise in total farm income is therefore due to the steady increase in direct payments (see Table 3).[7] Total income per farm has risen even more sharply.

Price support benefits are, of course, much more difficult to estimate than direct payment benefits, since they represent the difference between income actually earned by farmers in the sale of farm products and the income they would have earned under free market conditions. Without supply controls, production of most, if not all, price-supported crops would increase. Prices would fall, and with low price elasticities of demand, cash receipts of farmers would be reduced. The prices, output, and incomes that would prevail under these conditions must be estimated in order to measure price support benefits. The wide range of factors, about which some estimates must be made, includes:

1. Acreages planted and yields of various crops with acreage restrictions removed and CCC loans and purchases eliminated;
2. The price elasticities of demand, both domestic and export, for the commodities involved;
3. The impact of lower grain prices on livestock feeding, production, and sales;

7 This is not to say that income per farm, exclusive of direct payments, would have remained constant had farm programs been abolished and direct payments been eliminated. Because they were used in part to purchase reductions in farm output, direct payments helped keep farm prices and cash receipts from marketings at higher levels than would otherwise have prevailed.

4. The impact of lower returns from previously price-supported crops on the production and prices of other commodities. Because of the substitutability, both in production and consumption, among farm commodities, the effect of removing price supports would extend to returns from other commodities as well as from price-supported crops;

5. The changes in production expenses that would occur under free market conditions. On the one hand, increased output would tend to raise expenses. On the other hand, several factors would tend to reduce them: prices for purchased feed, seed, and livestock would be lower; removal of the acreage restrictions that are currently used to control supplies would improve the mix of inputs (land, labor, capital) and thereby lead toward lower costs; with sharply lower incomes, farmers' ability to purchase machinery and other capital would be curtailed.

In the short run the major impact of the removal of price supports would fall directly on the price-supported crops. After some period of time, livestock prices and cash receipts would drop as lower grain prices stimulated additional meat production. Also, the lower returns from planting the previously price-supported crops would induce larger production and lower prices for other crops. Even those relatively efficient farmers who today produce the bulk of farm output and earn returns on their investment and labor equivalent to what they would realize in nonfarm employment would, for some time at least, earn subnormal returns.

Over a longer period of time the reduced returns from producing farm commodities should lead to some restrictions of supply and to a partial recovery of prices. While the larger farmers who produce most of the agricultural output might not cut back their production, many marginal farmers would in the long run be forced out of farming altogether. The exodus from farming would be accelerated (unless unemployment rates outside of farming were high). Prices would rise more nearly to cover costs, including a reasonable return on investment and family labor for those who produced the bulk of farm output. Whether farming would eventually become as economically attractive as other sectors of the economy, and how long it would take for subnormal farm returns to be eliminated, is a matter about which there is much controversy and little knowledge. In any event, current farm programs are primarily designed precisely to avoid this long period of subnormal returns to large farmers.

The estimates of free market prices and incomes used in calculating price support benefits do not take into account the long-term adjustment. They cover a period long enough to allow the impact on livestock production and non-price-supported crops to accrue, but not long enough to allow for an accelerated exodus of farmers to other occupations. As a consequence the measure of price support benefits used here – however accurately it may portray the short- and intermediate-run effects of current farm programs – does overstate the long-run supplement to farmers' income these programs provide.

Free Market Estimates of Farm Prices and Incomes   In the early 1960s a number of pioneering efforts were undertaken to construct models of the farm economy that could be used to predict farm prices, output, and income under varying conditions. Some of these models were designed in response to congressional requests for estimates of the consequences of various alternative farm programs, including one without price supports or supply controls.

The Joint Economic Committee of the Congress in 1960 published the results of a model, constructed by George Brandow of Pennsylvania State University, that projected farm prices, output, and incomes to 1965 under the assumption that price supports and supply controls had been eliminated. Another model, developed by the U.S. Department of Agriculture to make the same projections under roughly corresponding assumptions, was also published in 1960 by the Senate Agriculture and Forestry Committee as Senate Document 77. Periodically since then, the Economic Research Service (ERS) of the Department of Agriculture has used a model of the farm economy to estimate the impact of removing price support and supply control programs; the results have been summarized in various congressional publications. The 1968 ERS model estimates what the major farm economic variables would have been under free market conditions during the period 1961 to 1967. In 1968 Professors Mayer, Heady, and Madsen of Iowa State University's Center for Agricultural and Economic Development (CAED) projected farm prices, output, and incomes to 1970 under alternative farm programs, including a free market set of conditions. Unlike the other models, the CAED model included a projection of the long-term consequence of removing farm programs, allowing for an accelerated exodus from farming. Essentially, this projection estimated the balance between free market demand and supply on the assumption that marginal farms would be abandoned to the point where prices rose to cover the costs of production, including an imputed return to family and hired labor and to investment in farm capital.

Table 4 shows, for the relevant period covered by each of the four models, the difference between actual farm income and farm income under free market conditions. The Senate and JEC models projected free market conditions in 1965.[8] Their comparisons of actual 1959 farm income and 1965 free market income are obviously an understatement of price support benefits in 1965, since they do not take account of the substantial rise in the level of supports between 1959 and 1965. Their comparisons of actual income in 1965 and free market income in 1965 reflect not only the models' predictions of the effect of dropping price supports but also any other variations between the assumed and actual conditions in 1965.

The ERS model does not run afoul of this problem. Its comparison of actual with free market conditions during the 1961–67 period, made in 1968, was based

---

8 In both models, land retired under the soil bank was assumed to be 30 million acres. Land retirements obviously do support prices. Hence the full impact of free market prices was not shown.

Table 4. Projected Decline in Realized Net Farm Income and
Major Government Payments with Removal of Major Price Support
Programs (In Billions of Dollars)

Income Comparison	Decline in Income, Excluding Payments	Decline in Government Payments[a]	Decline in Income, Including Payments
Senate model[b]			
1965 free market/actual 1959	4.4	0	4.4
1965 free market/actual 1965	5.2	1.8	7.0
JEC model[c]			
1965 free market/actual 1959	4.2	0	4.2
1965 free market/actual 1965	5.0	1.8	6.8
ERS model[d]			
1961−67 free market/actual 1961−67	3.3	1.7	5.0
1965−67 free market/actual 1965−67	3.4	2.5	5.9
CAED model[e]			
Short run: free market/actual	3.0	2.9	5.9
Long run: free market/actual	1.4	2.9	4.3

[a]Direct payments under the wheat, cotton, and feed grain programs (including wheat certificates purchased by processors).

[b]*Report from the United States Department of Agriculture and a Statement from the Land Grant Colleges IRM−1, Advisory Committee on Farm Price and Income Projections, 1960−65, Under Conditions Approximating Free Production and Marketing of Agricultural Commodities*, S. Doc. 77, 86 Cong. 2 sess. (1960). Price support programs were assumed to have been removed by 1960.

[c]*Economic Policies for Agriculture in the 1960's: Implications of Four Selected Alternatives,* prepared for the Joint Economic Committee, 86 Cong. 2 sess. (1960), Part I and App. A. Price support programs were assumed to have been removed by 1960.

[d]*Farm Program and Farm Bargaining,* Hearings before the Senate Committee on Agriculture and Forestry, 90 Cong. 2 sess. (1968), pp. 588−90. Price support programs were assumed to have been removed prior to the 1961 crop.

[e]Leo V. Mayer and others, *Farm Programs for the 1970's,* CAED Report 32 (Iowa State University, Center for Agricultural and Economic Development, 1968).

on known conditions. Free market income differs from actual income only because of the removal of price supports; the ERS model contains only the imperfections attendant on estimating the impact of removing price supports and not the additional disturbances that may be reflected in the other comparisons.

Despite the potential differences, the results of the three models are not markedly different. The ERS model assumes that price supports were removed after the 1960 crop season, so that by the 1965−67 period the prices of livestock and non-price-supported crops would have been affected. Farm income was estimated to be $6 billion lower under free market conditions. According to the Senate and JEC models, which assumed the removal of price supports after the 1959 crop season, farm income would have dropped $7 billion. The actual figures used in the ERS model show that the larger part of the income decline was due to the cessation of direct payments and the smaller part to price support actions. The other two models do not reflect the fact that direct payments grew steadily during these years and averaged a good bit higher during the 1965--67 period than they did in the year 1965 itself.

The CAED model shows, for the short run, the same total impact of eliminating commodity programs as does the ERS model. The long-run CAED model is not comparable with the others, however, since it assumes a major withdrawal of resources out of agriculture.[9]

The distribution estimates in this study rely upon the ERS model's estimates of price support benefits. At least for the period during which there is not a significant acceleration of the exodus from farming, the results of the model are roughly consistent with estimates made by other investigators.

The ERS model defined the free market as one in which price supports, supply controls, and direct payments were eliminated on all major farm commodities. However, sugar and wool subsidy payments were assumed to have continued, as were payments under the agricultural conservation program. Government-assisted exports of agricultural commodities under Public Law 480 were also assumed to have remained at the actual levels of the period. In this study, Public Law 480 shipments are assumed to remain unchanged. But sugar, wool, and ACP direct payments are assumed to have been eliminated. The marketing allotments and import quotas currently supporting domestic sugar cane and beet prices are eliminated, so that domestic sugar prices reflect world price levels during the period in question. For the 1965—67 period these additional assumptions would change the estimated ERS value of price support benefits from $3.4 billion to $3.5 billion (on account of removing the support from sugar prices) and the direct payment benefits from $2.5 billion to $3 billion (reflecting the value of the direct sugar, wool, and ACP subsidies).

Distribution of Benefits by Economic Class   The Department of Agriculture classifies farms into the following categories, according to the value of their sales receipts:[10]

Economic Class	Value of Sales (Thousands of Dollars)	Percent of Total Farm Sales, 1969	Percent of Total Number of Farms, 1969
I	40 and over	51.3	7.1
II	20—40	21.3	12.0
III	10--20	16.0	17.0
IV	5—10	6.3	13.1
V	2.5—5	2.4	9.6
VI	Less than 2.5	2.7	41.2

9 Actually, the CAED model even in the short run differs from the ERS 1965--67 model significantly, even though the total $5.9 billion income decline is the same in the two models. The CAED short-run model refers to the first year after the elimination of major price support programs and hence does not allow for significant repercussions in markets for non-price-supported commodities. Its $5.9 billion reduction is concentrated almost wholly in price-supported commodities.

For 1964, extensive census data are available on various characteristics of farms grouped by economic class, including data on production and sales of each major commodity by farms in each economic class. The distribution of benefits in 1964 was estimated from these data. The 1964 distributions were then applied to the Department of Agriculture's 1969 estimates of cash receipts, production expenses, and net income for each economic class to produce an estimate of the distribution of farm program benefits by economic class for 1969. Quite different approaches were used to distribute price support benefits and direct payment benefits.

Price Support Benefits   Price support benefits, reflecting the support of market prices afforded by farm commodity programs, were estimated from the data underlying the ERS model. For each major commodity group – wheat, feed grains, cotton, livestock, and all other commodities – estimates were made of the decline in net income that would have occurred during the 1961–67 period had price supports and acreage restrictions been removed. The loss was first distributed to each of the six economic classes of farms in proportion to its share in the production of that commodity group, according to the 1964 census data. The losses in the various commodities were then summed to give an estimate of total losses within each of the economic classes. In effect, the ERS model provided a rough measure of price support benefits for the 1961–67 period as a whole, and the 1964 census determined the distribution of those benefits by economic class. The resulting distribution of price support benefits is very similar to a simple distribution of cash receipts (excluding direct payments) for 1964, as the following percentages received by the various economic classes show:[11]

| | Economic Class | | | | | |
Distribution	*I*	*II*	*III*	*IV*	*V*	*VI*
Price support benefits	42.3	19.3	17.9	11.0	5.3	4.2
Cash receipts	40.7	20.0	19.0	10.9	4.9	4.5

The close similarity in the distributions of price support benefits and cash receipts is not surprising. The two distributions can be obtained by weighting the basic production distributions for individual commodities by their shares in total price support benefits on the one hand, and total cash receipts on the other. The

10 USDA, ERS, *Farm Income Situation*. FIS-216 (July 1970), pp. 68, 71. Class VI includes a number of categories that the Bureau of the Census shows separately (small commercial farms, part-time farms, and so forth); with one very minor exception these categories all have the common characteristic of selling less than $2,500 of farm products each year.

11 Cash receipts are from *Farm Income Situation*, July 1970, p. 71.

similarity of the aggregate distributions implies that, if the secondary effects on non-price-supported crops are taken into account, the aggregate distributions by economic class ought not to differ from each other. Thus it seems reasonable to use the aggregate distribution of cash receipts to approximate the aggregate distribution of price support benefits for 1969, a year for which no census data are available on individual crop distributions by economic class.

Direct Payment Benefits   A follow-up sample survey conducted by the Department of Agriculture in 1965 to augment the 1964 census data included information on the volume of direct government payments received by farmers in each economic class. This information is used as the basis for distributing direct payments. The data are by no means perfect. In particular, the total volume of direct payments received, as estimated from the sample responses in the 1965 survey ($1.6 billion), fell significantly short of the total payment outlays recorded on government books ($2.2 billion). There was, clearly, substantial under-reporting. The discrepancy may arise from the fact that the census reported only payments received by farm operators; some unknown amount goes to nonfarm landlords. Although there is no way of knowing whether under-reporting varied by economic class, the distribution of direct payments based on the survey data appears to be consistent with other information about direct payment programs; hence the survey data, with minor modifications, are used in the analysis.[1][2]

Total Benefits from Farm Programs, 1964

Table 5 presents the information on direct payments and combines it with the distribution of price support benefits to reach a distribution of total benefits from farm programs in 1964. The total benefits per farm are then compared to the average net income of farmers in each economic class.

Benefit Distribution, 1969

The basic distributions of price support and direct payment benefits for 1969 were made by using the 1964 data in a variety of ways.

Price Support Benefits   Since in 1964 the distribution of cash receipts (excluding government payments) reasonably well approximated the distribution of price support benefits, the cash receipts data were used to estimate the distribution of benefits in 1969. The aggregate value of price support benefits again represented the average difference, from the ERS model, between actual

---

12 In 1964 there was a small amount of direct cotton payments. These were distributed in accordance with cotton production and added to the 1965 survey distribution.

Table 5. Distribution of Farm Program Benefits and Income by Economic Class, 1964

Item	I	II	III	IV	V	VI	I & II	V & VI
				Economic Class				
Aggregate benefits				*(Billions of Dollars)*				
Price supports	1.44	0.66	0.61	0.37	0.18	0.14	2.09	0.32
Direct payments	0.34	0.44	0.58	0.38	0.19	0.26	0.78	0.45
Total	1.78	1.10	1.19	0.75	0.37	0.40	2.87	0.77
Distribution of benefits				*(Percent of Total)*				
Price supports	42.3	19.3	17.9	11.0	5.3	4.2	61.6	9.5
Direct payments	15.4	20.3	26.4	17.4	8.6	12.0	35.7	20.6
Total	31.8	19.7	21.3	13.4	6.6	7.2	51.3	13.8
Income and benefits per farm				*(Thousands of Dollars)*				
Farmer's net income	27.3	11.8	8.0	6.3	5.0	5.1	17.3	5.1
Net income from farming	23.3	9.5	6.0	3.5	2.0	1.0	14.4	1.2
Price supports	9.9	2.5	1.3	0.7	0.4	0.1	5.0	0.2
Direct payments	2.3	1.6	1.2	0.7	0.4	0.2	1.9	0.2
Total	12.2	4.1	2.5	1.4	0.8	0.3	6.9	0.4
Net income from farming under free market conditions	11.1	5.4	3.5	2.1	1.2	0.7	7.5	0.8

Source: Based on *Farm Income Situation*, July 1970.

and free market farm income (exclusive of direct payments) for the years 1965–67. (No estimate was available for the years beyond 1967.) If the ratio of benefits to cash receipts were assumed to have remained unchanged from 1966–67 to 1969, then because cash receipts increased over the period, the aggregate value of price support benefits would also have increased – from $3.6 billion to $4.5 billion. If the ratio in the single year 1967 were used, the value of benefits in 1969 would have been even larger, $4.7 billion. In the case of some major crops (particularly cotton), however, prices were closer to free market levels in 1969 than in the 1965–67 period. In view of this fact, and in an attempt to present conservative estimates, the 1969 estimate of $3.6 billion is used, implying a decline in the ratio of price support benefits to cash receipts over the period.

Direct Payments   The distribution of direct payments in 1969 under the cotton program was calculated separately from that for other programs. The voluntary diversion program for cotton was started in 1965, one year later than the period to which the sample survey data on direct payments refer. Since cotton production is much more highly concentrated among large farmers than is the production of wheat and feed grains, which dominated the 1964 census, the sample survey substantially understates the concentration of total direct payments in years after 1964. In order to estimate their distribution, 1969 cotton payments were assumed to be proportional to the distribution of cotton production in 1964. This method of distribution has two biases that, fortunately, run in opposite directions. On the one hand, farmers with less than 10 acres receive certain special benefits under the program, so that a production distribution tends to overstate the concentration of benefits among large farmers. On the other hand, the economic class boundaries are fixed in dollar terms; for example, Class I includes sales of $40,000 and over. Over time the average size and cash receipts of farms tend to grow – some farmers move up from one class to another, and those who leave farming tend to be principally in the lower economic classes. Hence a 1964 distribution understates the percentage of cotton production taking place in the top economic classes and overstates the percentage accounted for by the lower economic classes. Because the quantitative impact of the opposing biases may not be the same, the 1969 distribution of cotton payments by economic class must remain mildly suspect.

The distribution of direct payments for all other programs was determined from the ratio of direct payments (excluding cotton) to cash receipts in 1964 for each economic class. That ratio was applied to 1969 cash receipts, and the resulting figures were used to distribute the 1969 direct payments.

The results of both calculations are shown in Table 6. In 1969 Class I farms accounted for 7.1 percent of all farms. But they received 40.3 percent of the benefits from farm commodity programs. Average net income of these farm operators (from both farm and nonfarm sources) was $33,000, of which 42

Table 6. Distribution of Farm Program Benefits and Income by Economic Class, 1969

Item	\multicolumn{8}{c}{Economic Class}
	I	II	III	IV	V	VI	I & II	V & VI
Aggregate benefits	\multicolumn{8}{c}{*(Billions of Dollars)*}
Price supports	1.90	0.76	0.55	0.22	0.08	0.09	2.66	0.17
Direct payments	1.08	0.90	0.88	0.43	0.20	0.30	1.98	0.50
Total	2.98	1.66	1.43	0.65	0.28	0.39	4.64	0.67
Distribution of benefits	\multicolumn{8}{c}{*(Percent of Total)*}
Price supports	52.9	21.0	15.4	6.1	2.2	2.4	73.9	4.6
Direct payments	28.5	23.7	23.2	11.3	5.3	7.9	53.6	13.2
Total	40.3	22.5	19.4	8.8	3.8	5.3	62.8	9.1
Income and benefits per farm	\multicolumn{8}{c}{*(Thousands of Dollars)*}
Farmer's net income	33.0	13.7	9.6	8.1	7.0	8.1	20.9	7.9
Net income from farming	27.5	10.5	6.5	3.6	2.1	1.1	16.8	1.3
Price supports	9.0	2.1	1.1	0.6	0.3	0.1	4.7	0.1
Direct payments	5.1	2.5	1.7	1.1	0.7	0.2	3.6	0.3
Total	14.1	4.6	2.8	1.7	1.0	0.3	8.3	0.4
Net income from farming under free market conditions	13.4	5.9	3.7	1.9	1.1	0.8	8.5	0.9

Source: Based on *Farm Income Situation,* July 1970.

percent, or $14,000 per farm, could be attributed to farm·commodity programs. Class I and II farms taken together represented only 19.1 percent of all farms but received 62.8 percent of total benefits. Farm commodity programs contributed $8,000 of their $21,000 average net income.

At the other end of the scale Class V and VI farms accounted for 50.8 percent of total farms, but received only 9.1 percent of the subsidy benefits. The average net benefit per farm was only $400, about 5 percent of their average net income from farm and nonfarm sources.

The proportion of benefits received by large-scale farms rose between 1964 and 1969 (compare Tables 5 and 6). This change reflects in part the steady trend toward larger farms; the proportion of total production and cash receipts accounted for by Class I and Class II farms continued to rise. The concentration of direct payments also increased because the benefits of the cotton price support program enacted in 1965 were heavily concentrated among large producers.

By their very nature, current farm programs tend to provide benefits — paid for by both consumers and taxpayers — primarily to those larger farmers who produce the bulk of agricultural output. Conversely, the very large number of small farmers, who in the aggregate produce only a modest fraction of total farm output, are helped relatively little by these programs.

Capitalization of Price Support Benefits

Because the increase in land rents brought about by price support programs is capitalized into higher land prices, many of the benefits of the farm price support programs are not felt in farm income itself, as farmland gradually changes hands (at about 3 percent per year) and as farm landlords raise cash rents to their tenant farmers. The first generation owners capture the benefits in the form of capital gains when they sell. Second generation owners lose many of the benefits to higher carrying charges. Looked at another way, a large part of the benefits of price support programs are gradually realized as capital gains upon sale of farmland, so that over time net farm income less and less reflects the benefits of farm programs. Equally as disturbing is the fact that as price support benefits are translated into higher land prices, they necessarily become frozen into farmers' asset positions. A removal or reduction in price supports would cause substantial capital losses to second generation landowners who purchased land at the higher prices and typically are paying sizable carrying costs in the form of mortgage interest. Such farmers will be worse off after the removal of farm subsidies than they would have been if the subsidies had never been introduced at all.

Viewed in this light, the concept of parity income as a possible goal for agricultural policy becomes a dubious objective. Parity income would provide the farmer a return on his own labor and investment (including investment in land) equal to what he could earn in nonfarm occupations. Price support programs are presumably needed to attain this objective because, under free market conditions, too many farmers would remain in agriculture, creating a condition of excess production and depressed incomes. But this is equivalent to saying that too many farmers will accept a less-than-parity return on their own labor (and possibly on their equity investment) while still remaining in agricultural production. If this is true, then any attempt to increase income above that level by price support programs will result in a rise in land rents, which will gradually be capitalized into higher land prices. In turn, with higher land prices, a subsequent calculation of parity income will show that price support programs have not improved the relationship between actual and parity income, since the parity rate of return, applied to the higher land prices, raises the level of parity income right along with the rise in actual income.

Subsidies, the rights to which are salable, or which are attached to salable assets as farm program subsidies are attached to land, must eventually be dissipated in the form of capital gains to asset holders. The process may take time. The asset prices may only imperfectly reflect current subsidy values, because potential purchasers may be uncertain about whether the subsidy will continue. But, at least in rough measure, such subsidies will tend to benefit primarily those who held the asset when the subsidy was introduced or increased. In the long run, farm subsidy programs, related as they are to the production of farm commodities, tend to benefit farmers chiefly in their role as landowners and not in their role as farm operators. Only as subsidies are granted to individuals, and not to salable business enterprises as such, will the benefits of the subsidy escape capitalization into higher asset prices.

Transfer Costs and National Income Costs of Farm Subsidy Programs

Two quite different kinds of costs are associated with the farm price support programs. Transfer costs represent the amounts the nonfarm sector of the economy transfers to the farm sector. These costs are themselves of two kinds: taxpayers support the direct payments made by the federal government to farmers; consumers pay additional sums to farmers through the higher prices that result from acreage restrictions and other supply management techniques. Aside from the administrative costs involved, these amounts transferred from consumers and taxpayers to farmers do not represent a loss of national income, merely a redistribution of it. But there are, nevertheless, national income costs (or welfare losses) associated with the farm price support programs, arising from the diversion of resources caused by acreage restrictions that leads to a reduction in national income (or the national welfare). These national income costs are smaller than the transfer costs associated with the programs.

Figures 1 and 2, in a highly simplified fashion, illustrate the difference between the two kinds of costs. In Figure 1 the nationwide demand and supply (marginal cost) curves for a particular farm commodity are shown as *DD* and

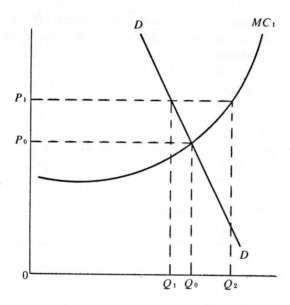

Figure 1. Effect of Price Supports on Farm Production

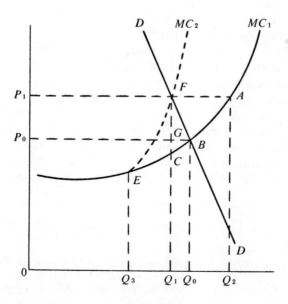

Figure 2. National Income Costs with Price Supports
and Supply Controls

MC_1, respectively. With no farm price support programs in existence, amount Q_0 would be produced and sold at price P_0. If, now, price support objective P_1 is established, production must somehow be cut to Q_1. Otherwise the government will have to buy, and hold off the market, the amount $Q_2 - Q_1$ (that is, at price P_1 farmers will produce Q_2, of which only Q_1 can be disposed of in the market place).

Figure 2 depicts the situation after the introduction of "voluntary" acreage restriction programs, designed to restrict production to level Q_1, consistent with price support objective P_1.[13] Farmers who agree to reduce their planted acreage by a certain percentage receive direct payments from the government. Since acreage is restricted, the cost of producing any given quantity of the farm commodity rises; more fertilizer or pesticide or labor must be applied to the remaining acres. The result is the new supply (marginal cost) curve MC_2 shown in Figure 2. The trick is to induce enough acreage reductions to make the new cost curve cut the demand curve at the desired price and quantity combination (P_1, Q_1).

Participation in the acreage restriction programs is voluntary; that is, any farmer may decide not to restrict his acreage and forego receiving payments as well as giving up the privilege of putting his crop under a Commodity Credit Corporation (CCC) loan.[14] From the viewpoint of the individual farmer, his participation in the program will depend upon whether the direct payments are large enough to compensate him for the income he might have earned by *not* restricting acreage and producing out to the point where his marginal cost curve cuts the new price line P_1. For all producers taken together, the amount of income loss that must be compensated through direct payments is the area *ABCEF* in Figure 2. As a matter of fact, however, the Department of Agriculture must set its direct payment formula high enough to generate an aggregate volume of payments larger than *ABCEF*, if it wishes to induce enough participation to shift production back to Q_1. Only if it could calculate, farm by farm, the income loss associated with acreage restrictions could it achieve a direct payment aggregate as low as *ABCEF*. But lack of data, political considerations, and administrative limitations make this impossible. Rather, with minor qualifications, it must set a common direct payment formula for all producers. This means that the formula must be set high enough to attract the marginal participants, and therefore substantially higher than absolutely necessary to attract the bulk of participants.[15] As a consequence, the sums

---

13 In actuality, because direct payments under the voluntary acreage restriction program contribute to farm income, the market price objective P_1 can be, and is, lower than in the purchase situation depicted in Fig. 1.

14 The latter privilege is generally valuable to the farmer because the actual market price may fall below the target (or "loan") price P_1 – that is, the government may miscalculate – and the CCC loan allows the farmer more flexibility in determining when to market his crop.

15 In technical jargon the Department of Agriculture cannot act as a discriminating monopsonist in buying participation. It must set a common price for all.

transferred to farmers by taxpayers, via direct payments, will be equal to area *ABCEF* plus a substantial additional sum, whose magnitude basically depends on the degree to which marginal cost curves differ among individual farmers.[16]

The consumer loses a sum equal to the area $P_1 FBP_0$, of which $P_1 FGP_0$ is transferred to the farmer and *FGB* is lost altogether (part of the national income loss discussed below).

Total transfer costs are therefore equal to the higher prices paid by consumers on the amount they consume (area $P_1 FGP_0$) and the amount paid by taxpayers in the form of direct payments (area *ABCEF* plus an additional sum necessitated by the inability of the program to discriminate in its payments).

The transfer costs of the program do not represent a loss of national output or welfare, but a redistribution of it. There are net losses to the society from the program, however. These are measured by the shaded area *FBCE*. For each unit of output lost $(Q_0 - Q_1)$ there was an excess of what consumers were willing to pay over the additional cost of that unit — that is, the difference between the demand curve and the marginal cost curve. The loss of welfare on the lost output is therefore the area *FCB*. In addition, on part of the output actually produced, marginal costs are higher. These additional costs are represented by area *FCE*. The sum of the two losses — the welfare loss on the output that would otherwise have been produced and the cost increase for the output actually produced — is the total national income loss, *FBCE*.

This diagrammatic presentation necessarily makes a number of simplifications and leaves out several important points:

1. It ignores the problem of exports. A significant proportion of price-supported products are exported. To some extent the foreign, not the American, consumer pays the transfer costs described above. But foreign tariff mechanisms (for example, variable "gate levies") are often such that changes in prices of American agricultural exports result not in price changes to foreign consumers but in changes in tariff revenue collected by foreign governments.

2. The price support programs provide a higher, more stable set of prices for farmers than would free markets. It is often asserted that the existence of relatively high and stable prices has stimulated the growth of productivity on farms, particularly through a faster acceptance of new techniques and a higher rate of investment than would otherwise have been the case. Even with acreage restrictions, farm costs may be lower rather than higher than they would be in a free market. Hence the diagram overstates the national income

---

16 Actually the department sometimes indulges in limited payment discrimination. In some years, and for some commodities, a two-layer payment scheme is offered: all participants are required to reduce acreage by a specified percentage and are thereby entitled to a specified amount of direct payments; in addition, participants may choose to retire still further acreage and receive payments based on the added acreage. The two levels of payment are different, the second level being lower and designed to attract out of production land on which the difference between price and cost is not very large — that is, the income loss to be compensated is not very great.

losses (part of which stem from higher costs). Whatever the validity
of this position, it is a strange argument to use in defense of a
program whose very existence is based on the proposition that the
growth of farm productivity so far outstrips the demand for farm
products as to require price support and supply restrictions.

3. The price support programs provide not only high prices but stable
    prices (at least relative to the volatility of farm prices in a free
    market). This price stability in turn is a benefit to the farmer and
    should be counted as an offset to the national income losses shown
    in the diagram. While this point has undeniable merit, it imme-
    diately raises the question of whether or not relatively stable prices
    could not be provided at lower average levels. Some of the national
    income losses associated with high price supports could thus be
    avoided, and some protection would be available against the
    extreme swings of free agriculture markets.

7

Roy W. Bahl and Jeremy J. Warford:
Real and Monetary Dimensions of
Federal Aid to States

Introduction

The objective of this paper is to define, measure, and explain interstate
variation in the impact of federal flows of funds to states. We begin by drawing
attention to the weaknesses of methods previously used to estimate the level of
per capita federal assistance to states in order to analyze federal distribution
policy. We define the flow of federal aid to include not only grants-in-aid to
state and local governments and to private organizations and individuals but also
a portion of direct federal expenditures. It is argued that the total dollar flow of
federal funds measured by adding these two components does not provide an
acceptable measurement of interstate differentials in the real benefits of federal
assistance. We therefore suggest a method of bringing federal grant and
expenditure data to a common basis in order to make interstate comparisons.

We then turn to the question of identifying the causes of interstate variation
in the real benefits accruing from the flow of federal funds. Here an important
distinction is made between "political" and "nonpolitical" determinants of aid.

Presented at the Symposium on the Grants Economy held between the Association for
the Study of the Grants Economy and the Public Choice Society in December, 1969, in
New York, New York. All rights reserved. Used by permission of the authors. Mr. Bahl is
affiliated with the International Monetary Fund and Mr. Warford with The Brookings
Institution.

The final section of the paper deals with the definition and measurement of the net impact of federal budgetary policy in redistributing real income among states.

Alternative Concepts of Federal Aid

The bulk of a voluminous amount of research on federal–state fiscal relations treats federal aid and federal grants-in-aid as synonymous, and ignores direct federal expenditures in states, even though such expenditures are clearly of some value to recipient states. This situation exists partly because research interest has centered on determining the distortive effects of intergovernmental flows on state government budgets, and direct federal spending is not generally included in this category of intergovernmental fiscal relations. Moreover, although grants-in-aid to states are reported annually by program,[1] interstate allocation of federal expenditures are less readily available and are certainly far less accurate. However, in a recent study, I. Labovitz and H. Halper present an interstate allocation of federal expenditures, based on a three-year average for the 1965–67 period.[2]

To estimate the total federal inflow by state, we use the Labovitz–Halper three-year average of direct federal expenditures and an average of federal grants for 1965, 1966, and 1967. We derive the per capita amounts by using a three-year population average. Hopefully, this method reduces the problem of abnormal expenditures in a given year. We then estimate the total federal inflow for each state and indicate the results of the allocation on a per capita basis (see Table 1, columns 1 through 3).

We have noted that for federal expenditures the impact is, theoretically, inflow of federal funds and the real benefits derived in that state from the money inflow. This divergence occurs for two reasons: First, some of the federal inflow ultimately results in public sector assets that are primarily of benefit to the residents in the state (for example, schools, sewers), whereas certain federal funds are used to purchase goods that yield benefits shared more uniformly on a national basis (for example, defense). Second, the money cost of a federal investment in a state exceeds the states' opportunity cost of undertaking the investment if productive factors are idle; for example, factor market prices of labor would not appropriately represent the unit cost sacrificed if there were unemployment. To the extent that there are interstate variations in idle capacity, interstate comparisons of federal money inflow will be spurious.

Consequently, to describe interstate variations in the real income effect of

---

1 *Annual Reports of the Secretary of the Treasury, GPO* (Annual).

2 See *Federal Revenue and Expenditure Estimates, For States and Regions, Fiscal Years 1965–67*, House of Representatives Intergovernment Relations Subcommittee, October 1968, pp. 30–31. I. M. Labovitz and H. J. Halper readily admit the imperfections of the method employed to allocate expenditures among states.

Table 1. Per Capita Federal Dollar Flows, Real Assistance,
and Federal Revenues by State (In Dollars Per Capita)

State	Grants	Expenditures	Total Flow	Adjusted Expenditures	Adjusted Total Aid	Revenues
Alabama	109	436	545	19	128	420
Arizona	120	545	665	24	144	586
Arkansas	128	314	442	15	143	394
California	90	794	884	42	132	781
Colorado	135	606	741	20	155	649
Connecticut	69	708	776	25	94	983
Delaware	86	510	597	16	102	1,301
Florida	66	592	658	17	83	672
Georgia	96	567	662	20	116	507
Idaho	150	366	516	15	165	515
Illinois	71	360	431	11	82	845
Indiana	69	357	427	11	80	659
Iowa	144	370	514	8	152	594
Kansas	163	545	708	17	180	572
Kentucky	108	414	523	18	126	460
Louisiana	114	403	518	19	133	457
Maine	81	499	580	22	103	577
Maryland	62	836	898	28	90	783
Massachusetts	86	522	608	23	109	783
Michigan	66	309	375	12	78	761
Minnesota	123	378	501	13	136	625
Mississippi	128	343	472	16	144	328
Missouri	108	539	647	19	127	688
Montana	218	536	754	26	244	570
Nebraska	194	463	658	13	207	605
Nevada	155	489	643	30	185	868
New Hampshire	73	434	507	10	83	703
New Jersey	49	456	505	21	70	826
New Mexico	177	558	736	29	206	505
New York	68	411	479	17	85	893
North Carolina	75	420	495	15	90	476
North Dakota	292	546	838	25	317	464
Ohio	65	359	424	12	77	702
Oklahoma	152	476	627	18	170	531
Oregon	121	336	457	16	137	661
Pennsylvania	66	366	432	14	80	703
Rhode Island	94	629	719	26	120	713
South Carolina	76	474	549	21	97	402
South Dakota	227	443	669	15	242	463
Tennessee	98	371	469	14	112	487
Texas	94	558	652	19	113	562
Utah	136	472	609	24	160	541
Vermont	144	433	577	17	161	631
Virginia	73	809	882	23	96	594
Washington	106	601	707	28	134	667
West Virginia	111	310	421	22	133	480
Wisconsin	66	305	372	10	76	644
Wyoming	273	580	853	24	297	664

the grant/expenditure process, we distinguish between grants-in-aid and direct federal expenditures:

1. Federal expenditures are assumed to be for items that are not *in themselves* of exclusive benefit to the inhabitants of the state in which they take place, although there may be an indirect value through an employment effect (for example, the construction and operation of a military installation).
2. Federal grants-in-aid are assumed to be of direct intrinsic value primarily to the inhabitants of the recipient state (for example, public assistance payments, grants for highway development, or agricultural price support payments).

Unfortunately, the distinction between federal grants-in-aid and direct federal expenditures is not always this clear-cut. For example, grants-in-aid for the interstate highway program may not be of exclusive benefit to the inhabitants of the state. On the other hand, federal expenditures within a state (for example, for a certain type of water resource development) may have an intrinsic net value to the inhabitants of that state, particularly if a price that recovers less than total costs is levied. Moreover, some military expenditures may be of marginally greater intrinsic benefit to the inhabitants of some states than of others. One way or another, the location of an ABM installation may be a case in point. Some justification for this classification is the usual rationale for the federal government's assuming direct responsibility: the benefits (costs) of undertaking (not undertaking) an investment spillover to such an extent that identification with a particular governmental unit is not possible.

Despite the spillover effect normally associated with federal expenditures, political representatives eagerly seek not only grants to but also expenditures within their constituencies. Hence both grants and expenditures should somehow be used in estimating the extent of federal aid. The next step is therefore to show how grants and expenditures may reasonably be brought to a common basis and summed to arrive at a total federal aid figure in order to facilitate interstate comparison. Here we deal with the problem of adjusting for interstate differences in levels of idle capacity.

Expenditures

As previously mentioned, we begin by assuming that direct federal expenditures do not normally result in the construction of assets that are of greater direct intrinsic value to the inhabitants of the state in which they take place than to the inhabitants of any other state. Nevertheless, federal expenditures do confer benefits within the state to the extent that resources that would otherwise be idle are now employed.[3]

---

3 For a more specific treatment of the growth effects of direct federal expenditures in a particular sector, see R. Bolton, *Defense Purchases and Regional Growth* (Washington, D.C.: The Brookings Institution, 1966).

We begin therefore with the proposition that federal expenditures within a state will be of greater benefit the higher the rate of unemployment in that state. If a state has full employment, we take the position that such expenditures merely involve a transfer of resources from other employment.[4] Consequently, if R is the real cost (or opportunity cost of the local resources employed in constructing a military installation, the maximum benefit would be realized if at the margin $R = 0$ — that is, if the factors employed would otherwise be idle. In these circumstances, an expenditure of x dollars would be matched by an equivalent gain to the state.

On a statewide basis, we can roughly estimate the local opportunity cost (R) of employing factors to implement a federal expenditure (E) as $E(1 - u)$, where u is the state unemployment rate. The total income received by local owners of factors who are affected will be E, the net gain to them therefore being $(E - R)$, or Eu. The initial impact of a federal expenditure, represented by Eu, can be taken as a strictly minimum estimate of the present worth of the additional intrastate consumption generated by that expenditure. At the very least, additional out-of-state purchases to the value of Eu could be made immediately and the benefits of further employment of idle factors exported to other states. We pursue the interstate incidence of benefits no further, implicitly assuming that the relationship between the initial benefit Eu and the discounted value (V') of the net intrastate consumption resulting from it is constant for all states — that is,

$$V' = k\,Eu$$

Finally, we consider only the opportunity cost of the labor factor and ignore both idle industrial capacity and the cost of diverting capital from the private to the public sector. We take the position that only the labor factor is perishable; idle industrial capacity may productively be claimed in a later period, so only a rate of return during the idle period is lost.[5] But even this omission will produce no error in our analysis if idle nonlabor capacity is proportional to idle labor capacity, because our concern is essentially with the interstate variance.[6]

---

4 This is only an approximation because to attract resources from other employment, factor incomes would normally have to be raised above their current level, bringing about a net gain on this account.

5 We ignore questions of technological obsolescence, which would suggest yet another opportunity cost.

6 For a different treatment of the opportunity cost associated with the nonlabor factors, see R. H. Haveman and J. V. Krutilla, *Unemployment, Idle Capacity, and the Evaluation of Public Expenditures* (Baltimore: Johns Hopkins Press), 1969.

Grants-in-Aid

Because no distinction is required between substitute grants and grants that augment state or local expenditures in the particular field concerned, we can distinguish, on a conceptual level, two elements of the benefits that could conceivably accrue from federal grants:

1. the intrinsic value of the product that results directly from the grant, and
2. the intrinsic value of the product yielded by the employment of resources that would otherwise be idle.

In the first instance, we assume the intrinsic value of the product yielded by the grant to be the monetary equivalent of the grant. If the grant (G) is immediately spent outside the state, the total benefit is also G, for any "employment" benefits are exported.

We have noted that for federal expenditures the impact is, theoretically, traced to the states of factor owners, so for a first round estimate the question of leakages and their repercussions on factor employment does not arise. To be consistent, therefore, as we have measured the *minimum* likely effect of direct expenditures on states, we should do the same for grants. Consequently, we do not estimate the direction of the expenditures resulting from additional state incomes or the propensity to export or import or therefore the gains from employing hitherto idle capacity. As for expenditures, we consider the base figure used for calculation of relative net benefits (V'') as the intrinsic value of the additional income if it were immediately spent outside the state, expressing the relation between initial and total net benefits as

$$V'' = kG.$$

Total Aid

We estimate the total value (V) of federal aid for any state as

$$V = k(Eu + G),$$

assuming that the ratio between the additional net intrastate consumption generated by federal aid and the federal aid itself ($Eu + G$) is constant for all states. Because our interest centers on interstate *differences* in the benefits resulting from federal grants, we make such an assumption *without specifying what that ratio is*. Therefore for comparative purposes we use the expression ($Eu + G$) as our estimate of total federal assistance. In other words, having arrived at the base figure of ($Eu + G$), we assume that the proportionate benefit, including multiplier effects, will be the same for all states.

An ideal method for calculating net benefits requires an estimation of the cost and benefit streams resulting from all forms of federal aid, but this method is clearly impracticable. We can reasonably expect many factors entering such a calculation to be randomly distributed among states, but our approach (in common with the other measures used) suffers from one particular weakness: Calculations made on this basis are likely to systematically underestimate the net gain to the highly industrialized states, which are the probable beneficiaries of the bulk of out-of-state purchases generated by federal aid.[7] Although this effect has not been quantified, we should however bear it in mind in interpreting our results, which are based purely on first-round effects.

Relation to Other Studies

Per capita federal aid to any state can now, for comparative purposes, be estimated statistically as $(Eu + G)/P$, where P is the total population of that state. Table 1, columns 4 and 5, shows the results, by state, of applying this adjustment to three-year averages of per capita grants and expenditures.

This method of aggregating federal assistance and adjusting for interstate differences in the level of idle resources sheds new light on the often investigated question of the ex post income equalization of federal assistance. On the one hand, the data provide further support for the argument that the long-term mood of Congress tends toward greater income equalization as far as grants-in-aid policy is concerned. James Maxwell[8] examined 1942 data and found a significant *positive* relationship between per capita aid and per capita grants, although Mark Haskell[9] could not find a statistically significant correlation between the variables in 1962. Our analysis of a three-year average of 1965–67 grants data shows a significant negative relationship (see Table 2, column 1). The money flow of per capita direct federal expenditures is directly (and significantly) related to per capita income, with a result that per capita total (dollar) federal assistance is neutral with respect to income (see Table 2, column 1). However, when per capita total federal assistance is adjusted for interstate variations in the level of idle resources, an overall pattern of income equalization is revealed. The state-to-state variance in the real benefits of federal grants is sufficiently equalizing to offset the neutral real income effect of direct federal expenditures (Table 2, column 2).

---

7 A recent evaluation of the benefits of public expenditures for water resources indicates that a substantial portion of total industrial demands and off-site labor costs accrue to the Mid-Atlantic and East–North Central regions, irrespective of the region wherein the water resource project is constructed. See Haveman and Krutilla, *op. cit.*, ch. 3.

8 J. A. Maxwell, "The Equalizing Effects of Federal Grants," *Journal of Finance*, 9 (May 1954).

9 M. A. Haskell, "Federal Grants and the Income-Density Effect," *National Tax Journal*, March 1962.

Table 2. Simple Correlation Coefficients between the
Logarithms of Selected Classes of Per Capita Federal
Assistance and Per Capita Income

	Per Capita Amounts (Not Adjusted for Unemployment)	Real Per Capita Amounts (Adjusted for Unemployment)
Total assistance	0.13	−0.32
Direct expenditures	0.25	0.01
Total grants-in-aid	−0.31	−

Statistical Model and Results

Political and Nonpolitical Determinants

We assume that the function of political representatives is to obtain as much aid for their constituents as possible. The relative political overrepresentation of states with small populations suggests that the total aid received per state will tend to be more equal than it would be under conditions of perfectly proportional representation. In other words, we might expect federal aid to vary, *on a per capita basis*, inversely with state population. The political philosophy that implies a tendency toward equal treatment of states irrespective of their size (exemplified by the senatorial system) and is designed to protect minority groups may therefore be expected to bias the structure of federal aid in favor of the inhabitants of smaller states.

The procedure followed here is to examine the component parts of federal aid and to define certain "needs" that we might reasonably expect to cause a variance in aid *on a per capita basis*. The criterion is necessarily our own, and we have used the terms *nonpolitical* and *political* to distinguish between those motives we consider to be reasonable underlying observed interstate variations in aid and those not so considered. Our criterion will certainly be questioned, but such questioning is inherent in the nature of the problem.

Our statistical objective is to partition the explained interstate variance in per capita federal assistance into a political and a nonpolitical component. We shall classify as nonpolitical the income equalizing or stabilizing role of federal assistance, which includes per capita aid that varies directly with state unemployment rates or inversely with state per capita income, as well as aid that reflects variations in physical circumstances and "needs" and may therefore perform a *real* income equalizing role. On the other hand, a negative and statistically significant partial relation between population and per capita assistance is taken to be evidence of purely political influences.

To classify as nonpolitical those forms of aid that tend to equalize interstate real income disparities implies that such measures have our approval. However, the distinction between what we have termed *political* and *nonpolitical* determinants of aid is not watertight, for even political machination, resulting in proportionately larger benefits to states with small populations, may produce effects generally considered desirable by parties not directly affected. Indeed, a more equitable distribution may be one such result. Because we cannot disentangle these influences, our estimation of political effects must be somewhat conservative.

We should accept as a legitimate (in our terminology, nonpolitical) role of the federal government the subsidization of a given state if net efficiency benefits (for the United States) are likely to result. However, apart from the case in which aid may particularly favor states with high unemployment (which we test directly), we assume such conditions, with respect to the variables that concern us here, to be randomly distributed among states.

For certain types of assistance we could conceivably explain an inverse per capita aid--population size relationship by economies of scale in the provision of public services. To maintain the same real assistance irrespective of state size (*real* income equalization), smaller states would need relatively greater monetary assistance. This possibility would come within our definition of a non-political explanation of interstate variation in aid. However, we ignore this possibility on the grounds that empirical analyses of state and local government expenditures have consistently failed to uncover any convincing evidence of economies (or diseconomies) of scale.[10]

State population is therefore initially used as our proxy for the political influence. The choice of nonpolitical variables is dictated by a desire to measure "need" factors that would constrain an aid-maximization objective function of congressmen. Per capita income and the current unemployment rate are included on these grounds, the latter because it may act as a proxy for the concentration of low-income population in any given state. Thus, we assume that congressmen attempt to maximize the flow of federal funds to their respective states, subject to the constraint that some minimal amount of income redistribution takes place and that congressional allocative decisions are sympathetic to interstate variances in the *potential* for increasing real income. That is to say, if the unemployment rates in *equally populated* states A and B were 5 and 10 percent respectively, we would expect the political process to work marginally in the direction of diverting a greater dollar amount of federal money to B.

There are often a priori reasons to expect certain types of federal aid to be closely correlated with other variables. For example, we might expect per capita agricultural aid to be correlated positively with the proportion of farm population in each state. Using this as an independent variable would no doubt improve the fit of our estimating equation considerably, but we have excluded it because there is no a priori objectively determined reason why the proportion of a state's population employed in farming should *in itself* be an important factor in determining the need for equalizing aid. Rather, this variable has been

---

10 For a summary of these studies, see R. W. Bahl, "The Determinants of State and Local Government Expenditures: A Review," in S. Mushkin and J. Cotton, eds., *Functional Federalism: Grants-In-Aid and PPB Systems* (State–Local Finances Project, George Washington University), November 1968.

subsumed within the political category; it is not used as an explanatory variable because it tells us nothing about income-equalizing or stabilizing motives of federal distributional policy. Briefly, aside from political motivation, it may be the effect, rather than the cause, of the grant structure. On the other hand, there is an a priori equalizing reason why per capita aid, irrespective of its primary objective (for example, water resource development, transportation,[11] defense expenditures) should vary inversely with income or directly with unemployment, just as HEW welfare grants might be expected to.

We compute least squares estimates for the following regression equation:

$$A = \alpha Y^\beta u^\gamma P^\delta,$$

where A = *per capita* aid (variously defined)
         Y = mean per capita income   all averaged
         u = unemployment rate   over 1965–67
and P = population.   for each state

The nonlinear form is used because it seems more reasonable to assume, for example, that the per capita federal aid response to interstate differences in per capita income is not independent of the level of income. Our interest centers on the partial effects of the population (political) variable with the goal of accepting the alternative statistical hypothesis that it is negative in sign and significantly different from zero. There is no evidence that our results are substantially biased by multicollinearity.[12]

The Results

Initially we analyze three forms of real per capita federal assistance:

1. grants plus expenditures, $\dfrac{G + Eu}{P}$

2. grants, $\dfrac{G}{P}$, and

3. expenditures, $\dfrac{Eu}{P}$.

---

11 In a side calculation, population density (D) was included as an additional independent variable for transportation grants, as is suggested by the form of the actual grant distribution formulas for highway and airport construction and is justified by real income equalizing or "need" factors. For FY 1966, the following regression equation was obtained for transportation grants (T) to state–local governments:

$$\ln\left(\frac{T}{P}\right) = 3.19 - 0.2120 \ln D + 0.4237 \ln\left(\frac{Y}{P}\right) + 0.5586 \ln u - 0.2337 \ln P$$
$$\quad\quad (6.020) \quad\quad (1.781) \quad\quad\quad (1.781) \quad\quad (5.296)$$
$$R^{-2} = 0.796, \text{ and } t\text{-values in parentheses.}$$

The correlation between $\ln D$ and $\ln P$ is low enough (0.28) for us not to exclude transportation for the following aggregated estimates.

12 The simple intercorrelation between $\ln Y$ and $\ln u$ is –0.25, between $\ln Y$ and $\ln P$ is 0.24, and between $\ln P$ and $\ln u$ is –0.14.

Table 3. Regression Equations of Measures of Federal Assistance on Per Capita Income, Percent of Labor Force Unemployed, and Population Size (In Logarithms with t Ratios Shown in Parentheses)

Equation Number	Dependent Variable (Per Capita)	Constant	Per Capita Income	Percent Unemployed	Population	Coefficient of Multiple Determination	Coefficient of Partial Determination of Population
1	Total grants and expenditures [G + Eu]	+4.8210	−0.2737 (1.164)	+0.2650 (1.512)	−0.2196 (5.513)	0.462	0.395
2	Total grants [G]	+5.3150	−0.4300 (1.623)	+0.1450 (0.735)	−0.251 (5.592)	0.463	0.402
3	Total federal direct expenditures [Eu]	+1.5150	+0.4022 (1.820)	+0.9917 (6.019)	−0.0317 (1.004)	0.467	0.000

In the case of (1) and (2), Table 3 shows a significant and negative partial relationship with the political variable (population): After we account for the effects of the "needs" factors, we tend to associate a smaller population with higher per capita federal assistance and with higher per capita grants-in-aid. In the case of direct federal expenditures, the relationship is negative although not significant.[13] A comparison of the partial elasticity coefficients for population for the expenditure and grant equations suggests that the political process influences the interstate distribution of real grant benefits to a significantly greater extent than it does the distribution of real expenditure benefits[14]

Alternatively, the division of direct federal expenditure benefits among states is more responsive to high levels of unemployment than is the division of grants-in-aid. Per capita income is related negatively to grants and positively to expenditures; however, only in the case of expenditures is the relationship significant. But the opposite signs of the partial income elasticity coefficients indicate a substitution of expenditure for grant benefits as the income level of a state rises; for example, a 1 percent higher per capita income is associated with grant benefits 0.43 percent lower and expenditure benefits 0.40 percent higher. But because a given injection of federal funds has a greater real benefit effect in the form of a grant-in-aid, the overall distribution is characterized by a 1 percent higher per capita income being associated with a 0.27 percent lower level of aggregate per capita aid.

Finally, years of seniority in the Senate and House of Representatives were employed as additional independent variables in the preceding regression equations. These were entered as mean seniority of senators and representatives separately and then as a mean figure for the seniority of senators plus representatives for each state. In no case was the seniority variable significant, nor did its inclusion contribute materially to improving the R^{-2}.

Net Benefit Flows

The preceding analysis is concerned essentially with the gross benefit flow to states resulting from federal grants-in-aid and direct expenditures. To determine the variance in the *net* flow of funds to states, we must take account of the cost side of the equation — that is, the federal outflows.[15]

---

13 Because, after our adjustment, grants are quantitatively so much more important than expenditures, the result for overall aid is more akin to that for grants alone than for expenditures alone.

14 A similar pattern emerged when unadjusted per capita expenditures were used as the dependent variable to test the hypothesis that certain congressmen place as much importance on federal expenditures within their states as on federal grants. This result could be that a more influential part of the community is likely to be the primary beneficiary of, for example, a military installation than a welfare grant. When per capita expenditure (E) was regressed on Y, u, and P, a nonsignificant multiple determination coefficient resulted.

15 Data on federal revenues, calculated as far as possible by state of origin for 1965–67, are found in Labovitz, *op. cit.*

Our approach to the measurement of the cost to states of federal taxes parallels that applied to the benefits from grants, previously described. We simply define the foregone value of intrastate consumption (c) as kR. For purposes of interstate comparison the relevant calculation to be made for the net effect of the budgetary process on the jth state is therefore

$$R_j - (G_j + E_j u_j)$$

For several reasons we would not expect that $\Sigma V_j = \Sigma C_j$. The most important reason is the assumption that if state money were retained, it would approximate a federal grant (the whole amount would be of intrinsic value to the state itself) rather than an expenditure. We would therefore expect redistribution, if calculated this way, to be negative for all states. This expectation is reinforced by the fact that about 12½ percent of federal expenditures could not be allocated by state,[16] which is only slightly offset by a budgetary deficit over the three-year period considered.

We may consider all unallocated expenditures as being, on a per capita basis, equal in benefit for the inhabitants of all states. Moreover, loans to the federal government by private individuals and organizations may be considered distributionally neutral. The (negative) real distributive effect for each state (Table 4, column 1) may be compared with the mean redistributive effect, by state, of a negative $496 per capita. This shows whether the state concerned is a relative gainer or loser in the redistribution of real benefits as defined here. Table 4, column 2 gives rankings of states. A regression of per capita income and unemployment rates on the (negative) real per capita redistribution (N) accruing from the budgetary process yielded the following result:[17]

$$N = 6946.0 - 2131.0 \ln Y + 8510 \ln u$$
$$\quad\quad\quad\quad (9.936) \quad\quad\quad (0.522)$$

$$R^{-2} = 0.694$$

To compare the real and purely monetary redistributive effects, note the rankings of states according to the difference between per capita total monetary inflow and tax outflow (Table 4, column 4). These further demonstrate that the distribution of federal assistance has a greater equalizing effect on real than on monetary income. Net per capita monetary flows of funds (M), which may be

---

16 Data on federal revenues, calculated as far as possible by state of origin for 1965–67, are found in Labovitz, *op. cit.*

17 For purposes of clarity, only the independent variables are expressed as logarithms. Population is not included as an independent variable, the assumption being that congressmen are less clearly identified locally with the revenue than with the expenditure side of the budgetary process.

Table 4. Net Redistributive Effect of Budgetary Process

State	Real Effect		Total Dollar Flow	
	Per Capita Real Distribution (Dollars) (1)	Ranking[a] (2)	Per Capita Dollar Inflow (-- = loss) (3)	Ranking[a] (4)
Alabama	291	5	125	11
Arizona	−442	21	79	17
Arkansas	−251	4	48	21
California	−649	39	103	13
Colorado	−494	27	92	16
Connecticut	−889	47	−207	38
Delaware	−1,199	48	−704	48
Florida	−589	34	−14	28
Georgia	−390	18	155	7
Idaho	−350	12	1	26
Illinois	−763	45	−414	46
Indiana	−579	33	−232	40
Iowa	−442	21	−80	33
Kansas	−392	19	136	10
Kentucky	−334	10	63	20
Louisiana	−324	8	61	19
Maine	−474	24	3	27
Maryland	−693	43	115	12
Massachusetts	−673	40	−103	35
Michigan	−683	41	386	44
Minnesota	−489	26	−124	34
Mississippi	−184	2	144	9
Missouri	−561	31	−69	30
Montana	−326	9	184	5
Nebraska	−398	20	53	21
Nevada	−683	41	−225	39
New Hampshire	−620	36	−196	36
New Jersey	−756	44	−321	44
New Mexico	−299	6	231	3
New York	−808	46	−414	46
North Carolina	−386	17	19	24
North Dakota	−147	1	374	1
Ohio	−625	38	−278	43
Oklahoma	−361	13	96	14
Oregon	−524	29	−204	37
Pennsylvania	−623	37	−271	41
Rhode Island	−593	35	6	25
South Carolina	−305	7	147	8
South Dakota	−221	3	206	4
Tennessee	−375	15	−18	29
Texas	−449	23	90	15
Utah	−381	16	68	18
Vermont	−470	25	−54	31
Virginia	−498	28	288	2
Washington	−533	30	40	23
West Virginia	−347	11	−59	32
Wisconsin	−568	32	−272	42
Wyoming	−367	14	209	6
Mean	−496		−93	

[a] Rankings are in order of per capita net benefits received or of per capita net dollar inflow, as the case may be.

positive or negative, when regressed upon Y and u, produce the following equation:

$$M = 5919.0 - 1709.0 \ \ln Y + 55.3 \ \ln u$$
$$\quad\quad\quad\quad (5.183) \quad\quad (0.221)$$

$$R^{-2} = 0.368$$

For example, West Virginia and Arkansas, where the opportunity costs of using federal assistance is relatively low, show a higher ranking when real benefits are considered. Conversely, in California and Maryland, where the opportunity cost of using federal funds is relatively high, the ranking in terms of monetary redistribution is clearly more favorable.

Concluding Remarks

There are, clearly, immense conceptual and empirical problems involved in defining and allocating real federal assistance among states. Nonetheless, although our "need" and "political" variables between them explain, for example, only about half the interstate variance in the real benefits of federal assistance, the foregoing analysis does substantiate the hypothesis that the federal allocation process tends to work in favor of states with small populations. In fact, we would argue that the bias in the federal fund distribution process is even greater than is usually thought; it is more pronounced in the case of real benefit distribution than in the case of monetary distribution. It also appears that expenditure-aid is relatively less responsive to population differences (political influence) than is grant-aid, although the population coefficient has in all cases an elasticity of less than unity. Moreover, although the interstate variance in per capita grants is significantly related only to population, the primary determinant of the level of direct federal expenditure benefits is the unemployment rate. Finally, our results indicate that the real interstate progressivity of the budgetary process is substantially greater than the progressivity observed when we consider only dollar flows.

The results of the analysis must, however, be tempered by the simplifying assumptions we found necessary to make interstate comparisons. First, the distinction between the benefits received from grants-in-aid and those from direct expenditures is probably not as clear-cut as we have assumed. Next, we may question our assumptions that interstate variations in idle capacity are proportional to unemployment rates and that after the unemployment adjustment all direct federal expenditures and grants-in-aid have similar employment generating effects.

Finally, and probably most important, is the failure to account for second round and subsequent benefits resulting from a given injection of federal funds. These problems, however, certainly suggest the direction in which further research may be applied to measure more accurately the real interstate variance in the impact of the budgetary process.

8

Patricia Burke Horvath and John R. Burke:
Federal Research and Development Funding:
The Grants Component and Its Distribution

With technological change an ever more common feature of the productive system, research and development (R & D) activities have assumed increasing prominence as a subject of economic inquiry. In recent years significant contributions have been made toward the measurement of innovation and its diffusion, the comprehension of research motivations within the private firm, and the application of decision theory in determining governmental R & D expenditure patterns [7, 8, 16]. Implications for the economy as a whole, however, have largely been left unexplored,[1] despite the fact that federal R & D outlays ($16.7 billion in 1968) have grown to two thirds of the national total and, in the decade of the 1960s, averaged more than 12 percent of the federal administrative budget. This paper brings the perspective of the grants economy to the R & D question. Specifically, we propose to sort out the unilateral and bilateral transfer components of federal R & D expenditures and to determine their distributional characteristics.[2]

R & D Grants – A Definition

In establishing conceptual premises for R & D grants, we must bear in mind the nature of returns to unilateral transfers. If we define *utility gains* as the sole compensation to grantors, we get the impression that the economic goods involved are wholly unidirectional. With respect to R & D, this idea suggests that grants would support only research contributed to "the arts and philosophy." Yet looking at conventionally accepted granting processes – for example,

Presented at the Symposium on the Grants Economy held between the Association for the Study of the Grants Economy and the American Association for the Advancement of Science in December, 1969, in Boston, Mass. All rights reserved. Used by permission of the authors. Patricia Horvath is from the University of Michigan, and Robert Burke is from Harvard University.

1 Difficulties in measuring returns to nonmarket investments and in determining with any precision the contribution of innovation to national product present substantial barriers to such investigations [6, pp. 229–55] [15, pp. 21–34].

2 Kenneth Boulding has suggested that we could view the fiscal process as a compound unilateral transfer system – that is, with taxes as initial (perhaps involuntary) grants from individuals and all government outlays because of their nonmarket character as reverse grants [2, pp. 234–35]. Although underlining the need for careful reevaluation of the motivations and benefits involved in the tax-expenditure process, we assume here that the provision of a substantial proportion of public goods occurs through collective exchange.

welfare payments or nonloan foreign assistance – we note that anticipation of economic benefit is not necessarily absent. The welfare recipient who moves into the labor force contributes to the national product; the international grant, by improving the productive capacities of the less advanced country, can create gains from trade. But in such questions even this economic component falls outside the grasp of exchange analysis. Returns are so diffused through space and time that any connection between the exchangeables created and the distinct past outlays is long dissipated. Grants in general, and R & D grants in particular, carry the potential for generating two kinds of utility. One could be called "social returns" and would describe those social, cultural, and political benefits outside the scope of conventional economic definition. The other, "economic returns," would describe the welfare gains from a general increase in available goods and services.[3]

The Knowledge Spectrum

The output of resources allocated to scientific research is knowledge. If we propose for the present to ignore social returns to this output, we must in some sense be talking about knowledge that eventually finds its way into the production process, embodied in either the capital or labor factor. The first step is to determine the circumstances in which this knowledge cannot be considered as an "investment" in the conventional sense of that word – that is, the purchase of a producer good. This requires an *economic* description of scientific knowledge.

Looking at the natural science classification, we note at one extreme "pure" knowledge, discoveries concerning basic natural phenomena for which no "practical" use is foreseen. At the other extreme is technical information that promises immediate application to process or product improvement. This contrast in itself points toward the output of any set of research activities as lying within a knowledge spectrum bounded by these extremes. Rather than trying to stuff the various newly discovered "facts" into separate boxes, we can envision a good whose composition varies more or less continuously throughout a range of "seeming applicability."

Considering this spectrum, we can see that information falling toward the practical end fulfills the criterion of an exchange activity. Its connection to research efforts is straightforward in terms of time span, patent rights, and original research purpose. We can attribute the cost of scientific inputs to a particular final goods flow. However, as we move along our ordering toward the extreme of pure knowledge, we can imagine that the various facts become ever more tenuous in their seeming usefulness. The potential for embodiment in the production process in the foreseeable future moves farther beyond our present

---

3 Martin and Anita Pfaff develop utility interdependence as the theoretical basis for a grants system [13, 14].

capacities for technical imagination. Years hence, such pieces of knowledge may serve as the vital underpinning of marketable products [5, 11, 17], but many successive stages of refinement undoubtedly will long since have obscured even the *strength* of ties to these economic returns.

Thus, we identify "grants knowledge" and "exchange knowledge." The basis for distinction is whether the "facts" involved are of such character that their only outlet is into the public domain as a social producer good. In such case, because exclusive rights cannot be maintained, we must view the original supporter of the research effort as providing a unilateral transfer of scientific resources, motivated by concern for long-run economic improvement. In effect, we attribute a greater or lesser degree of grants character to knowledge depending on the size of external economies relative to direct benefits.[4]

Role of Ex Ante Returns

So far we have only implied the unpredictability of research outcomes, although this treatment of scientific knowledge suggests several successive stages of uncertainty. That final goods produced with new techniques may not yield a positive return is the most familiar problem. But success in research intended to produce what we have called *exchange knowledge* is itself subject to a probability calculation. In turn, we should view grants knowledge, by improving general scientific understanding, as enhancing the likelihood that development of a device or process will even initially be considered as feasible.

Thus, although the proposed yardstick may seem hauntingly familiar as the traditional distinction between public and private goods, what we have actually developed is the probability version. Classification is in accordance with *anticipated* results. We recognize that even for establishing a measurement device, uncertainty precludes the evaluation of actual (ex post) returns to knowledge. To attempt otherwise would require that we select arbitrary points in time at which to assess results; the standard of judgment would be particular outcomes that are unpredictable on an individual basis.[5] We accept, rather, the proposition that efforts to a certain purpose do not change their essential nature simply because results are different from initial intentions.

Grants and exchange knowledge are determined, then, on the basis of returns judged ex ante. Whether the returns can concretely be conceived of at

---

4 Richard Musgrave has argued a comparable case for the conventional theory of public finance: ". . . [the] distinction between private and social wants is essentially one of degree . . . . In the case of private wants, the divergence between private and social product is a more or less marginal matter; in the case of social wants the divergence becomes of the essence" [9, 8]. Albert Breton has developed a theory of intergovernmental transfers predicated on *jurisdictional* externalities [3].

5 In fact, the return to any project can be determined only as an average among a statistical sample of similar projects. Patricia Horvath and John Burke discuss the probability distinctions between research for grants versus exchange knowledge incorporated into a normative allocation model [4].

the time research is initially undertaken becomes the criterion for determining the predicted ex post fact of the knowledge output as a social or a private producer good. This expectational measure is termed "the degree of expected embodiment."

The Research Spectrum

At this point let us bring to light the several levels of our definition. Character of new knowledge provides the substance for a measurement standard. But facts issue forth from research projects -- that is, from various collections of scientific resources. In turn, R & D accounts translate this information-gathering process into dollars of funding. If research is taken, however, as an endeavor pursued only along limited and generally well-defined lines of inquiry, we can assume a simple and logical connection between the objectives of the productive effort and the character of the output. Then we can specify R & D projects -- and their associated financial support -- in terms of the kind of knowledge we expected them to produce.

With this extrapolation, we can conceive of a research project spectrum along the lines of our earlier logic. We view projects not as homogeneous in their output but as producers of "units" of knowledge, subject to differing degrees of expected embodiment. Unlike the knowledge spectrum, points within the project spectrum are not definitive in any absolute sense. They provide instead a general measure reflecting the mixed character of the project output. Figure 2 visualizes this proposition. Projects are ordered according to the *average* expected embodiment of their knowledge output. Movement from higher to lower positions on the scale points toward an increasing proportion of the returns to various projects as highly diffused.

An advantage of this collective spectrum is that we can suppress concern as to the amount of expected embodiment to be associated with exchange versus grants knowledge. Not that the problem of arbitrary dividing lines is eliminated; but raised to the level of research projects as a whole, it is far less crucial conceptually. In this vein, we must point to our use of the terms *grants research* and *exchange research* as semantic conveniences, reflecting the majority character of the effort. Likewise, the magnitudes of *grants funding* and *exchange funding* should be viewed as issuing not only from entire projects but also from partial amounts among many projects.

Measurement of the Grants Component

This section develops a means of estimating the grants component of federal R & D funding. The six federal agencies with the largest total R & D outlays appear separately in the analysis. They are: Department of Defense, National Aeronautics and Space Administration (NASA), Atomic Energy Commission

(AEC), Department of Health, Education and Welfare (HEW), National Science Foundation (NSF), and Department of Agriculture. Funding by the remaining agencies is accumulated in a collective category. The years analyzed are fiscal 1957 through 1968. Earlier years have been discarded because data breakdowns are not in a form comparable to the later period; also, redefinitions pose increasing problems of consistency. The National Science Foundation annual surveys [10] are the data source.[6]

Table 1 brings together a picture of this funding, providing figures and percentages for total and agency R & D *obligations*, broken down by type of research.[7] Listing is by three year averages, with annual figures given for 1957 and 1968 to highlight movements over the entire period.[8] During these years, total funding (including R & D plant)[9] grew 3.8 times, or at an average annual rate of 12.6 percent. Compared with 1950, the outlays in 1968 were over thirteen times greater.

Rationale of Grants Indicator

In using expected character of returns to knowledge output as a standard for measuring grants and exchange components, we must obtain two sets of informations. The first, data on funding inputs, is available at least in an aggregate form from the NSF material. The second, indicators of expectations regarding the output of the various funding efforts, places more rigorous demands. We need a specifically designed sample survey stratified by agency and project to produce even embryonic estimates. Any analysis thus requires development of a proxy measure of expectation.

---

6 Regarding limitations of the data, the NSF observes: "... all data reported are estimates and accounting precision cannot be imputed to them .... There are often no clear-cut demarcations between categories .... Best judgment must be used .... Compensating for such factors, however, is the fact that the survey respondents, in general, are a continuing group who have participated in as many as 17 successive annual surveys" [10, vol. 17, p. 93].

7 Adjustments have been made in the NASA funding for the years 1957–62. In 1963, NASA instituted new definitions for the three research categories, which resulted in substantially different proportions (favoring the development category) as compared with the 1962 breakdown. The difference in relative amounts falling in the basic and applied research categories, as between 1962 and 1963, has been taken as the percentage overstatement because of the older set of definitions. Basic and applied research for 1957 through 1962 have been reduced accordingly, with the residual added to the development category.

8 In the process of estimating the grants component, averaging alleviates two phenomena: variations in annual levels of funding that are not reflections of longer-term trends; the substantial difference between current obligations and current expenditures that may occur when programs are expanding rapidly. Data available are for obligations only.

9 The term *R & D Plant* refers to acquisition and construction of, or major repairs to, research facilities and fixed equipment. Because these outlays are not classified by type of research, they are excluded from the analysis proper.

Table 1. Federal R & D Obligations, by Agency and Type of Research, 1957—68

Agency	Millions of Current Dollars[a]						Percentage[b]					
	1957	1957–59	1960–62	1963–65	1966–68[c]	1968	1957	1957–59	1960–62	1963–65	1966–68	1968
Total R & D[d]	4,390	5,453	9,625	15,118	16,686	16,747						
Total Research	3,933	5,046	9,006	13,985	16,021	16,230						
Defense	2,985	3,850	6,336	7,245	7,590	7 698	75.9	76.3	70.4	51.8	47.4	47.4
NASA	55	136	920	4,037	4,835	4,587	1.4	2.7	10.2	28.9	30.2	28.3
AEC	528	624	882	1,202	1,278	1,365	13.4	12.4	9.8	8.6	8.0	8.4
HEW	144	190	442	796	1,147	1,279	3.7	3.8	4.9	5.7	7.2	7.9
NSF	30	36	84	185	256	277	0.8	0.7	0.9	1.3	1.6	1.7
Agriculture	100	110	142	198	250	258	2.5	2.2	1.6	1.4	1.6	1.6
Other	91	101	200	321	666	765	2.3	2.0	2.2	2.3	4.2	4.7
Basic Research	259	356	794	1,668	1,984	2,093	6.6	7.1	8.8	11.9	12.4	12.9
Defense	84	111	182	245	264	246	2.8	2.9	2.9	3.4	3.5	3.2
NASA	12	36	145	535	602	645	20.9	26.5	15.8	13.3	12.5	14.1
AEC	56	72	154	256	299	314	10.6	11.5	17.5	21.3	23.4	23.0
HEW	38	54	144	300	370	413	26.4	28.4	32.6	37.7	32.3	32.3
NSF	30	36	84	184	237	251	100.0	100.0	99.5	99.4	92.9	90.8
Agriculture	17	23	41	75	101	103	17.0	20.9	28.9	37.9	40.2	40.1
Other	22	25	45	74	110	120	24.2	24.8	22.3	23.1	16.5	15.7

Applied Research	654	733	1,695	2,972	3,333	3,313	16.6	14.5	18.8	21.3	20.8	20.4
Defense	361	375	933	1,502	1,357	1,178	12.1	9.7	14.7	20.7	17.8	15.3
NASA	22	43	224	654	802	831	39.6	31.6	24.3	16.2	16.6	18.1
AEC	43	62	70	70	92	95	8.1	9.9	7.9	5.8	7.2	7.0
HEW	104	134	296	491	708	775	72.2	70.5	67.0	61.7	61.7	60.6
NSF	—	—	—	1	3	4	—	—	—	0.3	1.1	1.5
Agriculture	78	82	95	115	137	139	78.2	74.5	66.9	58.1	54.7	54.0
Other	46	37	77	140	234	290	50.5	36.6	38.2	43.6	35.1	37.9

Development	3,020	3,958	6,517	9,345	10,704	10,824	76.8	78.4	72.4	66.8	66.8	66.7
Defense	2,540	3,364	5,221	5,498	5,969	6,274	85.1	87.4	82.4	75.9	78.6	81.5
NASA	22	57	551	2,848	3,431	3,111	39.5	41.9	59.9	70.5	71.0	67.8
AEC	429	491	658	877	887	955	81.3	78.7	74.6	73.0	69.4	70.0
HEW	2	2	6	6	68	92	1.4	1.1	0.5	0.8	5.9	7.2
NSF	—	—	**	1	15	21	—	—	0.5	0.3	5.9	7.8
Agriculture	5	5	6	7	13	15	4.8	4.5	4.2	3.5	5.0	5.9
Other	23	39	79	108	322	355	25.3	38.6	39.4	33.6	48.3	46.4

Source: [10].

a Figures are three year averages of period indicated. Detail may not add to totals due to rounding.

b Boldface figures give percentage of total federal research; lightface figures give percentage of total agency research.

c 1968 figures are estimates.

d Includes R & D Plant.

** Less than $500,000.

The breakdown by type of research in the NSF data suggests the logic for such a proxy. The three relevant categories are defined as follows:

> In *basic research* the investigator is concerned primarily with gaining a fuller knowledge or understanding of the subject under study.
>
> In *applied research* the investigator is primarily interested in a practical use of the knowledge or understanding for the purpose of meeting a recognized need.
>
> *Development* is a systematic use of the knowledge and understanding gained from research, directed toward the production of useful materials, devices, systems, or methods, including design and development of prototypes and processes [10, vol. 17, pp. 83–4].

Suppose we consider these categories as discrete (and probably overlapping) boxes somehow squeezed onto our research spectrum. The dollar amounts falling in each category then become a statement of the *weight* accorded each class of research, or in our terminology, three general classes of expected embodiment. A larger *relative* funding in the direction of the first category, "basic research," would reveal a greater emphasis on creation of pure knowledge; the reverse, greater funding to "development," underlines a concern with the production of usable technology. Our observation is that funding distributions can reveal the existence of immediate product goals, or lack thereof, and therefore can be taken as an indicator of *motivations* – that is, of the general willingness of a spender to support research for high versus low embodiment knowledge. Motivations, in turn, can imply the nature of spender expectations vis-à-vis all classes of research.[10]

To illustrate the latter point, suppose we were to establish a "neutral" environment in which to rank all potential research projects on the basis of their average expected embodiment. Among sufficiently informed individuals the ordering of expectations would be fairly universal [15, 33]. We could anticipate that for government agencies supporting general scientific investigation this scale would serve the decision-making needs. However, the spender intent upon some well-defined final objective would choose projects of original low embodiment potential not according to any aggregate maximizing criterion but because of their connection to his particular purposes. We could raise our expectations of applicability far above those prevailing in the universal ordering.[11] Figure 1 pictures the process in which motivations determine the selection from the class of research projects and the effect on the relevant set of expectations. Spender *X* is assumed to be a general supporter of scientific research and *Y* mission-oriented. In Figure 2 we illustrate the hypothesis with respect to the research spectrum. Grants are a constant function of the degree of expected embodiment

---

10 For another instance of data used as a foundation for a proxy indicator, see the study by Ronald Black and Charles Foreman [1].

11 Richard Musgrave presents a prominent physicist's observations on differences in basic research supported by mission versus nonmission-oriented agencies [19].

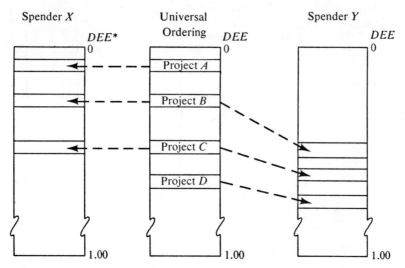

*"Degree of Expected Embodiment," expressed as a probability.

Figure 1. Effect of Motivations on Embodiment Expectations

attached by the spender to various projects. But depending on the interests of the funding agent, the boundaries of the scientific classification will fall at different points along the grants curve because projects within each of the three categories will be subject to substantially different sets of expectations.

On Calculation of the Grants Index

Having established that the available data breakdown can reflect the "grants orientation" of R & D spenders, we need a measure of the distribution of funding — that is, a grants index. Because we are representing a general concept rather than specific data, tractability is essential. A distributional indicator based on an elementary concept of expenditure concentration among the three categories of research is inherently as reasonable under the circumstances as any more complicated approach. Thus, we attack the problem in the following manner.

First, we assume that all expenditures for development by any agency fall too far along the spectrum of expected embodiment to be conceivable grants. This establishes a firm vantage point from which to view the relative size of the other two categories of research spending. As we observe that larger proportions of funding fall into these basic and applied research categories, we can conceive of this observation as representative of an increasing grants orientation. A simple addition of these funding amounts compared to total R & D would not quite serve our purposes, though. No distinction would be made as to the influence of basic versus applied research on the size of the index number; our scale would

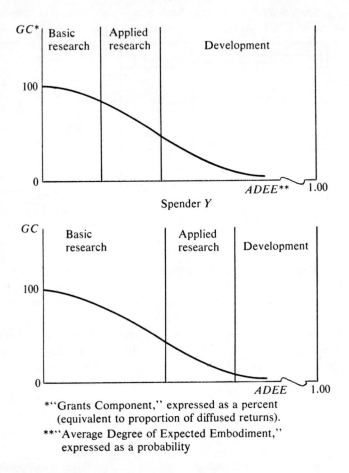

Figure 2. Variation of Grants Component Within Natural Science Classification Due to Spender Motivation

not be commensurate with the idea that funds devoted to basic research underline the strongest interest in production of grants-type knowledge. Consistency requires a weighting of the basic research category. Thus, the indicator proposed is:

$$I_i = \frac{2B_i + A_i}{T_i},$$

where I_i = the index number of the ith agency.
        B_i = expenditures for basic research of the ith agency.
        A_i = expenditures for applied research of the ith agency.
        T_i = total R & D expenditures of the ith agency, excluding R & D plant.

This index has two positive aspects. First, the weighting is not so large as to substantially discount calculated index numbers with respect to the theoretical limit (200). Of course, we reach this limit only when 100 percent of funding falls in the basic research category. Secondly, the index provides a convenient dividing line. Two categories of the scientific classification are to be evaluated. Intuitively we know that some level of the index must exist where the funding distribution is considered sufficiently "grants oriented" to implicate all the basic research expenditures and increasing amounts of applied research as a grant component. Although an arbitrary choice is necessary, the 100 mark not only offers the halfway point on the scale but also facilitates application of the index on a percentage basis; that is, we can use the first 100 points to evaluate basic research expenditures and the second, to evaluate applied research.

Table 2 lists the index numbers calculated from various combinations of a hypothetical $100 of R & D spending and illustrates the consistency of the scale (that is, increasing index values) as two phenomena occur. Increasing proportions of total funding fall in the basic plus applied research categories, or given a fixed proportion for these two categories, larger amounts go to basic research. Also provided are the proportions of basic and applied research that we would consider as grants in each case. We note, for example, that an index number of 80 indicates the grants component to be 80 percent of basic research

Table 2. Application of Grants Component Indicator $[(2B_i + A_i)/T_i]$ to Hypothetical Distributions of R & D Funding (Total Expenditure = $100)

Amount Allocated to Each Class of Research				Proportion of Expenditures Falling in Grants Category	
Basic	Applied	Development	Index Number	Basic	Applied
0	1	99	1	.01	—
1	0	99	2	.02	—
1	1	98	3	.03	—
1	9	90	11	.11	—
5	5	90	15	.15	—
9	1	90	19	.19	—
5	10	85	20	.20	—
10	20	70	40	.40	—
15	30	55	60	.60	—
20	40	40	80	.80	—
40	20	40	100	1.00	—
30	40	30	100	1.00	—
40	40	20	120	1.00	.20
30	60	10	120	1.00	.20
40	50	10	130	1.00	.30
45	45	10	135	1.00	.35
60	30	10	150	1.00	.50
90	1	9	181	1.00	.81
90	9	1	189	1.00	.89
97	1	2	195	1.00	.95
99	1	0	199	1.00	.99

expenditures alone; or a number of 130 includes in the grants component all basic research and 30 percent applied research. In addition we do not take equal grants orientation – that is, identical index numbers – for two different funding agents to mean necessarily that the grants component is the same proportion of total funding for each. Rather, that index number points to similar sets of expectations within the basic and applied research categories and implicates equal proportions of those categories.

Results and Observations

Table 3 lists the index number applied to each agency's expenditures for the four periods between 1957 and 1968. Except for AEC, these numbers reflect a degree of grants orientation that we might "expect," given familiarity with agency general purpose. For instance, in 1966–68 the Defense Department generates a rating of 24.9, whereas HEW receives 126.3 and NSF 189.0. The index number of 53.5 for AEC in this same period seems low considering its substantial support of basic research in high energy physics. This number results from the strikingly small proportion of funding the agency categorizes as applied research.

Table 4 gives the grants component of federal R & D funding, calculated by the previously described method. This component is less than 10 percent throughout the period, but we note a steady increase from 5.1 percent of total obligations in 1957–59 to 9.2 percent in 1966–68. A doubling in the proportion of funding to two general supporters of research (HEW and NSF) plus increases in the relative size of basic and applied research account for the

Table 3. Grants Orientation Index Numbers by Federal Agency and Major Performer, 1957–59 to 1966–68

	Index Number			
	1957–59	*1960–62*	*1963–65*	*1966–68*
Agency				
Defense	15.5	20.5	27.5	24.9
NASA	83.8	55.8	42.6	41.5
AEC	33.0	42.9	48.4	53.5
HEW	127.2	131.8	137.0	126.3
NSF	200.0	199.0	199.1	189.0
Agriculture	116.9	124.9	134.4	135.2
Other	85.8	82.9	89.1	68.1
Performer[a]				
Intramural			60.2	58.3
Industrial Firms			20.2	21.5
Universities & Colleges			146.6	150.2

Source: Table 1, [10].

[a] In pre-1963 data, breakdowns by performer and type of research are not sufficient for calculating index numbers.

Table 4. Grants Component of Federal R & D Funding by Agency and Total, 1957–59 to 1966–68

Agency	Millions of Current Dollars[a]				Percentage of Total Agency Obligations			
	1957–59	1960–62	1963–65	1966–68	1957–59	1960–62	1963–65	1966–68
Defense	17	37	67	66	0.4	0.6	0.9	0.9
NASA	30	81	228	250	22.0	8.8	5.6	5.2
AEC	24	66	124	160	3.8	7.5	10.3	12.5
HEW	91	238	482	557	47.6	53.8	60.5	48.5
NSF	36	84	185	240	100.0	99.5	99.7	93.9
Agriculture	37	65	115	149	33.8	45.7	58.1	59.5
Other	21	37	65	75	20.9	18.5	20.3	11.2
Total Grants Component	255	608	1,266	1,496				
Total Federal R & D	5,046	9,006	13,985	16,230				
Grants as Percent of Total R & D	5.1%	6.7%	9.1%	9.2%				

Source: Tables 1 and 3, [10].
a Detail may not add to totals due to rounding.

upward trend. The low level of the grants component, despite some rather high index numbers, results from the unequal distribution of total outlays. Agencies that absorb the largest proportion of R & D funding – Defense and NASA – show the lowest grants component; agencies for which high grants components have been calculated – HEW, NSF, and Agriculture – make under 10 percent of all R & D expenditures.

It may be argued that the method of calculating the grants component used here is a fanciful concoction. We do not raise a defense. What we have offered is a conceptual framework for viewing the difference between the grants and exchange components of research funding. Then, in the absence of any measurement system based on these premises, we have devised a means of approximation. The approach at least provides a single and consistent standard by which to evaluate the R & D funding of all federal agencies.

Distributional Effects of R & D Grants

Data recently published on federal research obligations by state enables some initial steps in evaluating the impact of R & D grants on equity. The figures available are for fiscal 1968 only. No breakdowns are given by type of research so that the amounts of grants and exchange research on a statewide basis cannot be derived. However, the techniques developed earlier can be used through comparison among federal agencies on the one hand and among R & D performers on the other, the latter a test to detect possible differences dependent on spender versus recipient status.

The premise on which the analysis rests is that consideration of any grants policy is not just a matter of cataloging the dollar results of transfers. The larger question of increase (or decrease) in welfare as compared with the alternative of a "less grants" or even pure exchange situation is always implied. We have noted that grants orientation differs among governmental units and among performers of research as well (see Table 3). Suppose that for each agent involved *total* R & D expenditures are correlated with income by state. The distributional impact of the "high grant" spenders (performers) versus the "low grant" spenders (performers) will point to the equity benefits or lack thereof in current R & D grants policy.

The potential distributional effects of R & D activities are twofold. Initially funds flow into a particular geographical area for personnel salaries and payments to suppliers. Local and regional income multiplier effects are generated.[12] Over the longer run the gathering together in one place of scientific

---

12 Burton Weisbrod has observed: "When government attempts to influence the production of particular goods and services – housing, highways, dams, schools, rivers and harbors, air traffic control systems, etc. – even though the motivation may be to enhance allocative efficiency, the fact is that these activities do affect the distribution of income sometimes in subtle though powerful ways" [20, p. 180]. H. Nieburg notes the pressures for maintaining previously established levels of R & D outlays in the interests of local income maintenance [12, p. 673].

minds and the continual production of knowledge that cannot be perfectly disseminated increases substantially the prospects for locally based "spin-off" industries. Encircling Boston, Route 128 is a favorite example. In this regard an initial maldistribution of grants funding, over time, will not be less inequitable than a similar distribution of exchange funding. Grants knowledge may be disseminated more widely before being put to practical purposes. But the ultimate user – someone with the capacity to recognize the value of the knowledge – is also likely to have been a beneficiary of high levels of R & D expenditures.

Specifically the hypothesis we test is that R & D grants funding is more equitably distributed by state than is exchange funding. That is, we presume grants funding to be *less* favorable to wealthier states and therefore on distributional grounds a more desirable form of research support. Because of its abstract nature grants research functions with smaller groupings of personnel and lesser amounts of scientific equipment. The spender allocates smaller discrete doses of funding and is therefore in a position at least to "even out" his expenditures and perhaps as well to support less prestigious efforts with smaller risk to overall objectives. Income redistribution per se is not presumed here because research spending is largely predicated on performance criteria.

Four R & D spenders are considered – two "high grantors," HEW and NSF, and two "low grantors," Defense and NASA. The three performers are Universities, Government (Intramural) Laboratories, and Industrial Firms.[13] Table 3 notes the "high" grants orientation of Universities along with "low" ratings for the latter two categories.

In the analysis, states are ranked in descending order of per capita personal income. The *total* R & D awarded in each state by individual spenders and received by individual performers is also reduced to per capita figure and appropriately tallied. Inspection of the raw data suggests *some* positive relationship between per capita state income and per capita R & D. For all spender–performer categories variations in per capita R & D among states adjacent and proximate to each other on the income scale are substantial. But with the exception of intramural laboratories the bulk of the *lowest* per capita R & D figures are found among the *lowest* income states. Table 5 lists the Spearman rank correlation coefficients calculated from these data. The size of the coefficients tends to confirm the above observations. Of course, none of the r' shows significant correlation, although evidence of income as an explicit criterion in allocating R & D would come as a matter of considerable surprise.

What is most interesting is that HEW and NSF, the high grant spenders, and Universities, the high grant performer, achieve the highest r', 0.523, 0.627, and 0.612 respectively as compared with Defense 0.455 or Industrial Firms 0.493. On a relative basis at least our hypothesis would seem to be denied. The Gini

---

13 Industrial firms and universities and colleges administer what are termed "Federally Funded Research and Development Centers." Examples are the Lincoln Laboratory, the Oak Ridge National Laboratory, or the Jet Propulsion Laboratory. The analysis does not include amounts allocated for these centers.

Table 5. Redistributional Effects of R & D Expenditures
by Spender and Performer

	Correlation Spearman r'	Inequality Gini Coefficient
Agency		
NSF	.627	.223
HEW	.523	.310
NASA	.427	.575
Defense	.455	.448
Performer		
University	.612	.180
Intramural	.136	.478
Industrial Firms	.493	.453
Total R & D	.422	.364

Source: [10, vol. 18, pp. 226, 229]; [18, pp. 12, 320].

coefficients also provided in Table 5 point to different conclusions, however. In this latter test, cumulative percentages of population on a state by state basis are calculated, starting with those states receiving the smallest total R & D from the particular spender and likewise for the particular performer. These figures are then compared with the accumulated percentage of R & D funds awarded. Results show our high grant categories with the lowest concentration of expenditures. Gini coefficients are 0.310, 0.223, and 0.180 for HEW, NSF, and Universities respectively, as contrasted with 0.478 for Intramural Laboratories or 0.575 for NASA.

The crux of the matter is that in our high grant categories discrimination is more consistent. Among low grantors and grantees, especially Defense and NASA, extraordinarily small amounts of R & D funds are awarded to a number of the poorest states. But a few other lower-income states rank among the most fortunate R & D recipients.[14] With substantial variation also among wealthier states – despite higher *levels* of per capita R & D – we can anticipate a low correlation of R & D expenditures with income. The high grantors-grantees, on the other hand, are subject to less radical extremes. Deviations among states proximate on the income scale are less pronounced as are differences between the highest versus the lowest per capita R & D recipient states (for instance, 114 times for NSF and 4,215 for NASA). An overall tendency to direct larger per capita allocations to high-income states, therefore, becomes more evident.

---

14 Some examples. Dollar R & D figures are on a per capita basis. Of the numbers in parentheses, the first indicates rank on the per capita income scale and the second indicates rank on the per capita R & D scale. Defense: Texas, $43.40 (32,12); Georgia, $52.70 (38,10); New Mexico, $186.22 (41,1); Maine, $0.05 (36,50); North Dakota, $0.27 (40,49); Arkansas, $0.06 (49,48). NASA: Texas, $30.90 (31,7); Louisiana, $64.12 (42,4); Alabama, $84.30 (48,1); North Dakota, $0.02 (40,50); West Virginia, $0.06 (46,49); Arkansas, $0.06 (49,48).

Conclusions

In this paper we have stressed that a working *economic* classification for R & D is the most immediate need. Using current definitions, which are still blunt instruments, we employ a functional outlook that gives little attention either to research interrelationships or to the outcomes of research efforts. A means for optimal allocation of R & D funds may be difficult to envision, but it is hardly attainable as long as dependence is placed on such generalized and noncomparable criteria as "basic research" or "development." Some kind of universal measurement device is the foundation stone for any effective evaluation of projects both within and among scientific disciplines. As a step in this direction, we have shown that, conceptually, a grants knowledge and an exchange knowledge can be distinguished by an ex ante measure of the character of returns -- the "degree of expected embodiment." Research projects, viewed as producers of units of knowledge, can then be described not through discrete categories but in terms of their widely varying composition.

We have amply illustrated the limitations the present structure of data imposes on analytical rigor. The expectations proxy circumvents a vital information roadblock. Although we may find some assurance that the relative structure of grant giving among federal agencies is accurately reflected, to express confidence in the absolute magnitudes requires courage. With respect to distributional effects, we might hope that grants and exchange components could be calculated explicitly on an agency--state basis over a substantial period; a breakdown for major urban concentrations would be even more eminently desirable. Aside from substantiating the equity characteristics of particular ongoing governmental expenditures, a broader view of efficiency in R & D funding might emerge. There could develop, for instance, vigorous discussion of the extent to which existing research structures are subject to economies or diseconomies of scale in promoting knowledge output as well as equity over the long run. All in all, our results suggest the prospect of high marginal returns to additional inquiry.

References

1. Black, R. P., and C. W. Foreman. "Transferability of Research and Development Skills in the Aerospace Industry." In *Technology and the American Economy*. Washington, D.C.: National Commission on Technology, Automation, and Economic Progress, 1966. Appendix vol. 5, pp. 75--130.

2. Boulding, K. "Grants vs. Exchange in the Support of Education." In *Federal Programs for the Development of Human Resources*. Washington, D.C.: U.S. Congress, Joint Economic Committee, 1968. Vol. 1, pp. 232–38.

3. Breton, A. "A Theory of Government Grants." *Canadian Journal of Economics and Political Science*, May 1965, pp. 175–87.

4. Horvath, P. and J. R. Burke. "The Grants Component of Federal Funds for Science." Paper presented at the AAAS meetings, Grants Economics Symposium, Boston, December 1969.

5. Byatt, I. C. R., and A. V. Cohen. *An Attempt to Quantify the Economic Benefits of Scientific Research.* U.K. Department of Education and Science, 1969.

6. Denison, E. F. *The Sources of Economic Growth in the United States and the Alternatives Before Us.* New York: Committee for Economic Development, 1962.

7. Mansfield, E. *Industrial Research and Technological Innovation, An Econometric Analysis.* New York; W. W. Norton, 1968.

8. Marschak, T., et al. *Strategy for R & D: Studies in the Micro-Economics of Development.* New York: Springer-Verlag, 1967.

9. Musgrave, R. A. *The Theory of Public Finance.* New York: McGraw-Hill Book Co., 1959.

10. National Science Foundation. *Federal Funds for Research, Development, and Other Scientific Activities.* Vols. 7–18, 1958–69.

11. Nelson, R. R. "The Link Between Science and Invention: The Case of the Transistor." In National Bureau of Economic Research, *The Rate and Direction of Inventive Activity.* Princeton, N.J.: Princeton University Press, 1962, pp. 549–83.

12. Nieburg, H. L. "Social Control of Innovation." *American Economic Review*, May 1968, pp. 666–77.

13. Pfaff, M., and A. Pfaff. "Grants Economy: An Evaluation of Government Policies." *Public Finance*, January 1971.

14. Pfaff, M. *The Grants Economy.* Belmont, Calif.: Wadsworth Publishing Co., forthcoming.

15. Scherer, F. M. "Government Research and Development Programs." In R. Dorfman, ed., *Measuring Benefits of Government Investments.* Washington, D.C.: The Brookings Institution, 1965, pp. 12–70.

16. Schmookler, J. *Invention and Economic Growth.* Cambridge, Mass.: Harvard University Press, 1966.

17. Townes, C. H. "Quantum Electronics and Surprise in the Development of Technology." *Science,* February 1968, p. 699.

18. *Statistical Abstract of the United States, 1969.*

19. Weinberg, A. M. "Scientific Choice, Basic Science, and Applied Missions." In National Academy of Science, *Basic Research and National Goals.* A Report to the Committee on Science and Astronautics, U.S. House of Representatives, 1965, pp. 279–88.

20. Weisbrod, B. A. "Collective Action and the Distribution of Income." In U.S. Congress, Joint Economic Committee, *The Analysis and Evaluation of Public Expenditures: The Planning–Programming–Budgeting System,* 1969, pp. 177–97.

9

Bruce C. Stuart: The Impact of
Medicaid on Interstate Income
Differentials

Introduction

The Problem

In recent years a number of studies have analyzed the effects of government expenditure policies on the distribution of regional and state incomes.[1] This should come as no surprise. Federal projects ranging from agricultural price supports to military procurements are, after all, highly regionalized in their impact. What is surprising is that similar attention has not been given the pure transfer programs whose primary purpose actually is the redistribution of income of services. Such unilateral transfers as public assistance deserve particular attention. Although we may assume that welfare payments tend to reduce income inequalities in any one state, the current practice of financing such payments through joint federal–state assistance programs raises the possibility of gross differences in benefit levels among the states. In fact, some would contend that this approach has augmented existing differentials in interstate incomes and more importantly has created serious inequities for the poverty populations in low-income compared to affluent areas of the country.

In this paper we attempt to gauge the direction and extent of such inequities in the system of joint federal–state welfare policy by analyzing the distributional impacts of the Medical Assistance program. Medicaid, as the program is popularly known, is the most recent and by far the largest program

This paper represents a revised and somewhat expanded version of a paper read at the American Association for the Advancement of Science symposium on the Grants Economy in December, 1970, in Chicago, Illinois. A revised version of the original paper also appeared as "Equity and Medicaid," *Journal of Human Resources*, vol. VII, no. 2 (Spring 1972), pp. 162–178. All rights reserved. Used by permission of the author. Mr. Stuart is from the Michigan Department of Social Services, Division of Research and Program Analysis.

1 See, for example, J. T. Bonnen, "The Distribution of Benefits from Cotton Price Support," in S. B. Chase, Jr., ed., *Problems in Public Expenditure Analysis* (Washington, D.C.: The Brookings Institution, 1968); W. W. Leontief, "The Economic Impact-Industrial and Regional of an Arms Cut," *The Review and Economics and Statistics*, 47, no. 3 (August 1965): 217 41: R. H. Haveman, *Water Resources Investment and the Public Interest* (Nashville: Vanderbilt University Press, 1965); M. C. McGuire, "Program Analysis and Regional Economic Objectives," in *The Analysis and Evaluation of Public Expenditure: The PPB System*, vol. 1, pt. III, *Some Problems of Analysis in Evaluating Public Expenditure Alternatives*, U.S. Congress, Joint Economic Committee Print (Washington, D.C.: Government Printing Office, 1969), pp. 592–610; and S. Engerman, "Regional Aspects of Stabilization Policy," in R. A. Musgrave, ed., *Essays in Fiscal Federalism* (Washington, D.C., The Brookings Institution, 1965).

within the panoply of welfare policies in America. In 1969, for example, over 41.9 percent of all public assistance funds from federal, state, and local governments combined was expended on this single program.[2] The impact of Medicaid has had a significant and expanding effect on the entire welfare system. But Medical Assistance is not only the largest of the joint federal–state welfare policies, it is also, in one respect, the most innovative.

Under the other categorical assistance programs, for example, the percentage of state funds, which the federal government agrees to match, is determined irrespective of individual state needs. In the adult welfare categories (Aid to the Blind, Disabled, and Aged) the current federal formula reimburses each state $31 of the first $37 spent per recipient per month and 50 percent of the remainder up to a maximum federal contribution of $50. The matching formula is similar under Aid to Families with Dependent Children (AFDC) except that the reimbursement rates are lower, reaching a maximum federal grant of $22 per recipient per month. Obviously it is to every state's advantage to establish and operate such assistance programs in order that they may partake of the lucrative matching funds available. *But* there is also an incentive for each state *not* to spend above the matchable limits. Given the two-stage reimbursement formula, we can even argue that a state faces a real incentive to stop spending when the first limit is reached ($37 in the case of adult programs, $18 for AFDC).

Historically these positive and negative incentives have played an important role in the amount of money states spend on their welfare recipients. Typically states in the low-income South and West have spent little more than the initial per recipient grant required to reach the maximum percentage reimbursement in federal funds. In addition, these same states have traditionally required the most stringent means tests for welfare eligibility. At the other end of the scale are the states in the rich industrial areas in the North (plus California), which, even though they face the same set of incentives, have tended to spend above the matchable limit on all programs. Because the wealthy states also have more liberal eligibility requirements, the net result is a welfare system that rewards the rich states with far greater federal welfare grants than their less affluent neighbors.

With its passage in 1965 Medicaid was designed in part to eliminate the inequity by establishing an alternative reimbursement formula based on per capita income. For high-income states the Act allowed 50 percent federal matching for a wide variety of covered medical expenses, but in those states with the lowest average incomes federal participation could reach as high as 83 percent. Not only was the alternative formula designed to act as an incentive for poor states to increase their expenditures on medical welfare, the law allowed (with certain restrictions) any state that wished to apply the formula to its other welfare programs, thus eliminating the disincentive to spend above the previous matchable limits.

As economic incentives go, the Medicaid reimbursement formula is indeed a carrot of rare quality. It represents perhaps the first instance where the federal

---

2 This figure may be contrasted with the 4.3 percent of welfare payments going to medical vendors in 1951.

government has overtly attempted to reduce regional and interstate differences in income and the level of welfare payments; and as a result it is all the more important to analyze the success (or failure) of the attempt.

Methodology

There are a number of ways to approach the issue of Medicaid-related income redistribution. Here we use techniques designed both to measure and to evaluate the distributional impact of Medicaid operations in fiscal 1968 — the latest year for which complete data are available. The first technique, often described as "fiscal incidence analysis,"[3] measures the current effect of Medicaid reimbursements and costs on state incomes. The second technique evaluates this impact in terms of distributive equity. Neither method is really new, but each takes on a slightly different connotation when the distribution of benefits and costs is measured among states rather than the more common analysis of impacts by income class. Moreover, in the case of fiscal incidence studies in particular there is a possible confusion over just what is being measured. Before we move ahead to the question at hand, placing each of these techniques into the proper context might prove helpful.

In general, the study of fiscal incidence may be approached from two points of view. We may, for example, consider the *net* or additive effect of a program such as Medicaid on government budgets at the federal, state, and local levels. No government policy is enacted in a vacuum. In most cases it results from a complex combination of new benefits and taxes, reductions in other budgeted programs, replacement of old projects, and other planned and unplanned adjustments in the final budget outcome. The measurement of interaction among each of these factors provides us with information about the redistributional impact of introducing a new program into a given governmental framework.[4] It does not, however, tell us how an existing program affects the current distribution of income.

---

3 See W. I. Gillespie, "Effects of Public Expenditures on the Distribution of Income," in R. A. Musgrave, ed., *Essays in Fiscal Federalism* (Washington, D.C.: The Brookings Institution, 1965); and the Tax Foundation, Inc., in *Tax Burdens and Benefits of Government Expenditures by Income Class, 1961 and 1965* (New York: The Tax Foundation, Inc., 1967).

4 An analysis of the introductory impact of Medicaid on federal, state, and local budgets would require the following information (in addition to contributory tax and expenditure figures): (1) estimates of the reduction (if any) in budgeted amounts for nonmedical programs at each level of government; (2) estimates of the benefits lost and taxes saved by state from replacing medical vendor payments under such programs as Aid to the Blind, Aid to Families with Dependent Children, Medical Assistance for the Aged, Old-Age Assistance, and Aid to the Disabled; (3) measurements of any Medicaid-related increase in government debt; (4) estimates of program-related reductions (if any) in public and private medical charity; (5) indication of the rise in provider incomes (and medical prices) that resulted from the Medicaid program. If we assume that these increases can be limited to Medicaid, then the following information is also necessary: (6) estimates of the medical price-related increase in income tax deductions for medical care; (7) estimates of the increase in income tax liabilities to medical providers arising both from higher incomes and from lower bad debt deductions.

For this purpose a second and superior approach is to isolate the program's expenditures and contributory tax revenues from the rest of the government budget. It is then possible to estimate the distribution of the burden of program costs and expenditure benefits by using appropriate assumptions of shifting and incidence. This study employs this static approach first to gain insight into the degree of current Medicaid-related redistribution among states and at a later stage to estimate the degree of redistribution among the poverty populations in each state. In both cases the measure of redistribution is the grant equivalent (net dollar gain) received or the tax equivalent (net loss) suffered by the inhabitants of each state. The Medicaid grant and tax equivalents are then compared for states with different average per household incomes to determine the direction and magnitude of redistribution in the system.

Although the use of fiscal incidence analysis allows us to calculate the actual amount of redistribution, it does not, in itself, provide the framework necessary for an evaluation of final outcomes. Such evaluation requires an explicit test of distributive equity. Ideally this test should incorporate standards of distribution for both benefits and costs, which reflect the "welfare function" of society with regard to the program under consideration. Because this welfare function is impossible to define, a second best solution is employed that approximates the original intent of the program designers. Naturally a set of standards of distributive equity developed in this manner is somewhat arbitrary, but it is, nonetheless, conceptually superior to no standard at all. In the first place, it forces us to consider the problems surrounding program evaluation. Second, it allows the analyst to make an explicit comparison between actual program performance and an alternative that at least some consider superior.

Because the standards are relative, it is best to understate rather than overstate the redistributional impact of any "ideal" Medicaid system that Title XIX legislation might imply. In this way the standards can be interpreted as a set of minimum criteria for distributive equity. For the present analysis these standards are as follows. First, program costs should be distributed among the states in such a manner that the burden is at least proportional to per capita state income. In other words, the financing of the Medicaid program itself should not aggravate existing interstate income inequalities. The provision of the federal matching formula mentioned previously suggests that this weak criterion of ability to pay is an appropriate minimal standard for the distribution of program costs. Second, program benefits should be distributed among the states on a basis proportionate with the medical needs of the poor in each state. This does not mean that health requirements of all poor persons have to be fulfilled in order to meet the standard (although this alternative is a possibility) but merely that what money is spent should be proportioned on the basis of need alone. Since the Medicaid legislation allows the state to develop programs that cover not only welfare recipients but all medically indigent persons,[5] this also is an appropriate standard of distribution. Unfortunately no commonly accepted cardinal measure of medical need exists. As a proxy I have used the distribution of households earning less than $3,000 per year in each state.[6]

Note that the combination of these standards implies a neutral economic impact only if the percentage distribution of poor households in all states is proportional to the distribution of average state incomes. However, because we know that the poverty populations in wealthy states represent a *smaller* percentage of total state population than in less affluent regions, the requirement of the combined standards is in fact "progressive." The relevant question is whether the required degree and direction of redistribution is obtained in actual Medicaid operations.

The test of this hypothesis is straightforward. First, the total value of tax contributions and expenditure benefits for Medicaid in fiscal 1968 are allocated among the states on the bases of the two standards of distribution. These figures may then be compared directly with the calculations of actual benefits and costs to gauge the extent of inequities arising from a maldistribution of Medicaid benefits and/or an inequitable distribution of the burden of Medicaid costs.

Estimation of Medicaid Benefits and Costs by State

Expenditure Benefits

The first step in this direction is an estimation of actual Medicaid benefits received by the state during the study period. In other, similar types of analysis, benefits from government programs are allocated among different population groups in terms of the current dollar value of program expenditures received by each group. The same practice is followed here. Total expenditures for assistance under Title XIX equaled $3.025 billion[7] for the thirty-seven states with approved programs in 1968. This total is allocated using the series for state Medicaid reimbursements published twice annually by the National Center for

---

5 The 1967 amendments to the Social Security Act revised the original Title XIX provisions for medically indigent persons. After July 1, 1968, federal matching funds covered only 133 $\frac{1}{3}$ percent of the highest amount ordinarily paid by the state to a family of the same size under the Aid to Families of Dependent Children (AFDC) Program. Although this revision effectively limits the coverage originally given medically indigent persons, its effects are not considered here because the provision became effective after fiscal 1968.

6 The correlation between low income and high rates of morbidity, disability, and so on is well documented. In every health survey by the National Center of Health Statistics (which began collecting national data on disability, morbidity, and utilization of medical services in 1957) this relationship holds. See, for example, U.S. Department of Health, Education and Welfare, Public Health Service, *Vital and Health Statistics Data From the National Health Survey*, National Center for Health Statistics Report, series 10, no. 47, *Disability Days, United States – July 1965--June 1966* (Washington, D.C.: Government Printing Office, 1968), pp. 28- 33. Note that price level differences among states may affect this relationship between income and medical need for a particular state. However, the effect will be minor.

7 This figure does not include amounts for administrative services and training, nor does it include expenditures for the Medicaid programs in Guam, Puerto Rico, and the Virgin Islands.

Social Statistics (see the second column in Table 2). Because of the minute possibility that these benefits may be transferred or shifted among states, the NCSS figures need not be adjusted.[8]

The Burden of Cost

Unfortunately we cannot say the same for the burden of Medicaid costs. The Medical Assistance program is funded from a bewildering variety of federal, state, and local levies. Of the total cost of $3 billion, the federal government financed half, the states 36 percent, and localities the remaining 14 percent.[9] In all, several thousand separate taxes are involved and, with relatively few exceptions, the shifting of tax burdens among states is a distinct possibility. The problem thus is really threefold: first to identify which taxes supported Medicaid at each level of government; second to determine the portion and amount of Medicaid-contributing revenue from each tax; and finally to determine the direction and extent of interstate tax shifting.

At the federal level the solution to these problems is quite straightforward. We know that all federal Medicaid revenues originate from the general fund. We may assume, therefore, that each tax finances Medicaid in direct relation to the importance of its revenues in the general fund. For example, if the personal income tax accounts for 40 percent of total general revenues I assume that 40 percent of federal Medicaid expenditures are financed from this tax. The question then becomes a matter of allocating the Medicaid-contributing component of each tax by state. The procedure is facilitated by the 1969 Tax Foundation study. With minor exception I have assumed the same tax incidence as contained in this study.[10] Table 1, column 2, shows the results by state.

---

8 The incidence of Medicaid benefits is assumed to remain in the state of original reimbursement. Although some Medicaid benefits may conceivably be shifted among states, as a result of lags in vendor payments combined with recipient or provider migration, the amounts are probably insignificant and are thus not considered in this analysis.

9 The federal share of total Medicaid expenditures is actually slightly less than 50 percent because a number of states included in their programs services not covered under the federal matching formula.

10 The following assumptions of shifting and incidence are used in this analysis: (1) the personal income tax is borne in the state of taxpayer residence; (2) one half of the corporate income tax is shifted backward to stockholders and the remaining half is shifted forward to consumers in the form of higher prices on retail sales; (3) the excise on automobiles is borne in proportion to state automotive sales; (4) estate and gift taxes are allocated on the basis of state personal income as are excises on alcohol and telephone and telegraphic messages; (5) excises on tobacco are borne in proportion to state population; and (6) all remaining excises and nontax receipts are allocated on the base of state retail sales. Considerable literature exists on the incidence of federal taxes by state. For a recent discussion, see R. Rosenberg, "The Geographic Incidence of the Federal Tax Burden" (unpublished Ph.D. thesis, University of Minnesota, 1969). The reasons for using the relatively simple assumptions of shifting and incidence contained in The Tax Foundation study, *Allocating the Federal Tax Burden by State* (New York: The Tax Foundation, Inc., 1963) are threefold: First, they can be applied to existing sources of data; second, with few exceptions they represent current thinking in the field; and third, if they do in fact somewhat oversimplify the actual complexities of tax incidence, this oversimplification makes little difference in the final estimates of federal Medicaid costs by state because these results are highly insensitive to alternate assumptions of tax shifting (see footnote 11).

Next to the federal government the states contributed the largest share of total Medicaid costs in 1968, and like Federal expenditures general revenues make up the bulk of state Medicaid costs (a few states earmark funds for welfare – a portion of which is used for Medicaid expenses). The tax base for state Medicaid contributions thus contains a similar array of individual taxes: personal and corporate income taxes, excises on tobacco products, alcoholic beverages, plus other types of levies such as general sales and severance taxes not

Table 1. Source of Funds for the Medicaid Program in Fiscal 1968

Region and State	Federal Costs ($000's)	State Costs ($000's)	Local Costs ($000's)
United States	1,509,476	1,086,102	429,135
North Central	432,367	287,081	48,954
Illinois	104,397	81,943	0
Indiana	36,510	2,758	0
Michigan	72,528	81,810	150
Ohio	82,707	40,869	0
Wisconsin	30,519	26,399	22,301
Iowa	17,443	8,724	0
Kansas	14,181	6,907	5,682
Minnesota	24,679	18,052	16,452
Missouri	33,750	10,294	0
Nebraska	9,476	4,593	3,929
North Dakota	3,001	2,716	439
South Dakota	3,177	2,017	0
Northeast	447,909	459,115	285,772
Connecticut	34,859	22,482	0
Maine	6,203	3,889	0
Massachusetts	49,857	61,159	24,697
New Hampshire	5,346	1,364	331
Rhode Island	7,308	10,877	0
Vermont	2,971	2,224	194
New Jersey	64,739	5,195	0
New York	184,479	296,975	249,816
Pennsylvania	92,148	54,950	10,734
South	366,499	115,923	2,977
Delaware	6,217	1,925	0
District of Columbia	8,313	894	0
Florida	46,668	5,200	0
Georgia	24,618	7,260	0
Maryland	32,752	31,203	2,977
North Carolina	25,581	2,242	0
South Carolina	11,497	893	0
Virginia	29,796	2,476	0
West Virginia	9,308	3,643	0
Alabama	15,567	1,198	0
Kentucky	15,861	7,473	0
Mississippi	8,227	679	0
Tennessee	20,769	1,671	0
Arkansas	8,215	700	0
Louisiana	19,089	11,363	0
Oklahoma	13,923	17,193	0
Texas	70,099	19,911	0

Table 1. (Continued)

Region and State	Federal Costs ($000's)	State Costs ($000's)	Local Costs ($000's)
West	262,701	223,983	91,432
Arizona	10,379	1,013	0
Colorado	14,198	1,260	0
Idaho	3,868	2,056	0
Montana	4,091	1,303	936
Nevada	3,952	1,580	1,181
New Mexico	5,147	3,547	0
Utah	5,665	3,427	0
Wyoming	2,208	558	63
Alaska	1,857	94	0
California	166,362	170,886	87,761
Hawaii	5,418	5,947	0
Oregon	14,174	6,457	1,492
Washington	25,382	25,858	0

Sources: U.S. Department of Health, Education and Welfare, Social and Rehabilitation Service, National Center for Social Statistics, *Recipients and Amounts of Medical Vendor Payments Under Public Assistance Programs*, NCSS A–7 and B–3 reports (Washington, D.C.: Government Printing Office, 1967 and 1968); U.S. Department of Commerce, Bureau of the Census, *Governmental Finances in 1967–68* (Washington, D.C.: Government Printing Office, 1969); U.S. Treasury Department, Internal Revenue Service, *Statistics of Income, 1967, Individual Income Tax Returns* (Washington, D.C.: Government Printing Office, 1969); U.S. Department of Commerce, *Survey of Current Business*, 49, no. 8 (August 1969); Sales Management, Inc., *Survey of Buying Power* (1967 and 1968); U.S. Department of Commerce, Bureau of the Census, *State Government Finances* (1967 and 1968) (Washington, D.C.: Government Printing Office, 1968 and 1969); The Tax Foundation, Inc., *Facts and Figures on Government Finance, 15th Biennial Edition of 1969* (New York: The Tax Foundation, Inc., 1969); U.S. Department of Commerce, Bureau of the Census, *Current Population Reports*, series P–25, nos. 384, 403, and 420 (Washington D.C.: Government Printing Office, 1967 and 1968).

found at the federal level. If we could be reasonably certain that the burden of these and other taxes is borne in the state of original payment, the process of allocating these tax burdens would be simple indeed. But we cannot make such an assumption. In fact, the majority of state taxes are probably shifted, to a certain extent, out of state. This results from the highly regional characteristics of manufacturing, mining, and wholesale trade, from population mobility, and from such structural anomalies as the one-way border trade between a state with and a state without retail sales taxation. The problem of identifying the burden of state taxes is at best extremely complex.

In the face of such complexity and lack of knowledge I have chosen to assume that the burden of all tax receipts that enter state general funds (or are earmarked for welfare) are borne instate with the exception of corporate income and severance taxes, which are allocated to each state one half on the basis of state retail sales and one half on the basis of state dividend income.[11] Based on this assumption states without Medicaid programs in 1968 actually bore a portion of the costs of those states using the program. Table 1, column 3 shows the distribution of the final burden of state Medicaid costs.

The financial support for the Medicaid program provided from local revenues was relatively insignificant in 1968. In fact, only seventeen states took advantage of the legislative option that allowed them to place a portion of the burden of Medicaid costs on municipal governments. In the allocation of this burden, we can reasonably assume that little or no out-of-state shifting occurred.[12] The actual amounts of local Medicaid costs by state are tabulated by the National Center so that we do not need to adjust these figures (Table 1, column 4) in this analysis.

Estimation of the Net Impact of Medicaid by State

Now that we have calculated federal, state and local Medicaid tax burdens individually, we need only sum the results to provide state-by-state estimates of total Medicaid costs. These estimates, provided in Table 2, are in turn compared with the NCSS calculations for Medicaid expenditure benefits by state. All differences represent the grant and tax equivalents mentioned previously. An analysis of these differences poses some interesting questions concerning the redistributional impact of the Medicaid system.

---

11 Although this assumption represents a gross simplification of the facts, it does account for the two taxes most likely to be shifted from the state of origin. As far as other state taxes are concerned the assumption allows for shifting out of state provided that in each case the shift is matched by an equal burden shifted in from other states. Again, the estimates are insensitive to alternative assumptions of tax incidence. In a recent study by the author an alternate set of shifting assumptions was employed to determine the burden of state Medicaid costs borne in Michigan. The estimates were based on an analysis by Richard Musgrave and Darwin W. Daicoff ["Who Pays the Michigan Taxes?," in H. Brazer, ed., *Michigan Tax Study: Staff Papers* (Lansing, Mich.: Secretary of Finance, 1958), pp. 131–83], in which the following percentages of Michigan taxes were assumed to fall on residents of other states: (1) corporate income, 42 percent; (2) corporate franchise, 43 percent; (3) business activities, 17 percent; (4) sales and use, 10 percent; (5) intangibles tax, 19 percent; and (6) taxes on insurance companies, 27 percent. The net difference in using these assumptions of outshifting was a reduction in state Medicaid costs of 3.9 percent for fiscal 1968. But because the results were not adjusted for an increased burden of other states' taxes shifted into Michigan, even this small change overestimates the actual effect of using the alternate set of assumptions. See Appendix E in B. Stuart and L. Bair, *Health Care and Income: The Distributional Impacts of Medicaid and Medicare Nationally and in the State of Michigan* (Lansing, Michigan: Department of Social Services, 1971).

12 Most localities derive the majority of their tax revenues from the residential property tax. In the short run at least a significant portion of such revenues is unlikely to shift to residents of other states. Some cities, on the other hand, derive revenue from local sales and business property taxes, which may partially be shifted to other states particularly if the city is located near a state border. Therefore, part of New York City's Medicaid costs (which represents a significant portion of all local Medicaid costs in New York State) is unlikely to shift to residents in New Jersey and Connecticut. The degree of shifting in this and other similar cases, however, is impossible to gauge; and because in the aggregate the amount of outstate shifting is probably quite small, it is best to consider that all local Medicaid costs are borne instate.

In the first place there is no evidence that Medicaid exerted a progressive influence on the distribution of interstate incomes. If anything the relationship was the other way around. For example, over 30 percent of all Medicaid reimbursements for the year went to the state of New York. Three other wealthy industrial states (California, Massachusetts, and Michigan) accounted for

Table 2. Medicaid Benefits and Costs by State and Region in Fiscal 1968

Region and State	Benefits[a] ($000's)	Costs ($000's)	B−C[b] ($000's)	B−C Hslds. ($)
United States	3,024,723	3,024,720	3	0.00
North Central	677,120	768,402	−91,282	−5.41
Illinois	146,848	186,339	−39,491	−11.65
Indiana	−[c]	39,267	−39,267	−25.67
Michigan	159,280	154,488	4,792	1.92
Ohio	71,732	123,576	−51,844	−16.20
Wisconsin	114,263	79,219	35,044	27.67
Iowa	19,287	26,167	−6,880	−7.91
Kansas	25,178	26,770	−1,592	−2.19
Minnesota	80,624	59,183	21,441	20.06
Missouri	23,219	44,044	−20,825	−14.23
Nebraska	19,940	17,998	1,942	4.18
North Dakota	10,216	6,156	4,060	22.53
South Dakota	6,533	5,195	1,338	6.53
Northeast	1,352,855	1,192,797	160,058	10.74
Connecticut	48,102	57,341	−9,239	−10.36
Maine	10,469	10,092	377	1.30
Massachusetts	192,022	135,713	56,309	33.98
New Hampshire	2,996	7,041	−4,045	−19.73
Rhode Island	24,502	18,185	6,317	22.50
Vermont	7,158	5,389	1,769	15.07
New Jersey	—	69,934	−69,934	−32.66
New York	914,549	731,270	183,279	31.70
Pennsylvania	153,057	157,832	−4,775	−1.35
South	329,960	485,404	−155,444	−8.67
Delaware	3,254	8,142	−4,888	−31.67
District of Columbia	—	9,208	−9,208	−33.65
Florida	—	51,868	−51,868	−25.79
Georgia	31,289	31,878	−589	−0.47
Maryland	58,152	66,932	−8,780	−8.30
North Carolina	—	27,823	−27,823	−20.44
South Carolina	—	12,391	−12,391	−18.13
Virginia	—	32,272	−32,272	−25.34
West Virginia	10,961	12,951	−1,990	−3.93
Alabama	—	16,765	−16,765	−17.00
Kentucky	35,381	23,335	12,046	13.23
Mississippi	—	8,906	−8,906	−14.26
Tennessee	—	22,440	−22,440	−20.00
Arkansas	—	8,915	−8,915	−15.06
Louisiana	41,821	30,452	11,369	10.98
Oklahoma	66,659	31,116	35,543	44.20
Texas	82,443	90,010	−7,567	−2.32

Table 2. (continued)

Region and State	Benefits[a] ($000's)	Costs ($000's)	B−C[b] ($000's)	B−C Hslds. ($)
West	664,788	578,117	86,671	8.15
Arizona	−	11,392	−11,392	−23.64
Colorado	−	15 458	−15,458	−24.71
Idaho	6,348	5,924	424	2.01
Montana	5,636	6,329	−693	−3.13
Nevada	4,915	6,713	−1,798	−11.47
New Mexico	13,331	8,694	4,637	16.15
Utah	8,691	9,092	−401	−1.40
Wyoming	1,019	2,829	−1,810	−17.10
Alaska	−	1,950	−1,950	−27.37
California	549,835	425,009	124,826	19.69
Hawaii	10,704	11,365	−661	−3.53
Oregon	16,883	22,123	−5,240	−8.03
Washington	47,426	51,239	--3,813	−3.78

[a] Source: U.S. Department of Health, Education and Welfare, Social and Rehabilitation Service, National Center for Social Statistics, *Recipients and Amounts of Medical Vendor Payments Under Public Assistance Programs*, NCSS B−3 reports (Washington, D.C.: Government Printing Office, 1967 and 1968).

[b] Benefits slightly exceed costs because of rounding errors.

[c] Dash indicates that state did not have Medicaid program during year.

an additional 30 percent of the total. These four combined received nearly two thirds of all Medicaid benefits despite the fact that together they contained less than one quarter of the nation's poverty households in 1967−68. In addition each of these states contributed considerably less than they received in benefits notwithstanding the federal matching formula, which supposedly favors low-income states. The net gain from Medicaid in New York, California, Massachusetts, and Michigan combined equaled an impressive $369 million for the year.

At the opposite end of the scale are those states with no Medical Assistance plans in fiscal 1968. The fourteen states (including the District of Columbia) in this category lost a total of $277 million as a result of being taxed for the Medicaid programs of other states. More surprising perhaps is the fact that several states with small programs actually lost more on the average than states without a program. In Delaware, for example, the average per household loss was $31.67, which exceeded per household losses in twelve states without any Medicaid program (Delaware itself has had an operative Title XIX program since October 1966). Other Medicaid states had similar losses. In fact the four states with the smallest programs (Delaware, New Hampshire, Wyoming, and Nevada) had benefits totaling $12.2 million but costs of $24.7 million, a poor rate of return indeed!

Equity in the Distribution of Medicaid
Benefits and Costs by State

The initial step in evaluating such distributional anomalies is to compare the actual state benefits and costs with the standards developed earlier. This comparison provides us with our first measure of inequity in the system and sets the stage for a final evaluation of the level of net Medicaid grants to the poor in each state. To reiterate, the standards for this analysis are (1) that benefits be distributed on the basis of the medical needs of the poverty population in each state as measured by the number of households earning less than $3,000 per annum and (2) that costs be distributed on a basis proportionate to state per household income. Table 3 shows the distributive series of standard benefits and costs and includes calculations of standard grant and tax equivalents (standard benefits minus standard costs) for all households in each state.

The interpretation of these figures follows directly from the previous definitions. For example, if the minimum standards of distribution had been met nationally in 1967/68 New York State would have lost a total of $90.7 million (as opposed to an actual gain of $183.3 million). Instead of an actual net loss of $7.6 million, Texas would have gained $61.4 million under the national

Table 3. Standard Benefits and Costs for Medicaid by State and Region in Fiscal 1968

Region and State	Benefits ($000's)	Costs ($000's)	B–C[a] ($000's)	B–C Hslds. ($)
United States	3,024,717	3,024,718	−1	0.00
North Central	758,170	886,309	−128,139	−7.60
Illinois	130,515	200,227	−69,712	−20.56
Indiana	67,827	78,639	−10,812	−7.07
Michigan	88,894	142,611	−53,717	··21.56
Ohio	136,424	163,567	··−27,143	−8.48
Wisconsin	55,238	65,078	−9,840	··7.77
Iowa	47,016	42,740	4,276	4.92
Kansas	39,566	33,963	5,603	7.70
Minnesota	52,925	53,867	−942	··.88
Missouri	90,693	67,012	23,681	16.18
Nebraska	24,664	21,817	2,847	6.12
North Dakota	10,534	8,046	2,488	13.81
South Dakota	13,874	8,742	5,132	25.05
Northeast	557,516	809,369	−251,853	−16.90
Connecticut	23,380	54,723	−31,343	−35.14
Maine	13,360	12,669	691	2.38
Massachusetts	45,475	90,941	−45,466	−27.43
New Hampshire	8,992	10,109	−1,117	ᴸ−5.45
Rhode Island	11,818	14.328	−2,510	−8.94
Vermont	5,909	5,627	282	2.40
New Jersey	67,056	122,589	−55,533	··25.93
New York	230,200	321,032	−90,832	−15.71
Pennsylvania	151,326	177,351	−26,025	−7.36

Table 3. (continued)

Region and State	Benefits ($000's)	Costs ($000's)	B–C[a] ($000's)	B–C Hslds. ($)
South	1,196,989	785,291	411,698	22.98
Delaware	6,166	8,806	–2,640	–17.10
District of Columbia	10,534	15,940	–5,406	–19.76
Florida	137,195	83,648	53,547	26.62
Georgia	80,416	56,433	23,983	19.09
Maryland	36,996	60,934	–23,938	–22.63
North Carolina	86,325	60,112	26,213	19.26
South Carolina	49,585	28,490	21,095	30.87
Virginia	72,708	61,755	10,953	8.60
West Virginia	35,969	20,605	15,364	30.37
Alabama	78,361	37,944	40,417	40.98
Kentucky	67,827	37,805	30,022	32.97
Mississippi	59,092	22,593	36,499	58.46
Tennessee	82,471	45,489	36,982	32.96
Arkansas	53,182	20,914	32,268	54.53
Louisiana	72,708	45,392	27,316	26.37
Oklahoma	59,862	32,277	27,585	34.31
Texas	207,592	146,154	61,438	18.80
West	512,042	543,749	–31,707	–2.99
Arizona	28,518	21,712	6,806	14.12
Colorado	30,317	29,891	426	.68
Idaho	12,075	8,781	3,294	15.66
Montana	13,360	9,540	3,820	17.26
Nevada	7,451	7,836	–385	–2.46
New Mexico	17,984	12,202	5,782	20.13
Utah	12,589	13,103	–514	–1.80
Wyoming	5,909	4,563	1,346	13.08
Alaska	3,597	4,827	–1,230	–17.26
California	290,320	338,176	–47,856	–7.55
Hawaii	5,909	11,633	–5,724	–30.59
Oregon	35,712	29,298	6,414	9.82
Washington	48,301	52,187	–3,886	–3.85

[a] Standard costs slightly exceed standard benefits because of rounding errors.

standards. The standards for other states show similar if less dramatic deviations from actual Medicaid benefits and costs. Table 4 shows the extent of such deviations; actual Medicaid benefits, costs, and the net grant and tax equivalents for each state are subtracted from the comparable figures in Table 3. In this way we can show both the direction and the magnitude of distributive inequities in the Medicaid program for the year under study.

Analysis of these figures suggests the following conclusions. First, *inequities* in the distribution of Medicaid benefits among the states (in terms of the established standard of medical needs) explain far more of the total distributive inequities in the system than does the maldistribution of Medicaid costs. In all but four states (North Dakota, Pennsylvania, Utah, and Washington) the dollar deviation in actual benefits from standard benefits exceeded the deviation in

Table 4. Comparison between the Standard and Actual Distributions
of Medicaid Benefits, Costs, and Grant Equivalents by State
and Region in Fiscal 1968

Region and State	Standard Minus Actual Benefits ($000's)	Standard Minus Actual Costs ($000's)	Standard Minus Actual Grant or Tax Equivalents ($000's)	Standard Minus Actual Grant or Tax Equivalents Per Hsld. ($s)
United States[a]	-6	-2	−4	0.00
North Central	81,050	117,907	- 36,857	−2.19
Illinois	−16 333	13,888	−30,221	−8.91
Indiana	67,827	39,372	28,455	18.60
Michigan	−70,386	−11,877	−58,509	−23.49
Ohio	64,692	39,991	24,701	7.72
Wisconsin	−59 025	−14,141	−44,884	−35.44
Iowa	27,729	16,573	11,156	12.83
Kansas	14,388	7,193	7,195	9.89
Minnesota	−27,699	−5,316	−22,383	−20.94
Missouri	67,474	22,968	44,506	30.41
Nebraska	4,724	3,819	905	1.95
North Dakota	318	1,890	−1,572	−8.72
South Dakota	7,341	3,547	3,794	18.52
Northeast	−795,339	−383,428	−411,911	−27.64
Connecticut	−24,722	−2,618	−22,104	−24.78
Maine	−2,891	−2,577	314	1.08
Massachusetts	−146,547	−44,772	−101,775	−61.41
New Hampshire	5,996	3,068	2,928	14.28
Rhode Island	−12,684	−3,857	−8,827	−31.44
Vermont	−1,249	238	−1,487	−12.67
New Jersey	67 056	52,655	14,401	6.72
New York	−684,349	−410,238	−274,111	−47.42
Pennsylvania	−1,731	19,519	−21,250	−6.01
South	867,029	299,887	567,142	31.66
Delaware	2,912	664	2,248	14.56
District of Columbia	10,534	6,732	3,802	13.90
Florida	137,195	31,780	105,415	52.41
Georgia	49,127	24,555	24,572	19.56
Maryland	−21,156	−5,998	−15,158	−14.33
North Carolina	86,325	32,289	54,036	39.70
South Carolina	49,585	16,099	33,486	49.00
Virginia	72,708	29,483	43,225	33.93
West Virginia	25,008	7,654	17,354	34.30
Alabama	78,361	21,179	57,182	57.99
Kentucky	32,446	14,470	17,976	19.74
Mississippi	59,092	13,687	45,405	72.72
Tennessee	82,471	23,049	59,422	52.97
Arkansas	53,182	11,999	41,183	69.60
Louisiana	30,887	14,940	15,947	15.40
Oklahoma	−6,797	1,161	−7,958	−9.90
Texas	125,149	56,144	69,005	21.12

Table 4. (continued)

Region and State	Standard Minus Actual Benefits ($000's)	Standard Minus Actual Costs ($000's)	Standard Minus Actual Grant or Tax Equivalents ($000's)	Standard Minus Actual Grant or Tax Equivalents Per Hsld. ($s)
West	–152,746	–34,368	–118,378	–11.15
Arizona	28,518	10,320	18,198	37.76
Colorado	30,317	14,433	15,884	25.39
Idaho	5,727	2,857	2,870	13.64
Montana	7,724	3,211	4,513	20.39
Nevada	2,536	1,123	1,413	9.02
New Mexico	4,653	3,508	1,145	3.99
Utah	3,898	4,011	–113	–.40
Wyoming	4,890	1,734	3,156	29.80
Alaska	3,597	2,877	720	10.11
California	–259,515	–86,833	–172,682	–27.24
Hawaii	–4,795	268	–5,063	–27.06
Oregon	18,829	7,175	11,654	17.85
Washington	875	948	–73	–.07

[a] Differences between standard and actual benefits and costs do not equal zero because of slight rounding errors.

actual from standard costs.[13] If the minimum criteria of equity in the Medicaid system are to be attained, then the major change must be an alteration in the distribution of program benefits.

Second, the *direction* of inequities in Medicaid grant and tax equivalents is strongly related to the level of state income. Of the seventeen states that received higher grants than standards "justified" most are wealthy industrial states (with exception of Oklahoma, North Dakota, Utah, and Vermont). The states that received less are primarily low-income agricultural states in the South and West. This finding suggests that the federal matching formula has not succeeded in providing positive gains to the lowest income states.

Third, the *magnitude* of inequities is highly correlated to per household state incomes.[14] The states with the greatest deviation from either standard are found at the extremes of the income range. For example, residents of Arkansas and Mississippi, which rank last and next to last in average per household income, would require actual grants of between $54 and $58 per household to meet the minimum national standards. Instead they sustained net costs of slightly over $14 per household. On the other end of the income scale we find Medicaid states with equal – but opposite – deviations from the standard.

13 For all states the mean deviation of actual benefits from standard benefits is $52.4 million. The mean deviation of actual costs from standard costs is only $23.0 million. This suggests that roughly two thirds of the distributive inequities in the system arise because of the maldistribution of Medicaid benefits.

14 Table 5 is a list of states by average per household income in fiscal 1968.

Table 5. Per Household Medicaid Benefits and Costs to the under $3,000 Income Class by State in Fiscal 1968

State and Region	Average Per Hsld. State Income	Per Hsld. Benefits to Under $3,000 Class	Per Hsld. Costs to Under $3,000 Class	Per Hsld. Net Benefits to Under $3,000 Class
United States	$9,305	$256.92	$7.30	$249.62
Northeast	10,077	623.44	14.80	608.64
North Central	9,758	229.45	7.02	222.43
South	8,133	70.82	3.28	67.54
West	9,503	333.56	8.93	324.63
Title XIX States				
Hawaii	$11,531	$465.39	$10.22	$455.17
Connecticut	11,385	528.59	11.76	516.83
Illinois	10,952	289.07	8.77	280.30
Maryland	10,689	403.83	8.12	395.71
Michigan	10,619	460.35	9.90	450.45
Delaware	10,585	135.58	6.75	128.83
New York	10,302	1,020.70	23.14	997.56
Massachusetts	10,180	1,084.87	14.98	1,069.89
California	9,894	486.58	11.29	475.29
Washington	9,590	252.27	8.55	243.72
Wisconsin	9,531	531.46	9.98	521.48
Ohio	9,481	135.09	6.16	128.93
Rhode Island	9,466	532.65	11.85	520.80
Minnesota	9,349	391.38	8.83	382.55
Pennsylvania	9,296	259.86	8.16	251.70
Nevada	9,276	169.48	7.21	162.27
New Hampshire	9,143	85.60	6.29	79.31
Iowa	9,118	105.39	4.80	100.59
Vermont	8,896	311.22	8.39	302.83
Nebraska	8,707	207.71	6.18	201.53
Kansas	8,658	163.49	5.87	157.62
Utah	8,515	177.37	5.37	172.00
Missouri	8,493	65.78	4.80	60.98
Georgia	8,331	99.96	3.26	96.70
Oregon	8,323	121.46	5.71	115.75
Texas	8,297	102.03	3.53	98.50
North Dakota	8,285	249.17	5.46	243.71
Louisiana	8,127	147.78	3.77	144.01
Maine	8,100	201.33	6.37	194.96
Montana	7,999	108.38	4.83	103.55
Wyoming	7,998	44.30	4.52	39.78
South Dakota	7,917	120.98	4.04	116.94
New Mexico	7,804	190.44	5.10	185.34
Idaho	7,745	135.06	4.74	130.32
Kentucky	7,702	134.02	3.29	103.73
West Virginia	7,557	78.29	3.29	75.00
Oklahoma	7,446	286.09	4.97	281.12

Table 5. (continued)

State and Region	Average Per Hsld. State Income	Per Hsld. Benefits to Under $3,000 Class	Per Hsld. Costs to Under $3,000 Class	Per Hsld. Net Benefits. to Under $3,000 Class
	States with No Title XIX Program			
Alaska	$12,559	0	$4.64	$—4.64
District of Columbia	10,811	0	4.32	—4.32
New Jersey	10,618	0	5.97	—5.97
Indiana	9,539	0	4.09	—4.09
Virginia	8,992	0	3.25	3.25
Colorado	8,863	0	4.16	—4.16
Arizona	8,356	0	3.98	3.98
North Carolina	8,192	0	2.62	—2.62
South Carolina	7,734	0	2.33	—2.33
Florida	7,712	0	3.31	—3.31
Tennessee	7,522	0	2.57	—2.57
Alabama	7,139	0	2.18	—2.18
Mississippi	6.714	0	1.83	—1.83
Arkansas	6,556	0	1.93	—1.93

Sources: Sales Management, Inc., *Survey of Buying Power* (1967 and 1968); U.S. Department of Health, Education and Welfare, Social and Rehabilitation Service, National Center for Social Statistics, *Recipients and Amounts of Medical Vendor Payments Under Public Assistance Programs*, NCSS B—3 reports (Washington, D.C.: Government Printing Office, 1967 and 1968); U.S. Department of Labor, Bureau of Labor Statistics, *Survey of Consumer Expenditures, 1960—61*, supp. 3, pt. A, *Reports, Consumer Expenditures and Income: Detail of Expenditures and Income*, nos. 237—34 to 237—38 and 237—89 to 237—92 (Washington, D.C.: Government Printing Office, 1964—1966); and sources for Table 2.

Massachusetts residents, for example, received an average of $61 more per household than the standard assumptions justified. For New York State the comparable figure was $47 per household. Far from reducing inequities in regional and interstate incomes the Medical Assistance program has, in fact, aggravated existing inequalities.

Program Impacts on Medicaid Recipients by State

Up to this point our concern has centered on the redistributional effects of Medicaid among states, without regard for the differential impact of the program on the recipient populations in each state. We know that Medicaid has been a boon to the rich industrial states as compared to the low-income agricultural states, but has it provided the same scale of grants to the poor in each area? In other words, does the program discriminate among poverty households in the same fashion as it does among states generally? To answer this question we must first measure program benefits, costs, and grant equivalents for poverty households in every state.[15] We do this on the assumption that all Medicaid benefits accrued to households with disposable income of less than $3,000 in 1967–68.[16] Program costs to these same households are calculated on the basis of estimates of federal, state, and local tax burdens by regional income class.

Table 5 shows the results of these calculations, which confirm our previous finding of gross inequalities in the level of grants among states with Medicaid programs. Moreover, the level of grants to poor households is much more strongly correlated to state income than were average grants calculated for all households in each state.[17] This correlation suggests that only a portion of the wide gap in benefit levels to the poor can be explained by the fact that Medicaid redistributes real income among the states. As expected, because the wealthy states have fewer poverty households in relation to their total populations, they can provide generally high benefit levels. The net result of these two factors can readily be seen. For non-Medicaid states the net loss (tax equivalent) suffered by poverty households is small in absolute terms, but in relative terms it is significant indeed. For example, compare Arkansas (the state with the lowest average income) with Massachusetts. As a direct result of Medicaid operations poverty households in Massachusetts received an annual increase in income-in-kind equivalent to $1,069.89 compared with an average loss of $1.93 for the poor in Arkansas. Similar disparities are obvious among the Medicaid states even though the poor in these states all received net gains from the program in 1967–68. In West Virginia (ranked forty-fourth in average income) the poor received an average grant of $75.00 from Medicaid, but in New York (ranked

---

15 To calculate these figures we employ the same benefit concept of money value of services received that we used in determining the impact of Medicaid by state. Although it might be argued that Medicaid "benefits" to recipients represent an ability to restore some previous level of health rather than a direct increase in real income, the money-value measure is justified in two respects: First, an increase in medical coverage may free funds that the recipient can then use for other purposes. Second, even if the new coverage does not free any income, it still allows the recipient to enjoy a higher level of health than might otherwise be the case. The money value of medical services used in this instance is at least a good proxy for the actual increase in recipient welfare.

16 The income limit of $3,000 is somewhat arbitrary. In most states with Title XIX programs the majority of benefits do go to households with earnings of less than $3,000. But there are exceptions to this generalization. First, large households (both in states with strict and liberal categorical assistance limits) may exceed the income limit of $3,000 and still receive Medicaid benefits. Second, states with liberal assistance statutes, such as New York, California, Massachusetts, and Michigan, offer Medicaid benefits to medically indigent households who, in some instance, may earn considerably more than $3,000. On the other hand, large numbers of single- and two-person households with income under $3,000 are not eligible for Medicaid benefits even in states with liberal assistance laws. On balance, therefore, the $3,000 limit offers a fair approximation of the relative distribution of actual per household benefits received by the poor in each state.

17 A rank correlation between average per household state income and average net grants to poor households in states with Medicaid programs yields a coefficient of 0.6255. A similar correlation between income and average grants calculated for all households (in the same Medicaid states) produces a coefficient of only 0.1183.

ninth) the poor gained an average of $997.56.[18] On a regional basis the same relationship holds. Average Medicaid grants in the Northeast (the most affluent region) exceeded those in the low-income South by more than $530 for each poverty household.

With the aid of our standard distributions we can also evaluate these and similar differences. At this final stage of evaluation the standard of costs may safely be ignored because the burden on poverty households is insignificant (the highest costs are found in New York where the poor contributed an average of $23.14 for the year). Standard benefits are $256.92 (the national average) per poverty household in each state. When we compare this figure to actual benefits received by the poor in each of the Medicaid states, we see that of the eleven "wealthy" states with average incomes in excess of $9,500 in 1968 all but two (Delaware and Washington) provided the poor with significantly more benefits than the national average. On the other hand, for the fifteen Medicaid states with average incomes below $8,500 per year only Oklahoma provided benefits that exceeded the same standard. Obviously if such disparities continue, the only result can be ever greater inequalities within the low-income sector.

Summary and Conclusions

As a redistributive mechanism Medicaid must be judged a failure. The program was designed to reduce inequities in the distribution of welfare payments among states. Instead it has widened an existing gap in assistance levels. Prior to the enactment of Medical Assistance, poor households in the rich industrial states of the North received far higher welfare grants than their counterparts in less affluent regions. After two and a half years of Medicaid these differences have become more, not less, pronounced. At the same time the Medicaid program has in many cases redistributed real income from the poor to the wealthy states. In so doing it has violated even the weakest standards of horizontal and vertical equity.

Ironically the root cause of these failures lies in the incentive concept, which was to ensure distributive equity in the system. The original intent of the program planners was to create a federation of state plans under limited national direction and control. They realized that the key to a successful federation lay in the financial incentive for states (particularly those with low incomes) first to establish and then to expand their own Medical Assistance programs. Success, in this case, meant first that all states would initiate plans for comprehensive health care under Medicaid shortly after the passage of the Social Security amendments in 1965 and second that, in relative terms at least, the rich states would help subsidize the medical welfare programs of their less affluent neighbors. Neither

---

18 If these figures could be adjusted for price level differences among the states, the gap might be reduced somewhat but not enough to alter the basic relationship between high average state income and large Medicaid benefits to the poor.

of these goals has or is likely to be met under the system of joint federal–state control. As of July 1968 only thirty-seven states had operative Medicaid programs. Those with none were primarily low-income Southern states, which stood the most to gain.

Since 1968 eleven states plus the District of Columbia have initiated Medicaid programs (only two, Alaska and Arizona, are currently not enrolled). But despite this fact Medical Assistance today suffers from the same distributive inequities that it did in 1967--68. In February 1970, for example, the four states with the largest programs (New York, California, Pennsylvania, and Massachusetts) received 56 percent of total benefits.[19] The combined population of these states, however, represents only 27 percent of the total population and a much smaller percentage of the poverty population in the country. In the same month the ten states ranked lowest in per capita income (with 14.5 percent of the population) received a mere 6.7 percent of total Medicaid benefits.[20]

Perhaps more serious, evidence exists that the formula for federal reimbursements under Medicaid has provided an impetus for even greater inequality in the distribution of nonmedical welfare grants among the states. Although in principle this formula decidedly favors the poor states, in practice it works to the advantage of the most wealthy. For years California, Massachusetts, New York, and a few other affluent states have provided welfare recipients with grants averaging well above the matchable limits of the "regular" reimbursement formula. By using the alternative Medicaid formula these states are now eligible to receive 50 percent matching for every dollar spent in excess of the previous limit. However, this ability to increase the effective rate of federal reimbursements is impossible for most states at the low end of the income scale. Virtually all the poorer states spend under the limits of the regular formula so that they already receive a higher percentage return than is offered by the alternative Medicaid approach. As a cursory glance at recipient welfare levels around the country will show, the new formula has not induced any of these states to increase the level of their welfare grants significantly.

In sum, the Medicaid program raises a host of new questions of the wisdom involved in continued reliance on joint federal–state welfare policy. If we consider equity a primary goal of public assistance, then we can purchase improvement only at the price of 100 percent federal financing of *all* welfare programs. Halfway measures, such as the proposed Family Assistance Plan and limited national health insurance for the poor, may have somewhat better results; but if the states are still allowed to determine recipient eligibility and the ultimate level of welfare grants, the system will compound rather than correct existing inequalities.

---

19 U.S. Department of Health, Education and Welfare, Social and Rehabilitative Service, National Center for Social Statistics, *Public Assistance Statistics, February, 1970,* Report A–2 (2–70) (Washington, D.C.: Government Printing Office, 1970), Table 12.

20 These include Arkansas, Mississippi, Alabama, Oklahoma, South Carolina, Tennessee, Kentucky, West Virginia, Florida, and Idaho.

3

Implicit Public Grants and Taxes

Part 3 investigates the intellectual continent of income distribution. Implicit public grants can only be estimated on the basis of a standard or norm which commands sufficient plausibility or general acceptability. "Hidden subsidies" result from real benefits conveyed to some groups but not to others — through the operation of the tax system, which provides "tax aids" or reductions to some; through the distributive consequences of fiscal and monetary policies, which affect some groups more than others; through taxation in kind, as in the case of the military draft system; or through administrative procedures that convey real benefits (=grants) to some and real costs (=taxes) to others. There is a wide and complex universe of such relations inherent in the interactions of individuals, families, corporations, foundations, nonprofit institutions, and government agencies. Of these, only some of the more significant implicit public grants will be discussed in the subsequent papers. The first group of papers, by Rudney, Pfaff and Pfaff, Aaron, and Muller, deals with implicit public grants conveyed by provisions in the budget and in tax laws. The second group of papers, by Hollister and Palmer, and Thurow, treats the consequences of "macroeconomic redistribution." Finally, Sjaastad and Hansen focus on the implicit taxes and transfers in kind resulting from the de facto operation of the draft system.

Gabriel Rudney provides an overview of implicit public grants conveyed through the tax system, termed *tax aids*, and relates them to other instruments for the attainment of public ends in general and to specific budget functions in particular. He notes that "efficiency as a tax policy goal must compete with the other important tax goals, such as fairness, equity, and simplicity." The economic aspects of tax aids result from impact on the size of budget deficits and surpluses, their "secondary effect on income of the private sector and the demand for goods and services through the 'multiplier'," and their distributive consequences. Rudney provides an overall picture reflecting Treasury compilations (which represent a "minimal selection of tax aids"). From these it is evident that tax aids increased significantly from 1968 to 1969 by all budget functions listed.

Martin and Anita Pfaff examine the equity in the distribution of implicit public grants conveyed by the special provisions, exemptions, and deductions of the U.S. individual income tax laws. They estimate that about $64 billion of implicit public grants were conveyed in 1965 due to the effects of the contribution deduction, real estate tax deduction, mortgage and other interest deduction; due to untaxed capital gains, imputed rent, the use of Tax Schedule 2, the exemption for self and spouse, and for children and other dependents, as well as several other minor provisions, and due to the joint effect of these provisions. In the absence of a generally accepted empirical equity norm, the authors estimate the distributive effect of these grants across income classes on hand of five alternative equity norms:

1. Under norm 1 "the maze of special provisions is abandoned and income is treated as the sole determinant of tax liability." "Tax under norm 1 would thus equal nominal tax . . . [and] exceed the 1965 tax yield by $64 billion."

2. "Norm 2 combines both the progressivity of the tax rate and the preference for the present tax yield. Under norm 2 we assume that actual taxes equal taxes under present law." Sixty-four billion dollars in implicit public grants, the authors observe, "are distributed in a rather regressive fashion."

3. For norm 3 they combine "the nominal progressivity of the tax schedule and the present desired tax yield, with a different distribution of implicit public grants. If the implicit grants were to be distributed equally to all tax units . . . this would provide us with a negative income tax system. Tax under norm 3 would have guaranteed everybody an income in the amount of the average implicit public grant of $911.60 in 1965 . . . . Up to a total income of $5,000 the income tax liability would be negative . . . . A tax unit with total income between $0 and $600 would receive $911.47 on the average under 1965 conditions; a tax unit in the $4,500–$5,000 total income class would receive an average transfer of $128.77. All groups with income above $9,000 would pay more tax than under present law, whereas individuals with income under $9,000 would pay less than under present law."

4. Under norm 4 a distribution of implicit public grants in proportion to a tax unit's income is proposed. "This would provide a larger share of implicit public grants for high income groups and a smaller share for low income groups. . . . Although tax liability . . . is less than under norm 3, it is higher than under norm 2 for high income classes . . . 77.4 percent of the population, who receive total income under $13,000, would pay less under norm 4 than under present law; the remaining 22.6 percent of the population would pay higher taxes."

   From a comparison of norms 2, 3, and 4 it is evident that the most equal distribution of income after taxes results from norm 3, followed by norm 4 and norm 2.

5. Norm 5, finally, assumes that the relative burden of taxation should equal the relative benefit of the implicit public grants. A "vertical equity index weight for each income class was derived by dividing the overall mean nominal tax by the income class nominal tax." The distribution of total income after taxes under norm 5 was found to be similar to that of norm 2. The authors conclude

that "under present law implicit public grants provide a vehicle of redistribution to the wealthy."

Henry Aaron analyzes the distributive effects of implicit public grants under the individual income tax laws as well as under the Federal Housing Administration and Veterans' Administration loan programs. He notes that "the value of tax concessions to homeowners ranges from an average of $27 for aged taxpayers in the lowest income bracket using the standard deduction to $3,505 for aged taxpayers in the highest income bracket who take itemized deductions." And he shows further that tax benefits reduce gross rents: "The plausible range of implicit subsidies to homeowners runs from about 5 percent of gross rent in the lowest income brackets to more than 50 percent in the highest brackets. Of course, the subsidy to households with no taxable income is zero. [Thus] the current tax treatment of income from homeownership raises the housing consumption of upper-income households, in both relative and absolute terms, by much more than that of lower income households."

Aaron defines "the implicit subsidy offered through government default protection . . . as the difference between actuarial cost of default protection and the cost to lender or borrower of such protection. The amount of redistribution [under FHA mortgage insurance] is modest in the aggregate. VA loan guarantees redistribute income from nonusers to users, because the charge for the guarantee is nominal. For the same reason, the per-household transfer under VA is considerably larger than under FHA. . . ."

Aaron concludes that "with respect to any conceivable policy objective, the pattern of tax benefits seems to be capricious and without rationale. . . . Even if one were to acknowledge that homeownership benefits society by making homeowners more stable or less antisocial than they otherwise would have been, the *pattern* of tax benefits is ill-suited to that objective. Tax benefits provide largest benefits to recipients of larger than average income whose experience with wealth is typically not limited to their own houses. They provide negligible aid to low-income households, most of whom have not experienced the salutary discipline of property management. [Furthermore] it is not clear what objective is served through the redistribution of income among users of the FHA program, [nor] why veterans who own their residence deserve such a subsidy [under the VA program], while veterans who rent their residence do not. . . . Why the subsidy should be tied to housing or, even more, to loans received for houses veterans occupy is equally obscure."

Thomas Muller studied the effect of several categories of implicit public grants under taxes on real property levied in the Montgomery and Prince George's counties of Maryland, as well as by zoning policies and assignment practices. Among these, fully exempt property owned by various levels of government or nonprofit institutions – private schools and colleges, religious organizations — preferential treatment of land used for farming, property tax exemptions for senior citizens, and other personal exemptions (including veterans), tax savings due to assessments of income producing property below the level provided by legislation (particularly for apartment buildings), and the increase in the market value of land due to rezoning for more intensive use are major sources of such implicit public grants. The effect of these lead to a loss of tax revenue of $19.7 million (of which about one-half are implicit public grants) in Montgomery County, and of $34.7 million in Prince George's County (for which about 21.4 percent of the total revenue collected were implicit public grants). Furthermore, "totally exempt property in Prince George's County was 47.3 percent of all property subject to taxation compared to 26.8 percent in the more affluent Montgomery County."

Turning to the distributive effects of the measures, Muller notes that "the substantial loss of tax revenue . . . adds an additional inequity to the county tax structure. The major beneficiary is not likely to be the small low-income marginal farmer, but the land speculator. Partial exemption for senior citizens, disabled veterans, and the blind" are not necessarily benefiting those "least likely to pay." "Tax concessions, to be equitable, should be extended to low-income families living in rented properties. Most of the tax savings accrue to families earning more than $10,000."

Robinson Hollister and John Palmer "attempt . . . to assess the impact of inflationary processes such as those experienced in the United States during the last twenty years on the economic well-being of the poor." In order to get a comprehensive picture of such an impact, three types of possible effects are examined in some detail: effects of expenditure patterns, effects related to the sources of income, and effects due to the nature of assets held by the poor.

In looking at expenditure patterns, the authors construct a Poor Price Index (PPI) and compare its movements with those of the Consumer Price Index. The comparison suggests that price rises have hurt the poor *less* than the nonpoor. On the income side, several types of evidence indicate that the benefits of tight labor markets which normally accompany inflationary pressures are very important to the poor. Simple regressions relating the incidence of poverty to unemployment, median family income, and price rises indicate that the gains to the poor from tight labor markets go beyond those strictly related to lower unemployment. It seems that the poor gain relatively *more* than any other group, probably because of increases in hours worked and narrowing of wage differentials. Public transfer payments, second only to wages and salaries as income sources for the poor, are found to have risen more than enough to offset the rise in the Consumer Price Index, although the position of Social Security benefits is somewhat unclear. The assets of the poor are found to be small in total value, and of the total a very small proportion is vulnerable to inflation. Thus negative wealth effects of inflation are extremely small.

Lester Thurow examines the effects of macropolicy instruments — fiscal and monetary policies — on black and white income equalization. In order to summarize the entire distribution of income, he employed the beta-distribution whose parameters — β and σ — he estimated for every year from 1949 to 1966. He estimates the effect of various factors which produce changes in these parameters — real growth of GNP, inflation, factor shares, labor force utilization, transfer payments, and government expenditures. He concludes: "Based on the evidence from this analysis there are no macropolicy instruments for equalizing black and white income distributions or for equalizing white incomes or black incomes, but macropolicy instruments have a large impact on the inequality or equality that actually exists. General growth results in higher incomes for both black and whites but does not have much impact on their relative incomes. A 1 percent increase in employment results in a 5 percent increase in median black incomes and a 1 percent increase in median white incomes, but this is an instrument that is inherently limited. Unemployment can only fall to zero. Transfer payments and government purchases lead to more equal incomes, but the coefficients are small enough that enormous expenditure increases would be necessary to equalize income using the current structure of transfer payments and government incomes. Regional economic policies that would increase job opportunities in relatively depressed states and the quality of the existing jobs can also have an impact on black–white income differentials.

"If society wishes to narrow its income distribution, any factor which lowered $\mathcal{S}$ or raised $\mathcal{G}$ would be acceptable. Growth would be a proper policy instrument for blacks, and inflation would be a proper policy instrument for whites. Realistically, macroeconomic policies can lead to a more equal distribution of income, but vigorous use of these instruments would still leave a widely dispersed income distribution. The major factor leading to increases in average incomes is, of course, growth for either blacks or whites."

Finally, Larry Sjaastad and Ronald Hansen study the taxation aspect of conscription: "By use of coercion the government acquires the personal services of large numbers of individuals under terms favorable to the general taxpayer but rather unfavorable to the individuals rendering these services." This special tax is discriminatory because it affects some but not others. Furthermore, it creates incentives for actions to avoid military service. The costs associated with avoidance may thus be viewed as the cost of collection of the conscription tax — representing deadweight welfare losses to the community.

The authors estimate the magnitude of the conscription tax under the assumptions that the confiscation of economic rent arising from the coercive nature of conscription does *not* constitute taxation, and alternatively, that it *does* constitute taxation. They note that "the Selective Service is a very inefficient taxation device, and that the tax itself is substantial. . . . [It] imposes a burden of about $2 billion on a small subset of the population and does so in a fashion so discriminatory as to make this tax unique. In addition to the tax itself, the coercive nature of conscription is estimated to have deprived first-term enlisted personnel of an additional $1.25 billion of income that they would have received were procurement of first-term enlisted personnel subject to the same rules that guide government procurement in other areas. . . . [Furthermore], our results indicate that these costs of collection exceed the tax itself, perhaps by as much as 100 percent and very likely by as much as 50 percent. As a tax, conscription under Selective Service is brutally inefficient -- virtually in a class by itself."

Turning to the distributive effects of the conscription tax, Sjaastad and Hansen conclude: "The conscription tax falls much more heavily upon lower income persons than upon the well-to-do, with the lowest income group paying nearly three times as much tax as do the highest income group. It is true, however, that conscription imposes a higher tax *rate* on the high-income inductee than it does on the true volunteer; that these two statements are consistent is due to the fact that higher income conveys with it greater success in escaping conscription."

The picture conveyed by Part 3 is thus even more dramatic than that resulting from Part 2. Implicit public grants tend to be even more regressive than many types of explicit public grants. Their very character as a "hidden subsidy" generally keeps them out of the limelight of public scrutiny. Furthermore, the absence of generally accepted explicit equity norms with which distributive patterns can be evaluated imposes considerable difficulties on the investigators. Nonetheless, as the papers constituting Part 3 may indicate, many plausible and well-supported assumptions can be marshaled to the task of analysis. Even where a *single* norm is not readily applicable, the economist qua public policy scientist can still estimate the implications of alternative norms in order to note how sensitive his conclusions are to the choice of his assumptions.

The messages voiced by the individual papers thus swell into an overall chorus: Their moral, loud and clear, calls for the elimination of the "perverse effects" of the public grants economy. At the least, equity considerations must be included more consciously in public allocations. Only thus can the public grants economy fulfill one of its avowed purposes, which is the remedy of some of the income inequalities wrought by the operation of the market economy.

The problem of poverty, moreover, could be attacked by a reform of the present jungle of tax laws themselves and more specifically, by the withdrawal of many types of implicit public grants that cannot be justified on efficiency, equity, or any other grounds. No doubt the elimination of poverty requires more than a reform of the public grants economy: It depends on job training that is designed to enhance working capacities, on education that truly equalizes opportunities of advancement for all income classes, on health measures that improve the capacity to work, on assistance to lower-income women in family planning, on the elimination of the myriad forces of discrimination, whether exercised against women or racial minority groups or on any other ground, and on a host of other social services that must be available to the poor.[1] But the key to the financing of all of these programs is the public budget which conveys benefits – or grants – to various groups. A reform of the public grants economy is thus the key to the more specific reforms required in some of these functional areas.

---

1 See W. J. Cohen, "Government Policy and the Poor: Past, Present, and Future," *Journal of Social Issue* 26, no. 3 (1970): 1–9, for some imaginative proposals along these lines.

10

Gabriel G. Rudney: Implicit Public
Grants Under the Tax System:
Some Implications of Federal Tax Aids
Accounting

Implicit public grants under the tax system are identified by a large variety of names: tax subsidies, tax preferences, tax exclusions, tax reliefs, tax remissions, tax expenditures, tax aids, and so forth. The Treasury currently prefers to identify these implicit grants as tax aids in order to have this designation consistent with the standard federal budget practice of identifying explicit government subsidies as public aids. The earlier use of the term *tax expenditures* had created some confusion. The same words (and also the term *tax transfers*) are often applied to another form of analysis, which is becoming more widely used as a measure of the combined burden and benefits of taxes and government expenditures according to income class.

Although tax aids have long been the subject of study and evaluation, interest in the program aspects of tax aids and their relative efficiency is renewed, largely because of the many new tax incentives being proposed to resolve critical social and economic problems. These alternatives include direct expenditures and credit aids, including direct loans, loan insurance and guarantees, and interest subsidies.

Other important forces continue to focus attention on tax aids. Because of the questionable redistributive as well as allocative effects, many people continue to exert strong pressures for reform of existing tax aids. Others are concerned about the sizable accumulation of tax aids, which erodes the tax base and results in high rates. On the other hand, still others are concerned about high rates but view many tax aids as necessary and appropriate adjustments of the high-rate situation. In addition, there are public demands for more information about tax aids, their magnitudes, and their functions.

Program Aspects of Tax Aids

Under the past administration, the Treasury compiled and classified tax aids with the purpose of demonstrating that these have the same program functions as other subsidies and public expenditures and that tax aids incur costs. As an

Presented at the Symposium on the Grants Economy held between the Association for the Study of the Grants Economy and the American Association for the Advancement of Science in December, 1969, in Boston, Mass. All rights reserved. Used by permission of the author.

initial effort, the Treasury was only concerned with the accounting of tax aids under the federal income tax — corporate and individual — which is by far the most important in terms of revenue and impact. Tax aids within its structure cover a wide spectrum of social and economic functions.

The compilation was published in the fiscal 1968 Report of the Secretary of the Treasury[1] and has served its purpose well. Although we cannot measure its influence, the compilation has no doubt helped create public discussion and improved understanding of the program aspects of tax aids. In fact, we can make a case to provide such data as supplemental budget information to make the program relationship between tax aids and government purchases and transfers more obvious.

The compilation also helps to stimulate program analysis of tax aids — an approach that has received the endorsement of Richard Nixon. In his tax message to the Congress of April 1969, Nixon stated: "Tax dollars the government deliberately waives should be viewed as a form of expenditure and weighed against the priority of other expenditures. When the preference device provides more social benefit than government collections and spending, that 'incentive' should be expanded; when the preference is inefficient or subject to abuse, it should be ended."

However, some difficulties in program analysis exist. The cost—benefit approach is a difficult and uncertain technical undertaking. And only limited progress has been made on the direct expenditure side. But in addition to the technical difficulties, a serious obstacle to program analysis exists in the tax area. Efficiency as a tax policy goal must compete with the other important tax goals, such as fairness, equity, and simplicity. On balance, the latter goals represent rather formidable political constraints.

Economic Aspects of Tax Aids

In addition to its value as a catalyst for program analysis, the compilation of tax aids has value for economic analysis.

As a unique grouping, distinguishing it from direct expenditures and general tax reduction, such compilations focus on tax aids as important determinants of the size of budget deficits and surpluses. The overall magnitude of foregone revenues due to tax aids is substantial and, if the budget is not balanced, the deficit or surplus is only a small fraction of that magnitude. Year-to-year changes in the magnitude of tax aids, either because of economic growth or through legislative actions, could affect substantially the size of the budget deficit (or surplus) and the expansionary (or restrictive) course of the economy.

---

1 U.S. Treasury Department, "The Tax-Expenditure Budget: A Conceptual Analysis," Exhibit 29, *Annual Report of the Secretary of the Treasury on the State of the Finances for the Fiscal Year Ending June 30, 1968*, Washington, D.C., 1969, pp. 326–40. In Congressional Testimony on June 1, 1970, Treasury Assistant Secretary Murray L. Weidenbaum presented more recent tax aid data (for fiscal 1968 and 1969).

The effect on the budget deficit or surplus position is the same whether a new transfer objective is accomplished explicitly in cash or implicitly as a tax aid. A cash transfer or a direct federal loan either increases the budget deficit or reduces the surplus by raising expenditures. The tax aid has the same deficit—surplus effect but reduces revenues instead of increasing expenditures. This effect differs, however, if a loan guarantee program is substituted for tax aids or direct expenditures. Except for administrative costs and defaults, loan guarantees do not require any government monies.

A systematic presentation of tax aids as implicit public grants supplements the conventional and more limited analysis of government receipts and expenditures on national income and product account. Government decision makers should know how implicit as well as explicit government actions affect level of private incomes and how such actions affect aggregate demand. Direct government purchase of services is output-generating. But if government provides a cash subsidy or a transfer payment, private incomes increase although the effect on output is uncertain, particularly if the transfer is made unconditionally with respect to consumption. Alternatively, the government could provide a tax reduction in the form of a tax aid. If granted unconditionally with respect to consumption – for example, as an increased personal exemption – disposable personal income increases as in the case of the cash transfer. The effect is also expansionary, but the extent is equally uncertain.

Tax aids, like government expenditures and general tax reductions, have a secondary effect on income of the private sector and the demand for goods and services through the "multiplier." For example, a tax credit for investment expenditure not only increases directly the level of investment output but also increases incomes as more resources are allocated to investment.

The systematic presentation of tax aids as implicit public transfers also provides a better measure of the degree to which the government provides direct and/or indirect support of aggregate demand. It alters the limited view of the role of government that is now presented. The national income and product account creates the impression of more demand supported by the marketplace than actually is the case. Income and profits items after tax do not reflect the implicit public transfers that are contained in these items.

This inadequacy handicaps analysts, particularly those interested in measuring trends in the structure of the economy and their impacts. For example, the relative role of government influence in the economy is a key consideration in the study of economic development.

The presentation also serves as an important frame of reference for distribution analysis of tax benefits, which is a necessary complement of the usual type of analysis of tax burdens and public transfers.

Identification of Tax Aids

The Treasury compilation would have more value if it were a full and complete accounting of tax aids in the income tax. But it is not intended to provide a full accounting. The Treasury in fact describes it as a minimal selection of tax aids – minimal in the sense of including acceptable and practical choices.[2]

Identification of tax aids is a rather subjective and uncertain undertaking. As a result, the identification criteria in the compilation inherently reflect a policy point of view. The assumptions made about the normative income tax structure are subject to question as so-called "tax ideals." Certain tax provisions may be omitted because inclusion would require controversial or highly theoretical justifications.

Surrey and Aaron discuss these uncertainties in their papers on tax aid inventories presented at the November 1969 Symposium[3] of the Tax Institute of America at Princeton, New Jersey. Surrey, who was formerly Assistant Secretary for Tax Policy, justifies the Treasury's choice of guidelines. For those tax provisions that are not clearly identifiable as tax aids, the criteria of public acceptability and practicality governed the choice, even though this choice differs from that of economists.

For example, the revenue loss resulting from tax exemption of imputed rents on owner-occupied residences was not included in the Treasury compilation on grounds of acceptability and practicality.[4] Aaron, guided by the precepts of economics, included this item and added others even though his inventory of tax incentives is more limited in coverage than is the Treasury tabulation of tax aids. Tax incentives, according to Aaron, include items primarily altering resource allocation; tax aids include these items but also include others that primarily affect income distribution.[5]

A definitive accounting of tax aids and other implicit public transfers will have to be the work of economists in developing a grants accounts system free of constraints of government policy and public acceptability. No doubt these economists will disagree among themselves – and this is as it should be – as to assumptions about normative tax structures in the case of tax aids and as to definitions of taxable items, such as income, wealth, consumption, and production.

However, at some time I predict that they will agree on most points such that a fully developed system will have practical and widespread use. In this

---

2 U.S. Treasury Department, *op. cit.*, p. 330.

3 Tax Institute of America Symposium, "Tax Incentives," Princeton, N.J., November 20–21, 1969.

4 S. S. Surrey, "Tax Incentives – Conceptual Criteria for Identification and Comparison with Direct Expenditures," paper presented at Tax Institute of America Symposium, Princeton, N.J., November 20, 1969, pp. 4–5.

5 H. Aaron, "Inventory of Existing Tax Incentives: Federal," paper presented at Tax Institute of America Symposium, Princeton, N.J., November 20, 1969, p. 11.

connection, the construction of the grants accounts in the 1970s may mirror the development of national income and products accounts of the 1930s.

This tax aid dilemma may appear to have been resolved when the Treasury chose its pragmatic norms and definitions. But these were decisions of policy makers. The society of economists should and must decide on the conventions of an acceptable and useful grants accounts system.

Estimated Tax Aids, Fiscal 1968 and 1969
(Millions of Dollars)

Tax Aids by Budget Function	1968	1969
National defense		
Exclusion of benefits and allowances to armed forces personnel	500	550
International affairs and finance		
Exemption for certain income earned abroad by United States citizens	40	45
Western Hemisphere Trade Corporations	50	55
Exclusion of gross-up on dividends of less-developed country corporations	50	55
Exclusion of controlled foreign subsidiaries	150	165
Exclusion of income earned in United States possessions	80	90
Total	370	410
Agriculture and rural development		
Farming: expensing and capital gain treatment	800	860
Timber: capital gain treatment for certain income	130	140
Total	930	1,000
Natural resources		
Expensing of exploration and development costs	300	330
Excess of percentage over cost depletion	1,300	1,430
Capital gains treatment of royalties on coal and iron ore	5	5
Total	1,605	1,765
Commerce and transportation		
Investment credit	2,300	3,000
Excess depreciation on buildings (other than rental housing)	500	550
Dividend exclusion	225	260
Capital gains: corporation (other than agriculture and natural resources)	500	525
Excess bad debt reserves of financial institutions	600	660
Exemption of credit unions	40	45
Deductibility of interest on consumer credit	1,300	1,600

Estimated Tax Aids, Fiscal 1968 and 1969
(Millions of Dollars) (continued)

Tax Aids by Budget Function	1968	1969
Expensing of research and development expenditures	500	550
$25,000 surtax exemption	1,800	2,000
Deferral of tax on shipping companies	10	10
Total	7,775	9,200
Community development and housing		
Deductibility of interest on mortgages on owner-occupied homes	1,900	2,200
Deductibility of property taxes on owner-occupied homes	1,800	2,350
Excess depreciation on rental housing	250	250
Total	3,950	4,800
Income security		
Disability insurance benefits	—	100
Provisions relating to aged, blind, and disabled: Combined cost for additional exemption for aged, retirement income credit, and exclusion of Social Security payments	2,300	2,700
Additional exemption for blind	10	10
"Sick pay" exclusion	85	95
Exclusion of unemployment insurance benefits	300	325
Exclusion of workmen's compensation benefits	150	180
Exclusion of public assistance benefits	50	50
Treatment of pension plans		
Plans for employees	3,000	4,000
Plans for self-employed persons	60	135
Exclusion of other employee benefits		
Premiums on group term life insurance	400	400
Deductibility of accident and death benefits	25	25
Privately financed supplementary unemployment benefits	25	15
Meals and lodging	150	165
Exclusion of interest on life insurance savings	900	1,000
Deductibility of charitable contributions (other than education)	2,200	3,000
Deductibility of child and dependent care expenses	25	25
Deductibility of casualty losses	70	80
Standard deduction	3,200	3,600
Total	15,550	18,905
Health		
Deductibility of medical expenses	1,500	1,600
Exclusion of medical insurance premiums and medical care	1,100	1,400
Total	2,600	3,000

Estimated Tax Aids, Fiscal 1968 and 1969
(Millions of Dollars) (continued)

Tax Aids by Budget Function	1968	1969
Education and Manpower		
Educational expense deduction	—	40
Additional personal exemption for students	500	500
Deductibility of contributions to educational institutions	170	200
Exclusion of scholarships and fellowships	50	60
Total	720	800
Veterans' benefits and services		
Exclusion of certain benefits	550	600
Aid to state and local government		
Exemption of interest on state and local debt	1,800	2,000
Deductibility of nonbusiness state and local taxes (other than on owner-occupied homes)	2,800	4,150
Total	4,600	6,150

Source: From a statement by Murray L. Weidenbaum, Assistant Secretary of the Treasury for Economic Policy, Before the Subcommittee on Economy in Government of the Joint Economic Committee, June 2, 1970.

11

Martin Pfaff and Anita Pfaff:
How Equitable Are Implicit Public Grants?
The Case of the Individual Income Tax

Introduction

This paper is addressed to questions of equity in the distribution of those hidden subsidies termed *implicit public grants* conveyed to some groups of the population by the special provisions, exemptions, and deductions of the U.S. individual income tax laws.

This is the first publication of this article. All rights reserved. Permission to reprint must be obtained from the publisher and authors. Martin and Anita Pfaff are from Wayne State University. The authors wish to acknowledge the assistance rendered by Mr. Keith Beyler, University of Chicago, in carrying out the programming work and in making many substantive contributions.

We may interpret the concepts of equity applicable to implicit public grants at two levels. First, implicit public grants are a device for reducing the amount to be paid in taxes. Equity in the distribution of implicit public grants thus assumes the same character as the more general concept of equity in the distribution of taxes. Second, we may contrast the psychology of implicit public grants with the psychology of taxation. This entails a study of the attitudes of taxpayers toward tax payment itself as distinguished from the set of attitudes toward activities that entail a search for and use of exemptions, deductions, or other special provisions in the intricacies of the tax law, which convey implicit public grants. The second view assumes that an additional qualitative factor is introduced into the attitudinal patterns of taxpayers and that it may have some profound effects on their perception of the equity of implicit public grants and more generally, the legitimacy of the whole tax-expenditure process.

If we subsume the concept of the distribution of implicit public grants under the concept of the equity of taxation, we are raising a time-honored problem in a slightly modified garb. The concept of equity in taxation has been an age-old question, which elicited spirited and often quite opposing reactions from scholars and policy makers. The main endeavor has been to find an objective criterion that would embody a socially acceptable equity norm. This search for an objective criterion is reflected in the thought of Thomas Aquinas, who examined the equity of taxation in general, as well as in the work of Adolph Wagner, who attempted to focus such equity norms on particular items of taxation. The works of continental schools – specifically the Romantic and the Historical–Ethical Schools of economics – also reflect a long tradition of normative inquiry. Largely due to the endeavors of many a good scholar who felt that his perceptions of equity could be marshaled to a sweeping analysis of the existing system, the ensuing reaction aimed at a "value-free" (*wertfrei*) approach to economics in general and public finance in particular. Max Weber and his followers rejected explicitly such normative approaches and thus led economics onto its long, seemingly nonnormative path.

On the other hand, we cannot readily deny that we – and therefore, by implication, others – have a sense of equity that pertains to questions of taxation and redistribution. We also cannot deny that this sense of equity represents a factor in our utility function, when we contemplate the reduction or increase of welfare resulting from a particular tax or exemption provision. Furthermore, some contemplation will lead to the conclusion that even the pure efficiency norm, which underlies much of the new welfare economics, is not entirely value free. The norm of efficiency subsumes commitment to some kind of rationality that would guide our evaluation of the system. The great advantage of the efficiency norm no doubt is that it can presumably be embodied in the anonymity of market operations, without the possibility of any individual or group's influencing the automatic operation of this invisible efficiency calculus. However, because of the imperfections of markets and the operation of factors of power reflected in monopoly and other market forces, the market price structure cannot guarantee general efficiency. In a society where a variety of explicit or implicit transfers influences markets, market efficiency becomes somewhat questionable as an "automatic norm." Furthermore, if we were to contemplate the welfare implications of the nature of the economic system in which we participate and the nature of society in which the economy operates the need for many more explicit value norms should be readily evident.[1]

The postulates of the value free economics dominant in the last decades thus stand in marked contrast with our personal experience, which suggests that equity norms are a factor in the determination of individual preferences. Fritz Karl Mann and others have already provided a viable synthesis of the extreme normative and nonnormative theses. They recognize that the problem of equity in taxation can be reduced to what is considered equitable in a *particular* socioeconomic setting.[2] This approach recognizes the necessity for evaluation of particular actions in the context of the norms of the society in which these actions take place. On the other hand, it separates the value judgments of the investigator from the analysis of the structures relevant for a particular situation. Accordingly, one may still say that this approach to the analysis of equity in taxation is "value free" in the sense that the views of the investigator do not color it directly. On the other hand, it is value oriented, or normative, because it pertains to the norms of the time and the society in which a particular process takes place.

The second major approach to the concept of equity and redistribution that we associated with the level of attitudes toward taxation and implicit public grants is related to the concept of normative structures. These normative structures, however, emanate from an inquiry into the attitudes prevailing in the relevant target population. Furthermore, an explicit separation into the attitudes toward taxation in general and toward hidden subsidies, in particular, is formulated. On theoretical grounds an individual could conceivably consider the de facto progressivity of a tax rate schedule, which results *after* the implicit public grants have been subtracted, as equitable, while he rejects the jungle of provisions that convey special advantages only to the legal wizard or to the individual wealthy enough to obtain the services of a legal expert or to the person adept at manipulating potential sources of income in order to conform to some obscure section in the tax law.

This second view is not entirely divorced from the first one. In fact, it could be a special manifestation of the concept of equity in distribution that emanates from an empirical inquiry into relevant normative structures. In particular,

---

1 The subdiscipline of grants economics starts precisely from this vantage point: It assumes a systemic nature of economic life, the interdependence of utility functions of individuals, and the multiplicity of norms that are reflected at the macro or systemic level as well as at the micro level. See M. Pfaff and A. B. Pfaff, *The Grants Economy*, Belmont, California, Wadsworth Publishing Company (forthcoming).

2 F. K. Mann, *Steuerpolitische Ideale.* Vergleichende Studie zur Geschichte der oekonomischen und politischen Ideen und ihres Wirkens in der oeffentlichen Meinung. Jena 1937. Also G. Schmoelders, *Allgemeine Steuerlehre*, 4. Aufl. Berlin 1966 and G. Schmoelders, *Finanzpolitik*, 3. Auflage, Berlin–Heidelberg–New York: Springer-Verlag, 1970.

however, we may identify it with the approach of the psychology of public finance and taxation reflected in the pioneering work of Guenter Schmoelders and Burkhard Struempel.[3] Their approach is based on the empirical methods of social science inquiry; it attempts to arrive at some general notions of equity on the basis of interviews of a sample population.

The approach based on the actual inquiry of taxpayers' attitudes could be likened to the construction of an empirical preference function for equity in redistribution. Although the authors know of no explicit method for constructing such a social equity function across the entire range of income levels and on the basis of some rating of opinions of a target population, such an endeavor may conceivably be quite appropriate for the task at hand. In the meanwhile, however, it may still be useful to postulate alternative theoretical equity norms and to pursue their implications for the distribution aspects, in general, and implicit public grants, in particular. Indeed, this is the purpose of this paper.

The empirical analysis was based on a stratified random sample of 34,000 individual income tax returns for the year 1965.[4]

The Distributive Pattern

An extensive number of special provisions characterizes the present income tax system. Over the years a number of exemptions and deductions were introduced to accord special tax benefits to some groups of taxpayers.

We can distinguish three overall ways for conferring these tax benefits. First, an item may be deductible from the income tax base; under this treatment the deduction reduces the income liable to taxation and consequently also the tax. Second, an item may give rise to a tax credit; that is, a certain amount may be deducted from taxes after they have been computed. (The item is considered part of the tax base.) Third, a differential tax schedule may be used for different groups of individuals.

The first group conveys by far the largest share of tax benefits. These include personal exemptions (exemptions for self, spouse, children; other dependents for blindness; and age) as well as all other deductions, such as medical expenses, charitable contributions, other payments, interest fees. Furthermore, it includes adjustments to income (moving expenses, unreimbursed employee benefits, sick pay), dividend exclusion, and 50 percent deduction of long-term capital gains. An item might belong to this group even though it never appears as explicit income; however, it ought to be treated as implicit income. Rent on owner-occupied properties is not included in income computations.

3 G. Schmoelders, *Finanz- und Steuerpsychologie:* Reinbeck bei Hamburg: Rowohlt Taschenbuch Verlag, 1970; and B. Struempel, *Steuersystem und wirtschaftliche Entwicklung*, Tuebingen, 1968.

4 The analysis was carried out at The Brookings Institution. The authors gratefully acknowledge the assistance and advice of Henry Aaron, Benjamin Okner, and George Sadowsky.

Furthermore, some types of income are exempted from taxation: Interest received on state and local bonds; fellowships granted for the purpose of pursuing a degree; or fellowships, prizes, or awards up to the amount of $300 per month are not liable to taxation.

Some of these items seem directly related to the taxpayer's ability to earn income; in other words, they constitute a cost of earning income. These items are not considered as giving rise to an implicit public grant from the government to the taxpayer in terms of the tax savings involved. However, other items do not seem to qualify under this criterion and therefore represent a subsidy or grant to the taxpayer in the amount of the tax savings.

In the second group we find three different tax credits: retirement credit, foreign income tax credit, and investment credit. The first is designed to provide for the equal treatment of all aged people irrespective of income source and therefore is not considered as giving rise to an implicit public grant. The second is designed to regulate income tax for income earned abroad in such a way as to avoid double taxation and to adjust tax liability on the foreign income so as to charge the higher of the domestic and foreign income tax. Investment credit was abolished temporarily between October 1966 and April 1967 and has since been abolished in 1970. In this analysis we have included implicit public grants conveyed by income tax credit, in view of the fact that this tax credit was in effect in 1965.

In the third group we find three exemptions from the standard income tax schedule (Schedule 1). Schedule 2, which applies to married couples filing joint returns and to some widows and widowers; and Schedule 3, which is in effect for certain heads of household.

A special tax computation for long-term capital gains provides that 25 percent of long-term capital gains are paid as taxes alternatively to using the tax rate under schedules 1, 2, or 3.

We could advance arguments in favor and against the equity considerations of using differential tax schedules for different tax units. In our analysis we consider schedules 2 and 3 as giving rise to implicit public grants to taxpayers. This implication was chosen in view of the fact that particularly in the case of schedule 2 income can be averaged between husband and wife, and in effect each can be taxed one half although only one spouse may in fact have earned income. Implicit public grants due to schedules 2 and 3 may be overstated in this analysis, because we could not split up income between husband and wife only, where both earn income and let both file single returns, but we did treat them as one tax unit and apply the norm of Schedule 1 to the combined income. Obviously this kind of tax computation would be a disadvantage to married couples. If the norms of schedules 2 and 3 were to be abolished, every taxpayer would most likely have to file an individual return, using Schedule 1 as the norm.

Table 1 provides a list of the items considered to give rise to implicit public grants together with the size of each implicit public grant.

We computed implicit public grants due to an item or a group of items by

Table 1. Sources and Amounts of Implicit Public Grants (1965)

Source of IPG	Amount (In $ Million)
(1) IPG due to contribution deduction	3,053.6
(2) IPG due to personal property tax deduction	195.3
(3) IPG due to real-estate tax deduction	2,162.5
(4) IPG due to gasoline tax deduction	504.4
(5) IPG due to 1/2 state and local income tax deduction	704.2
(6) IPG due to 1/2 state and local sales tax deduction	463.1
(7) IPG due to mortgage interest deduction	1,688.6
(8) IPG due to other interest deduction	2,046.5
(9) IPG due to items (1) – (8) jointly	11,100.7
(10) IPG due to dividend exclusion	243.3
(11) IPG due to untaxed capital gains	4,768.9
(12) IPG due to imputed rent	4,079.8
(13) IPG due to tax-exempt interest	372.3
(14) IPG due to alternative tax	378.0
(15) IPG due to Schedule 2	9,583.9
(16) IPG due to Schedule 3	102.2
(17) IPG due to exemption for self and spouse	11,356.5
(18) IPG due to exemption for children and other dependents	7,895.9
(19) IPG due to blindness	5.9
(20) IPG due to old age	669.2
(21) IPG due to all exemptions [(17) – (20)]	20,791.6
(22) IPG due to investment credit	417.6
(23) IPG due to items (1) – (8), (10) – (20) and (22)	63,958.0

disallowing deduction of the item and subtracting the actual tax under 1965 law from the tax liability under the modified law. Because of the progressivity of the income tax schedule, the sum of implicit public grants due to individual items does not generally equal the implicit public grants due to a group of items considered jointly [(9) is therefore not the sum of (1) through (8); and so on].

The deduction of mortgage interest rates, no doubt, leads to a sum total of itemized deductions exceeding $1,000. Thus we assume that among the taxpayers who used standard deductions none were eligible to deduct mortgage interest rates, and therefore the amount of the standard deduction was distributed to the other deductible items in the same percentage share as observed in returns of individuals who use itemized deductions. Table 1 includes these imputed implicit public grants due to items (1) through (8). These grants may be considered upper limits, because it is unlikely that many taxpayers would opt for the use of the standard deduction, if their itemized deductions would be far in excess of their allowable standard deduction. They are likely to use the standard deduction if their itemized deductions would approximately equal or be less than their standard deductions.

From the stratified random sample of the 1965 individual income tax returns, implicit public grants due to all items jointly were estimated to total almost $64 billion.

The most sizable implicit public grants appear to be due to exemptions for self and spouse. Taxpayers save $11.3 billion on account of this deduction. This item is considered as source of implicit public grants despite the fact that this deduction is available to everyone filing an income tax return, because the amount of the tax savings due to the standard $600 deduction for self and $600 for spouse gives rise to a highly unequal distribution of these implicit public grants. Table 2 shows the distribution of implicit public grants due to exemptions for self and spouse by thirty income classes. The average implicit public grant due to the personal exemptions deduction for an individual or a couple in the $0 to $600 total income[5] group amounts to $9.92. Because the tax rate for income under $500 equals 14 percent and the marginal tax rate for income between $500 and $1000 amounts to 15 percent, an individual with a taxable income of $600 before tax exemption could write off his whole income as personal exemption, thus receiving an implicit public grant in the amount of $90. [These rates would be applicable to individuals filing returns under Schedule 1.] This implicit public grant will be less for taxable income before exemption of under $600. By comparison individuals in the income groups above $100,000 show implicit public grants for personal exemption in the $500 and $600 range. Persons filing a single return with income before personal exemptions of over $100,600 can reap tax savings or implicit public grants in the amount of $420 as a consequence of the $600 reduction in the income tax base. For individuals in the same total income class, implicit public grants may vary depending on their taxable income.

As exemptions for self and spouse are combined into one item, some of the variability in the size of implicit public grants may be accounted for by the fact that for some returns one exemption was claimed, whereas others claimed two. In all groups of total income above $8,000 there are a large number of married couples filing joint returns. This may be deduced from inspection of a distribution of average exemptions by income class (Table 2, first half); the average exemption for self and spouse in these income groups exceeds $1,100 for all but two income groups (in the $150,000 to $200,000 income and in the above $1 million income bracket the average exemptions are between $1,000 and $11,000). Inspection of income group above $8,000 only, therefore, gives a fairly good illustration of the relative size of average implicit public grants in relation to the income level. Similarly the rich benefit much more than the poor from exemptions for children and other dependents, old age, and blindness.

Implicit public grants due to the use of Schedule 2 is another sizable item. However, this amount has been considered to be overstated insofar as it does not allow for the separate filing of married couples, where both earn income.

Implicit public grants due to deduction amount to a total of $11,001 million. Among deductions the contributions deductions are the most sizable. For an estimated $12.3 billion contributions (including the imputed contribution from standard deduction return) $3,053 million were received as in implicit

---

5 Total income is defined as Adjusted Gross Income, plus untaxed capital gains, plus imputed tax-exempt interest, plus imputed rent on owner-occupied property, plus dividend exclusion.

Table 2. Distribution of Personal Exemption for Self and Spouse by Total Income Class

Income Class	Personal Exemption for Self and Spouse				IPG Due to Personal Exemption for Self and Spouse			
	Absolute (Millions)	%	Cum. %	Per Capita	Absolute (Millions)	%	Cum %	Per Capita
-999999.- 0.	427.183	0.6	(0.6)	1001.44	3.964	0.0	(0.0)	9.29
0.- 600.	2269.023	3.4	(4.0)	649.22	134.664	0.3	(0.3)	9.92
600.- 1000.	1394.883	2.8	(6.9)	670.21	134.666	1.2	(1.5)	47.63
1000.- 1500.	2605.155	3.9	(10.8)	695.00	241.224	2.1	(3.7)	64.35
1500.- 2000.	2871.109	4.3	(15.1)	750.94	301.054	2.7	(6.3)	78.74
2000.- 2500.	2532.218	3.8	(18.9)	766.77	294.835	2.6	(8.9)	89.28
2500.- 3000.	2545.602	3.8	(22.7)	822.42	334.600	2.9	(11.8)	108.10
3000.- 3500.	2663.351	4.0	(26.7)	862.70	379.809	3.3	(15.2)	123.03
3500.- 4000.	2371.183	3.6	(30.8)	857.56	356.053	3.1	(18.3)	128.77
4000.- 4500.	2595.835	3.9	(34.1)	887.48	414.651	3.7	(22.0)	141.76
4500.- 5000.	2475.030	3.7	(37.9)	916.52	400.128	3.5	(25.5)	148.17
5000.- 6000.	4580.660	6.9	(44.7)	951.92	783.823	6.9	(32.4)	162.89
6000.- 7000.	4959.093	7.4	(52.2)	1005.73	891.675	7.9	(40.3)	180.84
7000.- 8000.	4974.754	7.5	(59.6)	1062.70	921.267	8.1	(48.4)	196.80
8000.- 9000.	4961.665	7.4	(67.1)	1110.61	937.889	8.3	(56.6)	209.93
9000.- 10000.	4313.398	6.5	(73.5)	1127.42	823.896	7.3	(63.9)	215.35
10000.- 11000.	3902.701	5.9	(79.4)	1162.23	769.567	6.8	(70.7)	229.18
11000.- 12000.	2786.728	4.2	(83.6)	1145.87	567.672	5.0	(75.7)	233.42
12000.- 13000.	2206.449	8.3	(86.9)	1164.95	462.747	4.1	(79.7)	244.32
13000.- 14000.	1707.203	2.6	(89.4)	1170.38	368.432	3.2	(83.0)	252.58
14000.- 15000.	1449.998	2.2	(91.6)	1159.55	324.962	2.9	(85.8)	259.87
15000.- 20000.	3006.477	4.5	(96.1)	1159.47	718.055	6.3	(92.8)	276.92
20000.- 25000.	966.103	1.4	(97.6)	1139.12	263.157	2.3	(94.5)	310.29
25000.- 50000.	1241.339	1.9	(99.4)	1152.99	433.038	3.8	(98.3)	402.22
50000.- 100000.	301.571	0.5	(99.9)	1155.96	147.474	1.8	(99.6)	565.24
100000.- 150000.	47.700	0.1	(99.9)	1135.72	26.693	0.2	(99.8)	635.55
150000.- 200000.	14.509	0.0	(100.0)	1095.87	8.387	0.1	(99.9)	633.50
200000.- 500000.	17.734	0.0	(100.0)	1110.09	9.906	0.1	(100.0)	620.10
500000.- 1000000.	2.988	0.0	(100.0)	1101.36	1.526	0.0	(100.0)	562.41
1000000.- *********	1.406	0.0	(100.0)	1087.24	0.663	0.0	(100.0)	512.62
Total	66693.039	100.0			11356.477	100.0		

Table 3. Distribution of Untaxed Capital Gains and IPG Due to Untaxed Capital Gains by Total Income Class

Income Class	Untaxed Capital Gains				IPG Due to Untaxed Capital Gains			
	Absolute (Millions)	%	Cum. %	Per Capita	Absolute (Millions)	%	Cum %	Per Capita
-999999.— 0.	-463.695	-4.7	(-4.7)	-1086.82	-17.206	-0.4	(-0.4)	-40.34
0.— 600.	15.000	0.2	(-4.6)	4.29	0.000	0.0	(-0.4)	0.00
600.— 1000.	6.385	0.1	(-4.5)	2.26	0.000	0.0	(-0.4)	0.00
1000.— 1500.	8.621	0.1	(-4.4)	2.30	-0.963	-0.0	(-0.4)	-0.26
1500.— 2000.	42.910	0.4	(-4.0)	11.22	3.138	0.1	(-0.3)	0.32
2000.— 2500.	18.595	0.2	(-3.8)	5.63	-0.870	-0.0	(-0.3)	-0.26
2500.— 3000.	92.446	0.9	(-2.9)	29.87	4.730	0.1	(-0.2)	1.53
3000.— 3500.	31.684	0.3	(-2.5)	10.26	2.051	0.0	(-0.2)	0.66
3500.— 4000.	89.690	0.9	(-1.6)	32.44	8.308	0.2	(-0.0)	3.00
4000.— 4500.	101.656	1.0	(-0.6)	34.75	12.162	0.3	(0.2)	4.16
4500.— 5000.	73.857	0.8	(0.2)	27.35	8.933	0.2	(0.4)	3.31
5000.— 6000.	403.014	4.1	(4.3)	83.75	30.557	0.6	(1.1)	6.35
6000.— 7000.	269.105	2.7	(7.3)	54.58	42.594	0.9	(2.0)	8.64
7000.— 8000.	92.311	0.9	(8.0)	19.72	14.947	0.3	(2.3)	3.19
8000.— 9000.	342.124	3.5	(11.5)	76.58	64.731	1.4	(3.6)	14.49
9000.— 10000.	207.765	2.1	(13.6)	54.30	37.569	0.8	(4.4)	9.32
10000.— 11000.	276.759	2.8	(16.4)	82.42	53.557	1.1	(5.5)	15.95
11000.— 12000.	260.028	2.7	(19.1)	106.92	59.525	1.2	(6.8)	24.48
12000.— 13000.	68.364	0.7	(19.8)	36.09	13.545	0.3	(7.1)	7.15
13000.— 14000.	262.206	2.7	(22.5)	179.76	53.960	1.1	(8.2)	36.99
14000.— 15000.	133.109	1.4	(23.8)	106.45	29.399	0.6	(8.8)	23.51
15000.— 20000.	486.405	4.9	(28.7)	185.27	125.651	2.6	(11.5)	48.46
20000.— 25000.	477.375	4.9	(33.6)	562.87	134.766	2.8	(14.3)	158.90
25000.— 50000.	1344.394	13.7	(47.3)	1248.71	475.578	10.0	(24.3)	441.73
50000.— 100000.	1446.188	14.8	(62.1)	5542.93	741.406	15.5	(39.8)	2841.65
100000.— 150000.	609.513	6.2	(68.3)	14512.43	368.029	7.7	(47.5)	3762.71
150000.— 200000.	336.450	3.4	(71.7)	25411.93	228.112	4.0	(52.3)	17229.29
200000.— 500000.	1056.351	10.9	(82.6)	66750.67	815.084	17.1	(69.4)	51022.04
500000.— 1000000.	570.616	5.8	(88.5)	210326.64	477.543	10.0	(79.4)	176020.45
1000000.— ********	1129.912	11.5	(100.0)	873868.53	982.084	20.6	(100.0)	759539.27

Table 4. Distribution of Actual Tax and Nominal Tax by Total Income Class

Income Class		Actual Tax				Nominal Tax			
		Absolute (Millions)	%	Cum. %	Per Capita	Absolute (Millions)	%	Cum. %	Per Capita
-999999.-	0.	17.206	0.0	(0.0)	40.34	.048	.00	.00	.12
0.-	600.	0.000	0.0	(0.0)	0.00	46.497	.04	.04	13.30
600.-	1000.	3.045	0.0	(0.0)	1.08	251.715	.21	.25	89.03
1000.-	1500.	81.068	0.1	(0.2)	21.63	603.246	.50	.75	160.94
1500.-	2000.	186.203	0.3	(0.5)	48.70	905.129	.75	1.50	236.73
2000.-	2500.	340.464	0.6	(1.1)	103.09	1047.652	.87	2.37	317.73
2500.-	3000.	418.525	0.7	(1.9)	135.21	1237.364	1.03	3.40	398.79
3000.-	3500.	579.245	1.0	(2.9)	187.63	1527.460	1.27	4.67	494.77
3500.-	4000.	687.927	1.2	(4.1)	248.79	1630.894	1.30	6.03	589.82
4000.-	4500.	939.467	1.7	(5.8)	321.19	2010.777	1.67	7.70	687.46
4500.-	5000.	943.491	1.7	(7.4)	349.38	2113.970	1.76	9.46	782.82
5000	6000.	2120.970	3.8	(11.2)	440.77	4492.872	3.74	13.20	933.68
6000.-	7000.	2755.348	4.9	(16.1)	558.80	5711.430	4.75	14.95	1158.31
7000.-	8000.	3059.415	5.4	(21.5)	653.55	6711.716	5.58	23.53	1433.75
8000.-	9000.	3497.575	6.2	(27.7)	782.89	7512.616	6.25	29.78	1681.61
9000.-	10000.	3387.091	6.0	(33.8)	885.31	7342.506	6.10	35.88	1919.17
10000.-	11000.	3503.550	6.2	(40.0)	1043.37	7407.856	6.16	42.04	2206.08
11000.-	12000.	2946.661	5.2	(45.2)	1211.63	6122.907	5.09	47.13	2517.66
12000.-	13000.	2580.247	4.6	(49.8)	1362.30	5378.601	4.47	51.60	2839.76
13000.-	14000.	2232.070	4.0	(53.8)	1530.21	4665.633	3.88	55.48	3198.44
14000.-	15000.	2212.983	3.9	(57.7)	1769.70	4453.919	3.70	59.18	3561.76
15000.-	20000.	5684.309	10.1	(67.8)	2192.20	11725.119	9.75	68.93	4521.83
20000.-	25000.	2709.118	4.8	(72.6)	3194.28	5656.132	4.70	73.63	6669.06
25000.-	50000.	6453.788	11.5	(84.0)	5994.47	13522.305	11.24	84.87	12559.92
50000.-	100000.	4204.692	7.5	(91.5)	16115.68	8084.072	6.72	91.59	30984.50
100000.-	150000.	1407.818	2.5	(94.0)	33519.98	2754.814	2.29	93.88	65591.77
150000.-	200000.	692.077	1.2	(95.2)	52272.33	1316.805	1.09	94.27	99,457.79
200000.-	500000.	1364.245	2.4	(97.6)	85398.01	2826.151	2.35	97.32	176,909.34
500000.-	1000000.	527.821	0.9	(98.6)	194552.50	1201.889	1.00	98.32	443,011.13
1000000.-	*******	796.041	1.4	(100.0)	615654.63	2031.380	1.69	100.01	1,571,060.18

public grants. Thus, about one quarter of all charitable contributions were paid for by public resources. The two next most sizable sources of implicit public grants among deductions are real-estate tax deductions and mortgage interest deductions. These two items, together with more than $4 billion of implicit public grants resulting from the exclusion of imputed rent from income subject to tax, amount to a sizable subsidy to homeowners through the income tax system.

Last but not least a large implicit public grant of a rather regressive nature is transferred by the exclusion of one half of the realized long-term capital gains from taxable income (for capital held for more than six months). This provision, in conjunction with alternative tax computations, results in implicit public grants of more than $5 billion, distributed almost exclusively to high-income groups. Table 3 shows the distribution by income class of implicit public grants due to realized long-term capital gains. The 0.5 percent of the population receiving the highest income obtain more than three quarters of the $4.8 billion implicit public grants due to this item. Nominal tax — that is, the tax liability if all items enumerated in Table 1 were to be disallowed — shows a far more progressive distribution than actual tax.

Table 4 presents a distribution by thirty classes of income of these two taxes. Total nominal taxes (actual taxes plus implicit public grants due to all items) are more than double the size of actual taxes. The progressivity of the nominal tax rate obviously involves an equity judgment on the part of the public decision maker.

Implicit Public Grants under Alternative Equity Norms

In the absence of a generally accepted equity norm that reflects the social preference function for the distribution of tax burdens and the allocation of implicit public grants, we shall formulate a set of norms on the basis of public acts.

As equity norm 1 we recognize the public decision maker's differential treatment of different income groups as reflected in tax schedule 1. The maze of special provisions is abandoned and income is treated as the sole determinant of the tax liability.

Only a limited number of items are retained as legitimate deductions or tax credits. These items include all those directly instrumental in increasing or maintaining the taxpayer's ability to earn income. Thus, they include all adjustments to income as well as certain medical expense deductions and certain other items. The first half of Table 5 presents the distribution by total income of taxable income or tax base under norm 1. The second half of Table 5 shows the distribution of taxable income under 1965 law. The tax base under norm 1 is more than $190 billion larger than the actual tax base used under 1965 law. Because norm 1 assumes that nominal tax is the desired tax, no implicit public

Table 5. Distribution of Taxable Income under Norms 1 and 2 by Total Income Class

Income Class	Taxable Income (Norm 2) Absolute (Millions)	%	Cum. %	Per Tax Unit	Taxable Income (Norm 1) Absolute (Millions)	%	Cum. %	Per Tax Unit
-99999.— 0.	84.932	0.0	(0.0)	199.10	0.344	0.0	(0.0)	0.81
0.— 600.	0.000	0.0	(0.0)	0.00	334.770	0.1	(0.1)	95.79
600.— 1000.	21.750	0.0	(0.0)	7.69	1778.993	0.4	(0.4)	629.22
1000.— 1500.	580.283	0.2	(0.2)	154.81	4132.218	0.9	(1.3)	1102.39
1500.— 2000.	1335.568	0.5	(0.7)	349.32	6041.729	1.3	(2.6)	1580.21
2000.— 2500.	2379.714	0.8	(1.5)	720.59	6770.239	1.4	(4.0)	2050.97
2500.— 3000.	2953.259	1.0	(2.6)	954.12	7778.309	1.6	(5.6)	2512.97
3000.— 3500.	3836.716	1.3	(3.9)	1242.76	9216.729	1.9	(7.5)	2985.42
3500.— 4000.	4483.889	1.6	(5.4)	1621.64	9668.991	2.0	(9.6)	3496.88
4000.— 4500.	5981.859	2.1	(7.5)	2045.13	11697.361	2.4	(12.0)	3999.19
4500.— 5000.	6058.984	2.1	(9.6)	2243.69	12007.834	2.5	(14.5)	4446.69
5000.— 6000.	13479.944	4.7	(14.3)	2801.32	24888.356	5.2	(19.7)	5172.14
6000.— 7000.	16954.817	5.9	(20.2)	3438.53	30136.130	6.3	(26.0)	6111.78
7000.— 8000.	18827.425	6.5	(26.8)	4021.89	33896.534	7.1	(33.1)	7240.92
8000.— 9000.	21316.583	7.4	(34.2)	4771.45	36586.696	7.7	(40.8)	8189.47
9000.— 10000.	20433.546	7.1	(41.3)	5340.87	34610.576	7.2	(48.0)	9046.42
10000.— 11000.	20816.778	7.2	(48.5)	6199.28	33726.738	7.1	(55.1)	10043.90
11000.— 12000.	17168.375	6.0	(54.5)	7059.43	26827.525	5.6	(60.7)	11031.16
12000.— 13000.	14735.587	5.1	(59.6)	7780.00	22747.802	4.8	(65.5)	12010.23
13000.— 14000.	12610.488	4.4	(64.0)	8645.19	19004.283	4.0	(69.5)	13028.88
14000.— 15000.	12101.580	4.2	(68.2)	9677.52	17540.613	3.7	(73.1)	14027.07
15000.— 20000.	29942.150	10.4	(78.6)	11547.42	42600.330	8.9	(82.0)	16429.14
20000.— 25000.	13088.305	4.5	(83.1)	15432.23	18057.474	3.8	(85.8)	21291.30
25000.— 50000.	26132.192	9.1	(92.2)	24272.37	35094.713	7.3	(93.2)	32597.03
50000.— 100000.	12412.705	4.3	(96.5)	47575.21	16581.516	3.5	(96.6)	63553.36
100000.— 150000.	3353.876	1.2	(97.7)	79855.37	4830.616	1.0	(97.6)	115016.34
150000.— 200000.	1469.961	0.5	(98.2)	111025.60	2166.639	0.5	(98.1)	163645.41
200000.— 500000.	2683.205	0.9	(99.2)	167961.29	4383.938	0.9	(99.0)	274422.50
500000.—1000000.	976.747	0.3	(99.5)	360024.73	1776.652	0.4	(99.4)	654866.26
1000000.—*********	1466.564	0.5	(100.0)	*********	2930.508	0.6	(100.0)	*********
Total	287687.766	100.0			477815.684	100.0		

grants would be conveyed to the taxpayer under this tax scheme. Tax under norm 1 would thus equal nominal tax whose distribution was shown in Table 4.

We obviously would have qualms accepting norm 1 as the expression of the public decision maker's equity judgment. Although his equity judgment was laid down in the tax law in terms of the progressivity, the public decision maker obviously also shows a certain preference for the size of the tax yield. Tax under norm 1 would exceed 1965 tax yield by $64 billion.

Norm 2 combines both the progressivity of the special tax provisions and the preference for the present tax yield. Under norm 2 we assume that actual taxes equal taxes under present law. In other words the tax loopholes are the expressed desire of the public decision maker; a set of criteria other than income alone become determinants of the tax burden.

Table 4 shows the distribution of actual tax — the tax liability under norm 2 — and Table 5 shows the distribution of taxable income under norm 2. Table 6

Table 6. Distribution of IPG Due to All Deductions, Exemptions, by Total Income Class

Income Class		IPG Due to All Deductions			
		Absolute (Millions)	%	Cum. %	Per Capita
−999999.−	0.	−17.150	−0.0	(0.0)	−40.22
0.−	600.	46.497	0.1	(0.0)	13.30
600.−	1000.	248.670	0.4	(0.4)	87.95
1000.−	1500.	522.178	0.8	(1.3)	139.81
1500.−	2000.	718.926	1.1	(2.4)	188.03
2000.−	2500.	707.188	1	(3.5)	214.14
2500.−	3000.	815.839	1.3	(4.8)	263.58
3000.−	3500.	948.215	1.5	(6.2)	307.14
3500.−	4000.	942.967	1.5	(7.7)	341.03
4000.−	4500.	1071.310	1.7	(9.4)	366.27
4500.−	5000.	1170.479	1.8	(11.2)	433.44
5000.−	6000.	2371.902	3.7	(14.9)	493.91
6000.−	7000.	2956.082	4.6	(19.4)	599.51
7000.−	8000.	3652.301	5.7	(25.3)	780.20
8000.−	9000.	4015.041	6.3	(31.5)	898.72
9000.−	10000.	3955.415	6.2	(37.7)	1033.86
10000.−	11000.	3904.306	6.1	(43.8)	1162.71
11000.−	12000.	3176.246	5.0	(48.8)	1306.03
12000.−	13000.	2798.354	4.4	(53.2)	1477.46
13000.−	14000.	2433.563	3.8	(57.0)	1668.34
14000.−	15000.	2240.936	3.5	(60.5)	1792.06
15000.−	20000.	6040.810	9.7	(69.9)	2329.68
20000.−	25000.	2947.014	4.6	(74.5)	3474.78
25000.−	50000.	7068.517	11.1	(85.6)	6565.45
50000.−	100000.	3879.380	6.1	(91.6)	14868.82
100000.−	150000.	1346.996	2.1	(93.9)	32071.79
150000.−	200000.	624.728	1.0	(94.7)	47185.46
200000.−	500000.	1461.906	2.3	(97.0)	91511.33
500000.−	1000000.	674.068	1.1	(98.1)	248458.63
1000000.	********	1235.339	1.9	(100.0)	955405.55

depicts a rather regressive distribution of $64 billion in implicit public grants. Although the group with negative total income receives a negative implicit public grant and the group of total income between $0 and $600 receives on the average $13.30 implicit public grants per tax unit, individuals in the highest income class (the group above $1 million of total income) receive, on the average, $955,405.55. Because under the present law the marginal tax rates of the taxpayer generally determine implicit public grants, the taxpayer can reduce his taxes at his highest rather than at his average tax rates.[6]

We can formulate a third norm, by combining both the nominal progressivity of the tax schedule and the present desired tax yield with a different distribution of implicit public grants.

If the implicit public grants were distributed equally to all tax units – that is, if all tax units were to receive equal tax savings – we would, in fact, have a negative income tax system. Tax under norm 3 would have guaranteed everybody an income in the amount of the average implicit public grant of $911.60 in 1965. (Because income and tax yield have risen since that time, the amount would be somewhat higher now.) Table 7 shows the distribution of actual tax under norm 3, which is computed as nominal tax minus an equal per tax-unit share of implicit public grants. This table indicates that up to a total income of $5,000 an income tax liability would be negative; in other words no tax has to be paid but the tax unit actually receives an explicit transfer from the public sector. This transfer would depend on the income level. A tax unit with total income between $0 and $600 would receive $911.47 on the average under 1965 economic conditions; a tax unit in the $4,500–$5,000 total income class would receive an average transfer of $128.77. This income tax scheme would naturally result in much higher tax payments of the higher income groups as compared to their tax liability under present law (norm 2). All groups with income above $9,000 would pay more tax than under present law, whereas individuals with income under $9,000 would pay less than under present law. This type of tax system would benefit 72.8 percent of the population. However, the main burden of this income tax scheme would fall on the 27.2 percent of the population who receive 58.7 percent of the total income. Considering that the surplus income is much larger for high income groups, this finding may not be as harsh as it seems at first sight. A modified system of this sort may, in fact, be a useful substitute for some social welfare payments which impose undue hardship on the recipients under the present system. Under this income tax system 54.1 percent of the population would have paid income tax in 1965, whereas 45.9 percent would have received a net transfer.

---

6 Historically many special tax provisions were introduced after the original tax law had been passed. A gradual erosion of the income tax base was experienced over time. As one pressure group was successful in attaining a tax benefit another group would lobby for a similar benefit, thus having the effect of making tax base erosion more and more likely. We could, therefore, argue that the present income tax system is not so much an expression of the public decision makers' equity concept but rather the result of varying applications of pressure by different groups.

Table 7. Distribution of Tax under Norm 3 by Income Class

Income Class		Absolute (Millions)	%	Cum. %	Per Tax Unit
−999999.−	0.	−388.804846	−.69	−.69	−911.470
0.−	600.	−3139.506482	−5.573	−6.263	−898.290
600.−	1000.	−2325.613194	−4.128	−10.391	−822.560
1000.−	1500.	−2813.759730	−4.994	−15.385	−750.650
1500.−	2000.	−2580.238803	−4.580	−19.965	−674.860
2000.−	2500.	−1962.838238	−3.484	−23.449	−594.360
2500.−	3000.	−1587.254968	−2.817	−26.266	−512.800
3000.−	3500.	−1286.824627	−2.284	−28.550	−416.820
3500.−	4000.	−889.706277	−1.579	−30.129	−321.770
4000.−	4500.	−655.565681	−.163	−31.292	−224.130
4500.−	5000.	−347.737332	−617	−31.909	−128.770
5000.−	6000.	106.297168	.187	−31.722	22.090
6000.−	7000.	1216.533390	2.159	−29.563	246.720
7000.−	8000.	2444.358367	4.339	−25.224	522.160
8000.−	9000.	3440.088220	6.106	−19.118	770.020
9000.−	10000.	3854.885208	6.843	−12.275	1007.580
10000.−	11000.	4346.810689	7.716	−4.559	1294.490
11000.−	12000.	3905.925300	6.933	2.374	1606.070
12000.−	13000.	3652.021465	6.482	8.856	1928.170
13000.−	14000.	3335.922230	5.921	14.777	2286.960
14000.−	15000.	3313.992532	5.882	20.659	2650.170
15000.−	20000.	9361.388102	16.618	37.277	3610.290
20000.−	25000.	4882.996669	8.668	45.945	5757.470
25000.−	50000.	12540.859989	22.262	68.207	11648.330
50000.−	100000.	7846.232729	13.928	82.135	30072.910
100000.−	150000.	2716.502879	4.822	86.957	64680.180
150000.−	200000.	1304.751688	2.316	89.273	98546.200
200000.−	500000.	2811.564056	4.991	94.264	175997.750
500000.−	1000000.	1199.416052	2.129	96.393	442099.540
1000000.−	********	2030.202126	3.603	99.996	157014.859
Total		56,332.89839	100.00		

We shall investigate a third type of distribution of implicit public grants in conjunction with the nominal progressivity of the income tax system as well as the present tax yield. This income tax scheme, under norm 4, would provide for a proportional distribution of implicit public grants. Each tax unit would receive implicit public grants in proportion to total income so that a larger share of implicit public grants would go to high-income groups and a smaller share to low-income groups. Table 8 shows a distribution of tax under this norm. An estimated 12.78 percent of total income of taxpayers was dispersed in the form of implicit public grants in 1965. If each family is allowed a tax credit of 12.78 percent, an actual tax would result, as the average column of Table 8 shows. The table also shows totals for each income class as well as the simple and cumulative percentages borne by different income classes.

Although tax liability under norm 4 is less than under norm 3, it is higher than under norm 2 for high-income classes. A comparison of the tax distribution under norms 2 and 4 shows that 77.4 percent of the population, who receive

Table 8. Distribution of Tax under Norm 4 by Income Class

Income Class		Absolute (Millions)	%	Cum. %	Per Tax Unit
−999999.−	0.	232.752	.41	.41	545.64
0.−	600.	−110.707	−.20	.21	−31.68
600.−	1000.	−42.112	−.07	.14	−14.90
1000.−	1500.	5.907	.01	.15	1.58
1500.−	2000.	53.668	.10	.25	14.04
2000.−	2500.	102.111	.18	.43	30.92
2500.−	3000.	146.752	.26	.69	47.41
3000.−	3500.	244.552	.43	1.12	79.21
3500.−	4000.	313.782	.56	1.68	43.48
4000.−	4500.	414.194	.74	2.41	141.61
4500.−	5000.	472.635	.84	3.25	175.02
5000.−	6000.	1096.506	1.95	5.20	227.87
6000.−	7000.	1627.300	2.89	8.09	330.03
7000.−	8000.	2205.858	3.91	12.00	471.21
8000.−	9000.	2656.693	4.71	16.71	594.67
9000.−	10000.	2707.915	4.81	21.52	707.79
10000.−	11000.	2922.778	5.19	26.71	870.41
11000.−	12000.	2549.195	4.52	31.23	1048.20
12000.−	13000.	2357.298	4.18	35.41	1244.59
13000.−	14000.	2151.637	3.82	39.23	1475.07
14000.−	15000.	2141.543	3.80	43.03	1712.57
15000.−	20000.	6094.085	10.82	53.85	2350.23
20000.−	25000.	3252.605	5.77	59.62	3835.10
25000.−	50000.	8867.925	15.74	75.86	8236.80
50000.−	100000.	5884.001	10.44	85.80	22552.10
100000.−	150000.	2112.848	3.75	89.55	50307.10
150000.−	200000.	1026.944	1.82	91.37	77563.80
200000.−	500000.	2242.506	3.99	95.35	140375.99
500000.−	1000000.	967.119	1.72	97.06	356476.02
1000000.−	********	1648.398	2.93	99.99	1274863.57
Total	$AT^{(4)}$ = 56,346.688		100.00		

total income under \$13,000, would pay less under norm 4 than they pay under present law; the remaining 22.6 percent of the population would pay higher taxes under this income tax scheme.

Because norms 2, 3, and 4 are based on the same tax yield, a comparison of the income distribution pattern after taxes is a meaningful exercise. Table 9 shows the distribution of income after taxes under norms 1, 2, 3, and 4. Figure 1 exhibits the corresponding Lorenz curves. The most equal distribution results from norm 3, whereas norm 4 occupies an in-between position, and norm 2 shows the least equal distribution of income.

Norms 3 and 4 are examples of separate and different treatments of aspects of taxation and implicit public grants. In an integral view of the psychology of taxation and the psychology of implicit public grants, we may apply yet an alternative equity norm (norm 5): The relative burden of taxation should equal the relative benefit of the implicit public grants. To give an empirical content to this view, we may formulate an index of vertical equity implicit in the nominal

$Y - T^1$ income after taxes under norm 1 (nominal taxes)
$Y - T^2$ income after taxes under norm 2 (1965 law)
$Y - T^3$ income after taxes under norm 3
$Y - T^4$ income after taxes under norm 4

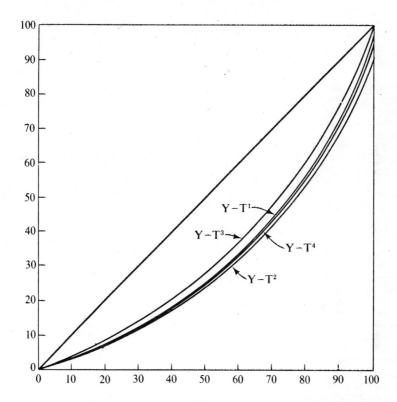

Figure 1. Distribution of Total Income after Taxes under
Norms 1 to 4

income tax and may apply it to implicit public grants. Alternatively we may derive the vertical equity index for implicit public grants and therefrom formulate a normative statement regarding the tax distribution. The former approach is more consistent with the treatment under norms 3 and 4.

Norm 5, therefore, involves the empirical derivation of the vertical equity index involved in nominal taxes and its application to implicit public grants. The resulting distribution of implicit public grants can then be compared to the present system.

A variety of parameters of nominal tax distribution may be chosen as base of the index. In this analysis we chose the mean nominal tax — an estimate from the sample average. For each income class we used the average nominal tax liability (see the second half of Table 4) as the representative value. We derived the vertical equity index weight for any income class by dividing the overall

Table 9a. Distribution of Total Income after Nominal Taxes,
Total Income after Actual Taxes (Norms 1 and 2)

Income Class		Total Income after Nominal Taxes			Total Income after Actual Taxes		
		Absolute (Millions)	%	Cum. %	Absolute (Millions)	%	Cum. %
-999999-	0	--1820.875	-.48	-.48	-2838.033	-.41	-.41
0-	600	1276.479	.31	-.17	1229.982	.28	-.13
600-	1000	2047.411	.54	.37	2296.081	.52	.39
1000-	1500	4070.966	1.07	1.44	4593.144	1.03	1.42
1500-	2000	5757.108	1.51	2.95	6476.034	1.46	2.88
2000-	2500	6350.781	1.67	4.62	7057.969	1.59	4.47
2500-	3000	7275.867	1.91	6.53	8091.706	1.82	6.29
3000-	3500	8511.042	2.24	8.77	9459.257	2.13	8.42
3500-	4000	8674.994	2.28	11.05	9617.961	2.17	10.59
4000-	4500	10482.036	2.76	13.81	11553.346	2.60	13.19
4500-	5000	10729.000	2.82	16.63	11899.479	2.68	15.87
5000-	6000	22082.751	5.81	22.44	24454.653	5.51	21.38
6000-	7000	26245.698	6.90	29.35	29201.780	6.58	27.95
7000-	8000	28545.493	7.51	36.86	32197.794	7.25	35.21
8000-	9000	30483.512	8.02	44.88	34498.553	7.77	42.98
9000-	10000	28922.020	7.61	52.49	32877.435	7.40	50.38
10000-	11000	27686.734	7.28	59.77	31591.040	7.12	57.50
11000-	12000	21840.277	5.57	65.52	25016.523	5.63	63.13
12000-	13000	18262.280	4.80	70.32	21060.634	4.74	67.87
13000	14000	15005.683	3.95	74.27	17439.246	3.93	71.80
14000-	15000	13639.800	3.59	77.86	15880.733	3.58	75.38
15000-	20000	32356.158	8.51	86.37	38396.968	8.65	84.03
20000-	25000	13150.781	3.46	89.83	16097.795	3.63	87.65
25000-	50000	22896.893	6.02	95.85	29965.410	6.75	94.40
50000-	100000	9130.888	2.40	98.25	13010.268	2.93	97.33
100000-	150000	2268.196	.60	98.85	3615.192	.81	98.14
150000-	200000	951.399	.25	99.10	1576.127	.35	98.50
200000-	500000	1740.518	.46	99.56	3202.424	.72	99.22
500000-	1000000	635.120	.17	99.73	1309.188	.29	99.51
1000000	and up	965.351	.25	99.98	2200.690	.50	100.01
Total		380051.344			444009.355		

mean nominal tax by the income class average nominal tax. Table 10 (second
column) shows this vertical equity index. We used the mean implicit public
grant - the sample average of $911.60 — as the corresponding base amount for
computing implicit public grants under norm 5. We then obtained the income
class average implicit public grants by dividing the overall mean implicit public
grant by the vertical equity weights derived from nominal taxes.[7]

Table 10 shows the distribution of implicit public grants and taxes under
norm 5. Comparing our results with norm 2 (actual implicit public grants under
1965 law) we find that lower-income classes (up to a total income of $5,000)
and the groups of total income above $500,000 on the average receive smaller

7 See the appendix for computational formulas used to derive the distribution of
implicit public grants under norms 3, 4, and 5.

Table 9b. Distribution of Total Income after Taxes under Norms 3 and 4

Income Class		Total Income after Taxes under Norm 3 Absolute (Millions)	%	Cum. %	Total Income after Taxes under Norm 4 Absolute (Millions)	%	Cum %
−999999.−	0.	−1432.022	.32	.32	−2053.579	−.46	−.46
0.−	600.	4369.489	.98	.66	1340.689	.30	.16
600.−	1000.	4624.739	1.04	1.70	2341.238	.53	.37
1000.−	1500.	7487.972	1.69	3.39	4668.305	1.05	1.42
1500.−	2000.	9242.476	2.08	5.47	6608.569	1.48	2.91
2000.−	2500.	9361.271	2.11	7.58	7296.322	1.64	4.55
2500.−	3000.	10097.486	2.27	9.85	8363.479	1.88	6.43
3000.−	3500.	11325.327	2.55	12.40	9793.950	2.21	8.64
3500.−	4000.	11195.594	2.52	14.93	9992.106	2.25	10.89
4000.−	4500.	13148.379	2.96	17.89	12078.619	2.72	13.61
4500.−	5000.	13190.707	2.97	20.86	12370.335	2.79	16.39
5000.−	6000.	26469.326	5.96	26.82	25479.117	5.74	22.13
6000.−	7000.	30740.595	6.92	33.74	30329.828	6.83	28.96
7000.−	8000.	32812.851	7.39	41.13	33051.351	7.45	36.41
8000.−	9000.	34556.040	7.78	48.92	35339.435	7.96	44.36
9000.−	10000.	32409.641	7.30	56.21	33556.611	7.56	51.92
10000.−	11000.	30747.779	6.91	63.14	32171.812	7.25	59.17
11000.−	12000.	24057.259	5.42	68.56	25413.989	5.72	64.89
12000.−	13000.	19988.860	4.50	73.06	21283.582	4.79	69.68
13000.−	14000.	16335.394	3.68	76.74	17519.679	3.95	73.63
14000.−	15000.	14779.724	3.33	80.07	15952.173	3.59	77.22
15000.−	20000.	34699.889	7.82	87.88	37967.192	8.55	85.77
20000.−	25000.	13923.916	3.14	91.02	15554.308	3.50	89.27
25000.−	50000.	23878.338	5.38	96.39	27551.273	6.21	95.48
50000.−	100000.	9368.727	2.11	98.50	11330.959	2.55	98.03
100000.−	150000.	2306.507	.52	99.02	2910.162	.66	98.69
150000.−	200000.	963.452	.22	97.24	1241.260	.28	98.96
200000.−	500000.	1755.105	.40	99.63	2324.163	.52	99.49
500000.−	1000000.	637.593	.14	99.78	869.890	.20	99.68
1000000.−	********	966.529	.22	99.99	1348.333	.30	99.99
Total		444008.94011	99.993		443995.150		

implicit public grants under norm 5. The "middle"-income groups would benefit from a distribution of this type.

Figure 2 shows the Lorenz curve for the income distribution after taxes, under norm 5. The broken line indicates the Lorenz curve for income after taxes, under norm 2. The closeness of the lines indicates a similar distribution. Table 11 shows the distribution of total income after taxes, under norm 5.

We can stipulate an infinite number of other equity judgments regarding the distribution of implicit public grants. However, the five norms under discussion in this paper seem representative of certain groups: Norms 2 and 5 show a distribution with regressive effect on the income distribution, norm 3 with a progressive effect, and norm 4 with a proportional effect. Norm 1 is in the latter group, too (with a proportion of 0.0 in tax savings).

Table 10. Distribution of IPG and Taxes under Norm 5

Income Class		Vertical Equity Weights	IPG's under Norm 5				Tax under Norm 5			
			Absolute (Millions)	%	Cum. %	Per Tax Unit	Absolute (Millions)	%	Cum. %	Per Tax Unit
Under 0		14,288.5833	.027	.00	.00	.06	.021	.00	.00	.06
0—	600	128.9105	24.715	.04	.04	7.07	21.782	.04	.04	6.23
600—	1,000	19.2577	133.835	.21	.25	47.34	117.880	.21	.25	41.69
1,000—	1,500	10.6531	320.758	.50	.75	85.57	282.488	.50	.75	75.37
1,500—	2,000	7.2425	481.240	.75	1.50	125.87	423.889	.75	1.50	110.86
2,000—	2,500	5.4046	557.026	.87	2.37	168.67	490.626	.87	2.37	149.06
2,500—	3,000	4.2993	656.307	1.03	3.40	212.04	581.057	1.03	3.40	186.75
3,000—	3,500	3.4653	812.156	1.27	4.67	263.07	715.304	1.27	4.67	231.70
3,500—	4,000	2.9068	867.133	1.36	6.02	313.61	763.761	1.36	6.03	276.21
4,000—	4,500	2.4940	1,069.127	1.67	7.69	365.52	941.650	1.67	7.70	321.94
4,500—	5,000	2.1902	1,123.992	1.76	9.45	416.22	989.978	1.76	9.46	366.60
5,000—	6,000	1.8363	2,388.850	3.73	13.18	496.44	2,104.022	3.74	13.20	437.24
6,000—	7,000	1.4802	3,036.753	4.75	17.93	615.87	2,674.677	4.75	17.94	542.44
7,000—	8,000	1.1958	3,568.616	5.58	23.50	762.32	3,143.100	5.58	23.52	671.43
8,000—	9,000	1.0196	3,994.469	6.24	29.75	894.11	3,518.147	6.25	29.77	787.50
9,000—	10,000	.8934	3,903.999	6.10	35.85	1,020.42	3,438.507	6.10	35.87	898.75
10,000—	11,000	.7772	3,938.767	6.16	42.00	1,172.97	3,469.119	6.16	42.03	1,033.11
11,000—	12,000	.6810	3,255.540	5.09	47.09	1,338.64	2,867.367	5.09	47.12	1,179.02
12,000—	13,000	.6038	2,859.797	4.47	51.56	1,509.90	2,518.804	4.47	51.59	1,329.86
13,000—	14,000	.5360	2,480.737	3.88	55.44	1,700.68	2,184.896	3.88	55.47	1,497.76
14,000—	15,000	.4814	2,368.166	3.70	59.14	1,893.80	2,085.753	3.70	59.17	1,667.96
15,000—	20,000	.3792	6,234.353	9.74	68.88	2,404.33	5,490.766	9.75	68.92	2,117.55
20,000—	25,000	.2571	3,007.397	4.70	73.58	3,545.98	2,648.735	4.70	73.62	3,123.08
25,000—	50,000	.1365	7,190.106	11.24	84.82	6,678.39	6,332.199	11.24	84.86	5,881.53
50,000—	100,000	.0553	4,298.623	6.72	91.54	16,475.69	3,785.449	6.72	91.58	14,508.81
100,000—	150,000	.0261	1,465.223	2.29	93.83	34,887.10	1,289.591	2.29	93.87	30,704.67
150,000—	200,000	.0172	700.498	1.09	94.92	52,907.72	616.307	1.09	94.97	46,550.07
200,000—	500,000	.0097	1,502.870	2.35	97.27	94,076.37	1,323.281	2.35	97.31	82,832.97
500,000—1,000,000		.0039	639.062	1.00	98.27	235,555.56	562.827	1.00	98.31	207,455.57
Over 1,000,000		.0011	1,081.375	1.69	99.96	836,330.28	950.005	1.69	100.00	734,729.90
Total			63,988.705	100.00			56,331.988	100.00		

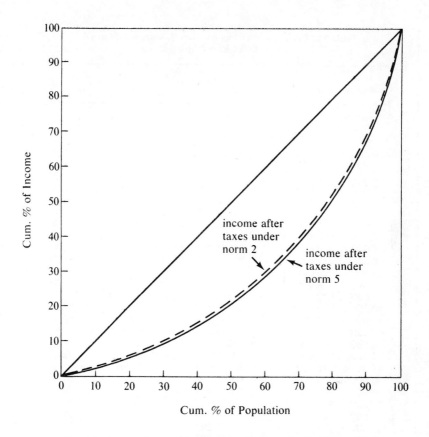

Figure 2. Lorenz Curve of Income after Taxes under Norm 5 and Income after Taxes under Norm 2 (Broken Line)

Conclusion

An examination of the individual income tax system lends support to the assertion that the federal government disperses a sizable amount of money through implicit public grants (or tax expenditures). Under present law implicit public grants provide a vehicle of redistribution to the wealthy.

If we accept the nominal progressivity of Schedule 1 as an aggregate reflection of the public decision makers' equity judgment and if the desired tax yield falls short of the amount collectible under nominal tax rates, we would have an infinite number of ways to distribute this surplus. In the absence of an empirically derived social equity function of the community at large, the isolation of any one norm has to be speculative and conditional.

In view of the fact that one important purpose of the tax-cum-expenditure process is a redistribution to low-income groups, it seems somewhat bewildering that more than one half of the nominal tax yield is devoted to redistribution to

Table 11. Distribution of Income after Taxes under Norm 5
by Income Class

Income Class		Absolute (Millions)	%	Cum. %
Under 0		−1820.848	−.41	−.41
0	600	1208.200	.27	−.14
600	1,000	2181.246	.49	.35
1,000	1,500	4391.724	.99	1.34
1,500−	2,000	6238.348	1.41	2.75
2,000−	2,500	6907.807	1.56	4.30
2,500	3,000	7929.174	1.79	6.09
3,000−	3,500	9323.198	2.10	8.19
3,500	4,000	9542.127	2.15	10.34
4,000	4,500	11551.163	2.60	12.94
4,500−	5,000	11852.992	2.67	15.61
5,000−	6,000	24471.601	5.51	21.12
6 000	7,000	29282.451	6.60	21.72
7,000−	8,000	32114.109	7.23	34.95
8,000−	9,000	34477.981	7.77	42.71
9,000−	10,000	32826.019	7.39	50.11
10,000	11,000	31625.471	7.12	57.23
11,000 −	12,000	25095.817	5.65	62.88
12,000−	13,000	21122.077	4.76	67.64
13,000−	14,000	17486.420	3.94	71.58
14,000−	15,000	16007.963	3.61	75.18
15,000	20,000	38570.511	8.69	83.87
20,000−	25,000	16158.178	3.64	87.51
25,000−	50,000	30086.999	6.78	94.28
50,000−	100,000	13429.511	3.02	97.30
100,000	150,000	3733.419	.84	98.15
150,000−	200,000	1651.897	.37	98.52
200,000−	500,000	3243.388	.73	99.25
500,000−1,000,000		1274.182	.29	99.53
Over 1,000,000		2046.726	.46	100.00
Total		444009.825	100.00	

the wealthy. However, a particular normative view of taxes and tax expenditures may explain (norm 5).

We can conceive alternative allocations of these $64 billion made in 1965. These are based on a more general consideration of the purpose of the tax-cum-expenditure system rather than a specific tie with taxation alone. Possibilities include a negative income tax for low-income groups.

In summary we conclude that, although we could advance an equity rationale for the present distribution of implicit public grants, the present pattern seems to violate rather flagrantly the purpose of redistribution.

On the other hand we can evaluate implicit public grants against norms other than equity: Although they appear to violate several of the equity norms described in this paper, we justify such grants, at least in part, on the basis of other social and economic criteria.

Appendix: Computation of Taxes under
Alternative Norms

Norm 1:   Items in Table 1 are disallowed and taxes are computed thereafter.

Norm 2:   1965 law

Norm 3:   Total implicit public grants under 1965 law (*IPG*) are divided by population (*P*) to yield: $\overline{IPG} = (IPG)/P$ (implicit public grants per tax unit). Average tax for the ith income class under norm 3 ($\overline{T}^{(3)}$) is obtained by subtracting $\overline{IPG}$ from the average nominal tax for the ith income class ($\overline{NT}_i$):

$$\overline{T}_i^{(3)} = \overline{NT}_i - \overline{IPG}.$$

Income class totals are:

$$T_i^{(3)} = NT_i - n_i\,\overline{IPG},$$

where $T_i^{(3)}NT_i$ are income class totals of tax under norm (3), and nominal tax and n_i are the number of returns in the ith income class.

Norm 4:   The ratio of implicit public grants to total income (*TY*) is computed:

$$r = \frac{IPG}{TY}.$$

Each taxpayer is allowed a reduction of 100 *r*% of his total income. Average tax for the ith income class under norm 4 ($\overline{T}^{(4)}$) equals average nominal tax of the ith income class minus average total income of the ith income class ($\overline{TY}_i$) multiplied by *r*:

$$\overline{T}_i^{(4)} = \overline{NT}_i - r\overline{TY}_{i}.$$

The income class total is

$$T_i^{(4)} = NT_i - rTY_i,$$

where $T_i^{(4)}$ and TY_i are tax under norm 4 paid by the ith income class and TY_i is the share of total income belonging to the ith income class.

Norm 5:   The vertical equity weights w_i implicit in the nominal progressivity of Schedule 1 are obtained by dividing the overall mean nominal tax NT by the income class average $\overline{NT}_i$:

$$w_i = \overline{NT}/\overline{NT}_i.$$

Average implicit public grants for the ith income class under norm 5 are computed as:

$$\overline{IPG}_i^{(5)} = \overline{IPG}/w_i.$$

The income class total $(IPG_i{}^{(5)})$ is computed as:

$$IPG_i{}^{(5)} = n_i(\overline{IPG}/w_i),$$

Where symbols bear the same meaning as above.

The average tax under norm 5 of the ith income class equals:

$$\overline{T}_i{}^{(5)} = \overline{NT}_i - \overline{IPG}_i{}^{(5)}.$$

The total tax burden of the ith income class is computed as:

$$T_i{}^{(5)} = NT_i - IPG_i{}^{(5)}.$$

12

Henry Aaron: Implicit Transfers to
Homeowners in the Federal Budget

Most Americans are generally believed to want their own home. Whether this belief is correct, without doubt the federal government has encouraged homeownership. The chief instrument is the federal personal income tax, By favorable personal income tax treatment of income from homeownership, the federal government implicitly transfers $7–9 billion to homeowners. In addition, the Federal Housing Administration and the Veterans' Administration provide approved lenders with default protection. This default protection enables homebuyers to obtain mortgages with lower downpayments and longer repayment periods than they could obtain without default protection.

Section I of this paper describes more fully the income tax benefits to homeowners. Section II goes into the value to the borrower of FHA and VA insurance. Section III raises some conceptual issues surrounding the estimates contained in Section II. Section IV presents some alternative policies suggested by the results of Sections I and II.

Presented at the Symposium on the Grants Economy held between the Association for the Study of the Grants Economy and the American Association for the Advancement of Science in December, 1969, in Boston, Mass. All rights reserved. Used by permission of the author.

The Brookings Institution, and Department of Economics, University of Maryland. The views expressed are those of the author and do not purport to represent the views of the other staff members, officers, or trustees of The Brookings Institution or the University of Maryland.

I

A homeowner occupant has a dual role – property owner and tenant. For tax purposes he keeps a single set of books, recording his transactions, as tenant or owner. As a result he will not record certain *implicit* transactions between tenant and owner. If he were required to keep one set of books as a property owner and another as a tenant, his books as a property owner would include gross rental income from the owned home and such deductible expenses as mortgage interest, property taxes, depreciation, and maintenance. Gross rent less these deductions, net rental income, would measure income from home-ownership. Net rent would be added to other income the property owner might have earned from other investments or from wages and salaries in reaching taxable income. If such separate bookkeeping were enforced, if the rent accurately measured the market value of the services of the house, and if equivalent security of tenure could be obtained, the person would remain a homeowner only so long as his after-tax income on his investment was not less than the after-tax income (adjusted for risk) he could earn on other investments. If alternative investments had higher yields, he could sell his house, retain occupancy or obtain similar housing at the same rent, and increase his investment income. House prices and rents would reflect this choice.[1]

The item imputed as income – net rent (NR) – is equal to gross rent (GR) less maintenance expense (M), depreciation (D), mortgage interest (I), and property and other indirect taxes (T) levied on the homeowner. If he were treated as other businesses, the homeowner would be required to report GR as income and would be permitted business deductions in the amount ($M + D + I + T$), generating income, positive or negative, of NR on which he would be required to pay tax. In fact, the homeowner is not required to report GR, but he is allowed deductions in the amount ($I + T$). Current tax treatment thus understates taxable income relative to other asset holders by ($NR + I + T$) = ($GR - M - D$).

Transfers – Ex post

Disallowance of deductions for mortgage interest would have raised revenues in 1966 by $1.5 billion; disallowance of deductions for property taxes would have raised revenues by $1.5 billion; disallowance of both deductions would have raised revenue by $2.9 billion[2]; inclusion in income of imputed net rent at 4 percent (6 percent) on owner's equity would raise revenues by $4.0

---

1 That imputed income from homeownership is real income properly subject to tax is well established. See [5, 17].

2 The Treasury Department [1] estimates that the revenue consequences of disallowing deductions for mortgage interest and property taxes would have raised revenues by $3.7 billion in 1968 and would raise them by approximately $4.8 billion in 1970.

Table 1. Change in Tax Collections Per Family from Inclusion in Adjusted Gross Income of Imputed Net Rent on Owner-Occupied Houses and Disallowance of Deductions for Mortgage Interest and Property Taxes, Change in Tax as Percent of Income, and Tax as Percent of Income, by Total Income Class[a]

$ = Average change in tax from current law per family in dollars
% = Average change in tax as percent of average total income
T = Tax as percent of total income under reformed law

	Total Income Mass									Total Tax Savings
	$0–3,000	$3,000–5,000	$5,000–7,000	$7,000–10,000	$10,000–15,000	$15,000–25,000	$25,000–50,000	$50,000–100,000	$100,000–9,999,999	(Millions of $)
All Returns										
Δ$	17	40	70	128	236	439	938	1,467	2,864	9,028
Δ%	1.2	1.0	1.2	1.5	2.0	2.4	2.8	2.2	1.3	
T	4.9	7.7	9.2	10.4	12.4	15.1	19.9	26.7	30.1	
Homeowners										
Δ$	59	107	119	181	292	513	1,053	1,592	3,024	9,028
Δ%	3.6	2.7	2.0	2.1	2.4	2.8	3.1	2.4	1.3	
T	6.1	7.6	9.1	10.3	12.3	15.0	20.0	26.8	30.2	
(A) Nonaged										
Δ$	62	108	117	181	293	518	1,059	1,531	2,831	8,255
Δ%	3.9	2.7	1.9	2.1	2.4	2.8	3.1	2.3	1.3	
T	6.7	8.2	9.2	10.4	12.3	15.1	20.1	27.0	30.0	
(1) Itemized										
Δ$	104	128	150	210	322	540	1,089	1,563	2,868	6,548
Δ%	8.3	3.1	2.5	2.4	2.6	2.9	3.2	2.4	1.3	
T	16.1	7.7	8.2	9.8	12.0	14.9	20.0	26.9	29.9	

Total Income Mass

	$0–3,000	$3,000–5,000	$5,000–7,000	$7,000–10,000	$10,000–15,000	$15,000–25,000	$25,000–50,000	$50,000–100,000	$100,000–9,999,999	Total Tax Savings (Millions of $)
(2) Standard Deduction										
Δ$	58	96	91	131	198	349	684	819	1,415	1,707
Δ%	3.6	2.4	1.5	1.6	1.7	2.0	2.0	1.3	0.8	
T	6.1	8.5	10.0	11.3	13.4	16.2	21.8	28.2	28.5	
(B) Aged										
Δ$	39	102	132	190	263	425	1,010	1,837	3,473	773
Δ%	2.1	2.7	2.2	2.3	2.2	2.3	3.0	2.7	1.4	
T	2.9	5.2	7.6	9.8	12.0	14.0	19.4	26.0	30.9	
(1) Itemized										
Δ$	72	102	143	207	288	454	1,024	1,863	3,505	662
Δ%	3.4	2.6	2.4	2.5	2.4	2.4	3.0	2.8	1.4	
T	4.6	5.0	7.3	9.3	11.7	13.9	19.4	26.1	31.0	
(2) Standard Deduction										
Δ$	27	103	88	132	188	310	840	1,057	1,671	111
Δ%	1.6	2.7	1.4	1.6	1.6	1.7	2.7	1.5	0.9	
T	2.2	5.6	8.7	11.7	12.7	14.5	19.1	22.1	24.2	

Source: The Brookings Institution Tax File. Estimating methods available from author on request.

a Total income equals adjusted gross income plus excluded dividends, excluded sick pay, and imputed net rent. Capital gains and losses are included in income in full in the year realized, but no losses carried forward from previous years are deducted. Total income does not include unrealized capital gains, tax exempt interest, or the excess of percentage over cost depletion on income from natural resources.

billion ($6.0 billion); and disallowance of both deductions and inclusion of imputed rent would raise revenue by $7.0 billion ($9.0 billion).[3]

Table 1 shows the distribution of tax benefits to homeowners in 1966 (assuming a 6 percent yield on equity in owned homes). The benefits are distributed among homeowners categorized in nine income brackets, two age groups (65 or over and under 65), and two filing classes (itemized deductions and standard deductions). The value of tax concessions to homeowners ranges from an average of $27 for aged taxpayers in the lowest income bracket, on the basis of the standard deduction to $3,505 for aged taxpayers in the highest income bracket who take itemized deductions. The range across income brackets for the nonaged is nearly as great. The tax benefits as a fraction of income are highest for taxpayers in the bottom brackets, which include disproportionate numbers of taxpayers whose incomes are temporarily depressed. Their housing outlays, to which tax benefits are related, depend at least partly on their normal income. Through the broad middle income range, from $5,000 to $50,000, which includes 72.8 percent of all taxpayers, tax benefits as a fraction of income rise with income.

Adjustments

Table 1 shows the distribution of tax benefits after market behavior and housing prices have adjusted to the tax benefits. These adjustments cannot be sorted out from other activity in housing markets. Nevertheless, some insights are possible. Let us ignore temporarily the effects of tax benefits on rental properties (principally excess depreciation deductions). Tax benefits to homeowners have induced some households to become homeowners who otherwise would have rented and have encouraged consumption of more housing than would have been consumed in the absence of these tax benefits. If resources can freely enter and leave the homebuilding industry as Muth [13] suggests, then tax incentives have not affected construction costs even though they raised housing consumption. If supply is not infinitely elastic even in the long run, then prices for all housing must have risen. The proportion of owned rather than rented housing has increased, and total housing consumption has also increased. The size of the shift between renting and owning depends on the cross-price elasticity

---

3 Even the 4 percent yield implies imputed net rent far in excess of the amounts reported in the national income accounts ($21.2 billion versus $12.1 billion in 1966). Yields on long-term government bonds, high-grade corporate securities, and mortgages were much above 4 percent throughout 1966 and have remained high since then. Consequently tabulations presented here embody the 6 percent assumption. Those who find the 6 percent estimate implausibly high may reduce the reported estimates. More detailed estimates showing separately the distribution of benefits from deductibility of mortgage interest and of property taxes and the exclusion of imputed rent are available from the author on request.

of demand between owning and renting.[4] The size of the increase in housing consumption will depend on the price elasticity of demand for housing and on the size of the price reduction represented by tax benefits.

No estimates have been made of the cross-price elasticity of demand between owning and renting. Estimates of the aggregate price elasticity of demand for housing range between -1.0 and -1.5;[5] that is, a drop in the price of housing services by 10 percent will cause consumption of housing services to rise by 10 to 15 percent. None of the cited studies contain estimates of price elasticities of different socioeconomic groups. Moreover, the accuracy of the estimates declines as one moves away from observed price levels.

Table 2 shows how much tax benefits reduce gross rent. The size of the price reduction depends on the marginal tax rate to which the taxpayer is subject and the proportion of gross rent that consists of tax favored items (see note to Table 2). According to Shelton [15] tax favored items constitute from three eighths to five eighths of gross rent for most properties. The fraction may well rise with income, because land, which depreciates less than structures, constitutes a larger proportion of total property value on high-priced than on

Table 2. Subsidy as a Percent of Gross Rent[a]

Imputed Rent Plus Deductible Expenses as a Fraction of Gross Rent	Tax Brackets				
	14%	20%	30%	50%	70%
$1/8$	1.8	2.5	3.8	6.2	8.8
$1/4$	3.5	5.0	7.5	12.5	17.5
$3/8$	5.2	7.5	11.2	18.8	26.2
$1/2$	7.0	10.0	15.0	25.0	35.0
$5/8$	8.8	12.5	18.8	31.2	43.8
$3/4$	10.5	15.0	22.5	37.5	52.5
$7/8$	12.2	17.5	26.2	43.8	61.2
1	14.0	20.0	30.0	50.0	70.0

[a]Current income tax provisions understate income of homeowners by the amount $NR + I + T = GR - M - D$, and tax liability by $t(NR + I + T) = t(GR - M - D)$, where t is the marginal rate on excluded income. The size of these tax benefits as a percent of gross rent is $100 \cdot t(NR + I + T)/GR$.

4 The owner-occupant is required not only to consume housing services but also to maintain, bear risk, and accept a return on investment in exchange for favorable tax treatment. Because the homeowner and the tenant receive different bundles of utilities, we speak of a cross-elasticity.

5 See, for example [9, pp. 72–75; 14, p. 381; 13, pp. 85–87; and 7, pp. 76–77]. The dependent variables in these studies are per capita net new construction of nonfarm housing [13], real households expenditure on rent [14], per family gross real nonfarm residential construction [9], per capita real rental value of owner-occupied housing [7]. The price variables are the Boeckh index of residential construction costs – brick [9, 13], the rent component of the consumer price index [14], the implicit price deflator for imputed rent divided by the implicit price deflator for personal consumption expenditures [7].

low-priced structures. Table 2 indicates that the size of the price effect of tax benefits is acutely sensitive (in fact, proportional) to the marginal effective tax rate. The plausible range of implicit subsidies to homeowners runs from about 5 percent of gross rent in the lowest income brackets to more than 50 percent in the highest brackets. Of course, the subsidy to households with no taxable income is zero.

The estimates of the subsidy value of favorable tax treatment of income from homeownership suggest that these tax factors will raise consumption of housing services by varying amounts, depending on the tax bracket of the homeowner. If we accept previously estimated elasticities as applicable to each income class, we can estimate the increases in demand by multiplying the figures in Table 2 by 1.0 to 1.5. Price elasticities of demand for housing may differ among income brackets, however. Unless elasticities of lower-income households vastly exceed those of upper-income households, the current tax treatment of income from homeownership raises the housing consumption of upper-income households, in both relative and absolute terms, by much more than that of lower-income households.

The shift from renting to homeownership is offset, but the increase in general demand for housing services is reinforced, by tax provisions which favor investment in rental property. The major provisions concern deductions for depreciation. Investment in rental housing is encouraged to the extent that the excess on rental property of deductible depreciation over true depreciation is greater than the excess on other depreciable assets of deductible depreciation over true depreciation. Table 3 shows the value of excess depreciation on real estate if actual tax deductible depreciation on other assets happens to equal true depreciation. As is apparent, the tax benefits on rental property may approach those on homes owned by middle-bracket taxpayers only if true depreciation is nearly zero on rental housing, if rental properties are owned by taxpayers

Table 3. Subsidy Equivalent of Tax Benefits from Excess Depreciation[a] on Rental Property as Percent of Gross Rent

True Depreciation	Marginal Tax Bracket			
	14	25	50	70
4.5%	0	0	0	0
4.0	0.4	0.8	1.6	2.2
3.0	1.3	2.3	4.7	6.6
2.0	2.2	3.9	7.8	10.9
1.0	3.1	5.5	10.9	15.3
0.0	3.9	7.0	14.1	19.7

[a]Property is assumed to be useful for forty years. Gross rents are assumed to equal 16 percent of market price. Depreciation at double-declining balance is taken to be the unweighted, undiscounted average of the first five years, 4.5 percent. Estimates assume no recovery of excess depreciation through income taxation at time of later sale.

subject to rates near 70 percent, and if deductible depreciation equals true depreciation on other assets. Under no circumstances can tax benefits on rental properties approach those for high-bracket homeowners.

II

The federal government protects lenders from losses due to defaults on certain mortgages. The largest such programs are the basic program of mortgage insurance administered by the Federal Housing Administration (FHA)[6] and loan guarantees offered to home buying veterans by the Veterans' Administration.[7]

The FHA charges one-half percent per year of the outstanding mortgage balance for this default protection. The VA charges a one-time rate of one-half percent of the loan when it guarantees the loan for veterans who served after 1955 or for servicemen; other veterans are charged nothing. The terms of FHA mortgage insurance and the manner in which it covers losses differ somewhat from those of VA loan guarantees.[8] There is no clear consensus as to which form of default protection gives greater assurance against loss to lenders.

The availability of such default protection is widely credited with the liberalization in mortgage terms that has occurred in the United States since the 1920s and 1930s. This liberalization has resulted in longer repayment periods and lower downpayments and virtually no change in mortgage payments relative to income between 1920 and the present (compare lines 1 and 4, Table 4). During this period, terms on conventional loans (those without government default protection) have also been liberalized but to a much smaller extent.

The degree to which FHA and VA have caused this liberalization is not clear. On the one hand, reduced economic instability in the form of less variation in unemployment and income has diminished the real probability of default. The government's commitment to sustain prosperity may also have affected subjective concern of lenders about depression. For these reasons, we would expect some liberalization in mortgage terms to have occurred even without government default protection. On the other hand, FHA and VA indirectly created mortgages with more liberal terms than were previously available. Although private mortgage insurance companies have sprung up recently and grown rapidly, none might have arisen except for the evidence of FHA's experience that mortgage insurance can be offered profitably. Even now private mortgage insurance companies might fail to offer coverage on certain classes of loans perhaps because of uncertainty regarding default risks. Whether private mortgage insurers would have arisen spontaneously, FHA and VA did offer a new service at the time of their creation. They may well have helped remove a market imperfection if there were economies of scale in the pooling of

---

6 Section 203, Public Law 479, 73d Congress, 48 Stat. 1246, 12 U.S.C., 1701 et seq., as amended.

7 Chap. 37, Title 38, U.S.C.

8 For a discussion of these differences, see [4, 6, 10].

Table 4. Relation of Downpayment and Monthly Payments to Annual Income (Price of House Equals Two and One-Half Times Annual Income)

Type of Loan	Downpayment	Annual Mortgage Payments
	(as Percent of Annual Income)	
1. Savings and Loan Association, 1920s L/V = .6; repayment period 11 years fully amortized	100	20.0
2. Banks and Insurance Companies, 1920s L/V = .5; repayment period 5 years unamortized	125	7.5 + 125.0 in fifth year
3. Conventional mortgage, 1960s L/V = .75; repayment period 20 years fully amortized	62.5	17.7
4. FHA mortgage, 1960s L/V = .95; repayment period 30 years fully amortized	12.5	20.1

Note: A "base" interest rate of 7 percent is used for lines 1 and 3. Because interest rates on mortgages held by banks and insurance companies ran about one percent below those held by savings and loan associations, a 6 percent interest rate is used. Since FHA charges a 0.5 percent insurance premium, a 7.5 percent interest rate is used for line 4.

mortgage risks that most lenders were too small or too ill-informed to capture. This paper does not attempt to evaluate the historical importance of FHA and VA in this respect. Rather it focuses on the implicit subsidy offered through government default protection, where the subsidy is the estimated difference between actuarial cost of default protection and the cost to lender or borrower of such protection. This definition is quite narrow since it excludes increases in consumer surplus that would be generated if default protection, offered at actuarial cost, removed market imperfections.

The probability of default and the size of the lender's loss in case of default depend on certain characteristics of the borrower and on the terms of the mortgage. Some of the more important factors are the income and wealth of the borrower, his occupation, the ratio of the loan to the value of collateral (the loan—value ratio, or L/V), and the term of the loan.[9] For example, loans with high L/V, loans to borrowers with low or irregular income, and loans with lengthy repayment periods tend to have relatively high default rates and relatively large losses in case of default.[10] The actuarial cost of default protection varies among loan classes. Nevertheless, as noted earlier, FHA and VA each charge the same amount to all borrowers within each program (except for the difference between veterans who served before 1955 and others eligible for VA guarantees). Accordingly, some loan categories must be receiving positive or

9 Other factors such as property location are believed to influence default risk. Other explanations of the practice of "red lining" may also occur to the reader.

10 On this subject, see [3, 4].

negative subsidies. The difference between the average cost of insuring a category of loans and the total premiums paid for such insurance represents an implicit subsidy if the difference is known to exist. In precisely the same sense, an implicit subsidy could be given through life insurance if twenty-five and fifty year olds were charged the same amount for term life insurance. To calculate the implicit subsidy on default protection, we must know the actuarial cost of default protection for each class. Full actuarial calculations are enormously laborious. They are also highly uncertain with respect to mortgage defaults, because such future economic contingencies as rates of unemployment and inflation are major determinants of mortgage defaults. Hence I have estimated the implicit subsidy for different loan classes under the assumption that FHA's one-half percent insurance fees in the aggregate just equal the aggregate actuarial cost of default protection.[11] The relative default rates and relative costs per default have been computed for eighty FHA loan categories, defined on the income of the borrower (ten classes), the L/V (four classes), for new and existing one- to four-family houses, from data compiled by Von Furstenberg [3, 4] (see Table 5). This functional relationship relating default rate to L/V and income of borrower was assumed to apply also to VA guaranteed loans.[12]

The subsidy (positive or negative) will accrue to the borrower if markets for home mortgage credit are reasonably competitive. In that case, lenders would charge borrowers the opportunity cost of loanable funds plus a risk premium based on default experience. If unusual profits were earned on a certain class of loans, perhaps because the government was absorbing default risk worth more than the premium charged for default protection, competition among borrowers would lower the interest rate. The power of custom in financial markets and the lack of good data on the determinants of default risks suggest that competition may not quickly remove any extraordinary profits. Nevertheless the following tables are computed on the presumption that subsidies accrue to borrowers.

Tables 6 and 7 show income redistribution in 1966 through FHA and VA default protection. If FHA is actuarially sound, then no redistribution occurs between users and nonusers of FHA mortgage insurance. Redistribution among users occurs because the same premiums are charged borrowers with widely different default risks. The amount of redistribution is modest in the aggregate. Even at the two extremes of the income distribution, the positive or negative

---

11 This assumption is questionable for two conflicting reasons. On the one hand, FHA has accumulated substantial and growing reserves, which have been judged adequate to meet conditions of all but the most severe depressions. On the other hand, since the last independent evaluation of the adequacy of FHA financing [2], L/Vs have risen markedly and repayment periods have lengthened. This liberalization in terms has occurred partly because of changes in the law governing FHA and partly because private mortgage insurers have begun to compete with FHA for relatively low L/V mortgages. In addition, rising real-estate prices have held down default rates. We may expect that as inflation is brought under control, default rates will increase without further liberalization in terms.

12 The L/V for VA loans is not directly comparable to the L/V on FHA insured mortgages. The FHA appraised value includes estimated closing costs; the VA appraisals do not. The estimates reported in this paper are adjusted for this difference.

Table 5. Index of Relative Default Probabilities[a]

Income/L/V	Less than $4,000	$4,000–4,999	$5,000–5,999	$6,000–6,999	$7,000–7,999	$8,000–8,999	$9,000–9,999	$10,000–11,999	$12,000–14,999	$15,000 and over
					New					
.76—.89	39	36	33	31	30	28	27	26	24	22
.90—.92	54	50	46	44	41	40	38	36	34	31
.93—.95	71	65	60	57	54	51	49	47	44	40
.96—.97	100	91	85	80	76	73	70	66	62	57
					Existing					
.76—.89	26	25	23	22	21	20	20	19	18	17
.90—.92	35	33	31	29	28	27	26	25	24	22
.93—.95	44	41	38	37	35	34	33	31	30	28
.96—.97	59	55	52	49	47	46	44	42	40	37

[a]Index = 100 for mortgage class with L/V = .96—.97, Y < $4,000.
Estimating methods available from author on request.

Table 6. Income Redistribution through Home Mortgage Insurance
by FHA Under Section 203, 1966

Income Class	Assumption A Actuarial Soundness		Assumption B 20% Actuarial Deficit		Assumption C 20% Actuarial Surplus	
	Total ($000)	Per Household	Total ($000)	Per Household	Total ($000)	Per Household
Less than $4,000	$625	$142	$1,029	$233	$220	$50
4,000– 4,999	2,194	137	3,802	237	587	37
5,000– 5,999	4,310	110	8,278	211	341	9
6,000– 6,999	5,528	82	12,680	187	−1,623	−24
7,000– 7,999	2,760	46	9,179	152	−3,658	−61
8,000- 8,999	416	9	5,361	114	−4,529	-97
9,000– 9,999	−1,669	−36	3,101	66	−6,438	−138
10,000–11,999	−4,556	−86	677	13	-9,788	−185
12,000–14,999	-6,033	−172	−2,670	−76	-0,396	-268
15,000 and over	−3,574	−263	−2,378	−175	−4,773	−352
All classes			39,059	+102	-39,059	−102

Table 7. Income Redistribution through VA Loan Guarantee Program
for Those Who Paid a Fee, Those Who Paid No Fee; and
Total Averages, 1966

Income Class	Total		Without Fee		With Fee	
	($000)	Per Household	($000)	Per Household	($000)	Per Household
Less than 4,000	$1,922	$261	$1,371	$280	$551	$225
4,000–4,999	9,011	332	6,383	353	2,628	290
5,000- 5,999	16,485	430	11,602	454	4,883	382
6,000- 6,999	15,488	508	10,905	536	4,583	451
7,000- 7,999	12,530	599	8,789	631	3,741	537
8,000–8,999	8,838	662	6,193	696	2,645	595
9,000 and over	15,030	778	10,511	816	4,519	701
Total	79,304	505	55,754	533	23,550	450

subsidies amount to only a small fraction of housing costs. These subsidies accrue at the time a loan is negotiated; they are not repeated annually for each cohort of borrowers as a tax benefit to homeowners. VA loan guarantees redistribute income from nonusers to users because the charge for the guarantee is nominal. For the same reason, the per-household transfer under VA is considerably larger than under FHA (see Table 7).

III

The foregoing estimates of income redistribution may be misleading in two major respects. First, the implicit transfers to homeowners through the tax system are based on revenue consequences of altering certain provisions, without allowance for the adjustments in demand for housing in general and in demand for owner occupancy in particular. Similarly the measures for redistribution through FHA and VA estimate what budget costs would be if the government engaged in accrual accounting of actuarial liabilities, again without allowance for the market responses that would occur if these programs did not exist.

The market adjustments to subsidies or taxes may have brought major distributional consequences of their own. Because the provision of housing services is a highly capital intensive industry, policies that encourage consumption of housing relative to other commodities require reduction in capital labor ratios in all industries if the output mix changes in response to incentives.[13] This adjustment increases yields on capital relative to wages and salaries on labor. Accordingly, policies that encourage consumption of housing raise incomes of owners of capital relative to income of recipients of wage and salary income. Such changes in income will affect everyone, whether they directly benefit from tax benefits to homeowners or from VA or FHA loan guarantees. Furthermore, because housing is highly capital-intensive, incentives to the consumption of housing services tend to raise the cost of housing (exclusive of incentives) relative to the cost of other, less capital-intensive goods. For renting households, therefore, incentives to homeownership raise housing costs. Whether complementary tax benefits on rental property offset this effect is a topic for useful further research.

Second, the phrase *income redistribution* is somewhat ambiguous when benefits are in-kind or tied to the purchase of specific goods. In particular, although prices may continue to measure marginal cost in the general market, they no longer reflect marginal rates of substitution of consumers.

As always in cases involving price change, we may value the change in consumption caused by a subsidy at the prices including subsidy, which consumers actually face (and hence measure marginal rates of substitution), or at prices excluding subsidy, which producers face (and hence measure marginal rates of transformation).

Let AB be a budget line reflecting the market price of housing and the marginal rate of substitution of housing for income in the absence of any subsidy; OX units of housing are consumed. As a result of a housing subsidy, the budget line shifts to AC and households move to point E. Given the marginal rate of substitution between housing and income at E, the income value of the subsidy is DA. The value of the subsidy at the marginal rate of transformation represented by line AB is AF, which necessarily exceeds AD. Accordingly the income value to homeowners of favorable tax treatment on income from homeownership or of subsidized default protection is smaller than the cost estimates that this paper presents. The difference, representing deadweight loss, is not estimated here.[14] A measurement of deadweight loss derived in this

---

13 For the theory underlying this section, see [11]. For an illustration of its possible quantitative significance, see [12].

14 For such estimates see [8, 16].

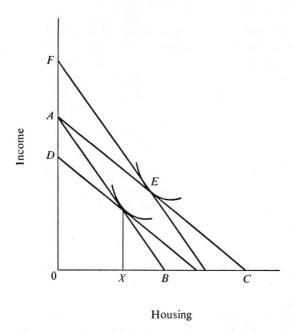

Housing

fashion would be incomplete, however, to the extent that it ignores real external benefits or costs from housing consumption.

Despite these shortcomings, estimates of the implicit subsidies represented by tax treatment of homeowners and by default protection not provided at cost are useful because we can compare them to direct government expenditures undertaken to increase the quantity and quality of housing and to redistribute income. In 1966 direct expenditures on Housing and Community Development were $3.4 billion, much less than the implicit transfers estimated here. Direct budget expenditures only partially, and sometimes deceptively, describe government efforts to achieve particular objectives.[15] They are particularly deficient in the case of housing.

IV

This paper is intended primarily to describe and measure certain implicit transfers. Nevertheless, we might briefly consider their efficiency in achieving public objectives; particularly, because of their "implicitness" they are not subject to scrutiny as regularly as are explicit budget outlays.

With respect to any conceivable policy objective, the pattern of tax benefits seems to be capricious and without rationale. Apart from the alleged, but unsubstantiated, benefits accruing to the community when households purchase their own homes, there appears to be no reason for subsidizing homeownership

---

15 For an effort to relate direct expenditures and tax provisions with similar objectives, see [1].

rather than other investments or for the consumption of housing services rather than the consumption of other commodities. Even if we acknowledge that homeownership benefits society by making homeowners more stable or less antisocial than they otherwise would have been, the *pattern* of tax benefits is ill suited to that objective. Tax benefits provide largest benefits to recipients of larger than average income whose experience with wealth is typically not limited to their own houses. They provide negligible aid to low-income households, most of whom have not experienced the salutary discipline of property management.

A clearly preferable course would be to tax income from homeownership as other income is taxed – through disallowance of deductions for mortgage interest and property taxes paid and inclusion in taxable income of net imputed rent – and to use the proceeds to promote housing expenditures or encourage homeownership in some less bizarre pattern, or to advance other public objectives.[16]

Other questions arise with respect to the provision of default protection. What public objective does the government provision of default protection preserve at actuarial cost? Why should the premium be the same for classes of loans with radically different risks?[17] With respect to the first question, much the same objective – perfecting a market where information is crucial and scarce – could be accomplished through a program with premiums set equal to actuarial cost in each loan category. With respect to the second question, what objective is served through the redistribution of income among users of the FHA program is not clear. Unless there is a persuasive answer, the FHA should charge a premium for default protection related to actual risk on each category of loans; because risk differs, so would premiums.

The implicit subsidy through VA loan guarantees, like other veterans' benefits, presumably results from the desire to make partial financial amends to men who were forced involuntarily into a socially useful, but underpaid, occupation. Why veterans who own their residence deserve such a subsidy, whereas veterans who rent their residence do not, is far from clear. Why the subsidy should be tied to housing or even more to loans secured for houses veterans occupy is equally obscure.[18]

In summary, this paper has estimated implicit subsidies in two federal programs that provide implicit transfers to homeowners.[19] Tax benefits to homeowners dwarf all other housing policies. Default protection serves to

---

16 Measurement of imputed net rent for tax purposes is difficult but administratively feasible. Perhaps the easiest way would be to subtract from appraised market value all house debts and multiply that difference by the estimated rate of return. Whether we should take into account debt repayment terms is a difficult question. This course would require considerable improvement in property appraisals. For a somewhat fuller discussion of these issues, see [5].

17 The subject here is the basic program of mortgage insurance, not the host of other mortgage insurance programs; however, similar questions can be raised in evaluating them.

18 Furthermore, the VA guarantee is transferable even if the veteran sells his home to a nonveteran.

19 I am extending this analysis to other housing programs in a manuscript now in preparation.

perfect the market for mortgage credit and may continue to do so; it also serves to transfer income to veterans and among users of FHA mortgage insurance. The case for either set of policies in terms of plausible public policy objectives seems weak.

References

1. Barr, J. "Statement of the Secretary of the Treasury Before the Joint Economic Committee." Supplement on "Tax Expenditures: Government Expenditures Made Through the Tax System," January 17, 1969.
2. Fisher, E. M., and C. Rapkin. *The Mutual Mortgage Insurance Fund: A Study of the Adequacy of Its Reserves and Resources.* New York: Columbia University Press, 1956.
3. Furstenberg, G. von. "Default Risk on FHA-Insured Mortgages as a Function of the Terms of Financing: A Quantitative Analysis." *Journal of Finance* 24, no. 3 (June 1969): 459–77. Also The Brookings Institution Reprint No. 163.
4. ————. "Mortgage Default Risk – An Analysis of the Experience of FHA and VA Home Loans During the Decade 1957–66." Unpublished manuscript.
5. Goode, R. "Imputed Rent of Owner Occupied Dwellings under the Income Tax." *Journal of Finance* 15 (December 1960): 504–30.
6. Haar, C. *Federal Credit and Private Housing.* New York: McGraw-Hill Book Co., 1960.
7. Houthakker, H., and L. Taylor. *Consumer Demand in the United States, 1929–1970 – Analysis and Projections.* Cambridge, Mass.: Harvard University Press, 1966.
8. Laidler, D. "Income Tax Incentives for Owner-Occupied Housing." In A. C. Harberger and M. J. Bailey, eds., *The Taxation of Income From Capital.* Washington, D.C.: The Brookings Institution, 1969.
9. Lee, T. "The Stock Demand Elasticities of Non-Farm Housing." *Review of Economics and Statistics* 46, no. 1 (February 1964): 82–89.
10. Maisel, S. *Financing Real Estate.* New York: McGraw-Hill Book Co., 1965.
11. Mieszkouski, P. "On the Theory of Tax Incidence." *Journal of Political Economy* 75, no. 3 (June 1967): 250–62.
12. ————, "The Property Tax: An Excise Tax or a Profits Tax." Mimeograph.
13. Muth, R. "The Demand for Non-Farm Housing." In A. C. Harberger, ed., *The Demand for Durable Goods.* Chicago: University of Chicago Press, 1960, pp. 29–96.
14. Reid, M. *Housing and Income.* Chicago: University of Chicago Press, 1962.
15. Shelton, J. "The Cost of Renting versus Owning a Home." *Land Economics* 44, no. 1 (February 1968): 59–72.
16. Tinney, R. W. "Taxing Imputed Rental Income on Owner Occupied Homes." In A. B. Willis, ed., *Studies in Substantive Tax Reform.* American Bar Foundation, 1969.
17. White, M., and A. White. "Horizontal Inequality in the Federal Income Tax Treatment of Homeowners and Tenants." *National Tax Journal* 18, no. 3 (September 1965): 225–39. Also The Brookings Institution Reprint No. 114, with additional detail.

13

Thomas Muller: Implicit Grants
to Property Owners at the Local Level:
A Case Study

Introduction

The public sector element of the grants economy at the county level is usually associated with federal and state grants to these jurisdictions or with payments such as county welfare benefits to needy individuals. Counties and municipalities also provide implicit grants to the federal and state government as well as to selected corporations and individuals in the private sector, by partially or fully exempting their property from real-estate taxes. Private sector owners of land are beneficiaries of implicit grants when local authorities are persuaded to approve more intensive use of their land. The public sector increases the value of privately held land by providing or expanding public services and facilities. However, because zoning ordinances usually constrain the type of land use, the rezoning action, which permits a more intensive land use than previously allowed, provides an immediate implicit grant. The implicit public grant element is the difference between the original land value and its increased value as a direct result of the public action.

Savings that result from nonpayment of property taxes for which individuals or enterprises in the private sector would be liable under a more general frame of legal provisions are considered to be implicit public grants.[1] In the region examined as part of this study, owners of farmland, aged owners of real property, and nonprofit enterprises including private schools are among recipients of implicit public grants. The revenue losses that result from exemptions of these and other properties are offset either by increasing the tax rate of nonexempt property owners or by reducing public services.

This study initially estimates the value of implicit grants associated with property taxes. Following this estimation is a discussion of fiscal and income distribution effects of these grants in two contiguous counties forming the state of Maryland portion of the Washington, D.C., Standard Metropolitan Statistical Area (SMSA). Montgomery County, the less populous of the two, is one of the

Presented at the Symposium on the Grants Economy held between the Association for the Study of the Grants Economy and the American Association for the Advancement of Science in December, 1969, in Boston, Mass. All rights reserved. Used by permission of the author.

1 Martin Pfaff defines this category of implicit grants in the "Association for Study of Grants Economy," Newsletter No. 1, October 15, 1969. Tax savings under federal income tax provisions noted in the newsletter are also found in the Maryland State Income Tax and the associated county income tax surtax.

highest per capita income areas in the nation. Its neighbor to the east, Prince George's County, is considerably less affluent. Both counties have undergone rapid development in the last two decades. The major employment source, however, remains the federal government, although Montgomery County has a substantial number of industrial and commercial facilities within its borders.

Value of Implicit Grants

The public sector provides implicit grants by total or partial exemption of real property from taxation as well as by zoning policies and decisions. Government and certain nonprofit property is totally exempt from taxation in all parts of the nation. In the two counties examined, as well as in a number of states and counties. Older citizens and certain veterans are partially exempt from taxes on agricultural land and property. Also, certain owners of income-producing properties are provided implicit grants as a result of assessment practices. The total value of these implicit grants in the two-county area is estimated in this section.

Fully Exempt Property

The assessed value of fully exempt property in Maryland increased from 20 percent of all property in 1966 to 23 percent in 1969. This increase is representative of other cities and regions that have reported rises in exempt property as a share of all real estate in the past decade.

Prince George's County estimates the assessed value of property in 1969 to be $813 million, or 30 percent of all exempt and nonexempt property value, considerably above the state average. Federal land and structures account for 51 percent, whereas state and local property comprise 37 percent of the total. The balance, or 12 percent, is nonprofit property owned by religious institutions, veterans and other lodges, clubs and civic organizations.

In Montgomery County, the value of exempt property has risen, sharply, from $150 million in 1963 to $547 million in 1969, twice the rate of increase in the taxable assessment base during this period. However, the exempt property represents only 17 percent of the total property value, below the state mean. The assessed value of the 36,315 acres of exempt land has been estimated at $151 million, the balance of exemptions representing improvements on this land. The federal government accounts for 45 percent and private nonprofit property 20 percent of the exempt total. Private schools, colleges, and nonprofit research facilities comprise about half the exempt property in the private sector not owned by religious institutions. The distribution of tax-exempt property varies considerably within the county. Thus, in the highly urbanized Wheaton district only 11 percent of the tax base is exempt, whereas in the Gaithersburg district, which includes the Federal Bureau of Standards complex, 46 percent of the property is tax exempt.

For purposes of computing the value of implicit grants to the federal government, funds received by each of the two countries under provisions of the Federal Impact Aid formula are considered as offsetting, in part, losses from federal property tax exemptions. This legislation, designed to offset property tax losses in areas with large concentrations of federal employees, provided approximately $9.1 million in 1969 to Prince George's County.[2] Therefore, the implicit grant value is the difference between this amount and the loss in real-estate taxes – or $6.9 million. In Montgomery County the difference between lost tax revenues and Federal Impact Aid funds in 1969 resulted in a $2 million implicit grant to the federal government.

Agricultural Land

Maryland was the first state to modify its property tax laws for preferential treatment of land used for farming, a practice now required in six other states. The original Maryland legislation, approved in 1960, did not restrict preferential assessment to owner-operated farms or to what would be considered "bona fide" farms. Nor did the legislation make provisions to recapture any tax loss at the time of rezoning, which would indicate its use for more intensive development, or at the time of sale to land developers.[3]

The annual value of the implicit grant to owners of property nominally valued as "agricultural" is the difference between property taxes based on the market value of the land and property taxes based on farm use of the land.

Two previous studies estimated the difference between market value and preferentially assessed value for agricultural property in both Montgomery and Prince George's counties for 1961 and 1966.[4, 5] A more recent analysis by a member of the Montgomery County staff established the market value of

---

2 Payments under Public Laws 815 and 874 were designed primarily to substitute for the real property tax revenues that might have been derived if the federally connected residence of public school pupils, or their parents' workplace, was not tax exempt. The contribution rate is based on the assumption that approximately half the real property base required to meet the local share of education costs is derived from residential property, half from commercial and industrial property.

3 In 1969 the Maryland State Assembly amended the earlier bill by providing for "recapture" of tax losses when land use is changed. However, the legislation limits the tax payment (state and local) at the time of the use charge to 5 percent of the full market value; this is equal to *total* property taxes for a two-year period in Montgomery and Prince George's counties.

4 Peter House, *State Action Relating to the Taxation of Farmland in the Rural Urban Fringe,* United States Department of Agriculture, ERS 13, August 1961. This paper estimates value of land by election district in both Montgomery and Prince George's counties in 1960.

5 P. House, "Partial Tax Exemptions for Farmland Properties in the Rural–Urban Fringe," *Appraisal Journal,* July 1968. The estimated aggregate loss in the Montgomery County tax base in 1965 is $83 million, the loss to Prince George's County totals $59 million.

preferentially assessed land at $205 million, or about 8 percent of the total tax base.[6]

The approach used in this study to determine the implicit grant element associated with preferential farm land assessment considered the level of urbanization in each of Montgomery County's election districts:

> In the four most urban election districts in the county (which contain 81 percent of the population, 24 percent of the land area) the value of tax-exempt land was calculated as the difference between its preferentially assessed value and its value if the land were zoned for single-family residential construction. The total number of acres zoned as farmland in the four election districts is 7,364 acres, providing a 4–5 year land reserve for one-family homes based on the rate of construction in the 1960 decade. The computed value of tax-exempt land is conservative, because a considerable portion of the land held vacant in areas presently urbanized, is, in fact, more valuable than its assumed best alternative -- single-family construction. For example, an agricultural area presently surrounded by single-family homes is an ideal site for a shopping center. Many farms in urbanized areas of the county either front or are close to existing roads. This land has a potential for multifamily, commercial, or industrial purposes. In some cases, land has already been rezoned for more intensive use, but remains agricultural. Table 1 shows the value of this land, as well as land zoned for agricultural use.

The assessed value of farmland in the two semiurban areas is

Table 1. Value of Preferentially Assessed Farmland in Montgomery County, 1969

Present Zoning	Type of District	Number of Acres Preferentially Assessed	Average Assessed[a] Value of Preferentially Assessed Land Per Acre	Value of Assessed Land Not Taxed (In Thousands)
Agricultural				
	Urban	7,364	$215	$32,867
	Semiurban	14,351	129	24,573
	Semirural	138,341	92	38,149
Intensive Use				
	Urban	708[b]	$136	$11,275
	Semirural	1,048[b]	130	7,200
	Total	161,812		$114,064

Source: [a]Assessor's Master File, Montgomery County.

[b]William Sussman, Background Data—Farmland Assessment Program, Montgomery County, January 1968 (unpublished).

---

6 W. Hussman, Background Data – Farmland Assessment Program (unpublished informal memorandum); Office of Program Coordination, Montgomery County, January 1968. The procedure used to determine exempt land value does not consider intracounty locational differentials.

estimated to have appreciated 180 percent since 1960, or about 15 percent per annum. Land in semirural areas has appreciated about 130 percent, or 11 percent per annum (in historical dollars).

The total assessable value of land not taxed is calculated to be $114 million. The implicit tax grant in 1969 represents a revenue loss to the county of $3.0 million.

In Prince George's County, 90,450 acres of land, comprising 28 percent of the total county area, were preferentially assessed in 1969. The method for calculating the value of the resulting implicit grant was essentially the same as outlined for Montgomery County, although the value of rezoned land could not be established. The preferential assessment per acre in Prince George's County in 1968 was $251 per acre, considerably above Montgomery County's average of $100 per acre. The assessed value of agricultural land not taxed is estimated to be $65 million, representing a tax loss in 1969 of $2.3 million.

Senior Citizens and Other Personal Exemptions

Maryland is one of several states that allow property tax exemptions to senior citizens. Counties within the state have the option to exempt property on the basis of age alone or on the basis of age and income. Prince George's and Montgomery counties have elected to exempt, upon application, up to $5,000 of assessed resident unit value owned by citizens over 65 years old. The value of this grant during 1969 in Prince George's County was $539,800, or 0.7 percent of the total assessable tax base. Presumably the dollar value of this grant in Montgomery County does not deviate considerably from this amount because the number of owner-occupied residences in the two counties is about the same.

Property-owning veterans in thirty-two states are eligible to receive some form of tax exemption. This group of citizens were recipients of over $2.1 billion in property exemptions nationally in 1965. No offsetting form of tax relief is provided for veterans who rent their residences in any of the states. Both Prince George's and Montgomery counties limit veterans' exemptions to a share of the private residence value owned by *disabled* veterans. Because of this constraint the total value of this grant in both counties does not exceed $50,000 and thus does not seriously erode the tax base. Nonveteran blind are the only additional group eligible to receive personal exemptions on property in the two counties.

Income-Producing Property

Income-producing property can be grouped into industrial, commercial, and multifamily residential land and improvements. New industrial enterprises are exempt from local taxation for specified time periods in a number of counties and municipalities in the nation on the premise that this induces industry to locate in these areas. Such direct real property exemptions are not provided in either of the two counties examined. However, Prince George's County reduced, and, in 1970 totally eliminated, personal property taxes on business inventories.

Tax savings that result from assessments below the level that legislation provides are considered implicit grants. This study did not attempt to determine implicit grants, if any, associated with industrial and commercial property. The Bureau of the Census in 1966 calculated the ratio of assessed value to sales price of 432 commercial and industrial properties as 44.2 percent, considerably below the level of residential structures and the state requirement of 60 percent.[7] These statistics, which imply considerable implicit grants, aggregate data from counties in the Baltimore SMSA as well as Prince George's and Montgomery counties. Implicit grants, if any, associated with the third category of income-producing properties — apartments — cannot be estimated from Bureau of Census data, because single- and multiple-unit dwellings are aggregated. In view of the large number of apartment units in the two-county area, tax savings associated with these properties are calculated.

Although building costs for apartments have risen at almost the same rate as single-family homes since the 1950s, assessment records for the two counties do not indicate a parallel rise in assessment value. In Prince George's County multiple-family units were assessed at 111 percent of single-unit residences in 1953 but only 38 percent of single unit residences in 1968. In Montgomery County the change was from 52 percent in 1953 to 41 percent in 1968.

To determine individual changes in the assessed value of apartments, all high-rise structures on the Assessor's rolls during the 1963—64 period in Prince George's County were compared to their assessed values in 1968. These structures were assessed in 1963 on the basis of either cost or income.[8] The analysis indicated practically no change in assessments during the five-year period. The increase in assessment, which includes all apartment units between 1961 and 1968, is only 8 percent. During the same time span, apartment-unit construction costs in the county increased 55 percent.

To determine the assessment level that would more closely reflect the state's required share of market value, annual appreciation of apartment structures was estimated using three variables: increases in rents reflecting gross income changes, changes in cost of construction, and sales value less physical obsolescence. The assessed value (land and improvement) of apartment structures sold for over $1 million in 1968 was 47.6 percent of the sales price.[9]

---

7 Bureau of the Census, *1967 Census of Governments,* vol. 2 (Washington, D.C.: Government Printing Office, February 1968).

8 Apartments only partially occupied after construction are assessed on the basis of *reported* construction cost. After the building is occupied, assessment is modified on the basis of income.

9 This percentage is based on ten reported sales of apartment buildings in 1968. Total assessment value was $12.9 million whereas total sales price was $27.1 million. However, sales price does not necessarily denote market value because of intricacies in federal tax laws, which encourage certain extralegal practices.

On the basis of these variables the appropriate assessment for all apartment structures is conservatively estimated at $436 million. The difference between this value and actual assessments in 1968 is $88 million, indicating an implicit grant, or county tax loss, of at least $3.1 million in 1969.

State and county officials give two reasons for low apartment assessments in Prince George's County: numerous apartment vacancies and deterioration of structures in certain districts. In fact, apartment vacancies in the county during 1968 were 5.1 percent of the total, below the level of Montgomery County or the District of Columbia. The policy of not assessing vacant units and federal tax regulations tend to encourage overbuilding without reducing rents for tenants, whereas lack of building maintenance in older areas tends to encourage urban blight.[10] Owners of one- or two-unit structures available for rent are not offered the privilege of reduced assessments given to apartment owners. Neither reason given for low total assessment should affect the assessment level of land, which represents only 12.6 percent of the total assessed apartment value in the county. This compares to land comprising 22.6 percent of total assessed apartment value in Mongtomery County, close to the national average of 20 percent.[11]

In comparison to national levels, apartment assessments in both counties are low. In 1968 the effective tax rate in the two counties for all real estate ranged from 1.5 to 1.6 percent of market value. Nationally, median assessments for single-family residences were estimated at 1.6 percent of market value. However, this percentage increased to 2.7 percent for apartments containing fifty or more units.[12] This effective tax rate differential between single and multiple units tends to substantiate the view that apartment owners in the two counties are recipients of implicit grants because income is the criterion nationally, as well as in Maryland, for determining apartment worth.

In Montgomery County the difference between the assumptive and actual assessed value for apartments is considerably smaller — $38 million, representing a tax loss of $1.1 million.

Single-family residences, particularly those in subdivisions, are usually assessed at close to the state required level in both counties.

---

10 In the Point Pleasant district of Prince George's County, which comprises a major part of the Model Cities area, per unit assessments of apartments in 1968 are below the 1953 level, although two thirds of all apartments were built since 1953.

11 If we assume that the total assessment of property, both land and improvements, represents the approximate share of market value, the allocation between land and improvements has no effect on local tax revenue. However, the allocation does affect federal tax payments by property owners because land, unlike improvements, is not subject to depreciation. The following example illustrates this point: The useful life of a new apartment is $150,000. Improvements are depreciated over a useful life of forty years, according to a double-declining balance method. In case A land forms $33\frac{1}{3}$ percent of the total value. In case B land forms $16\frac{2}{3}$ percent of the total $150,000 value. First-year depreciation under case A is $5,000, but it increases to $6,250 in case B.

12 D. Netzer, *Economics of the Property Tax* (Washington, D.C.: The Brookings Institution, 1966), p. 299.

Land Rezoned for Intensive Use

The most valuable, and probably most controversial, implicit grant by the public sector to the private sector is based on the legal power of county or municipal government to approve a change of land use from less intensive to more intensive development. Official constraints on the quantity of land for which rezoning approval is granted results in a public sector quasi-monopoly over land use. The potential worth of this "benevolent" form of implicit grant is the greatest in or near expanding urban areas, such as Prince George's and Montgomery counties. The monetary worth of the grant to the property owner is the difference in the value of land before and after rezoning, less costs (such as legal fees) associated with obtaining rezoning approval. Although the rezoned land remains unimproved, the net worth of the county increases as a result of higher tax revenues from the land. However, once the land is improved, the fiscal impact may be favorable or detrimental.[13] The net worth of the final land user is decreased by an amount equal to the worth of the implicit grant, as the increased value of land is likely to be shifted to the ultimate user in the form of higher rent or purchase price.

Between 1961 and 1969 about 8,376 acres in Montgomery County were rezoned, primarily from agricultural or rural residential to multifamily, commercial, or industrial. As Table 2 shows, the assessed value of land rezoned to intensive use between 1961 and 1968 was $165.6 million, based on land value. For purposes of determining the implicit grant value of rezoning, we assume that land owners can easily rezone from rural–agricultural to single-family residential. (That is, the quasi-monopoly power of the county to restrict this land use would not be evident.) We also assume that in these areas water and sewer facilities will be provided a reasonable premise in the bicounty area. Subtracting the value of single-unit residential land from the total results in an implicit grant of $149.6 million assessed value, or approximately $274 million market value.

The difference between the assessed value of land in use and vacant in Montgomery County is not substantial. In fact, industrial land zoned but vacant, as Table 2 shows, is assessed higher than industrial land in use. This is an indication that the value of vacant land goes up after rezoning because of its *potential* land use and not because the land is improved. Within the county, the value of land zoned for alternative land use varies sharply, as Table 3 shows. This is a clear example of "location rents," where land value in a given category is a function of the desirability of the location.

Prince George's County rezoned 11,001 acres for intensive use between 1961 and 1968, or considerably more than its neighbor. However, as Table 2

---

13 For example, rezoning for three- and four-bedroom garden apartments is likely to result in a fiscal loss in suburban Washington, D.C., counties because costs of public services will exceed revenues. However, rezoning for research and development industry is likely to result in a fiscal surplus. See the reference cited in note 23 for examples.

Table 2. Assessed Value of Land Rezoned for Intensive Use

Land Use	Quantity Acres Zoned		Status		Assessed Value Per Acre[b]		Assessed Value of Land Rezoned 1961–69 (In Millions)
	Total	1961–69[a]	In Use	Vacant	In Use	Vacant	
Montgomery County							
Apartments	3,112	2,856	2,191	921	$23,174	$17,892	$61.3
Commercial	2,976	1,695	2,105	871	46,928	30,747	64.0
Industrial	5,992	3,825	3,341	2,651	10,069	10,698	40.3
Total/Mean	12,080	8,376	7,637	4,443	$23,988	$16,120	$165.6
Prince George's County							
Apartments	8,180	4,515	4,591	3,589	$8,674	$4,898	$30.6
Commercial	6,380	3,528	4,339	2,041	11,368	11,760	40.1
Industrial	6,117	3,038	3,057	3,060	5,234	5,241	15.9
Total/Mean	20,677	11,081	11,987	8,690	$8,772	$6,630	$86.6

[a]Prince George's County data for 1961–68.

[b]For Prince George's County, acres vacant author's estimate.

Source: Assessor's Offices, Prince George's and Montgomery counties.

Table 3. Assessed Value Per Acre of Land by Use,
Montgomery County 1969

Election District	Industrial	Commercial	Apartment	Single Family	Agricultural
Urban					
Potomac	—	$ 28,203	$28,320	$ 3,414	$ 398
Colesville	$ 9,530	25,150	18,925	3,975	166
Rockville	25,301	42,630	21,504	3,765	220
Wheaton	70,916	33,491	28,951	7,624	315
Bethesda	73,934	144,379	36,449	15,433	1,141
Nonurban					
Barnesville	$ 849	$ 1,183	—	$ 568	$ 85
Damascus	3,938	8,307	—	1,099	91
Laytonsville	4,504	11,075	$ 2,819	783	97
Clarksburg	3,724	13,780	—	926	87

Source: Assessor's Master Tape, Montgomery County.

Table 4. Assessed Value of Tax-Exempt Property in Montgomery
and Prince George's Counties 1968—69 (In Thousands)

	Montgomery County		Prince George's County	
	Total	Implicit Grant Element	Total	Implicit Grant Element
Fully tax-exempt public				
Federal	$243,737	$90,286	$410,830	$182,320
State	5,651	—	160,555	—
County and local	189,937	—	198,058	—
Fully tax-exempt private				
Religious organizations	$76,852	$76,852	$87,322	$87,322
Other nonprofit	29.654	29.654	5.417	5.417
Partially exempt				
Farm preferential	$114,100	$114,100	$65,000	$65,000
Nonveteran blind & disabled veteran	1,809	1,809	767	767
Senior citizen	15,500*	15,500*	16,188	16,188
Apartments	38,500	38,500	88,000	88,000
Total	$717,550	$366,701	$982,905	$445,014
Total assessed taxable property—1969	$2,678,177	$2,678,177	$2,078,912	$2,078,912
Percent exempt of tax-paying	26.8	13.7	47.3	21.4
County tax loss	$19,661	$10,047	$34,696	$15,708

*Estimate
Source: Maryland Legislative Council Committee on Taxation and Fiscal Matters, 1969
Report.

shows, the assessed value of the rezoned land was only $86.6 million, of which $70.1 million is considered an implicit grant. This is partially due to liberal rezoning policies, which have resulted in a large reserve of vacant land.

Total Value of Implicit Grants

Table 4 shows the total assessed value of exempt property and associated implicit grants as a result of tax savings in both counties. In Montgomery County the loss of tax revenue in 1969 was $19.7 million. The implicit grant element is approximately one half of this total.

The loss of tax revenue in Prince George's County was $34.7 million. Of this amount, $15.7 million, or 21.4 percent of the total revenue collected, can be considered an implicit grant. Totally exempt property in Prince George's County was 47.3 percent of all property subject to taxation, compared to 26.8 percent in the more affluent Montgomery County.

Market value, which totals over $3.2 billion in the two counties, illustrates the magnitude of tax-exempt property. Per capita exemptions of $2,839 in this region no doubt exceed the national average, in view of the demand for land created by the rapidly expanding population and the presence of large federal facilities.

Fiscal and Income Distribution Effects of Implicit Grants

Implicit grants discussed in the previous section have differing fiscal and income distribution effects in the two counties examined. These differences are attributable to factors including the value of exempt property as a share of all property and the characteristics of fully or partially exempt property.

Total Tax-Exempt Public and Private Property

Measurement of the fiscal impact of tax-exempt public property requires a determination of benefits from government facilities relative to the loss in local revenue. The exemption of county and municipal property is fiscally neutral because payment of real-restate taxes on this property would result in taxing oneself. State property is generally a small share of total exempt property, and the major beneficiaries of services provided by these facilities are frequently residents of the county. In the two counties examined, federal and private property comprises the bulk of tax exemptions. Federal facilities can be grouped into two general categories: those facilities that serve the "common (national) welfare" (military installations, research laboratories) and those that serve primarily a local need (post offices). In both counties the services provided by over

90 percent of the tax-exempt federal facilities are linked with the common welfare.

The conclusions of a previous study indicate that in rapidly growing areas, potential tax revenues from federal property are likely to exceed income from federal grants.[14] Nevertheless the impact of federal tax exemptions on the local fiscal structure in growing areas is greatly affected by local labor market conditions and the income structure of federally employed personnel. Relatively full employment, concurrently with an expansion of federal employment in the Washington, D.C. SMSA, in recent decades has increased in-migration, particularly to suburban communities. Most federal facilities in Montgomery County attract relatively high-income professional personnel. In Prince George's County, however, facilities such as Andrews Air Force Base engage military personnel with relatively low incomes. In addition, two large facilities employing a high ratio of professional personnel, Goddard Space Flight Center and the Agricultural Research Center, are physically close to the Montgomery County boundary. A previous study has shown that higher-income senior faculty members at the University of Maryland, adjacent to the two aforementioned federal facilities, live in Montgomery county and commute to the university.[15] A similar pattern may exist at other government facilities in Prince George's County, which would reduce the locational benefit of these installations. Apparently federal facilities in Prince George's County are capital intensive because the assessed value per at-place federal employee is $16,700 compared to $6,800 in Montgomery County. An indepth analysis, outside the scope of this study, would be required to determine the collective impact of federal installations on the fiscal structure in the two counties.

Tax exemptions to religious and charitable institutions shift the tax burden to other property owners. Regardless of the motivation for these exemptions, real-estate tax losses from the exemptions of these properties, although beneficial to users of their facilities, tend to promote additional inequities in the property tax. The exemption of structures such as private schools are more likely to benefit higher-income families than other county residents. Other exemptions benefit members of what are essentially social clubs.

On an aggregate level the cost of tax exemptions in both counties is borne by residents of single-family structures that provide 58 percent of the total tax base. Owners of these properties pay a higher share of their income in property taxes relative to apartment dwellers.[16]

---

14 J. E. O'Bannon, "Payments for Tax-Exempt Property," in R. W. Lindholm, ed., *Property Taxation USA* (Madison: University of Wisconsin Press, 1967), p. 201.

15 J. H. Cumberland, *Economic Development in Prince George's County, Maryland,* rev. ed. County Study Governmental Study Commission, June 1967.

16 Doxiadis-System Development Corporation, *Fiscal and Land Use Analysis of Prince George's County,* draft final report, December 1969. If the value of imputed rents is added to homeowners' income, the gap in the share of income paid for housing between single family and apartment residents is reduced. The report also supports Netzer's hypothesis that the property tax is regressive among jurisdictions in a single metropolitan area ("The Property Tax and Federal Tax sharing," in H. L. Johnson, ed., *State and Local Tax Problems*).

Preferential Taxation for Selected Groups in the Private Sector

Preferential assessment of farmland represents the greatest real-estate tax loss from the private sector in the bicounty area. A major justification for preferential assessment legislation has been that it would reduce urban sprawl and encourage the maintenance of farmland, thus preserving open space near urban areas. However, this justification has been challenged. Based on an analysis of preferential assessment in Maryland, Peter House points out that "the effectiveness of tax measure in preserving open land depends on area-wide planning and control over land use."[17] Frederick Stocker shares this view. He points to the "opportunities for developers and speculators to hold tracts of undeveloped land, while hiring a nearby farmer to cut hay or pasture a cow."[18] An examination of the growth pattern in the bicounty area lends little credence to the argument that the preferential tax has reduced urban sprawl. In fact, limited evidence indicates that owners of such property occasionally choose to wait to sell or build on the property, while development "skips" their land into previously rural areas.

The substantial loss of tax revenue, despite recent legislative changes, adds an additional inequity to the county tax structure. The major beneficiary is not likely to be the small low-income marginal farmer but the land speculator.

Partial tax exemptions for senior citizens, disabled veterans, and blind individuals are based primarily on the premise that these groups may not be able to afford the burden of real-estate taxes. However, it is by no means certain that those who are least likely to be able to pay are the beneficiaries of these grants.

The largest percentage of low-income families in both counties live in rental property, and thus tax concessions, to be equitable, should be extended to these tenants. In addition, statistical findings dispute the argument that the aged as a group are at an economic disadvantage relative to the total population.[19] Perhaps the most sound fiscal argument for the senior citizen exemption is that persons over 65 are not likely to have children in public schools, which is the major county service cost. Applying this criterion, however, would justify reduced tax assessments to single individuals as well as childless couples.

Impact of Implicit Grants on Income in the Bicounty Area

Implicit grants had two major effects on income in the two-county area: Exemptions of certain properties from taxation transferred the burden to other

---

17 House, *op. cit.*

18 F. D. Stocker, "Taxing Farmland in the Urban Fringe," *Journal of Farm Economics.*

19 Yung-Ping Chen, "Property Tax Concessions to the Aged," in R. W. Lindholm, ed., *Property Taxation USA* (Madison: University of Wisconsin Press, 1967), p. 226.

property owners in the county, thus reducing their income. Secondly implicit grants as a result of rezoning and assessment practices affected the income structure of migrants in one of the two counties examined.

This section of the study measures the income distribution impact of property tax exemptions on resident income. The following sections discuss the potential effects of an increment land value tax as well as fiscal problems in one county linked with past rezoning and assessment practices.

If we were to discontinue the implicit grants shown in Table 4, what impact would this move have on the distribution of income in the bicounty area? Presumably the federal government would provide a direct grant equal to the real-estate revenue loss from its property, and other full and partial exemptions (except those involving state and local property) as well as grants under Federal Impact Aid would be eliminated. If we also assume that revenues from the expanded tax base would not be used to increase the quantity or quality of public services, the real-estate tax in Prince George's County could be reduced from the $3.53 to $2.91 per $100 assessed value, with a tax reduction in Montgomery County from the present $2.74 to $2.41. Because the real-estate tax is generally regressive, a change in the tax rate is likely to have the greatest relative effect on lower-income families in both renter-occupied and owner-occupied residential units. In suburban areas of the Washington SMSA during 1960, renters with earnings below $3,000 spent 34 percent of their income for housing in contrast to residents earning $15,000 or more, who paid only 12.5 percent of their income for rental housing. In the same year the value of homes associated with 9 percent of families and individuals in owner-occupied units exceeded their owners' income by a ratio of 4.0 or more. Families and individuals comprising this group were primarily those earning $4,000 or less. Conversely 24 percent of owner-occupied dwellings had a value less than 1.5 times the income of their residents, the majority families and individuals with earnings exceeding $10,000. The income distribution impact of eliminating implicit grants, other than those associated with rezoning, is shown in Table 5. Although the mean one- to two-family unit assessment in 1968 within Prince George's County was $11,700, the average tax savings for these residences assuming elimination of implicit grants would be $73. Although the greatest percentage income increase from the property tax reduction is shown for families earning less than $10,000, most of the aggregate tax savings would accrue to families earning above this amount. This result is particularly evident in the more affluent Montgomery County, where the majority of owner-occupied residents earned over $12,000. Although apartment assessments in both counties would be raised if implicit grants were eliminated, the offsetting effect of the reduced tax rate would result in only minor increases in tax payments. In addition to owner-occupied dwellings, industrial and commercial property owners would be major beneficiaries of lower tax levels.

A number of groups would find their financial burden increased, or services reduced, by the elimination of implicit grants. Thus, residents who use these facilities would have to absorb real-estate taxes on presently exempt nonprofit

Table 5. Owner-Occupied Housing Unit Tax Reduction Resulting from Implicit Grant Elimination

Median Income	Ratio[a] Value of Home / Income 1960	Tax Saving as Percent of Income (1968)[b] Before Income Tax Offset	After Income Tax Offset	Number of Units 1969	Total Tax[a] Savings (In Thousands)
Prince George's County					
Under $3,000	8.3	2.8	2.4	3,920	$ 196
$3,000–$3,999	3.8	1.3	1.1	980	44
$4,000–$4,999	2.9	1.0	0.8	980	44
$5,000–$5,999	2.6	0.9	0.7	1,960	98
$6,000–$6,999	2.4	0.8	0.6	2,940	156
$7,000–$7,999	2.2	0.8	0.6	6,860	391
$8,000–$9,999	2.0	0.7	0.5	18,620	1,154
$10,000–$14,999	1.9	0.6	0.4	42,140	3,160
$15,000 +	1.7	0.6	0.4	19,600	1,920
Total				98,000	$7,163
Tax saving per unit					$73

Montgomery County

Under $3,000	8.3	1.5	1.3	1,920	$ 52
$3,000–$3,999	3.8	0.7	0.6	960	23
$4,000–$4,999	2.9	0.5	0.4	960	23
$5,000–$5,999	2.6	0.5	0.4	2,880	75
$6,000–$6,999	2.4	0.4	0.3	3,840	108
$7,000–$7,999	2.2	0.4	0.3	2,880	86
$8,000–$9,999	2.0	0.4	0.3	5,760	179
$10,000–$14,999	1.9	0.3	0.2	32,640	1,338
$15,000 +	1.9	0.3	0.2	44,160	3,356
Total				96,000	5,240
Tax saving per unit					$54

[a]Ratios are based on a comparison of owner-occupied housing values and income in the suburban parts of the Washington, D.C., SMSA from the *1960 Census of Population*. This area includes Montgomery, Prince George's, and Fairfax counties as well as the city of Alexandria and Falls Church. Seventy percent of all owner-occupied dwellings in this suburban area were located in Maryland. Ratios were also obtained by relating aggregate median single-family housing values and median income for census tracts containing 90 percent or more single-family dwellings in Prince George's and Montgomery counties. A comparison between the two sets of ratios shows that in affluent census tracts within Montgomery County (median income $15,000 and over) the median house value was 2.2 times median income, considerably above the total suburban area ratio of 1.7 for this income category.

Total tax savings were obtained by estimating the number of owner-occupied residences in each income category based on values from Federal Housing Administration, *Analysis of Washington, D.C.–Maryland–Virginia Housing Market* (Washington, D.C., Government Printing Office, February 1969).

[b]Assessed value of homes estimated at 55 percent of market value. Difference in tax payments resulting from elimination of implicit grants converted to percentage of median income for each income grouping.

property. The elimination of preferential farm assessment would affect most directly owners of farmland already zoned for intensive use. In Montgomery County, these owners are primarily large land developers.[20] Taxpayers nationally would share the cost of increased direct federal grants to offset property tax losses.

Tax on Rezoned Land

The average value of land rezoned annually between 1960 and 1968, based on 1968 assessment levels, was close to $38 million in Montgomery County, $18 million in Prince George's County. The potential income distribution impact on county residents of this capital gain, most of it considered an implicit grant, depends on the method by which the public sector recovers part or all of this increment in value. Total recovery is theoretically feasible by open, competitive bidding. Under this scheme the county would "auction off" land rezoned to the highest bidder, who would presumably pay the market value of land. From the proceeds of the sale the county would pay the original owner the highest value of the land prior to rezoning. This means of recapturing capital gains has considerable legal and administrative limitations. However, in Montgomery county the incremental land value as a result of rezoning is close to half the *total* county real-estate revenue, whereas in Prince George's County, it is about 25 percent of the revenue derived from the real property tax. Thus the approach offers a potential new source of considerable revenue to expanding urban and suburban areas requiring large capital outlays to meet the demand for public services.

Alternatively the Prince George's County delegation to the 1969 Maryland legislature proposed to impose a county tax on the land value increment resulting from rezoning. A 20 percent tax on this land in Prince George's County would have produced sufficient revenues to lower the tax rate by about 5 percent. The average real-estate tax payment by one- to two-family owner-occupied residents could thus be reduced by $21, with an average $8 tax reduction per apartment unit. In Montgomery County average savings resulting from a 20 percent land tax are potentially greater: $55 for one- to two-family residences, $21 for apartment units. These tax savings assume that county services would not be improved or expanded as a result of the additional revenues. Renters would only benefit from the tax reduction if apartment and other income-producing property owners shifted the savings to their tenants.

---

20 Hussman, *op. cit.*

Rezoning and Apartment Assessment
Policies

Implicit grants associated with rezoning and apartment assessments are discussed jointly because as the following discussion indicates, their collective effect accelerated apartment construction. The increased building activity, in turn, had a negative impact on the fiscal structure of Prince George's County. Between 1961 and 1967 over 3,000 acres of land were rezoned in the county, mostly from previous agricultural or rural—residential use, for the construction of garden apartments. This rapid conversion of land for apartment use was justified primarily on the basis that garden apartments were fiscally profitable, with the beneficiaries of a fiscal surplus single-family homeowners. To substantiate this view a widely circulated report was produced, which indicated a net profit to the county from apartment units and a considerable fiscal loss from single-family structures.[21] As a result of liberal zoning, over 47,000 garden apartment units were constructed between 1960 and 1968, a number exceeding the total built in all other suburban counties within the Washington SMSA during this period. Approximately 7,500 high-rise units were also constructed between 1962 and 1968. Because the quantity of land rezoned, despite the construction boom, was considerably more than required, developers had available numerous alternative sites and thus could exert considerable influence in determining the pattern of population growth within the county.

In 1968 over two thirds of migrants to the county since 1960 and 43 percent of all county residents were estimated to live in apartments. Migrants accounted for approximately 70 percent of the total county population growth between 1960 and 1968. The balance of population growth was attributable to natural increases, although the percentage of population fourteen years of age or under was reduced from 35 percent in 1960 to 30 percent in 1968.

A large share of in-migration appears to result from the availability of housing and not from the expansion of intracounty employment opportunities. New housing was concentrated in garden apartments, at rentals somewhat below the level of other suburban jurisdictions, and within commuting distance to the District of Columbia, the major employment center in the region.

In contrast to contiguous suburban areas, at-place—employment increases in Prince George's County comprised less than half the expansion in the labor force of the county. The number of commuters from the county therefore increased from 69,861 in 1960 to an estimated 165,852 in 1970. In other jurisdictions within the SMSA, all of which had lower percentage and absolute growths in population, at-place–employment increases absorbed most or all the growth in the resident labor force.

Despite increases in federal civilian and military personnel in the region

---

21 J. H. Deckman, *A Study of Income and Expenditures by Family Dwellings, Apartment and Business Units for the Fiscal Year 1963–1964*, Prince George's County Economic Development Committee, October 1963.

since the mid-1960s, this expansion did not greatly influence at-place employment in Prince George's County. Total civilian government employment at all
levels increased by only 14,000 since 1960, military personnnel by about 3,500.
A factor for apartment growth in one district adjacent to the University of
Maryland was increased student enrollment, which accounted for about 2,000
units, or only 3 percent of the increase in apartments.

The policy of encouraging rapid physical growth by accelerated construction
activity had serious fiscal implications for the county. Both median family
incomes and county revenues derived from apartment tenants are sharply below
the level of single-family residents. The gap in income between single- and
multiple-unit residents is the widest in Prince George's County relative to two
contiguous suburban counties.[22] A recently completed study has shown that the
cost of services exceeds real-estate revenues and income-tax collections from
apartment tenants, resulting in a per unit fiscal loss from newer apartment units
exceeding that of single-family units.[23] Because the per pupil cost of public
services, particularly education, in Prince George's County during the past
decade increased at about the rate of contiguous jurisdictions without a
concurrent expansion of the tax base, the nominal tax rate had to be increased
thus:

	1960	1969
Prince George's County	$2.42	$3.53
Montgomery County	$2.53	$2.74

Moderate income groups may have benefited by the availability of units at
rents below those in Montgomery and Fairfax counties. However, any short-term
monetary advantages were offset by higher real-estate and income tax surtax
rates as well as qualitative factors including increased traffic congestion and
fewer recreational facilities.

The slow rise in income for Prince George's County is also attributable to
the relatively low wage level in industrial and commercial enterprises. Between
1961 and 1968, 6,500 acres of land were rezoned for industrial and commercial
use, on the premise that this rezoning would attract new industry that would
contribute to an expansion of the tax base and thus reduce the tax burden on
residents. In addition, a tax on all business inventories, historically providing
considerable revenues, was eliminated on the basis of the same argument.[24]

Despite these measures to attract new enterprises, industrial and commercial

22 Federal Housing Administration, *op. cit.*

23 Doxiadis-System Development Corporation, *op. cit.*

24 The growth rate of industrial and commercial property assessments in Montgomery
county, which retained the business inventory tax, has been considerably above Prince
George's since 1967. There is no evidence that the elimination of this tax had any impact on
industry location within the SMSA.

property as a share of the tax base increased from only 11.0 percent in 1961 to 12.2 percent in 1968, an additional cause for the increase in tax rates. Wages in nongovernment enterprises, including manufacturing industries above the level of adjoining communities in 1958, were found to be below their level ten years later.

The rapid population growth can only be attributed in part to the effects of implicit grants. Nevertheless, as John Cumberland points out, the coalition of public and political forces as well as private special interest groups were the major beneficiaries of the highly successful rapid growth policy.[25] Frequently these groups were the direct recipients of specific implicit grants that contributed to the growth pattern and rate.

Between 1963 and 1967 an apartment boom was also in full swing in Montgomery County. As Max Neutze, in his study of apartment growth in the county, states: "it appeared that the legal costs of a good zoning lawyer could possibly be regarded as the cost of getting rezoning."[26] This growth was also justified fiscally despite a somewhat dated study which showed that the fiscal loss per apartment unit in the county exceeded single-family homes.[27] However, the effects of this apartment boom do not appear fiscally detrimental for a number of reasons. The total number of units constructed was considerably below, and the average assessment per unit about 50 percent above, the value of apartments constructed in Prince George's County. After 1964 most multiunit structures built were so-called luxury "hotel apartments," whose relatively high-income residents had an average of only 0.07 children attending public schools. Finally a change in the political structure forced modification in zoning practices and thus reduced the rate of construction.

Conclusion

This study has identified six implicit grant categories associated with taxes levied against real property by two political jurisdictions in one state. However, owners of property also benefit from additional implicit grants in this region. Thus, county income-tax payments are lowered as a result of deducting real-estate taxes and mortgage interest from gross personal income. Approval of variances from county ordinances also result in unequal privileges. For example, certain property owners, by special exemption, may build more bedrooms per residential unit or more residential units per acre than is allowable under existing legislation -- a privilege denied others meeting the same criteria for land development.

---

25 Cumberland, *op. cit.*

26 M. Neutze, *The Suburban Apartment Boom,* Resources for the Future (Baltimore: Johns Hopkins Press, 1969), p. 45.

27 Homer Hoyt Associates, *Economic Survey of Montgomery and Prince George's Counties, Maryland*, January 1955.

Although comparative data are not presently available, the implicit grant share of the total property tax base found in the bicounty area may be conservative relative to other political jurisdictions, particularly those exempting industrial facilities for limited time periods. However, the magnitude of these grants is only one element of its effect. The study has demonstrated that the same implicit grant categories can have differing impact on such factors as income distribution and construction activity even in contiguous areas. Therefore, no preliminary conclusions are reached as to the aggregate impact of implicit grants to property owners.

Implicit grants provided to property owners can be grouped into those that benefit more affluent groups, such as land developers, those that are neutral with respect to income, and those that favor lower-income segments of the population. In the region examined the more affluent groups appear to receive the largest dollar share of implicit grants. Additional research is required to establish whether these groups are also the major beneficiaries of local property tax related implicit grants in other regions of the nation.

14

Robinson G. Hollister and John L. Palmer:
The Impact of Inflation on the Poor

I.   Introduction

The objective of this study is to determine how the processes associated with what is generally known as inflation affect the economic well-being of a particular subgroup of the United States population, the poor. We are concerned here both with the technical problems of determining the impact of inflation on the poor and with the relevance of the findings to questions of public policy.

Despite the fact that much of the rhetoric in public discussions about the evils of inflation is focused on particular subgroups of the population — the aged and the poor[1] — the formal economic literature on the distribution of the effects of inflationary processes is rather thin. The literature in existence tends to focus on only one or two types of inflationary impacts rather than on an

This is the first publication of this article. All rights reserved. Permission to reprint must be obtained from the publisher and authors. Prepared under support from the Institute for Research on Poverty, University of Wisconsin, through funds granted pursuant to the Provisions of the Economic Opportunity Act of 1964.

1 For two recent examples see, E. L. Dale, Jr., "The Dreadful Economic Choice That Faces Mr. Nixon," *New York Times Magazine*, November 24, 1968; and E. A. Robert, Jr., "How Inflation Hits Hardest at the Poor," *The National Observer*, March 3, 1969.

assessment of the overall impact on the economic well-being of a particular group.[2] In this paper we attempt to be more comprehensive by seeking to determine the impact of inflationary processes on the economic well-being of the poor in three broad areas: expenditure effects, income effects, and wealth effects. In the first area we examine how the impact of inflation on the poor is conditioned by the ways in which they (and other groups) spend their income; in the second we examine the ways in which inflationary effects are reflected in the sources of income of the poor; and in the third we estimate the way in which the assets of the poor might create inflationary effects on their economic well-being.

Our concern here is with that group of the population whose incomes and family characteristics are such that we would designate them as poor according to the official (Social Security Administration) poverty lines.[3] We have not attempted to determine the total impact of inflation on other groups, although our framework for analysis would be applicable for other population groups as well.

In section II we examine the expenditures of the poor, develop special price indexes for various groups of the poor, and compare our indexes with the Consumer Price Index. In section III we review the various sources of income of the poor and attempt to determine how the major sources of income have behaved in various inflationary periods. In section IV we examine the distribution of such wealth as the poor hold among various types of assets and attempt to estimate the extent to which "wealth effects" might be created for this group during periods in which the price level is rising. In the final section we draw together a number of policy considerations, which follow from the findings of the previous sections.

II.   The Poor Man's Price Index

The major indication that inflationary processes are under way is generally taken to be a substantial rise in the Consumer Price Index (CPI), which is designed to reflect the pattern of expenditures of a "typical family." It seems curious, therefore, that discussions of the effects of inflation on various parts of the population have rarely included any careful examination of the expenditure patterns of particular groups and the way in which differences among these expenditure patterns might generate relative differences in inflationary impacts. Obviously any given change in prices of various products will have different

---

2 See, for example, G. L. Bach and A. Ando, "Redistributional Effects of Inflation," *Review of Economics and Statistics*, February 1957; T. Scitovsky and A. Scitovsky, *Inflation, Growth and Income*, *Research Studies for the Commission on Money and Credit* (Englewood Cliffs, N.J.: Prentice-Hall, 1963).

3 For a description of the poverty lines and their rationale, see M. Orshansky, "Counting the Poor: Another Look at the Poverty Profile," *Social Security Bulletin*, January 1965, and "Who's Who Among the Poor: A Demographic View of Poverty," *Social Security Bulletin*, July 1965.

effects on the amount of consumption (or real income) of groups to the extent that they spend their incomes on quite different combinations of goods and services.

We might reasonably expect that the expenditure patterns of the poor would be somewhat different from those of the "typical family" used as the basis for the CPI. We, therefore, have attempted to construct a Poor Man's Price Index (PPI), which would reflect the expenditure patterns of the poor and would allow us to compare the extent to which price changes had expenditure effects on the poor which, in various periods, differed from those reflected in the CPI.

As a first approximation to a PPI, we simply reweighted the broad categories of the CPI, using as weights the expenditure pattern for an urban family of five with money income after taxes of $1,000 to $3,600 in 1960–61. Table 1 shows the results of this first approximation.

Although the results are interesting, we do not pause here to comment because this first approximation has at least two shortcomings. First, the weights are for broad categories of goods and, as Snyder has argued,[4] more disaggregated expenditure data would yield considerable differences in price relatives within the broad categories. Second, the group in the $1,000–$3,600 income range includes some individuals who are only "temporarily poor" (that is, whose incomes are low for a year or two but whose expenditures are related to their past and anticipated higher incomes) and excludes those with larger family size who have higher incomes but still fall below the official poverty standard. We might better estimate the expenditure patterns of the poor if the "temporarily poor" could be removed and the large-family poor included.

Table 2 (drawn from the Survey of Consumer Expenditures, 1960–61, hereafter referred to as the SCE) tabulates the degree to which families, defined as poor according to their income, had levels of expenditure exceeding the poverty line relevant to their family size. We include data for those families with incomes just above the poverty line as well, to give some indication of the extent to which drawing a sharp distinction at the poverty threshold may distort the picture.

This table is of some interest beyond the concerns of this paper, in that it seems to suggest that as much as 22 percent of the groups defined as poor on an income basis have expenditures exceeding the official poverty level.[5] (Of course, this group should be somewhat offset by those persons whose income exceeds the poverty standards but who continue to hold expenditures below poverty standard level — that is, those we could to some extent call the

---

4 See, for example, E. M. Snyder, "Cost of Living Indexes for Special Classes of Consumers," *The Price Statistics of the Federal Government*, NBER 73, General Series, 1961.

5 For an attempt to develop a poverty measure that takes into account the fact that low current income may reflect only temporary poverty, see W. L. Hansen and B. Weisbrod, "An Income–Net Worth Approach to Measuring Economic Welfare," *American Economic Review*, December 1968.

Table 1. First Approximation of Poor Price Index, Percent Change in Indexes

	Inflationary Period					Expenditure Weights of Poor	Expenditure Weights of Urban Family of Five with After-Tax Income of $7,500–$10,000
	1940–43	1945–48	1950–52	1956–58	1965–67		
Poor Price Index	21.6	30.5	10.2	6.1	5.9		
CPI	23.6	33.6	10.4	6.3	5.8		
Food	42.9	51.0	13.2	7.6	5.9	32.0	26.5
Housing	8.3	18.2	8.1	4.9	5.3	32.3	26.1
Clothes	27.5	35.5	7.9	2.2	6.7	10.8	12.0
Transportation	12.1	29.2	13.4	9.2	4.3	6.7	14.1
Medical	8.3	8.3	21.4	10.5	11.8	4.7	6.1
Personal	26.3	24.4	10.6	7.2	5.1	3.7	2.8
Reading, Recreation	17.3	15.6	3.5	7.9	4.3	4.8	7.3
Miscellaneous	5.5	17.2	9.7	4.2	6.1	5.1	5.2

Table 2. Unit[a] Income and Expenditures in Relation to
Poverty Standards

Income Poverty Line	Total Expenditures/Poverty Line Percentage of Raw Total					
	0–100	100–120	120–140	140–160	160–300	
0–1.0	78.6	9.5	4.5	3.1	4.3	100
1.0–1.1	35.6	31.5	16.0	8.6	8.3	100
1.1–1.2	28.8	32.5	15.9	9.6	13.2	100
1.2–2.0	8.5	8.8	22.8	19.3	40.6	100

[a]Consumer units: families and unrelated individuals.

Source: U.S. Department of Labor, Bureau of Labor Statistics, *Survey of Consumer Expenditures*, 1960–61.

"temporarily nonpoor." Table 3 facilitates the comparison of these two groups.)

Using the combination of expenditure and income levels as applied to the relevant poverty standard, we have tried to separate a group that would have expenditure patterns most closely representative of those of the "longer term poor." This group with incomes *and* expenditures below the poverty line is labeled "poor" in the tables. The group labeled "near-poor" includes those with incomes up to 1.2 times the poverty line and expenditures up to 1.6 times the poverty line. For these groups we have examined expenditure patterns. We used these new estimates to derive a refined set of weights for the broad categories of the price index, which we used in the first approximation. Table 4 shows the results of this second approximation.[6]

Note that Table 4 reports several different indexes. The Aged-Poor Index is for

Table 3. Distribution of Consumer Units by Income
and Expenditures

Income Poverty Line	Total Expenditures/Poverty Line Percent of Total		
	0–100	100–300	Subtotal
0–1.0	26.3	7.1	33.4
1.0–2.0	8.6	58.0	66.6
Subtotal	34.9	65.1	100.0

Source: U.S. Department of Labor, Bureau of Labor Statistics,
Survey of Consumer Expenditures, 1960–61.

6 The source of the price series is the U.S. Department of Labor, Bureau of Labor Statistics, *Handbook of Labor Statistics, 1968.* The listing of price series for Recreation and Reading (combined) presented difficulty. We simply applied the Recreation and Reading Index to the three weights from the SCE for which we had separate data. A glance at the expenditure weights on Table 3 will suffice to demonstrate that with the exception of the wealthy price index this procedure could make little difference relative to any other arbitrary one.

Table 4. Second Approximation Poor Price Indexes

	Year												Expenditure Weight			
	1947	1948	1950	1952	1956	1958	1960	1964	1965	1966	1967	1967[a]	Poor	Aged Poor	Near Poor	Wealthy
Consumer Price Index	77.8	83.8	83.8	92.5	94.7	100.7	103.1	108.1	109.9	113.1	116.3					
Poor Price Index	77.4	83.1	83.9	92.4	94.8	100.8	102.9	108.2	110.0	113.7	116.6	116.3				
Aged-Poor Price Index	76.6	82.3	83.4	91.9	94.8	100.8	103.1	108.4	110.3	114.1	117.1	116.3				
Near-Poor Price Index	77.1	80.6	83.8	92.2	94.7	100.6	103.1	108.4	110.2	113.8	116.8					
Wealthy Price Index[b]	76.5	82.2	83.9	92.0	94.5	100.6	103.4	108.9	110.6	113.8	117.0					
Food	81.3	88.2	85.8	97.1	94.7	101.9	101.4	106.4	108.8	114.2	115.2		.349	.344	.317	.219
Alcoholic beverages	75.4	78.9	82.6	96.6	97.1	99.6	102.1	104.7	105.8	107.7	109.9		.007	.004	.010	.018
Tobacco	73.0	76.3	80.0	86.6	94.1	99.7	107.1	114.8	120.2	126.1	130.9		.023	.016	.021	.013
Housing	74.5	79.8	83.2	89.9	95.5	100.2	103.1	107.2	108.5	111.1	114.3		.356	.422	.339	.278
Clothing	89.2	95.0	90.1	97.2	97.8	99.8	102.2	105.7	106.8	109.6	114.0		.078	.036	.087	.118
Transportation	64.3	71.6	79.0	89.6	91.3	99.7	103.8	109.3	111.1	112.7	115.9		.051	.033	.074	.160
Medical	65.7	69.8	73.4	81.1	91.8	100.1	108.1	119.4	122.3	127.7	136.7		.058	.086	.066	.062
Personal care	76.2	79.1	78.9	87.3	93.7	100.4	104.1	109.1	109.9	112.2	115.5		.033	.025	.032	.027
Recreation[c]	82.5	86.7	89.3	92.4	93.4	100.8	104.9	114.1	115.2	117.1	120.1		.023	.013	.027	.048
Reading[c]	82.5	86.7	89.3	92.4	93.4	100.8	104.9	114.1	115.2	117.1	120.1		.008	.011	.008	.009
Education[c]	82.5	86.7	89.3	92.4	93.4	100.8	104.9	114.1	115.2	117.1	120.1		.003	.0003	.005	.020
Miscellaneous	75.4	78.9	82.6	90.6	95.8	101.8	103.8	108.8	111.8	114.9	118.2		.011	.010	.014	.029

[a] Adjusted for Medicare

[b] Incomes of $10,000+ in 1960

[c] Reading and Recreation Index used

Source: Year data from U.S. Department of Labor, Bureau of Labor Statistics, *Handbook of Labor Statistics, 1968*; and Expenditure Weight data from U.S. Department of Labor, Bureau of Labor Statistics, *Survey of Consumer Expenditures*, 1960–61.

a subset of the poor, including those families with heads aged 65 and over and unrelated individuals aged 65 and over, whose income and expenditures fall below the poverty line for their family size. The Near-Poor Index is based on the expenditure patterns of the group of near-poor as defined in the previous paragraph. The Wealthy Index is based on the expenditure patterns of units with incomes of $10,000 and above.

Comparisons of the Near-Poor and Wealthy Index with both the CPI and the PPI make possible some idea of relative differences in expenditure effects of price level changes for groups at different income levels. The CPI is based upon the expenditure patterns of urban wage and salary earning units with incomes below $10,000 (income limit was revised upward after 1961). Thus the CPI group includes many poor units. If we wish to get some indication of how expenditure effects of price level changes are altering the relative position of the poor, it is useful to remember that the gap between the CPI and the PPI will tend to underrepresent any relative changes since the poor units are averaged into the CPI base.[7]

The picture that emerges from this second approximation is one that leaves the PPI generally close to the CPI. The Aged-Poor Index is more consistently above the CPI, and this difference began to widen after 1965. This gap between the Aged-Price Index and the CPI led us to make a rough adjustment in the former index to account for the effects of Medicare[8] on the Aged-Poor Index. The Medicare adjustment reduced the Aged-Poor Index back to the CPI level. In line with the change in the Aged Index we adjusted the PPI to account for the influence of the aged subset of this group on the overall weights. This adjustment brought the PPI down by a lesser extent but still to the level of the CPI (the results of these adjustments are reported in Table 4 in the column headed 1967[a]).

The process of making these adjustments brought to light another consideration. The aged are a considerable portion of the poor as we have defined them by income and expenditure. This finding suggests that if a Nonaged-Poor Index had been constructed, it would have fallen below the CPI in most years because the Aged-Poor segment is pulling the PPI up. Second, besides highlighting the importance of age differences in this group, it raises some questions about the relation of the SCE sample to the officially defined poverty population, because both the poor and the near-poor seem to contain substantially higher percentages of aged units. Third, the Medicare adjustment does not take into account the possible effects of Medicaid on the nonaged

---

7 Note that the CPI from 1947 to 1958 is the Bureau of Labor Statistics series and reflects adjustments made by the BLS for shifting expenditure weights over that period. Since we could only estimate expenditure weights for the other indexes on the SCE of 1960–61 those indexes are *fixed* weight indexes. Thus in the 1947–58 period comparisons between the CPI and other indexes are subject to bias due to differences in weighting procedures. We return to this point later.

8 For this approximation we simply followed S. Waldman in *Social Security Bulletin*, June 1967, p. 11, and cut the medical series weight by 40 percent to approximate effects of Medicare.

Table 5. Disaggregated Price Indexes for the Poor

Year	CPI	All Poor	Aged Poor	Rural Nonaged Poor	Rural Aged Poor	Urban Nonaged Poor	Urban White Poor	Urban Nonwhite Poor
1953	93.2	93.8	93.2	94.3	93.7	93.7	93.4	93.8
1954	93.6	94.3	93.9	94.3	93.9	94.2	94.0	94.3
1955	93.3	94.1	94.0	93.7	93.6	93.9	93.8	94.1
1956	94.7	95.4	95.2	94.9	94.9	95.1	95.1	95.4
1957	98.0	98.2	98.0	97.9	97.9	97.9	98.0	98.1
1958	100.7	100.9	100.7	100.7	100.8	100.6	100.7	100.7
1959	101.5	101.4	101.2	101.3	101.3	101.1	101.3	101.2
1960	103.1	102.9	102.7	102.6	102.7	102.6	102.9	102.7
1961	104.2	103.9	103.8	103.5	103.7	103.6	103.8	103.7
1962	105.4	104.9	104.7	104.5	104.5	104.7	104.8	104.6
1963	106.7	106.4	106.0	105.9	105.8	106.1	106.2	106.0
1964	108.1	107.5	107.1	107.0	107.0	107.2	107.4	107.1
1965	109.9	109.1	108.8	108.7	108.6	108.9	109.1	108.7
1966	113.1	112.5	112.0	112.1	112.0	112.2	112.4	112.0
1967	116.3	114.7	114.2	114.6	114.3	114.7	114.9	114.3
1966[a]			111.8		111.2			
1967[a]			113.5		112.4			

[a] Adjusted for Medicare.

segment of the poor group and in this sense may represent a conservative estimate of the effects of this important social legislation.

We have been able to move beyond this second approximation of the PPI by carrying out some further refinements. With the exception of the food category, the SCE provides a more detailed breakdown of expenditure categories than that used in Table 4. Wherever these disaggregated weights were compatible with detailed price series in the *1968 Handbook of Labor Statistics*, we used the information to construct a better price index for the poor.[9] Table 5 reports these final disaggregated price indexes. The difference between the disaggregated PPI (Table 5, column 3) and the second approximation of the PPI (Table 4) is quite striking. The effect of disaggregating to take into account detailed differences in expenditure patterns within the broader categories was to reduce the PPI almost two full points (in 1967) below the value that Table 4 reports. This reduction occurs even without the Medicare adjustment taken into account. The primary reason for this drop appears to be the exceedingly high index for hospitalized illness (200 in 1967) and the disparity between the food-prepared-at-home and the food-away-from-home price indexes (112 versus 129 in 1967). Because the poor spend a lower portion of income on hospitalized illness and a smaller portion of their food budget on meals eaten away from home, the impact of rises in these detailed indexes is considerably smaller for them.

---

9 When price information was not available to correspond with a detailed expenditure weight we applied the price index of the broader category (food, housing, and so forth) to the detailed expenditure weight.

In the last two rows of Table 5 we have made an adjustment for the impact of Medicare on the Aged-Poor Price Index. That the Medicare adjustment lowered their estimated price index by .7 points in 1967 reflects the substantial benefits of this legislation in protecting the aged poor from expenditure effects due to rising medical costs.

. That the disaggregated indexes for the poor are lower seems to cast some doubt on the theory sometimes proposed[10] that a more detailed calculation of a price index for the poor will yield a greater negative impact of inflation on the poor. (The inability of the poor, as compared to the wealthy, to substitute for items within a broad expenditure category, assuming differential price increases of these detailed items, is due to their putting a greater proportion of their money into "necessities.") This argument, however, would seem to be most applicable (if valid) within the food-prepared-at-home category. But because we do not have a breakdown of expenditures here we cannot assess the validity of it. We can only point out that the disaggregation we were able to accomplish seemed to reduce the estimates of the impact of inflation on the poor rather than to raise them.

Table 5 also shows indexes estimated for the poor group further subdivided by location, age and race.

Even with our most refined results we are forced to use a fixed set of weights for every period and all PPIs. Thus up to 1960 we use a Paasche Index and after 1960 a Laspeyre Index. As such we have only an approximation to the appropriate "true index" for the group in these years.[11] The CPI is adjusted by the BLS for the 1950–60 period to reflect shifting expenditure weights with a rising income over the period (after 1960 this is possible only to the extent that they raise the upper-income cutoff for units included in the base; they do not have new expenditure pattern data after 1960). We can probably say that using the fixed weight PPI to compare with the shifted weight CPI in the 1950–60 period tended to reduce the differences between the indexes in that period because the CPI procedure takes account of the lower levels of average income in the earlier period whereas the fixed-weight PPI does not.

We have not been able to make any estimates of price indexes for the poor that would take into account the elements of the contemporary controversy over whether the poor pay more. That controversy is concerned with the question of whether, or to what extent, the poor pay higher *prices* for any given good or set of goods. In constructing the PPI, we have used the same price series used for the CPI because we have no conclusive data on the *prices* the poor actually pay and, above all, no time-series data on such prices. However, we make clear that only under special circumstances would this shortcoming bias our conclusions. We are investigating the effects of price *changes*, thus the poor-pay-more phenomenon will only affect our results if the prices they pay

---

10 E. M. Snyder, *op. cit.*

11 For a discussion of price indexes, see N. Leviatan and D. Patinkin, "On the Economic Theory of Price Indexes," *Economic Development and Cultural Change*, 1961.

not only are higher in *level* but *rise faster* than the prices paid for the same goods in outlets used by the nonpoor – that is, only if the gap between what the poor pay for a given set of goods and what the nonpoor pay *increases* as the general price level increases.

Our final, disaggregated PPI estimates indicate that the expenditure effects of the type of inflation we have experienced since World War II, in general, have not been adverse for the poor. Particularly in the 1960s the expenditure effects of rising price levels have fallen somewhat less heavily on the poor than on other income groups.

A different set of factors in different periods can generate rises in a general price index, such as the CPI, and as a result the pattern of rises in detailed categories of prices can vary from one inflationary period to another. Although evidence seems to indicate that this has not happened in the United States post–World War II period, conceivably an inflation that would cause greater rises in those price categories in which the poor spend a greater portion of their income could be generated. The distributional effects of inflation (on the expenditure as well as other sides) could also differ substantially according to the differential forces generating the inflation. Just as the character of inflations may differ, so the policies for dealing with them could differ accordingly. We should certainly want to ask, what distributional effects of the particular inflation do we face at a given time; what forces generate the inflation, and what policies are available to deal with these forces; most importantly, what distributional effects are the *policies* we select likely to generate? We will return to these policy considerations. As far as the *expenditure effects* of recent inflations are concerned, the poor have not clearly been hurt the most by price rises, and their *relative* position may well have improved.

III.   Income of the Poor

We turn now to an examination of the sources of income of the poor. Although we must necessarily proceed in piecemeal fashion – considering first expenditure effects, then income effects, and finally wealth effects – we urge the reader to bear in mind that the inflationary process generates all these effects simultaneously. In assessing the impact of inflation or the policies adopted to contain inflation, we need to take into account these simultaneous effects in order to determine the *net* effect on the economic well-being of the group – in this case, the poor.

First, we examine the relative importance of various types of income for the poverty population. Table 6 shows a profile of the income sources of the poor and the near-poor (as defined in the previous section), based upon data from the 1960–61 SCE. Because there are likely to be significant differences in the relative importance in various types of income for the aged, as opposed to the nonaged units, there is a separation, for both the poor and the near-poor, of aged and nonaged units reported in Table 6.

Table 6. Income Sources of Various Groups,[a] 1960

| | Poor | | | | | | | | | Near-poor | | | | | | | | |
| | Aged | | | Nonaged | | | Total | | | Aged | | | Nonaged | | | Total | | |
	1	2	3	1	2	3	1	2	3	1	2	3	1	2	3	1	2	3
Frequency (000's)		2,959			3,558			6,517			4,470			7,088			11,557	
Total money income before personal taxes (Mean for all)		$1,176			$1,885			$1,643			$1,366			$2,938			$2,331	
Wages and salary	19.9	$ 454	7.7	74.3	$1,689	66.7	49.6	$1,465	44.3	22.5	$ 517	8.5	77.2	$2,140	56.3	56.1	$1,888	45.4
Self-employment	5.0	421	1.8	10.2	955	5.2	7.9	800	3.8	7.1	340	1.8	17.6	2,358	14.1	13.6	1,949	11.3
Rent, roomers	16.6	334	4.7	6.9	176	.6	11.3	281	1.9	19.9	371	5.4	10.7	295	.1	14.2	336	2.1
Int., dividends, prof. from stocks, bonds, & owned not operated business	21.6	140	2.6	5.5	83	.2	12.8	127	1.0	29.4	173	3.7	11.2	1,183	4.5	18.3	554	4.3
Public employment Social Security	73.8	905	58.5	29.6	748	10.9	49.7	854	25.8	79.3	1,021	59.2	27.2	751	7.0	47.4	926	18.8
Priv. pen., ret. annuities & trust funds	3.6	420	1.3	1.0	306	.2	2.2	391	.6	5.9	492	2.1	1.3	3,000	1.4	3.1	1,159	1.5
Pub. soc. ass't. private relief	20.5	822	14.3	23.7	1,203	7.4	22.3	1,044	14.1	15.7	796	9.2	15.5	1,155	6.1	15.6	1,015	6.8
Rect. of cash gifts	27.3	153	3.6	21.9	156	1.8	24.3	154	2.3	24.3	166	2.9	22.4	496	3.8	23.2	362	3.6
Military allotments, pensions, etc.	5.0	842	3.6	6.7	901	3.2	5.9	878	3.2	7.9	860	4.9	7.3	793	2.0	7.5	820	2.7
Other money incomes	13.0	184	2.0	17.5	398	3.7	15.4	316	3.0	12.2	239	2.1	19.1	589	3.8	16.4	489	3.4

1 Percent of those units reporting nonzero income from source.
2 Mean of source of those units reporting nonzero from source.
3 Percent of total mean income from source for all units.

Source: U.S. Department of Labor, Bureau of Labor Statistics,
Survey of Consumer Expenditures, 1960—61.
[a] Consumer units: families and unrelated individuals.

Briefly, Table 6 yields these significant observations:

1. Wage and salary income is important to the nonaged poor, as we would expect. Approximately three fourths of the units report income from this source, and they are highly dependent upon it.

2. Wage and salary income is also important to the aged-poor; one fifth of them report income from this source. Among the near-poor this fraction is one fourth, implying that those units with incomes just above the poverty line derive considerably more income from wages and salaries than those below the line. This, undoubtedly, is a primary factor in their being above the line.

3. Various forms of public assistance are the most important income source to the aged-poor; nearly 95 percent of the units report income in this category. For the nonaged this is the second most important source, although lagging far behind wages and salaries.

4. Contrary to popular belief, only a small percentage of the aged poor (about 10 percent) receive money from pensions, annuities, and other forms of fixed valued income. The data also suggest that the actual amounts accruing annually in this category are much less than 10 percent of the mean income of the aged-poor.

These results lead us to conclude that undue emphasis has been placed on the prevalence of aged-poor persons who live primarily on income of a fixed-value and thus have their purchasing power seriously eroded by inflation. (The case of public assistance income is somewhat different. See section B.) We need to stress the important primary role of wage and salary income for the poor as well as the secondary role of public transfer income. Accordingly we now turn to the experience of the poor with regard to these major income sources.

A.   Wage and Salary Income of the Poor

The area of wage and salary income is one of the most frustrating faced in this study. It seems to us that unquestionably considerable gains to the poor exist in terms of wage and salary income during the periods of tighter labor markets that usually accompany inflationary periods (in post–World War II America). However, data that will permit us to pin down with a high degree of precision the magnitude of such gains are difficult to obtain. Therefore, at the moment, we can only present the configuration of evidence at hand. This area of the study warrants considerably more attention, for soon far richer data than we have so far used will be available.

A few economists have written articles that discuss the harmful effects of unemployment on the poor and imply that a mild rate of inflation may be a small price to pay for the benefits of a tight labor market.[12] These

---

12 The most eloquent of these is perhaps "Unemployment and Poverty" by Harry G. Johnson, a paper presented at West Virginia University Conference on *Poverty Amidst Affluence*, May 3–7, 1965. See also Scitovsky, *op. cit.*; and J. Tobin, "On Improving the Economic Status of the Negro," in the *Daedalus* issue on *The Negro American*, 1965.

economists mention considerations, other than the more obvious ones we are attempting to measure, that bear upon the importance of lower unemployment rates for the poor. For this reason we should bear these in mind as strengthening the thrust of our evidence. Specifically, we refer to their arguments concerning:

1.   The dependence on a tight labor market of the success of the myriad of training and hiring programs aimed at the "marginal worker" and the "hard-core unemployed." We trust that this point need not be emphasized. Any analysis of the post–World War II American economy would tend to underestimate the effect of a low unemployment rate on the poor because government and private industry has never made such a massive effort to use special programs to facilitate their participation in the labor market.

2.   The damaging effects of a fluctuating unemployment rate upon the poor. Again, an examination of historical data might result in an underestimation of future harm, if the unemployment rate were to fluctuate more often than in the past. And we are in danger of promoting such cyclical movements if we apply fiscal and monetary brakes every time a mild inflation occurs. To quote Harry Johnson: "fluctuations in the unemployment rate . . . leave a residue of poverty that is not compensated for by periods of high demand for labor. Specifically, there are two major groups of victims of cyclically heavy unemployment: the youthful entrants to the labor force, whose failure to find work permanently impairs their future earnings because they miss the opportunity to obtain the on-the-job training necessary to fit them for higher-paying employment later in their careers, and the older workers, who find it difficult to become re-employed, or re-employed in as high-paying jobs, in the subsequent period of cyclically high employment. For both groups, cyclical unemployment not only increases the current incidence of poverty, but increases the future incidence of poverty."[13]

3.   The psychological consequences of unemployment. We are concerned in this paper with measuring the economic effects of unemployment on the poor. Although unquantifiable, the psychic harm is considerable and is ultimately a primary concern of society.

Aggregate Time Series Regressions   As a first step in exploring the income side of the inflationary impact question, we ran some crude regressions to see if we could find any gross relationships between the incidence of poverty and changes in the CPI.

The first regression that we tried on data for 1947–66 was:

$$\%P = a + b_1 t + b_2 U + b_3 \%\text{CPI}$$

where $\%P = \%$ of population below poverty lines (SSA standard in constant dollars). $U =$ unemployment rate; $\%\text{CPI} = \%$ change in the CPI.

---

13 Johnson, *op. cit.*

The results were:

$$\%P = 31.01 - .9117\% + .5749U - .0715\%CPI$$
$$SE = (1.13)\quad (.04)\quad (.21)\quad (.10)$$
$$t = 27.5\quad -23.2\quad 2.76\quad -.71$$

where $R^2 = .97$; d.w. $= .7859$.

The Durbin–Watson statistic indicated serial correlation of the residuals. In a simple attempt to remove serial correlation we took first differences and got:

$$D\%P = -.8539 + .6676DU - .1238D\%CPI$$
$$SE = (.183)\quad (.159)\quad (.058)$$
$$t = -4.65\quad 4.19\quad -2.12$$

where $R^2 = .69$; d.w. $= 2.3514$.

As we can readily see, the %CPI coefficient is statistically significant and negative. There are three important points about this result:

1. If inflationary processes had adverse effects on the incomes of the poor, we would expect the price index term in this regression to be positive by the following logic. The poverty lines used to determine the incidence of poverty were deflated (in constant dollars). Therefore, for inflation to "hurt" the poor (for the incidence of poverty to increase), we would expect, after allowing for the linear effects of a general time trend changes in the level of unemployment, that during inflationary periods the incomes of the poor would rise less than the price level – thus an increase in the incidence of poverty – and consequently that the coefficient on the %CPI term would be positive.

2. Even if the price term had not been statistically different from zero, we could not thereby infer that the poor *were* hurt by inflation. The price term could have failed to be significant for a completely different reason: the tighter labor markets associated with rising prices may already have adequately been represented by the unemployment term. To the extent that tighter labor markets can only be attained with higher percentage price changes, in other words, the poor should be willing to tolerate those rising prices (offset by rising incomes).

3. The first two points highlight the third. That the coefficient price term is both negative in sign and statistically significant indicates that even after the direct effects of a lower unemployment rate had been taken into account, the secondary effects of tighter labor markets – through higher participation rates, more full-time employment, narrowing wage differentials, increase in share to labor (any of which the price-index term might have picked up) – may be important in significantly raising the incomes of the poor.[14]

---

14 We were further encouraged by the fact that Charles Metcalf obtained similar price level effects in his work on income distributions. See his "The Size Distribution of Personal Income in an Econometric Model of the United States," Ph.D. thesis, Massachusetts Institute of Technology, 1968.

We decided to run an even more stringent test of the effects of the inflationary process on the incidence of poverty by replacing the time trend variable with median family income. Now, to the extent that tighter labor markets result in higher labor force participation rates and reduced part-time (or increased overtime) employment, which are broadly shared across all income classes, the median family income term should help to pick up these effects. Thus the median family income term and the unemployment term would be likely to pick up even more of the effects of tighter labor markets than did the time trend and unemployment variables combined.

Once again — and even more so in this case — even if the price term failed to have significance, we would *not* conclude that on the income side inflation was neutral or detrimental with respect to the incidence of poverty; an insignificant price term could reflect a positive relation of price rises with rises in median income, and through rises in median income a negative relation with the incidence of poverty. A prior hypothesis of an adverse impact of inflation on the incidence of poverty would lead to a prediction of a *positive* coefficient on the price term. The results of the regressions with median family income in place of the time trend were:

$$\%P = 54.22 - 0.0041M + .0214U - .0978\%CPI$$

$$SE = (1.733) \quad (.0002) \quad (.2146) \quad (.1068)$$

$$t = 31.28 - 21.987 \quad .099 - .915$$

where M = median family income; $R^2 = .97$; d.w. = .5088.

Due to the Durkin–Watson value we again took first differences:

$$D\%P = -.0038DM + .1789DU - .1318D\%CPI$$

$$SE = (.0005) \quad (.1424) \quad (.0440)$$

$$t = -7.09 \quad 1.263 \quad -2.996$$

where $R^2 = .87$, d.w. = 1.66.

On this basis, even when the change in median income picks up any general indications of tightness in labor markets, a higher rate of change in the price level would seem to be associated with further reductions in the incidence of poverty. The poverty-reducing effects of tighter labor markets associated with higher percent changes in the CPI survive even this more stringent test. We find these results quite compelling.

We should hasten to add, however, that we are aware of the weaknesses inherent in this approach, which focuses on gross aggregate relationships within a single regression equation framework. We mention here just three potentially serious shortcomings. First, a potentially important aggregation error exists because of subgroups within the poverty population (for example, aged and female-headed families) whose response to the tighter labor market variables may be different from those indicated by the aggregate figures. (However, it is not clear, *a priori*, whether having lower labor force participation they benefit less or, on the contrary, being marginal workers in looser labor markets they get relatively greater benefits when markets are extraordinarily tight.) Second, such a single equation relationship is implicitly a reduced form of an unspecified set of structural economic relationships. Without specification of the entire structure we must be cautious in interpreting the meaning of the observed coefficients. Third (but related to the second point), we have specified a linear relationship between the incidence of poverty and the other variables. However, this relationship may not be a proper specification, that is, one or more of the independent variables may, in fact, be related to the incidence measure in a nonlinear fashion. If such were the case, the price index term could simply be picking up some of the nonlinear effects of other variables.

To check this possibility we have experimented with other functional forms for the regression equations. Although in one case the results with alternative functional forms were somewhat weaker with respect to the price index term, in no case did they contradict (indicate a significant positive coefficient) the aforementioned results and in most cases they yielded similar results.

Despite these potential weaknesses, we feel the regression results are quite important. At a minimum they do provide certain simple results. The negative price index term serves to reject, at least on this level, the idea that during inflationary periods price-level rises outstrip rises in income of the poor. Even if it were colinear with median family income and/or the employment rate, the price index term would seem to characterize the important benefits to the poor of tighter labor markets. And if the direction of the economy is such that the benefits of tighter labor markets are only attained with higher rises in prices, then the fact that the benefits to the poor do occur must be kept clearly in focus. Finally, at least in the post–World War II period in the United States, in periods of tight labor markets that characterize the inflationary process, the poor seem to gain not only through decreased unemployment but also through some narrowing of wage differentials or *relative* increases in hours worked; these type of gains are reflected in the results we obtained with the price index term.

We might appraise these results in a somewhat different light. Instead of asking the question "Does inflation hurt the poor?" we might ask the question "Will a policy to stop inflation be helpful for the poor?" Nothing in these results suggests that the poor would gain from a reduction in inflationary pressure. If the results have any validity, they suggest that a policy to reduce inflation, especially if coupled with even a "slight" rise in unemployment, could result in serious losses for the poor. We will explore this point in more detail later in the paper.

Studies of Specific Labor Force Effects   Having examined some broad aggregate relationships, we now review some studies of the specific form labor force effects on wage and salary income might take.

We can divide the means by which the poor (or any other group) make gains in wage and salary into two broad types: changes in labor force status and increased remuneration for those already employed. We can separate gains resulting from changes in labor force status into several categories: (a) increased labor force participation, (b) reduction in unemployment for those already in the labor force, (c) changes in part-time employment status for those already employed.

The responsiveness of labor force participation rates (LFPR) of various subgroups of the population to the overall unemployment rate is a subject that has recently received considerable attention in the economic literature.[15] Differences in sex, age, employment status of other family members, and income seem to explain the significant individual differences in this sensitivity. Few studies deal explicitly with income as an independent variable, thus focusing on the poor; and the findings of such studies are the subject of considerable controversy.[16] For example, some of the gross evidence suggests that the LFPR of poor males are negatively related with the unemployment rate more strongly than are those for nonpoor males; that is, lower unemployment brings greater labor force participation for poor males. However, more refined analysis later overturned a similar gross result originally found for female workers. Thus we should be cautious about accepting any firm conclusions on these questions at this time.

We need to be clear about the relevance of these labor force participation questions to the issues we are addressing in this report. Without doubt the labor force participation rates of the poor (and most other groups) are likely to increase with tightening labor markets. Because the unemployment rate is the ratio of the number unemployed to the total in the labor force, this sensitivity of the LFPR means that the decline in the unemployment *rate* is likely to understate the actual gains in numbers of employed from these groups. However, in the regression in the previous section the unemployment term would pick up these gains in employment because of their correlation with the unemployment rate. The question of the *relative* sensitivity to LFPR of the poor, as opposed to the nonpoor, relates to two points of interest in this paper. First, that in the second set of regressions the price term was significantly negative even after the inclusion of a median family income term in the regression is suggestive of *relatively greater* gains for the poor than for the nonpoor from tight labor market situations characterized by rising price levels. A higher sensitivity of LFPR for the poor would suggest that a given reduction in unemployment would understate the gains in employment more for the poor than the nonpoor.

---

15 See, for example, the works of Bowen and Finegan, Cain, Mincer, Strand, and Dernburg, Tella, and Barth.

16 The only two studies familiar to us that attempt to focus explicitly on the poor are Parker and Shaw, "Labor Force Participation Within Metropolitan Areas," *Southern Economic Journal*, 1968; and Mooney, "Urban Poverty and Labor Force Participation," *AER*, March 1967. Cain and Mincer have challenged the validity of Mooney's findings in a comment that will appear in a forthcoming *AER* issue.

Relatively greater LFPR sensitivity would seem to be commensurate with the suggestion of relative (as well as absolute) gains for the poor that emerged from the second set of regressions. However, this is only one possible explanation of the relative gains (others being relatively greater reduction in unemployment or relatively greater movement from part time to full time or relative greater increases in wages), and in light of the controversy previously noted, it should be regarded as one of the less likely explanations. The second point on relative LFPR sensitivity has to do with the study by Mooney and Metcalf,[17] who assume greater LFPR sensitivity to obtain their results (although we should note that they make other assumptions, adjustments to counterbalance any error that might prove to result from this relative LFPR sensitivity assumption).

Let us consider the Mooney and Metcalf study. In their work, carried out for the Office of Economic Opportunity, they attempted to construct some estimates of the change in poverty status for the population as a whole, which would result from a given change in the overall unemployment rate. Essentially this study provides estimates for the gains to the poor from *changes in their labor force status* associated with a reduction in unemployment.

They made use of the cross-section LFPRs of Bowen and Finegan[18] for the various population subgroups of the poor in 1964 that Orshansky profiled.[19] Two critical assumptions were necessary in the Mooney and Metcalf study. In light of the previous discussion, one should make us cautious about putting much weight on the results: the assumption that the LFPRs for the poor are the same in all cohorts as for the population at large, but *with their sensitivity increased by 25 percent*. The other one is that the unemployment within each population subgroup of the poor would fall proportionately to the national rate. To estimate the number of people removed from poverty they simply attributed the same incidence of poverty that existed at the higher unemployment rates for the various units classified by labor force status to the new distribution of units resulting from the lower employment rates. Tables 7 and 8 present their results.

Assuming that the decline in part-time employment all flows into full-time employment, they estimate that in moving from a 5.4 to a 3.5 percent national unemployment rate full-time employment would increase to 1,042,000 for the poor. Similarly, if the move were from 4.5 percent to 3.5 percent, the gain would be 518,000. These gains in employment translate into 1,811,000 and 958,000 (respectively) people moved out of poverty. Although the precise size of these quantities is questionable, we believe that the order of magnitude is reasonable primarily because it compares favorably with the estimates of the

---

17 C. E. Metcalf and J. D. Mooney, "Aggregate Demand Model," unpublished working paper for the OEO, 1965.

18 W. G. Bowen and T. A. Finegan, "Labor Force Participation and Unemployment," in A. M. Ross, ed., *Employment Policy and the Labor Market* (Berkeley: University of California Press, 1965), pp. 115–61.

19 M. Orshansky, "Counting the Poor: Another Look at the Poverty Profile," *Social Security Bulletin, January 1965, pp. 1–29.*

Table 7. Labor Force Status of the Poor at National Unemployment

Categories	Total Population	Employment Status	Full-time Employment	Part-time Employment	Unemployed	Labor Force
				5.4% Unemployment Rate		
Male heads of families	5,222	3,154	1,781	1,373	324 (9.3)[b]	3,478 (66.6)[a]
Female heads of families	1,958	574	143	431	76 (11.7)[b]	650 (33.2)[a]
Unrelated individuals (male)	1,441		232	333	114 (16.8)[b]	679 (47.1)[a]
Unrelated individuals (female)	3,474		190	738	90 (8.9)[b]	1,018 (29.3)[a]
Wives and non-wives (female) in families headed by a male	6,338	1,152			217 (15.9)[b]	1,369 (21.6)[a]
Males (nonheads) in houses headed by a male	1,450	451			126 (21.8)[b]	577 (40.2)[a]
Females (nonheads) in houses headed by a female	860	186			33 (15.1)[b]	219 (25.5)[a]
Males (nonheads) in families headed by a female	750	226			107 (32.0)[b]	333 (44.4)[a]

[a]Labor force participation rates in percentages.
[b]Unemployment rates in percentages.
Source: C. E. Metcalf and J. D. Mooney, "Aggregate Demand Model," unpublished OEO paper.

impact of a change in the unemployment rate that emerged from our first set of regressions in the previous section.

The Mooney and Metcalf study provides estimates of gains resulting from changes in labor force status associated with tighter labor markets. We previously noted that gains were possible beyond those due only to changes in labor force status. For that reason we now focus our attention on wage and salary increases to the already-working poor due to increased remuneration during times of low unemployment and inflationary pressures. This particular method of improving their income status is important to the poor for two reasons: First, because wage and salary earnings play a crucial role in the overall income picture of the poor (see Table 6); and second, although the benefits to many of the poor (through labor force status changes), which occur with a movement to lower unemployment, are striking, the already-employed poor (see Table 9 for percentages) must depend on the effects on remuneration of a continuing tight labor market for gains in their real wages.

Rates of 5.4%, 4.5%, and 3.5% (In Thousands of Persons)

	4.5% Unemployment Rate					3.5% Unemployment Rate			
Employment Status	Full-Time Employment	Part-Time Employment	Unemployed	Labor Force	Employment Status	Full-time Employment	Part-time Employment	Unemployed	Labor Force
3,243	1,966	1,277	272 (7.7)[b]	3,514 (67.3)[a]	3,343	2,175	1,168	213 (5.9)[b]	3,556 (68.1)[a]
603	180	423	65 (9.8)[b]	668 (33.9)[a]	635	220	415	52 (7.6)[b]	687 (34.7)[a]
	282	314	96 (14.0)[b]	692 (47.8)[a]		338	292	76 (10.9)[b]	706 (48.6)[a]
	243	726	77 (7.4)[b]	1,046 (30.1)[a]		304	713	63 (5.8)[b]	1,080 (31.1)[a]
1,234			188 (13.2)[b]	1,422 (12.4)[a]	1,330			152 (10.3)[b]	1,482 (23.4)[a]
499			110 (18.1)[b]	609 (42.0)[a]	544			88 (13.9)[b]	632 (43.6)[a]
196			28 (12.6)[b]	224 (26.0)[a]	200			23 (9.8)[b]	231 (26.9)[a]
252			92 (26.7)[b]	344 (45.8)[a]	284			74 (20.6)[b]	358 (47.7)[a]

In light of the result reported in the previous section we would expect that poor workers have at least held their own, or even gained, during times of mild inflation. We define "holding their own" as realizing wages increases that keep the real value of their wage income in line with the generally rising standard of living as reflected in the growth rate of median income. Rises in the real wage and salary income of the already-employed poor could occur either because the general wage level rises in those industries in which they are concentrated or because wage differentials within industries have narrowed in their favor. (Alternatively we could look at wage levels and differentials classified along occupational rather than industrial lines.) Because most theories of wage determination relevant to this study are couched in terms of relative wages, we focus on this latter aspect.

Minsky[20] and others have argued both that wage differentials tend to

20 H. Minsky, "Tight Full Employment: Let's Heat Up the Economy," in H. P. Miller, ed., *Poverty: American Style*, (Belmont, Calif.: Wadsworth Publishing Co., 1966), pp. 294–300.

Table 8. Reductions in Poverty Status of Families and Unrelated Individuals When the National Unemployment Rates Fall from 5.4 to 3.5 %

	Total Population (March 1964) at 5.4% (Unemployment Rate)	Change to 4.5% (Unemployment Rate)	Change to 3.5% (Unemployment Rate)
Members of male-headed families	22,100,000	−612,000[a]	−1,302,000
Members of female-headed families	7,600,000	−160,000	−341,000
Unrelated individuals (females)	3,500,000	−47,000	−95,000
Unrelated individuals (males)	1,400,000	−34,000	−73,000
Totals	34,600,000	−853,000	−1,811,000

[a]This figure means that 612,000 people (including heads and children) would be moved above the poverty line.

Source: C. E. Metcalf and J. D. Mooney, "Aggregate Demand Model," unpublished OEO paper.

Table 9. Percent of Total Poor (1964)

Employment and Work Experience of Head	Families (7,180,000)	Unrelated Individuals (11,182,000)
Not in labor force	42.5	65.4
Unemployed	5.6	4.2
Employed	51.9	30.4
Worked in 1963	64.3	36.2
Full-time jobs	50.0	23.6
Part-time jobs	14.3	12.7
Did not work in 1963	35.7	63.8
Number of earners		
None	27.5	
One	45.7	
Two or more	26.8	

Source: *Current Population Survey,* 1964.

narrow in tighter labor markets and that as the overall unemployment rate drops, the preponderance of unemployment rates in those occupations with a heavy concentration of poor drop disproportionately more. Hence the poor wage earners are aided relatively more by both the initial drop in unemployment and the continued operation of the economy at the lower rate. The point with regard to those benefits resulting from a change in labor force status is unlikely to be contested. However, we must examine the question of narrowing wage differentials as caused by a drop in the unemployment rate and by a continued tight labor market. Reder[21] points out that it is one thing to propose that occupational wage differentials narrow as the unemployment rate decreases and quite a different matter to stipulate that these differentials will continue to narrow with the unemployment level constant at the lower level. Briefly, his theory is that in a period of excess demand the supply of skilled workers can be augmented by lowering hiring requirements and by substituting less skilled for more skilled workers. However, this procedure cannot be used to increase the supply of the unskilled. Faced with a relatively inelastic supply of unskilled, the competition for labor during a rapid expansion leads to proportionately larger wage increases for the unskilled than for the skilled. Thus the former proposal regarding the narrowing of wage differentials is consistent with Reder's theory, whereas the latter need not be. In fact, the post—World War II American experience seem to bear out this former proposition, although some economists

21 M. W. Reder, "A Theory of Occupational Wage Differentials," *American Economic Review*, 45 (December 1955).

will put more emphasis on institutional factors as causal than they will on the elements of Reder's theory.[22]

Some schools of thought rely upon institutional factors to maintain that a mild inflation tends to narrow relative wage differentials even though there need not be any particular excess demand in the labor market. Perlman argues that "... under conditions of a wage and price inflation, with much smaller rises in real income, conditions that have prevailed since the end of World War II, there is a powerful tendency for wage increases to be distributed in such a way that narrows the percentage skill differential."[23] Under such conditions labor is more interested in wage levels than wage structure, and across-the-board wage increases of an equal amount to all workers decrease the relative wage differentials. In any event, most models of wage determination, whether or not they are primarily institutional, predict a narrowing of relative wage differentials in times of falling unemployment and, at worst, nonwidening relative differentials in labor markets with a constant low rate of unemployment and mild inflation.

In sum, then, we can say that studies of the specific labor force effects of tight labor markets associated with inflationary processes lend support to the results obtained in the previous examination of aggregate relationships between the incidence of poverty and rising price levels. The tighter labor markets associated with inflationary processes seem to provide both absolute and relative gains in income for the poor as a result of improved labor force status and a probable narrowing of wage differentials in favor of the poor worker.

B.   Transfer Income

Table 6 clearly shows that public transfer payments of various types are second only to wages and salaries as a source of income for the poor. To see how public transfer sources of income behave over the long term and in inflationary periods we have graphed, in Figure 1, indexes of average payments for various types of public transfers for the period 1947–66 in constant prices (reported in Table 10). We have also graphed an index of disposable income per capita *deflated by the CPI* as a rough indicator of changes in the general standard of living level.

Deterioration of real income from a given source occurs only when the slope of a portion of the curve for that source in Figure 1 is actually negative. With the exception of General Assistance, there are few negatively sloped portions on any of the curves (except for the 1950–51 period). Thus there have been surprisingly few cases in which even for a given year rises in public transfer payments have lagged behind rises in the price level.

22 M. Segal, "Occupational Wage Differentials in Major Cities During the 1950s," in M. Perlman, ed., *Human Resources in the Urban Economy, Resources for the Future*, 1963.

23 R. Perlman, "Forces Widening Occupational Differentials," *Review of Economics and Statistics*, 40: 112.

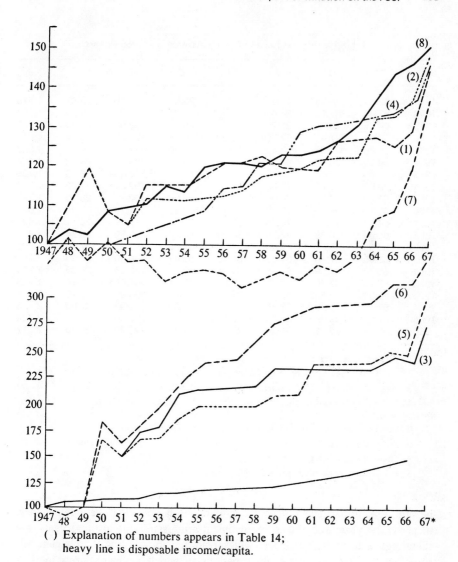

( ) Explanation of numbers appears in Table 14;
heavy line is disposable income/capita.

*Reflects recent passage of Social Security Bill
resulting in across-the-board 13% rise.

Figure 1. Indexes of Various Forms of Public Assistance and
Per Capita Disposable Income

It is noteworthy that the long-term trend in payments, as represented by the overall slope of the curves, is positive, and *because these are all constant dollar figures*, in the long term the real value of these monthly payments has been increasing. In addition, many of the slopes of the average monthly payments curves are as great as, or greater than, that of the disposable income per capita curve, indicating that in the longer term these payments have been a force working toward the raising of the relative income position of the recipients. To

Table 10. Various Forms of Public Assistance — 1966 Dollars

Year	1	2	3	4	5	6	7	8
1947	52.50	25.85	34.95		29.58	70.76	29.87	1,513
1948	57.40	28.55	34.65		27.81	67.23	30.24	1,567
1949	62.35	30.25	36.25		28.29	68.54	28.90	1,547
1950	56.70	27.45	57.75	28.03	49.28	126.77	30.04	1,646
1951	55.40	27.35	52.45		45.00	117.25	28.63	1,657
1952	60.20	28.90	60.75		49.65	129.32	28.43	1,678
1953	59.95	28.45	62.60		49.49	135.40	26.68	1,726
1954	59.95	28.60	72.80		56.02	157.91	27.65	1,714
1955	61.40	28.85	75.95	30.30	58.93	163.83	28.19	1,795
1956	63.50	29.55	75.20	32.15	56.62	167.79	27.91	1,839
1957	64.25	29.40	74.75	32.40			26.11	1,844
1958	64.80	30.35	75.30	34.25	58.13	169.90	26.94	1,831
1959	63.55	30.60	81.60	33.76	62.94	197.25	27.81	1,881
1960	65.05	31.30	81.75	36.16	63.47	206.80	27.34	1,883
1961	63.20	32.30	83.05	36.84	70.74	206.34	28.50	1,909
1962	66.75	31.75	82.60	36.98	70.51	204.05	28.14	1,958
1963	66.95	31.65	81.95	37.40	70.91	204.05	29.10	2,013
1964	67.10	33.20	81.75	37.76	71.30	203.07	32.03	2,123
1965	65.20	33.95	86.70	38.31	75.12	226.39	32.60	2,232
1966	68.05	36.25	84.35	39.76	74.30	221.90	36.20	2,317

1 Old-age assistance per recipient — average monthly payment.

2 Aid to families with dependent children — average monthly payment.

3 Average monthly retired workers' benefit under OASDHI.

4 Unemployment insurance — state summary — average monthly payment for total unemployed.

5 Survival families — aged widow only — average monthly payment.

6 Survival families — widow with two children — average monthly payment.

7 General assistance per recipient.

8 Per capita disposable income (1958 dollars).

be sure, rises in particular types of payments do lag behind price index changes in particular years and thus some recipient groups are hurt in those years, but these lags seem to be much less widespread and long lasting than is generally supposed and are offset by other periods in which payment levels increase considerably more than the price index.

It is also worth noting that in attempting to assess the effects of changes in the price level on the economic well-being of recipients of public transfer payments, we must select with care the standard for basing an assessment. In evaluating the effects of price level changes over a given period, we must look at more than a single year to see whether the payment rose in that year by as much as the price index; this would seem to be far too rigorous a standard. We have often made an assessment by looking at the value of the payment at the end of the period, deflating it by the price index rise over the period and then comparing it to the value at the beginning of the period. We would argue that even this assessment involves a somewhat biased standard for it weights heavily the position at the end of the period and ignores what may have transpired at other points in the period. A more general standard for the longer period effects would be one that cumulates the real income gains and the real income losses for each year over the whole period. Although in some years the price level rises while the money amount of the transfer payment remains constant, in other years the money value of the payment rises by considerably more than the price index rises. Thus a standard that balances years of real income gain (rise in money payment above rise in prices) against those of real income loss (rise in money payment less than rise in price levels) would more accurately reflect the real income of the recipients.

With respect to most of the types of transfer payments reported in Table 10 and Figure 1 this choice among standards of assessment is not of crucial importance. As we have already noted, for most of the payments there were few *single* years in which there was real income deterioration of the payment resulting from price level rises, and in most cases long period rises have exceeded not only price level rises but rises in per capita disposable income.

However, for one type of payment the data presented in Table 10 and Figure 1 could be seriously misleading. Waldman has pointed out[24] that in the case of Social Security (OASDI), changes in average monthly payments do not reflect changes in the level of the benefits actually received by particular groups of retirees. The increases in average monthly benefits reflect primarily the higher benefit levels for new retirees with higher past earnings records. Once drawing Social Security, the retiree only receives increases in benefits through specific amendments in the Social Security legislation. In recent years such amendments have raised benefits by approximately 7 percent in 1959, 7 percent in 1965 and 13 percent in 1968. Thus, although by 1968 a pre-1959 retiree had received benefit increases sufficient to offset increases in the CPI, for a number of interim years he suffered real income losses. Even the 1968 increases, although sufficient to keep up with rises in the price index, were not sufficient to keep this income source in line with the increases in disposable income per capita over this period for such a retiree. On the other hand, a 1964 retiree would have had benefit increases more than enough to offset price increases in all but one year, and his position relative to disposable income per capita would probably be about the same by the end of 1968 as it was in 1964.[25] Moreover, as previously noted, to get an overall assessment for a given period for a given retiree cohort, one would have to cumulate the yearly real income gain and loss

---

24 Waldman, "OASDI Benefits, Prices and Wages: A Comparison" and "OASDI Benefits, Prices and Wages: 1966 Experience" *Social Security Bulletin*, August 1966 and June 1967.

25 We should note, of course, the relevance of our discussion of price indexes in section II of this paper. Our Aged-Poor Index differs from that calculated by Waldman (*ibid.*, June 1967 p. 10), in that we calculate an index taking account of age, income, expenditure, and family size. Our Aged-Poor index in Table 5 is considerably below the CPI in 1967 even before the adjustment for Medicare is made. With the Medicare adjustment there is even more substantial difference. The Aged-Poor Index results suggest that rises in prices affect the relative position (however measured) of poor Social Security recipients less than has previously been suggested.

for this source. To make a precise estimate of the net overall effect of amendments raising benefit levels, of changes in the price index, and of growth in disposable income per capita on the relative position of Social Security recipients as a group, we would need to take account of the distribution of retirees according to the year of retirement, their survival rates, the cumulative value of each cohort survivor's yearly real gains and real losses from this source. We do not have the information such an assessment would require, and on the face of it we cannot see what the outcome of such an assessment would be.

We would conclude on the basis of the evidence provided in Table 10 and Figure 1 that, in general, public transfer payments have more than kept pace with rises in the price level (although with respect to Social Security we must reserve our judgment on the issue). *It is important to be clear about the fact that regardless of the historical relationship between transfer payments and the price level, public transfer payments are policy variables. If our objective is to protect low-income transfer recipients from the effects of inflation in the short term, a policy decision can be made to do so quite readily. Legislation can simply be passed to tie the payment levels for the transfer payments to the appropriate sort of price index.* In fact, in terms of policy we can, if we wish, go even further and offset the effects of price increases on other sources of income by raising transfer payments by some multiple of the changes in the price index. We will return to these considerations later in the paper.

IV.   Assets and Wealth Effects

In this part of the paper we attempt to estimate the extent to which negative "wealth effects" created by rising price levels might diminish the economic well-being of the poor. The common picture, conjured up in public debate, of those hurt by inflation is one of a family living on a meager, fixed income derived from accumulated assets. In this light an evaluation of the magnitude and distribution of various types of assets held by the poor is useful.

For the poor, asset incomes that inflation would adversely affect have a fixed monetary value: for example, cash, checking and savings deposits, life insurance, fixed value pensions and bonds. In general, assets with variable monetary value such as stocks, automobiles, and housing would be assumed to rise in money value as the price level rises. Balancing any deterioration in the real value of fixed value assets during inflation would be the real value gains that accrue to individuals with fixed monetary debts.

On the basis of data drawn from the *Survey of Financial Characteristics of 1961* (SFC), we could examine the distribution of assets for the poor (defined in terms of current income in relation to the Social Security Administration poverty lines and excluding those with net worth greater than $50,000). In Table 11 we present the data on the distribution of net worth of poor families. Not surprisingly the distribution is skewed; the median value of net worth is less than

Table 11. Net Worth of Families with Income Below the Poverty
Line (and Net Worth below $50,000), 1961

				Distribution				
Net Worth	Negative	0--999	1,000– 4,999	5,000– 9,999	10,000– 19,999	20,000– 49,999	Mean	Median
Percent	12.3	26.5	22.5	19.3	13.0	6.4	$5,845	$2,594

Median Values by Age and Race of Head

Nonaged White	2,356
Nonaged Nonwhite	1,474
Aged White	5,083
Aged Nonwhite	5,014
All Poor	2,434

Source: *SFC*, 1961.

half the mean. For this reason we concentrate on median values of assets as most
representative for the population. In Table 11 we also present the median values
for various age and race categories. In general, as we might expect, the poor have
relatively low net worth. Not all of even this low net worth is vulnerable to
inflation.

To assess more directly the potential "wealth effects" of inflation, we
segregated the assets of the poor into fixed value and nonfixed value categories
and estimated the median and means for each category. These are reported in

Table 12. Value of Types of Assets for Families with Income
below the Poverty Line (and Net Worth below $50,000), 1961

	Median Values			Mean Values		
	Nonaged Heads	Aged Heads	All Heads	Nonaged Heads	Aged Heads	All Heads
Net worth	1,823	5,121	2,434	5,539	6,418	5,845
Fixed value assets	790	607	743	2,932	2,224	2,686
Nonfixed value assets	317	2,384	611	3,516	4,570	3,883
Fixed value claims	58	17	23	910	376	724
Amount vulnerable to inflation	366	501	422	2,023	1,849	1,962
Income	1,336	1,059	1,164	1,660	1,149	1,482

Source: *SFC*, 1961.

Table 12. We also netted, for each observation in the SCF data tape, fixed value assets against fixed value claims and then found the median and mean of the resultant net distribution. These values are reported in Table 12 in the category "Amount Vulnerable to Inflation."

. Now, to get an idea of what the order of magnitude of potential "wealth effects" might be, let us pose a simple example. Let us make the generous assumption that the poor realized a 10 percent return on the value of their assets. If we focus on the median values in Table 12, we see that the amount of assets vulnerable to inflation is estimated at $366 for nonaged headed families and $501 for families with aged heads. A 10 percent yield on these assets would amount to $37 a year for nonaged family heads and $50 a year for aged heads. Comparing this finding to the estimated yearly income for these units reported in Table 12 we find that the amount of yearly income from assets, assuming a 10 percent yield, which is subject to negative "wealth effects" due to rising price levels is about 3 percent of annual income for families with nonaged heads and about 5 percent for families with aged heads.

Note that this finding *does not* mean a 3 to 5 percent decline in real income; this is the amount of income which is vulnerable. To determine the actual reduction in real income due to inflation, we multiply these percentages by the percentage rise in the price level. We can make the example extreme again by assuming a high (in United States terms) rate of inflation, say 5 percent. A 5 percent rate of inflation would, according to our estimates, generate negative "wealth effects" for the poor amounting to about one sixth of 1 percent of annual income for families with nonaged heads and one fourth of 1 percent of annual income for families with aged heads.

To be sure, these small estimates of the "wealth effects" of inflation on the poor are based upon the median values as most representative. Undoubtedly many individuals fall specifically into the category of small income from fixed value assets. (The skewness of the assets distributions resulting from the considerable difference between medians and means and the relationship among the medians of the various categories of assets seem to suggest such subgroups may exist.) We must therefore be careful *not* to give the impression that substantial negative "wealth effects" could not exist for individual families. However, we must not err in the other direction and let the possibility of these individual cases stand as indicative of the situation of the entire poor population. Contrary to the impression given by the usual public discourse our evidence indicates that most poor families and even most poor aged families do not receive substantial portions of their income from fixed value assets that are vulnerable to inflationary erosion in real value. In making policy decisions that will affect the broad group of the poverty population, we must remember that as a whole the poor are likely to suffer little from inflationary negative "wealth effects." We must balance even these small losses against the other effects of inflation on this group – the "expenditure" and "income effects" – to arrive at an overall assessment of the impact of inflation, or the impact of anti-inflationary policies, on the poor.

Summary and Conclusions

Our objective has been to assess the impact on the economic well-being of the poor of inflationary processes such as those experienced in the United States in the last twenty years. A comprehensive assessment of such an impact must take account of possible effects resulting from the characteristics of expenditure patterns, effects related to the sources of income, and effects related to the character of assets held by the poor.

Because we have noted a number of weaknesses in our data and procedures at several points in the paper, we will not repeat these reservations here but simply summarize our results, however tentative they may be.

On the expenditure side, we examined past movements of several "Poor Price Index" measures (based on weights derived from the expenditure patterns of poor families) relative to the CPI. The comparison suggests that the "expenditure effects" of price rises hurt the poor less than the nonpoor; the *relative* real income of the poor improves as a result of the expenditure effects of general price rises.

With respect to income, the beneficial effects of tight labor markets, which normally accompany inflationary pressures, are important to the poor. The results of some simple regressions relating broad aggregate measures of poverty, unemployment, and price rises indicate that a drop of 1 percent in the unemployment rate would remove a million to a million and a half people from poverty who would not have been removed otherwise. This estimate coincides with those of another study reviewed. The regressions provide some further suggestions that the gains to the poor from the tight labor markets associated with inflation go beyond those strictly related to lower unemployment. Both the regressions and some other studies reviewed suggest that during such inflationary periods the poor *gain relatively more than other groups*, probably because of movements from part-time to full-time employment and because of a narrowing of wage differentials between the employed poor and the nonpoor.

The next important income source for the poor, behind wages and salaries, is public transfer payments. Historically, average public transfer payments have risen more than enough to offset the rise in the CPI and in most cases have risen faster than disposable income per capita (the exact position of Social Security benefits is rather unclear, however). Moreover, regardless of what has occurred historically, policy decisions tying payments to price indexes could readily be made and thereby could specifically prevent erosion of the real value of such transfer payments.

An examination of the assets of the poor show the assets to be small in total value and the proportion vulnerable to inflation to be a small portion of these small assets. The potential negative "wealth effects" due to rising price levels are estimated to be extremely limited for the poor as a whole and even for the aged poor as a group.

On both the expenditure side and on the income and asset side, then, the relative position of the poor is likely to improve during periods of inflationary pressure similar to those experienced during the past twenty years. With the exception of two periods (one of only slight price rise, 1953–54, and one of substantial price rise, 1957–58), disposable income per capita has risen faster than the price level. Thus we may generally conclude that because the relative position of the poor seems to improve during inflationary periods and overall real income gains per capita occur during such periods, the poor as a whole must be gaining both absolutely and relatively in economic well-being during periods in which inflationary processes operate.

15
Lester C. Thurow: The Effects of Public Policy Instruments on Black and White Income Equalization

Governments have a wide variety of policy instruments that can influence the distribution of income. These instruments can be divided into micropolicy instruments and macropolicy instruments. Micropolicy instruments concentrate on altering the structure of demands and supplies for labor and capital, whereas macropolicy instruments concentrate on controlling the economic environment in which income is distributed.

Although both sets of policy instruments are used to influence the distribution of income and both sets must be analyzed to determine the total impact of government on the distribution of income, this paper examines only the impact of macropolicies, not that macropolicies are more important than micropolicies but simply as a division of labor. To list the micropolicies (education programs, training programs, specific expenditure programs, the structure of taxes, and so forth) is to be aware of their importance. Many studies exist analyzing the income effects of micropolicies, but all too often the income distribution impacts of macropolicies have been ignored. Although they are not as direct, they are just as real.

Macropolicy instruments (fiscal and monetary policies) are used to control economic output, its unemployment rates, its rate of inflation, and a variety of other measures of the economic environment of a country. These factors, in turn, have a major impact on the distribution of income. When output per employee rises, some incomes rise faster than other; when unemployment rises, some incomes fall faster than others; and similarly when inflation occurs, some

This article is a revised version of a paper presented at the Annual Meeting of the American Economics Association in December, 1969. All rights reserved. Used by permission of the author. Mr. Thurow is from Massachusetts Institute of Technology. Part of the work on this paper was financed under National Science Foundation grant # NSF–GS–2811.

people gain and others lose. The question in each case is "Who gains and who loses" and "How are the gains and losses distributed across the distribution of income?"[1]

To analyze the impact of the economic environment on the distribution of income, some summary measure of the distribution of income must be found. One technique is to summarize the distribution of income in terms of its median,[2] but the environment may have different impacts on rich and poor that are not reflected in the median income. As a result some technique that will summarize the entire distribution of income and not just some segment of it needs to be used.[3] The technique used here is to fit formal analytic distributions to the observed distribution of income. Then an attempt can be made to explain what has caused changes in the parameters of these formal distributions.

Because whites and blacks have different distributions of income, the analysis will separate whites and blacks to investigate whether macropolicy instruments have different impacts on the two groups. Such will in fact prove to be the case.

The Beta Distribution

A number of analytic distributions can be used to describe changes in the distributions of income for blacks and whites,[4] but the beta distribution seemed most desirable.[5] It fits the observed income distributions well and has only two parameters. These two parameters are ρ and σ (see Equation 1). By placing incomes on a scale between 0 and 1, the proportion of the population, ρ, who have some particular income is easily calculated (see Equation 2).

Complete Beta Function

$$\beta(\rho, \sigma) = \int_0^1 t^{\rho - 1}(1 - t)^{\sigma - 1}dt \tag{1}$$

where $\rho > 0; \sigma > 0$.

---

1 This is true of my own work as well as the work of others.

2 For example, the existing analysis of the impact of education on incomes looks at the difference in mean or median incomes between education cells. The analysis explicitly assumes that there is no income variance within education cells, yet the actual income variance within education cells is often greater than the variance between cells. Often medians are not statistically significantly different. Both regression techniques and tabular techniques for isolating the returns to education have this problem. If individual observations are used, the coefficient of determination in regression analysis provides some indication of the magnitude of the problem, but the regression coefficients are based on mean values.

3 C. Metcalf, *The Size Distribution of Personal Income in an Econometric Model of the U.S.*, unpublished thesis, M.I.T.

4 Metcalf uses what he calls the displaced log normal distribution. This distribution has three parameters with an infinite upper tail.

5 For a more detailed discussion of the beta function see M. G. Kendall and A. Stuart, *The Advanced Theory of Statistics* (London: Charles Griffin and Co., 1963), p. 150.

$$f\beta(p \mid \rho, v) = \frac{1}{\beta(\rho, \sigma)} \, p^{\rho - 1}(1 - p)^{\sigma - 1} \tag{2}$$

where $0 \leqslant p \leqslant 1; \sigma = v - \rho; \rho, \sigma > 0$.

The impact of changes in ρ and σ on the distribution of income is easily determined. Increases in ρ (see Appendix A, Chart I) result in higher median incomes and smaller relative income differences between the top and bottom of the income distribution. In the ranges under consideration in this paper a 1 percent increase in σ (holding ρ constant) results in an approximately 0.8 percent increase in the median income and a 0.4 percent reduction in the relative income gap between the 25th and the 75th percentiles of the income distribution. Increases in ρ (see Appendix A, Chart II) result in lower median incomes and larger relative income differences in the income distribution. A 1 percent increase in ρ results in a 0.4 percent reduction in the median incomes and a 1 percent increase in the relative income gap between the 25th and the 75th percentiles of the income distribution. When both ρ and σ rise in the same proportion (see Appendix A, Chart III), median incomes remain constant but relative income differences increase. The dispersing impact of ρ dominates the concentrating impact of σ. More precisely, a 1 percent increase in both ρ and σ results in a 0.2 percent increase in the income gap between the 25th and the 75th percentiles of the income distribution.

Estimating ρ and σ

The beta distribution was fit to U.S. Bureau of Census constant dollar (1959) income distribution statistics for households (families and unrelated individuals) for every year from 1949 to 1966.[6] Any number of observations could have been used in the estimating process, but ten were actually used. These ten observations were the proportion of the population who had incomes less than 0.05 through 0.95 of the income scale. As a finite distribution, the beta distribution has a maximum income implicit in its estimation. The maximum income can be adjusted, but it was set at $15,000 in this work. Thus individuals with income over $15,000 are given income of $15,000 for the year pose of the analysis. This constraint is not serious because less than 5 percent of the population have incomes over $15,000 (1959 dollars) in 1966. A $25,000 income limit works just as well but seemed inappropriate over the period under consideration. The proper income limit depends on the focus of the analysis. The larger the income limit the more weight is put on the upper tail of the

---

6 J. W. Pratt, H. Raiffa, and R. Schlaifer, *Introduction to Statistical Decision Theory* (New York: McGraw-Hill Book Co., 1965), p. 91. The income data are from U.S. Bureau of the Census, *Trends in the Income of Families and Persons in the United States, 1947 to 1960*, USGPO, Table 11; U.S. Bureau of the Census, *Current Population Reports, Consumer Income*, Series P–60, various issues.

income distribution in the estimating process.[7] Because this analysis did not focus on the factors that influence the incomes of the wealthy, a relatively low income limit was chosen.

Between 1949 and 1966 the median incomes of white households rose from $3796 to $6084 (1959 dollars) and from $1885 to $3429 for black households. Measured in terms of Gini coefficients[8] or relative incomes, almost no changes have occurred in the distribution of either white or black incomes (see Appendix A, Chart IV).

The beta distribution fit the actual income distributions well. The coefficient of determination (R^2) improves over the period but averages .96 for whites and .92 for blacks (see Appendix B, Table 1). Rho and sigma rise for both whites and blacks. Median incomes have grown, and the dispersion of income has remained relatively constant over the period under consideration, but this constancy was a product of two offsetting forces. Increases in ρ lead to a greater income dispersion, and increases in σ lead to less income dispersion. Although the distribution impacts of ρ and σ offset each other, the σ dominated ρ in terms of growth in absolute incomes.

The ρs and σs differ substantially between blacks and whites. Rho is relatively higher for blacks, whereas sigma is lower, reflecting that the income distribution for blacks is much more disperse than the distribution for whites. The same differences can be seen in Gini coefficients. The Gini coefficient for blacks is substantially higher than it is for whites.

Growth of the two parameters is also substantially different. The white ρ rose from .666 to 1.044, whereas the black ρ rose from .930 to 1.104. The white σ rose from .258 to .955, whereas the black σ rose from .160 to .514. Thus, by the end of the period, the ρs are rather similar, but the black σ is only half as large as the white σ. Thus, the σ parameter produces most of the differences in income level and dispersion.

The beta distribution works almost as well across states in 1960 as it does over time (Appendix B, Table 2).[9] Among whites, all R^2 are above .95 and most are above .98. The results are not quite as good among nonwhites. Of 51 observations the R^2 is above .90 in 33 and below .80 in only 2. As Table 2 in Appendix B indicates, a significant amount of variation in both ρ and σ for whites and nonwhites exists across states.

Factors Producing Changes in ρ and σ Over Time

In this analysis the impact of macroeconomic factors is separated into five parts: a real growth component (measured in terms of constant dollar *GNP* per

---

7 As the maximum income limit increases, the number of upper income observations used in estimating ρ and σ increases.

8 The Gini coefficient is the area between the diagonal and the Lorenz curve divided by the area under the diagonal.

9 Cross-sectional state data are from the 1960 U.S. Census.

employee, GNP/E); an inflation component (measured in terms of the implicit price deflator for GNP, I); a factor shares component (measured in terms of the share going to personal income, PI/GNP); a utilization component (measured in terms of the proportion of the labor force employed, E/LF); a transfer payment component (measured in terms of the transfer payments per household, TP/H); and a government expenditures component (measured in terms of government purchases of goods and services per household, GP/H).[10] The model is given in Equation 3.[11]

$$\rho \text{ or } \sigma = A \left(\frac{GNP}{E}\right)^{b_0} (I)^{b_1} \left(\frac{PI}{GPN}\right)^{b_2} \left(\frac{E}{LF}\right)^{b_3} \left(\frac{TP}{H}\right)^{b_4} \left(\frac{GP}{H}\right)^{b_5} e, \qquad (3)$$

where

A	= intercept
GNP	= gross national product
E	= total employment
I	= implicit price deflator for GNP
PI	= personal income
LF	= total labor force
TP	= transfer payments
H	= households
GP	= government purchases of goods and services
$b_0 \ldots b_5$	= elasticities

Table 1 gives the results of estimating Equation 3. Whenever variables had t-statistics less than 1, that variable was dropped from the model. The same variable can, of course, be instrumental in explaining both ρ and σ. Growth can lead to both a more dispersed and a more concentrated income distribution. To determine the net impact of growth on the income distribution, its impact on the two parameters must be combined. Thus, for whites the elasticity of ρ with respect to GNP/E is 1.20, and the elasticity of σ with respect to GNP/E is 2.94. Because the income dispersing effect of ρ is roughly twice as large as the income concentrating effect of σ, the income dispersing effects cancel each other. Growth leads to higher real incomes but does not have any major impact on the dispersion of income.

The rate of inflation also has two conflicting tendencies for whites. A 1 percent increase in inflation results in a 1.55 percent reduction in ρ and a 0.64

---

10 These data are standard national income and products account data and standard labor force data taken from *Employment and Earnings*, U.S. Department of Labor. The employment rate is not the normal unemployment rate because it is total employment divided by the total labor force rather than civilian employment divided by the civilian labor force.

11 The first four terms in this equation yield current dollar percent income per member of the labor force:

$$\left(\frac{GNP}{E}\right)\left(\frac{PI}{GNP}\right)(I)\left(\frac{E}{LF}\right) = \frac{PI}{LF}$$

Table 1. Time Series Distribution Elasticities

		White		Black	
		ρ	σ	ρ	σ
A		3.97	−3.24	−1.47	.05
		(2.44)	(2.21)	(.93)	(.50)
GNP/E	b_0	1.20	2.94	−.73	
		(.60)	(.43)	(.18)	
I	b_1	−1.55	−.64	.68	
		(.57)	(.55)	(.23)	
PI/GNP	b_2	−2.43			1.56
		(1.50)			(1.18)
E/LF	b_3	−2.52			6.23
		(1.94)			(1.37)
TP/H	b_4	.49	.39	.26	.73
		(.22)	(.13)	(.07)	(.06)
GP/H	b_5				.37
					(.08)
R^2		.96	.99	.95	.99
S_e		.04	.05	.02	.04
d.w.		1.82	1.59	2.13	2.05
d.f.		12	14	14	13

percent reduction in σ. Reductions in ρ lead to a more concentrated income distribution, and reduction in σ leads to a more dispersed income distribution. Because the ρ effects are roughly twice as powerful as the σ effects in terms of income dispersion, inflation seems to be a powerful force leading to a more equal *real* distribution of income.

The offsetting impacts of business cycles on white incomes can be seen in the *PI/GNP* and *E/LF* terms. In booms, employment rises but the proportion of income going to persons falls. Rising employment leads to a lower ρ and more equality, but a falling share for personal income leads to a rising ρ and more inequality. Because of these two offsetting forces, the distribution of white income does not change markedly over the course of a business cycle.

Transfer payments present a bit of a problem for whites. They have an impact on both ρ and σ, but the results indicate that increasing transfer payments leads to a greater dispersion of incomes for whites. Because most government transfer payments do not go to the very rich or the very poor, such a result is not impossible but it is surprising. Evidently government pensions, veteran's benefits, and social security benefits to the middle class dominate welfare payments to the poor for whites.[12]

---

12 In 1968 government transfer payments totaled $48.6 billion. Direct relief was only $4.9 billion.

Such is not the case for blacks. Transfer payments influence both ρ and σ, but the impact on σ is three times as large as that on ρ. Consequently transfer payments lead to a more equal distribution of black income. Given the size of central city welfare payments, such a result is not surprising.

Government purchases of goods and services lead to higher, more equal black incomes, whereas they had no impact on the level or distribution of white incomes. Direct and indirect employment on government projects is a major cause of increases in black incomes.

Business cycles have conflicting impacts on the level and distribution of black incomes, but the impacts do not balance out as they did for whites. The employment elasticity (b_3) is four times as large as the share elasticity (b_2). Full employment is a powerful force, leading to higher black incomes and more equal black incomes, because blacks suffer more than their share of unemployment and consequently are differentially aided by its elimination.

Inflation, however, leads to more unequal black incomes. Instead of being negatively related to ρ as it is for whites, inflation is positively related to ρ for blacks. Because black incomes are almost entirely wage and salary earnings and because rich blacks are lower middle class by white standards, results may simply indicate that the incomes of those people who are lower middle class by white standards rise relatively in inflationary periods. Thus, if inflation and employment are related to each other, as in the Phillip's curve, part of the equalizing impact of full employment will be offset by the concomitant inflation, even though employment elasticity is almost nine times as large as inflation elasticity. Adjusting for the differences in the impact of ρ and σ on the distribution of income still means a powerful equalizing impact from full employment.

General growth has a different impact on incomes of blacks and whites. Growth (GNP/E) is negatively related to the black ρ parameter rather than positively related to both ρ and σ as for whites. For whites, growth leads to higher incomes but did not have much, if any, net impact on the distribution of income. For blacks, growth leads to higher real incomes, but it also leads to more equal incomes – primarily because black incomes, rich and poor, are dependent on wage and salary earnings. Thus, the growth of capital incomes, which prevents growth from equalizing white incomes, does not affect black incomes.

Some of these results are based on a loose definition of statistical significance (t-statistics greater than 1), but the important results are based on coefficients that are easily significant at the 1 percent level. These include the growth effects, the inflation effects, the transfer payments effects, and the government purchases effect.

Factors Producing Changes in ρ and σ Across States

The cross-sectional model relies on six explanatory variables: the percentage of families living on farms, the percentage of the population aged 14 and above who work 50 to 52 weeks per year, an index of the industrial structure,[13] the percentage of families with no one in the labor force, the percentage of family heads with 0 to 7 years of education, and the state and local general expenditures per capita (see Equation 4).[14] The first two factors represent the level of productivity in a state, the second two represent the labor force participation characteristics of a state, the fifth represents the quality of the labor force, and the final characteristic reflects the quality of public services in a state.

The model was applied to the 51 state observations using weighted regressions.[15] Table 2 gives the results.

$$\rho \text{ or } \sigma = a + bF + cL + dE + eW + fI + g\left(\frac{E}{C}\right) + u, \tag{4}$$

where

F = percentage of families living on farms
L = percentage of families with no one in the labor force
E = percentage of family heads with less than eight years of school completed
P = percentage of population aged 14 and above who worked 50 to 52 weeks per year
I = index of the industrial structure of the state
u = error term
$\dfrac{E}{C}$ = state and local government general expenditures per capita

For whites, increasing the percentage of families living on farms and percentage of families with no one in the labor force leads to lower median incomes and more dispersed incomes. Neither of these two factors seem to have any impact on nonwhite income distributions. Because of lower black incomes,

---

13 The index is defined as follows:

$$I = \sum_{i=1}^{n} X_i W_i$$

where

X_i = percentage of the state's labor force in industry i
W_i = ratio of the U.S. median income in industry i to the general U.S. median income. This index measures the prevalence of high-wage industries in the state.

14 The independent variables refer to the state as a whole and not to either the white or the nonwhite populations in the state.

15 A regression using Equation 4 needs to be weighted by the population of each state because the dependent variable and most of the independent variables are in percentage terms. Because a large state provides more of the total number of families living in poverty, it needs to have a larger weight in the regression. The intercept term is a scaling f factor in a weighted regression.

Table 2. Cross-Sectional Distribution Parameters

	a	Percent of Families Living on Farms	Percent of Families with No One in Labor Force	Percent of Family Heads with 0–7 Years of School Complete	Percent of Population 14 and Above Who Worked 50–52 Weeks Per Year	Index of Industrial Structure	State and Local Expenditures Per Capita	R^{-1}	d.b	S_e
Whites										
ρ	.4414 (.1149)	.4723 (.1133)	1.9053 (.3045)	.3441 (.0985)	.3915 (.2661)		.0351 (.0153)	.99	45	.006
σ	−1.1894 (.2126)			.1636 (.0992)	.6776 (.2476)	1.3042 (.1995)	.0678 (.0145)	.98	46	.006
Nonwhites										
ρ	3.0180 (.3178)				−.9257 (.4086)	−1.6691 (.3381)		.97	48	.012
σ	−.2792 (.2036)			−.4363 (.0950)	.3849 (.2371)	.4837 (.1910)	.0248 (.0139)	.94	46	.006

being on a farm òr in a family with no one in the labor force is not the relative handicap it is for whites.

Increasing the percentage of the population working full-time and improving the industrial structure lead to higher median incomes and less income dispersion for whites and blacks, but the effects are much stronger for blacks than for whites. A 1 percentage point increase in full-time work and in the industrial structure would raise white incomes approximately 1.4 percent and reduce the income differential between the 25th and the 75th percentiles by 0.4 percent. For blacks, the corresponding improvements are 1.7 percent and 2.9 percent. Being at the end of the hiring queue, blacks gain relative to whites with tighter labor markets and improvements in industrial job opportunities. The difference between rich and poor blacks depends upon the supply of jobs; the difference between rich and poor whites does not depend on the supply of jobs to the same degree.

Increasing state and local government expenditures per capita raises the incomes of whites without affecting the dispersion of income, but for blacks, increasing public services both raises their incomes and reduces the dispersion in incomes. Better public services probably increase the probability of finding jobs for blacks and this reduces the income dispersion among blacks. For richer whites jobs have the same impact.

Education plays its expected role for blacks. The greater the proportion of poorly educated people in a state the lower are median black incomes and the greater is the income dispersion among blacks. Among whites, increasing the proportion of poorly educated people does not have a great impact on the median family income, but it does increase the dispersion of incomes substantially. The median white family head is not poorly educated, and thus changes in the proportion of poorly educated people over the ranges that are encountered in the fifty-one states do not affect his income.

The effective instrument for closing the income gaps between blacks and whites are providing full-time jobs and improving the industrial index (productivity levels) of a state.

Conclusions

Based on the evidence from this analysis there are no macropolicy instruments for equalizing black and white income distributions or for equalizing white incomes or black incomes, but macropolicy instruments have a large impact on the inequality or equality that actually exists. General growth results in higher incomes for both black and whites but does not have much impact on their relative incomes. A 1 percent increase in employment results in a 5 percent increase in median black incomes and a 1 percent increase in median white incomes, but this is an instrument that is inherently limited. Unemployment can only fall to zero. Transfer payments and government purchases lead to more equal incomes, but the coefficients are small enough that enormous expenditure increases would be necessary to equalize incomes using the current structure of transfer payments and government incomes. Regional economic policies that would increase job opportunities in relatively depressed states and which would improve the quality of the existing jobs can also have an impact on black–white income differentials.

If society simply wishes to narrow its income distribution, any factor which lowered ρ or raised σ would be acceptable. Growth would be a proper policy instrument for blacks, and inflation would be a proper policy instrument for whites. Realistically, macroeconomic policies can lead to a more equal distribution of income, but vigorous use of these instruments would still leave a widely dispersed income distribution. The major factor leading to increases in average incomes is, of course, growth for either blacks or whites.

As indicated, macropolicies have large impacts on the distribution of income, but they are even more important than these impacts might indicate. First, they represent a costless method of narrowing the distribution of income. A full-employment policy creates economic resources in the process of narrowing the distribution of income. Micropolicies, such as education, typically use resources. Second, the macroeconomic environment is a basic determinant of the effectiveness of micropolicy instruments. The world's best training program will be a failure in an economy with high unemployment. Even if the workers who are trained find jobs, they will simply be displacing other workers, with no net improvement in the distribution of income. As a consequence, all policies for equalizing the distribution of income depend upon establishing macroeconomic policies for equalizing income.

Appendix A
Distribution Parameters and the Distribution of Income

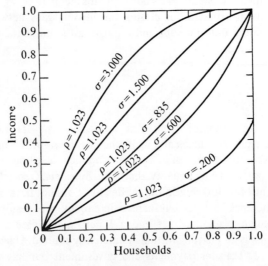

Chart I

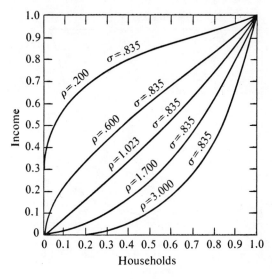

Chart II

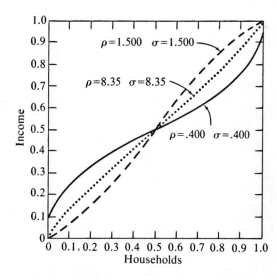

Scale:

Households
1.0 = 100 Percent of Households

Income
1.0 = $15,000

Chart III

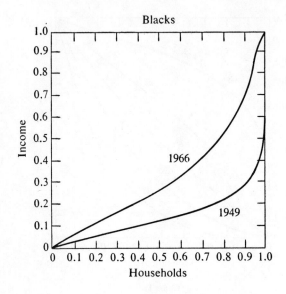

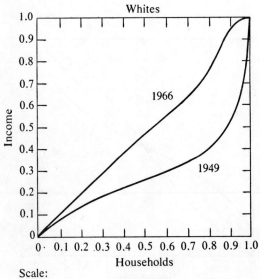

Scale:

Households   1.0 = 100 Percent of Households
Income   1.0 = $15,000

Chart IV
Actual Income Distributions
(Constant 1959 $)

Appendix B

Table 1. Time Series Distribution Parameters

	Whites			Blacks		
	ρ	σ	R^2	ρ	σ	R^2
1949	.666	.258	.92	.930	.160	.88
1950	.687	.279	.93	.930	.172	.86
1951	.625	.269	.93	.908	.182	.88
1952	.649	.298	.94	.921	.205	.89
1953	.667	.327	.95	.920	.228	.89
1954	.697	.334	.96	.929	.217	.89
1955	.718	.368	.96	.913	.225	.96
1956	.731	.411	.97	.978	.249	.94
1957	.728	.406	.96	1.025	.269	.94
1958	.750	.411	.96	1.075	.276	.92
1959	.765	.460	.97	1.051	.286	.95
1960	.815	.504	.97	1.061	.330	.94
1961	.979	.622	.98	1.173	.346	.93
1962	.971	.663	.98	1.107	.338	.91
1963	.985	.712	.98	1.073	.356	.94
1964	1.017	.785	.99	1.095	.406	.94
1965	1.029	.842	.99	1.124	.452	.95
1966	1.044	.955	.99	1.104	.514	.96

Table 2. State Distribution Parameters

	Whites			Blacks		
	ρ	σ	R^2	ρ	σ	R^2
Maine	.927	.400	.96	.866	.184	.79
New Hampshire	.915	.474	.97	.884	.240	.88
Vermont	1.035	.443	.96	1.454	.308	.91
Massachusetts	.939	.589	.98	.979	.339	.94
Rhode Island	.953	.495	.97	.956	.250	.91
Connecticut	.868	.674	.98	.919	.340	.95
New York	.978	.674	.98	.916	.327	.93
New Jersey	.886	.695	.98	.955	.363	.95
Pennsylvania	.922	.548	.98	.958	.319	.94
Ohio	.921	.602	.98	.992	.361	.95
Indiana	.970	.572	.98	.960	.348	.95
Idaho	.997	.706	.98	1.060	.410	.96
Michigan	.928	.634	.98	1.028	.373	.95
Wisconsin	.957	.560	.98	.951	.372	.95
Minnesota	1.029	.538	.98	1.119	.370	.95
Iowa	1.062	.494	.97	1.042	.355	.95
Missouri	1.131	.554	.98	1.135	.310	.93
North Dakota	1.025	.426	.96	1.111	.243	.88
South Dakota	1.114	.426	.96	1.541	.295	.92
Nebraska	1.024	.467	.97	.918	.294	.93

Table 2. (continued)

	Whites			Blacks		
	ρ	σ	R^2	ρ	σ	R^2
Kansas	1.032	.521	.97	1.039	.296	.93
Delaware	.956	.690	.98	1.071	.290	.90
Maryland	.953	.700	.98	1.052	.339	.94
D.C.	1.162	.764	.98	.992	.422	.96
Virginia	1.121	.605	.98	1.081	.243	.89
West Virginia	1.120	.484	.97	1.216	.271	.93
North Carolina	1.019	.441	.96	1.137	.191	.83
South Carolina	.991	.446	.97	1.229	.175	.80
Georgia	1.041	.519	.97	1.074	.195	.82
Florida	1.053	.525	.97	.933	.192	.84
Kentucky	1.221	.480	.97	1.140	.223	.88
Tennessee	1.090	.441	.98	1.146	.210	.86
Alabama	1.073	.508	.97	1.228	.212	.87
Mississippi	1.139	.446	.96	1.316	.159	.72
Arkansas	1.149	.400	.95	1.230	.162	.77
Louisiana	1.061	.553	.98	1.068	.200	.83
Oklahoma	1.129	.500	.97	1.197	.242	.87
Texas	1.108	.564	.98	1.086	.223	.88
Montano	.963	.487	.97	1.117	.294	.91
Idaho	.904	.460	.97	1.343	.387	.92
Wyoming	.902	.543	.98	.746	.212	.89
Colorado	.981	.547	.98	.986	.355	.95
New Mexico	1.047	.590	.98	1.442	.345	.93
Arizona	1.015	.576	.98	1.364	.303	.92
Utah	.885	.533	.97	1.242	.412	.95
Nevada	.958	.671	.98	1.083	.387	.95
Washington	.967	.591	.98	1.077	.393	.95
Oregon	.947	.538	.98	1.108	.376	.96
California	1.028	.711	.99	1.001	.421	.96
Alaska	1.219	.862	.99	1.466	.431	.95
Hawaii	1.248	.652	.97	.950	.698	.98

16

Larry Sjaastad and Ronald W. Hansen:
The Distributive Effect of Conscription:
Implicit Taxes and Transfers under
the Draft System

I.   Introduction

The use of conscription for military manpower procurement raises a great number of issues, only two of which are dealt with in this study. One of the issues is the taxation aspect of conscription: by use of coercion the government acquires the personal services of large numbers of individuals under terms very favorable to the general taxpayer but rather unfavorable to the individuals rendering those services. Through its military conscription power, the government subjects draftees and draft-motivated volunteers to a special tax, one which is discriminatory insofar as only some persons are not required to render these services to the government. The discriminatory aspect of the tax raises the second issue: when all eligible individuals are not required to render military service, incentives are created for activities to avoid that service. These activities are, in general, socially useless despite their private value. In public finance terms, the resources devoted to avoidance of conscription can be referred to as the cost of collection of the conscription tax. As in the case of collection costs of all taxes, these costs represent deadweight welfare losses.

This study attempts to measure the magnitude and distribution of the conscription tax associated with a peacetime force of 2.5 million men and the cost of collection of that tax under the Selective Service system. The estimates obtained refer only to first-term enlisted men; no attempt is made to estimate the tax borne by noncareer officers.

Section II of this paper is devoted to an abstract comparison of a number of possible conscription devices in terms of the magnitude of the conscription tax as well as the (social) costs of collection. The third section of the paper presents various estimates of the conscription tax, derived from three radically different approaches, together with the results of an attempt to quantify the relationship between the tax itself and the associated costs of collection. In Section IV, some tentative results on the distribution of the conscription tax are presented. All estimates are based upon pre-Vietnam data and are intended to refer to a peacetime military establishment. A brief summary completes the paper.

This paper is an abridged version of a report prepared for the President's Commission on an All-Volunteer Armed Force; in addition to the financial support received from the commission, Larry Sjaastad wishes to acknowledge that this research was also supported in part by the Bureau of Naval Personnel Contract No. N00022–69–C–0007. This is the first publication of this article. All rights reserved. Permission to reprint must be obtained from the publisher and authors.

II. The Components of the Conscription Tax

The narrowest concept of the conscription tax is the difference between the earnings the draftee or draft-motivated (reluctant) volunteer receives from the military (including income in hand) and the earnings that would cause that individual to be willing to enter the military.[1] This latter amount may be more or less than his civilian earnings depending upon a number of factors, such as his attitude toward military service, the risks he faces in military relative to civilian employments, the amount of training he receives in the military at no (additional) cost to him, and the level of postseparation benefits provided by the Veterans' Administration.

This narrow definition of the conscription tax reflects an implicit assumption that the confiscation of economic rent does not constitute taxation. Conscription can be viewed as a means of coercion whereby the government reduces the budgetary cost of military manpower procurement, and only part of that reduction takes the form of tax as defined above, the remainder being rents foregone. A persuasive argument can be made, however, that the tax should also include foregone rents. In procurement of manpower for civilian functions (that is, the post office) or procurement of materials, the government does not normally employ coercion; that is, the government abides by the ethical norm of our society that surpluses, be they generated in production or consumption, are properly the property of the person to whom they normally accrue. While it is true that these rents are not necessary to attract the affected individuals to military service, it is also true that similar rents are in fact collected by the sellers of goods and services to the government in virtually all other cases. It is only in the case of certain military manpower procurement that coercion is systematically employed to reduce rents. Hence, if one refuses to treat rent foregone as part of the conscription tax, he should logically treat as a subsidy those rents actually collected by other sellers of goods and services to the government.

An additional element to be taken into account when discussing the conscription tax is the cost of collection of that tax. These costs will vary widely depending upon the rules under which conscription is practiced. In some cases collection of the tax will be costless in the sense that only transfers are involved; in others, real resource costs will be involved.

Estimation of the conscription tax poses a major problem. As the tax is at

---

1 Several different definitions of the implicit tax have been used by various writers. Walter Oi [6, p. 57] defines the tax as "the difference between . . . minimum supply price and current first-term pay . . .," which is the same definition as above. Hansen and Weisbrod [4, p. 396] define the tax as the "difference between their civilian opportunity cost and military renumeration," a definition shared by Davis and Palomba [2, p. 150]. Fisher [3, p. 239] defines the tax as "the maximum amount (the draftee or reluctant volunteer) would be willing to pay to buy his way out of military service." Fisher's definition of the tax cannot exceed but may fall short of Oi's definition, whereas Oi's definition may either exceed or fall short of the Hansen-Weisbrod, Davis-Palomba definition, the outcome depending upon tastes with respect to military service.

once collected and expended, it will not generally be true that explicit trans-actions occur, permitting direct measurement of the tax. Rather, the measure-ments must be based upon estimates of the underlying structure of supply and demand forces, causing the results to be subject to both measurement and estimation errors. Many conscription schemes are possible and indeed have been used from time to time. One variation of some interest is that in which every member of the eligible group receives a draft notice, but as the government wishes to recruit only $s_1 N$ men, it offers to sell exemptions at a fixed price, P_E. This situation is depicted in Figure 1, where SS is the supply function of new recruits to the military as a fraction of the number of persons entering the pool of eligibles each time period. On the vertical axis we measure the supply price, and first-term military pay is taken to be the numeraire. Anyone whose supply price is less than $1 + P_E$ will not find it worthwhile to purchase an exemption, but everyone else will. In this case the tax proceeds under the narrow definition are equal to ABC; under the wider definition they are equal to $FGDE$. In this case there is no redistribution of income within the group, but again it is true that estimation of the tax is relatively simple, as only a portion of the supply function must be approximated.

The type of conscription existing prior to the recently installed lottery is in some respects similar to the scheme just mentioned. By bearing costs, it was possible under that system to avoid military service. These costs took such forms as going to school, entering sheltered occupations, bearing legal and court fees as one fought induction, going to jail, immigrating to Canada, and incurring disabilities. Under such a system, persons unwilling to bear these costs become draftees and reluctant volunteers; these people fall into the s_0' to s_1 range of the

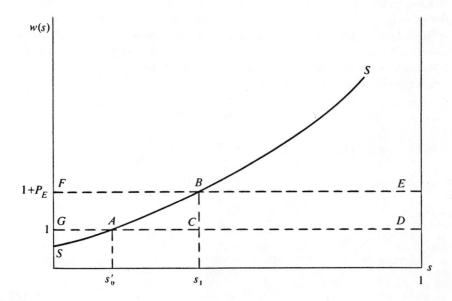

Figure 1.

horizontal axis of Figure 1. Persons willing to bear these costs avoid the military by so doing, and they fall into the s_1 to unit range of the horizontal axis. To the extent that the cost function is the same for everyone, and that by bearing a given cost one could avoid the military altogether, the solution is exactly the same as in the above case. The cost of avoiding the military becomes the distance $BC(= P_E)$, and the total expenditure made to avoid military service is the rectangle $BCDE$. The essential point is, of course, that these costs are real resource costs rather than mere transfer payments; hence, the social cost of conscription is increased by the area $BCDE$. The lottery, to the extent that it permits deferments in the same manner as did the system it replaced, leads to similar results. People will have incentives to enter activities to avoid induction, and the costs so incurred are real costs from a social point of view.

As social policy, the selling of exemptions to the highest bidder or the practice of hiring substitutes is considered to be morally repugnant, and has not been engaged in by the United States since the Civil War. The basis for this view apparently lies in the idea that the distribution of the costs is significantly different using the lottery or prelottery system of conscription. As is obvious from the above analysis, this view is not necessarily correct except when the comparison is to a system permitting the hiring of substitutes; ironically, the lottery and prelottery systems are highly regressive by comparison.

The preceding model does not accurately describe either the lottery or prelottery Selective Service system of the United States. There is, for example, no fixed amount of cost that one can incur that will guarantee avoidance of the draft, nor is the amount that persons are willing to spend the same for all. A crude but somewhat more realistic model is one in which the probability of being inducted is a declining function of the cost incurred to avoid induction. For simplicity, let us assume constant marginal utility of income, and also that the supply price to the military just equals civilian income foregone. Under these circumstances, utility is maximized when income is maximized. Letting the military wage be unity, the civilian wage be w, and the costs of avoiding induction be c, we have expected income as:

$$y^E = (1 - p)(w - c) + p(1 - c) \tag{1}$$

where p is the probability of induction. By cancellation,

$$y^E = w - c - pw + p, \quad \text{and}$$

$$\frac{\partial y^E}{\partial c} = \frac{\partial p}{\partial c}(1 - w) - 1. \tag{2}$$

Setting $\partial y^E / \partial c$ equal to zero, we obtain

$$\frac{\partial p}{\partial c} = \frac{1}{1 - w}. \tag{3}$$

A plausible functional form for $p(c)$ is

$$p = e^{-\beta c}, \quad \beta > 0, \tag{4}$$

as $p(0) = 1$, and $p(c) > 0$, $\partial p / \partial c > 0$ for all positive and finite c.[2] Using (4), we obtain

$$\frac{\partial p}{\partial c} = -\beta p,$$

and the marginal condition becomes

$$p = \frac{1}{\beta(w - 1)}. \tag{5}$$

This condition cannot be satisfied for a $w \geqslant 1$, as the values of w "near" unity would require $p > 1$. The appropriate interpretation of cases where (5) implies $p > 1$ is that of a corner solution; persons who cannot satisfy condition (5) are those for whom the gains associated with reducing the probability of induction are so small that no expenditure to do so is justified. These persons will simply permit themselves to be drafted, or they may even volunteer, but they would not do so in the absence of conscription.[3] Persons able to satisfy (5) enter the military only as draftees.

By setting p equal to unity in equation (5), we obtain

$$w^* = 1 + 1/\beta \tag{6}$$

as the supply price above which a person enters the military only as a draftee after having failed in his efforts to evade induction. Such persons lie on the supply curve above point B in Figure 2.

All true volunteers lie on the supply function up to point A, Figure 2, and all are inducted. Persons on that supply curve between points A and B will not be willing to incur costs to oppose induction and will be inducted. Persons on the supply curve above point B will oppose induction, and all such persons generally are not drafted. The narrow definition of the tax is the sum of the differences between supply for those persons who are drafted (or volunteer reluctantly) and the military wage; the broad definition will also include the area $ABDE$. Given our assumptions, this case is very similar to the purchased-exemption system discussed above. As in the case of the exemption system, the tax under the narrow definition is the area ABC for persons who are neither true volunteers nor successful draft evaders; for all potential draftees (all persons)

---

2 It is assumed that any eligible person who makes no effort to evade induction will in fact be inducted.

3 The incentive to volunteer arises from the greater options offered to volunteers.

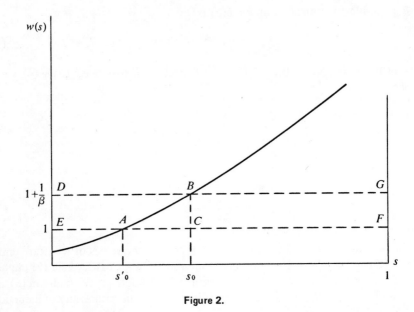

Figure 2.

above B on the supply function, the expected tax is the amount of the tax times the probability of paying it, or $p(w - 1)$. From (5), we have $t = p(w - 1) = 1/\beta$. Hence, the average tax that will be paid by draftees is the rectangle $BCGF$. If we include foregone rents, the tax becomes the rectangle $DEFG$, a result very similar to that obtained under the purchased-exemption system.

The costs borne by potential draftees can also be defined. Setting equation (4) equal to (5), we obtain

$$e^{\beta c} = \beta(w - 1),$$

and taking logarithms we obtain

$$c = \frac{1}{\beta} \left[\log \beta + \log (w - 1) \right] \tag{7}$$

as the density of costs. Costs incurred to avoid the draft are obviously

$$\text{Costs} = \int_{s_0}^{1} c(w)ds. \tag{8}$$

To evaluate the tax and costs of collection, it is necessary to specify $w(s)$ and also the parameters of the probability function.

In the following section three separate estimates of the conscription tax are described. All estimates refer to a peacetime force of 2.5 million men, including officers, but tax estimates have been made for enlisted men only. The first estimate is based upon a comparison of military compensation with civilian earnings for the immediate pre-Vietnam period, based upon the military population existing then. The second estimate is obtained by computing the annual accessions that would be required to maintain a 2.5-million-man force and then estimating the tax that will be paid during their first term by the recruits obtained in the course of one calendar year. This estimate is based upon the concept of supply price rather than civilian earnings. The final estimate of the tax is based upon the preceding behavioral model. As a number of additional assumptions are required to implement this model, the emphasis is placed upon the relation between the tax and costs of collection of that tax.

III.   Estimates of the Conscription Tax

It is frequently asserted that military service carries with it a great deal of training that can be beneficial in subsequent civilian employment. To the extent that on-the-job training of a general nature is greater in the military than in civilian occupations for persons of the same age and education, it is not appropriate to estimate the tax by comparison of military and civilian earnings. Fortunately, a major study of earning profiles of veterans and nonveterans recently made by Phillips Cutright [1] reports the effects of military service on the subsequent earnings of individuals. He has tabulated an approximately 1 percent sample of males who were registered with the Selective Service system in 1953 and were also given a preinduction examination. The sample is limited to persons born between 1927 and 1934 for whom Armed Forces Qualification Test (AFQT) scores are available. From Selective Service records he obtained information on the age, education, race, region of origin, mental score, and veteran status of individuals. Using Social Security numbers, he pairs these data with earnings data for these individuals from Social Security records. (Income is reported to the Social Security Administration on a quarterly basis but only up to the amount for which persons are liable for Social Security taxes. Incomes in excess of this amount are estimated by using the income from the last quarter in which the total reported income was below the ceiling as an estimate of the income of subsequent periods. No income figures were available for persons not covered by Social Security programs.)

Using income data for 1958 and 1964, Cutright attempts to measure the effects of education, mental score, mobility, and military service on earnings. Although the results are still preliminary, they indicate no net positive effect of the military service on future earnings except possibly for persons in the lowest mental groups. For the higher mental groups, nonveterans did consistently better than veterans when differences in education were standardized. His preliminary conclusion is that the positive effects of military service for these groups are not sufficient to outweigh the effect of having been removed from the civilian labor force.

As the draftees and reluctant volunteers tend to be concentrated in the higher mental groups, the results obtained by Cutright indicate that the conscription tax will not be significantly underestimated as a result of ignoring the effects of military service on subsequent earnings. Hence, the remainder of this section will focus solely on income comparisons for the period of active military service.

A. The Financial Burden of Conscription

Because persons entering the military forego the opportunity to earn wages in the civilian sector for the duration of their period of service, one of the components of the burden imposed by the military draft consists of the difference between potential civilian earnings and actual military earnings. Although military compensation will completely offset this loss of wages for some individuals, many servicemen will suffer a net deterioration in their income position. We can refer to this income loss as the financial burden of the military draft.[4]

The income a serviceman could earn in the civilian sector will vary from individual to individual depending on such factors as skills, education, age, and job preference. Although it would be impossible to accurately predict the earning potential of each serviceman individually, we can obtain a reasonable estimate of the earning potential of the group as a whole by comparing servicemen with civilian counterparts who have the same age and education characteristics, factors that strongly influence potential civilian income. The first-term force was categorized by education and age at the time of entry, using three age brackets – 17–18, 19–21, and 22 and over – and three education classifications – less than high school, high school graduate, and some college. College graduates constitute a tenth category in addition to the nine produced by the above cross classification. Using the 1964 force composition as derived from the 1964 NORC survey of the armed forces, we have estimated the age and education distribution of the approximately 1.29 million first-termers in a 2.5-million-man armed forces with the 1964 composition. This distribution is presented in Table 1.

Potential civilian income was estimated, using survey results from the Current Population Survey (CPS) administered in March 1965. The ages are reported for the survey date, although the incomes are for the calendar year 1964. An income distribution by two-year age groupings (age brackets: 19–20, 21–22, 23–24, 25–26, and 27–28) was constructed, using incomes for individuals in the full-time labor force plus persons who had completed school during the year and subsequently entered the full-time labor force. Individuals in this latter group were considered to have been in the labor force six and one-half

---

4 It should be noted that the financial burden so defined is not the same as the more inclusive measure of the conscription tax discussed above, because civilian and military activities with the same financial compensation would not be considered as equally attractive to most individuals.

Table 1. Estimated Distribution of First-Term Enlisted
Servicemen by Education, Age of Entry, and Service for a
2.5-Million-Man Force

Education and Age at Entry	Service					
	Regular Army	Army Draft	Navy	Air Force	Marines	Total
Less than high school	112,825	58,885	92,235	62,675	32,782	359,402
17–18	80,784	7,448	75,502	47,647	28,342	239,723
19–21	25,572	16,995	14,938	12,619	4,044	74,168
22 & over	6,469	34,442	1,795	2,409	396	45,511
High school	126,005	89,829	149,990	233,340	40,517	639,681
17–18	63,473	3,318	95,274	131,278	25,760	319,103
19–21	52,024	27,784	49,273	88,602	13,858	231,541
22 & over	10,508	58,727	5,443	13,460	899	89,037
Some college	55,820	66,491	44,438	80,648	14,253	261,650
17–18	7,805	1,219	8,801	12,810	3,365	34,000
19–21	35,503	21,372	28,689	54,033	9,259	158,856
22 & over	12,512	33,900	6,948	13,805	1,629	68,794
College						
21 & over	9,050	10,472	2,779	5,698	563	28,562
Total	303,700	225,677	289,442	382,361	88,115	1,289,295

Note: The first term stock by service for a 2.5-million-man draft army force was derived by first scaling the average strength of each service in 1964 by the factor .9283, which is the ratio between 2.5 million and 2.693 million, the actual 1964 total force strength. These numbers were then multiplied by the fraction of each force represented by enlisted personnel. To obtain the number of first-termers in the enlisted ranks, we multiplied the number of enlisted personnel by the ratio of the average first-term length of service to the average number of man-years generated by an accession in each service. To obtain the nondraft component for the army, we first subtracted from the 1964 army stock figure our estimate of the number of army man-years generated by draftees. This figure was obtained by multiplying the average FY 1962–FY 1964 inductions by 1.91, the average length of stay for inductees.

months, and their incomes were increased to a full year equivalent. Part-time workers and others not in the full-time labor force were excluded from the calculations of the income distribution.[5] The distribution of mean civilian incomes in 1964 computed as described is presented in Table 2.

Military compensation includes not only base pay but also income in kind received while in the service, such as food, housing, clothing, and medical care, plus eligibility for several programs administered by the Veterans' Administration, and a variety of other less important benefits such as commissary privileges.

---

5 An addition adjustment was made to eliminate a part of the transitory elements in the income distribution arising from abnormal illness or unemployment. The incomes of all individuals were adjusted by the ratio of the average number of weeks worked by full-time or full-time equivalent persons in the same age and education classification to the number of weeks actually worked by the individual.

Table 2. Mean Civilian Income in 1964

Age in March 1965	Education			
	1–3 Years High School	High School	Some College	College Graduate
19--20	$2,508	$2,995	$3,059	--
21–22	3,284	4,022	4,053	—
23–24	3,664	4,393	4,855	$5,662
25–26	4,781	5,521	5,938	6,586

Source: Tabulations from responses to the Current Population Survey of March 1965.

Food supplied by the military has been estimated at factor costs, including labor and equipment for preparation, to have a value of $2.57 per day or $938 annually. Military housing has an estimated value of $30 per month or $360 per year for a serviceman with no dependents. Clothing, medical services, and PX and commissary privileges add an additional $227 per year for a single serviceman.[6] These payments in kind have an estimated total value of $1,525 per year. For army draftees, who are in the service for an average of 1.91 years, the average annual pay in 1965 was approximately $1,150. First-term army enlistees, whose average first-term stay was 2.77 years, receive an average annual pay of approximately $1,450. The estimated average annual first-term base pay for enlistees in the navy, air force, and marines was $1,425, $1,475, and $1,275 respectively. Adding in $1,525 for services in kind, the military pay ranges from $2,675 for army draftees to $3,000 for air force personnel.

The range of military compensation narrows when benefits from Veterans' Administration programs are included. Since eligibility for V.A. hospitalization care is not altered by an increase in the length of service (although there may be an increase in the need for subsequent service-related hospitalization), lengthening the term of service has the effect of lowering the average annual contribution of these benefits to military compensation. Based on figures derived in a separate study on benefits from Veterans' Administration programs, we estimate that these programs will add the following amounts to total military compensation: army draft, $400; army regular, $310; navy, $275; air force, $260; and marines, $290.[7] Total annual military compensation is thus

---

6 These estimates were supplied in an unpublished memo by Rodney Weiher, a commission staff member. The valuation of food received was derived from a study prepared by DUP (comptroller); the evaluation of PX and commissary privileges was taken from the Hubble Committee report.

7 Disability compensation and service-related death benefits have an annual value of $104 and $34.57 respectively when a 5 percent discount rate is used and $60 and $20.46 when a 10 percent discount rate is employed. We used an average of these estimates, or $110 for the combined value of these benefits. For the annualized value of eligibility for hospital care, we divided out estimates of the present value of this eligibility, or $550, by the average length of stay of first term in each service. See Larry Sjaastad and Ronald W. Hansen, "Estimates of Veterans Benefits," Appendix B of [7].

approximately: army draft, $3,075; army regular, $3,285; navy, $3,250; air force, $3,260; and marines, $3,090. Since total compensation does not differ significantly among services, we have elected to use $3,250 as the annual compensation in all services.

To estimate the financial burden we need to know the number of persons with potential civilian earnings in excess of military compensation plus the probable distribution of their potential income. As a proxy for the number of individuals with potential earnings above the military wage we used the number of persons who involuntarily entered the services. The age and education distribution of these individuals, as derived on the basis of the 1964 NORC survey, is presented in Table 3. Undoubtedly some of these individuals did not

Table 3. Estimated Distribution of First-Term Reluctant Volunteers by Education, Age at Entry, and Service for a 2.5-Million-Man Force

Education and Age at Entry	Regular Army	Army Draft	Navy	Air Force	Marines	All Services
Less than high school	26,701	42,990	16,260	15,502	4,910	106,363
17–18	14,396	2,444	10,276	8,858	3,401	39,375
19–21	9,641	11,529	5,877	5,347	1,377	33,771
22 & over	2,664	29,017	107	1,297	132	33,217
High school	46,567	76,723	54,571	75,045	10,396	263,302
17–18	15,913	1,787	28,001	31,454	4,822	81,977
19–21	23,541	22,939	23,119	34,209	5,021	108,829
22 & over	7,113	51,997	3,451	9,382	553	72,496
Some college	33,347	59,429	26,391	44,920	7,215	171,302
17–18	2,946	105	4,621	3,898	1,170	12,740
19–21	21,419	28,000	16,467	31,971	5,043	102,900
22 & over	8,982	31,324	5,303	9,051	1,002	55,662
College	6,969	9,891	2,223	2,411	563	22,057
Total	113,584	189,033	99,445	137,878	23,084	563,024

The 1964 NORC survey of the armed forces was used to calculate the percentage of reluctant volunteers in each classification. These rates were applied to the force distribution reported in Table 1.

have potential civilian incomes in excess of $3,250; however, others who entered the service voluntarily had civilian income opportunities greater than $3,250. For purposes of this calculation, we assumed that the persons in the military with potential civilian income above $3,250 had a potential civilian income distribution similar to the actual distribution for civilians in the same age and education categories with incomes above $3,250. The means of civilian incomes above $3,250 by age and education categories are presented in Table 4. The financial burden imposed on reluctant volunteers is measured by the difference

Table 4. Means of Civilian Earnings above $3,250 in 1964[a]

Age in March 1965	Education			
	1–3 Years High School	High School	Some College	College
19–20	4,504	4,675	4,610	—
21–22	4,648	4,883	5,045	—
23–24	4,947	5,148	5,644	5,994
25–26	5,462	5,980	6,359	6,833

[a] Calculated from responses to the 1965 Current Population Survey.

between $3,250 and the mean civilian earnings above $3,250 of persons with similar education in the relevant age range; the results are presented in Table 5. The estimated financial burden is $411 million for draftees and $699 million for enlistees, or $1.1 billion total.

It should be noted that both of these estimates of the financial burden are based on incomes and military pay in 1964–65. Civilian and military earnings have risen approximately 30 percent since then in nominal terms. Part of this represents an increase in real earnings and part is the result of inflation. Increasing these estimates by 30 percent produces an estimate of $1.42 billion for the financial burden.

B. Supply Function Estimate of the Conscription Tax

The approach in obtaining an estimate of the conscription tax employed in this section involves the use of estimates of the flow supply of manpower to all branches of the military. Both cross-section and time series analyses were employed, and although the particular studies yielded elasticity estimates with considerable dispersion, the staff of the commission agreed upon a mean estimate of 1.25 as the elasticity of the flow supply of military manpower. The interpretation of this elasticity is that if first-term military compensation were to be increased by 10 percent, the annual accessions of true volunteers would increase by 12.5 percent, other things equal, including draft pressure.

The estimates were made on the bases of four groups defined by education and mental score on the Armed Forces Qualification Test. The education groups were persons with less than high school and those completing high school or more; the mental groups were AFQT I–III and AFQT IV. Persons below AFQT IV are generally not permitted to enter the armed forces. On the basis of 1960 census data and the Korpinos [5] data on rejection rates for physical and mental reasons, we estimated the annual (gross) additions to the pool of eligible persons of each education and mental category, as of 1964. Annual accessions of true volunteers were estimated from the distribution data described above in Part A

Table 5. 1964 Financial Tax of the Military Draft — Second Concept
by Education, Age at Entry, and Enlistment Status

Education, Age of Entry, & Enlistment Status	Number of Reluctant Accessions	Mean Civilian Income above $3,250 Minus $3,250	Total Financial Tax in Thousands of Dollars
Draftees			
Less than high school			
17–18	2,444	$1,254	$ 3,065
19- 21	11,529	1,398	16,118
22 & over	29,017	1,955	56,728
High school			
17- 18	1,787	1,425	37,459
19–21	22,939	1,633	127,133
22 & over	51,997	2,445	167,138
Some college			
17–18	105	1,360	143
19–21	28,000	1,795	50,260
22 & over	31,324	2,751	86,172
College			
21 & over	9,891	3,163	31,285
Enlistees			
Less than high school			
17–18	36,931	1,326	48,971
19–21	22,242	1,563	34,764
22 & over	4,200	1,955	8,211
High school			
17–18	80,190	1,529	122,610
19–21	85,890	1,765	151,596
22 & over	20,499	2,445	50,120
Some college			
17–18	12,635	1,577	19,925
19–21	74,900	2,095	156,916
22 & over	24,338	2,751	66,954
College			
21 & over	12,166	3,163	38,481
Total	563,024	—	1,109,447

of this section. Annual required accessions were estimated for a 2.5-million-man
force (including officers) under a Selective Service system, given the composition
of accessions and an average length of service for each type of accession (draftee,
three-year enlistment). These requirements were also computed using composition and length of service estimates for an all-volunteer force provided by other
study groups. Reluctant accessions — draftees and reluctant volunteers — were
then computed as a residual for the Selective Service system. These estimates of
required accessions were made subject to the constraint that the education and
mental score composition of the force (as opposed to accessions) be the same as
in the immediate pre-Vietnam period. The estimates are presented in Table 6.

Table 6. Flow Data for Selective Service and All-Volunteer Force Accessions[a]

Mental Category and Education	Annual Pool	True Volunteers	Requirements S.S.[b]	Requirements AVAF[c]	Reluctant Accessions
I--III					
Less than high school[d]	260,000	74,550	116,429	94,929	41,878
High school +[e]	520,000	108,971	268,076	217,120	159,105
Total	780,000	183,521	384,505	312,049	200,984
IV					
Less than high school[d]	32,560	10,426	26,635	13,376	16,209
High school +[e]	44,540	14,006	36,429	22,941	22,423
Total	77,100	24,432	63,064	36,317	38,632

[a] See text for method of estimation.

[b] Annual accessions required under Selective Service, 2.5-million-man force.

[c] Annual accessions required under an all-volunteer system, 2.5-million-man force.

[d] Less than high school education.

[e] High school education or more.

The number of true volunteers for each education and mental score group was treated as a point on the supply function for that group, and the remainder of the function was obtained by extrapolation using the (constant) 1.25 elasticity. The estimate of total first-term compensation was based upon pay data plus estimates of income in kind and estimates of the average number of years of service generated by a single accession. These estimates are in 1969 dollars but for 1964 levels of compensation; hence, the tax estimates refer to pre-Vietnam conditions. For persons with less than high school, average total first-term military compensation is estimated at $10,662; for persons with a high school education or more, this estimate is slightly higher — $11,018. No distinction on the basis of mental category was possible.

The estimate of the conscription tax under the procedure employed here is limited to rent foregone and the narrow definition of the tax. Rent foregone was based upon estimates of average total military compensation that would produce the required number of voluntary accessions for an all-volunteer armed force. The estimate of the narrow definition of the tax was initially made by assuming that, under Selective Service, the draftees and reluctant volunteers are uniformly distributed along the supply function above the point corresponding to first-term military compensation. This estimate was subsequently revised using a procedure to be described below.

The general procedure for estimation is to determine the amount of conscription tax that will be paid by all persons joining the military for the first time over a single calendar year. As the estimates of accessions presented in Table 6 correspond to a steady-state force of 2.5 million men, the resulting tax estimates are also equal to the tax levied on first-termers during an average calendar year under Selective Service. As the major portion of the conscription tax is estimated from persons of mental categories I–III and possessing at least a high school education, the estimation for this group only will be described in detail. The results for the other groups are presented in tabular form.

At current (1964) levels of compensation, the group under consideration produced 108,971 true volunteers, which represents 20.96 percent of the annual flow (520,000).[8] All-volunteer force requirements of this group are estimated at 270,120, or 41.75 percent of the annual flow. To obtain the required increase in true volunteers, the assumed 1.25 supply elasticity indicates a 66.8 percent increase in military compensation. Such an increase will raise the income of current true volunteers by $802 million annually; in addition, persons who are currently draftees or reluctant volunteers but who would be true volunteers after the pay increase would experience increase in income of about $310 million annually, of which $135 million is estimated to represent rent currently foregone.[9] These estimates are obtained by integration of the area under the supply function, adjusted according to the assumption that draftees and reluctant volunteers are randomly selected and represent 38.71 percent of the annual flow of those persons who do not become true volunteers.

The narrow definition of tax does not include any of the $802 and $135 million of annual foregone rent estimated above, as that definition includes only the excess of the supply price of draftees and reluctant volunteers over military compensation. Using the data at hand, the narrow tax estimate that emerges is $2.288 billion for those first-termers in mental categories I–III possessing at least a high school education. Little can be done to test the validity of the constant elasticity assumption, as the enlistment data did not strongly discriminate among the various functional forms, and no observations exist at the far end of the distribution owing to the low level of military compensation during the entire sample period. However, we did test the random selection assumption in an indirect manner. It is reasonable to assume that the distribution of supply prices is well correlated with the distribution of civilian income. If this correlation is high, then the fraction of persons possessing a college education should be about the same among draftees and reluctant volunteers as it is among all eligible persons entering the pool, excluding the 20.96 percent at the bottom end of the income distribution. For persons possessing at least a high school education, the latter fraction is 22 percent, whereas for the former group it is estimated by the authors to be only 7.4

---

8 The terms *current* and *currently* are intended to refer to the immediate pre-Vietnam situation.

9 The $135 million of rent foregone is a tax levied only on persons currently in the military; in addition, there is rent foregone by persons who are currently civilians but who would be true volunteers after the pay increase. This latter figure, estimated at $215 million, is not included because it is not borne by military personnel.

percent.[10] Clearly, the Selective Service system is indeed selective, and to fail to take this into account introduces an upward bias into our estimate of the conscription tax.

To deal with this problem, we first assumed that the orderings of individuals by civilian income and by supply price are one and the same, and then we estimated the density of college graduates as a function of income percentiles from the CPS data. The linear function

$$z(s) = 0.385 \, s \tag{9}$$

fit the data well over the relevant range, where $s = 1$ corresponds to the 100th percentile.[11] In addition a second function was set up relating the probability of entering the military to one's position on the income scale (supply function). This function had to satisfy two constraints. The first constraint is that the integral of the probability function over the relevant range produce 159,105 draftees and reluctant volunteers out of the 389,349 persons available, or in fraction terms,[12]

$$\int_{.2187}^{1} p(s)ds = .4086. \tag{10}$$

The second condition is obvious:

$$\int_{.2187}^{1} p(s)z(s)ds = .074. \tag{11}$$

---

10 The parent population estimate is obtained from the 1965 Current Population Survey described above in Part A of this section. This estimate is too high for our purposes because (a) many people escape the enlisted ranks by becoming officers, and (b) the NORC survey described indicates that about 15 percent of the enlisted accessions of college graduates are true volunteers. Hence, of the 90,420 college graduates in the upper 79 income percentiles entering the pool annually, 36,751 entered as officers, of which 21,680 are estimated to be true volunteers, and another 2,240 entered the enlisted ranks as true volunteers. Eliminating the true volunteers, we have then 68,740 college-educated persons "available" to enter the enlisted ranks as reluctant volunteers and draftees. This number represents less than 16 percent of the original base and less than 18 percent of the base adjusted for officer accessions of true volunteers. The 7.4 percent estimate is obtained as follows. Of total accessions of reluctant volunteers and draftees of *all* mental categories and with at least a high school education, 12.6 percent came from category IV. It is assumed that the frequency of college graduates in the category IV group would be no more than half as great as in categories I–III, and hence that about 6 percent of the reluctant accessions of college graduates to the enlisted ranks came from the category IV group, leaving 11,820 to come from categories I–III. This number represents 7.4 percent of the 159,105 reluctant accessions of persons in categories I–III and with at least a high school education.

11 Due to the removal of the 21,680 officers from the pool of 520,000, that pool is reduced to 498,320; hence, the 108,971 true (enlisted) volunteers represent 21.87 percent rather than 20.96 percent of the pool. When equation (9) is integrated from $s = .2187$ to unity, and the integral is divided by the base, we obtain 23.5 percent having college degrees, slightly greater than the true value of 22 percent.

12 The assumed 389,349 persons available is net of the 21,680 officers accessions removed from the original pool of 520,000.

Several functional forms were investigated, and one rather simple form that can satisfy these constraints is

$$p(s) = a(1 + bs)^\alpha. \tag{12}$$

The coefficients a, b, and α can be estimated from the simultaneous solution of equations (10) and (11), together with the constraint that

$$p(.2187) = 1.0, \tag{13}$$

that is, the probability of entering the military is unity if one is the marginal true volunteer. The function $p(s)$ is defined by (12), of course, only for $1 \geqslant s \geqslant .2187$.

The parameters of (12) have been estimated as[13]

$$a = 1.656,$$
$$b = -.5416,$$
$$\alpha = 4.0.$$

Using these parameters together with the assumed supply function, computation of the tax is a matter of evaluating the integral

$$\int_{.2187}^{1} p(s)w(s)ds \tag{14}$$

and subtracting out military compensation. The result that emerges is $1.35 billion, nearly $1 billion less than the adjusted estimate.

The adjustment described in the above paragraphs has not been carried out for the remaining three groups. This omission is due partly to the complexity of the calculations and partly to the expectation that the random selection assumption is much more reasonable for persons of lower education or mental categories or both than for the group treated above. A summary of the calculations for all four groups is contained in Table 7. The treatment of category I–III persons with less than high school is identical to that described above for the group with high school. Mental category IV persons, however, posed special problems. The supply elasticity estimate is not applicable to this group, as the accessions of mental category IV persons is demand rather than supply determined — that is, fluctuations in these accessions do not represent movements along a supply function. In the absence of any hard information concerning this supply elasticity, we assumed it to be 1.25 for both category IV groups, and we assumed further that the pay increase would be independent of

---

13 Although the functional form of (10) is arbitrarily chosen, the results do not depend critically upon that form so long as equations (10), (11), and (13) are satisfied. Note that $p(1) = .073$; the individual most adverse to the military has a probability of only 7 percent of being forced to join. This limiting value does not appear to be unreasonable.

Table 7. Supply Function Estimates of the Conscription Tax and Income Foregone as of 1964 for a 2.5-Million-Man Force in Millions of 1969 Dollars

Mental Category and Education	Rent Foregone	Tax — Narrow Definition	Total
I–III			
Less than high school[a]	$ 177	$ 396	$ 573
High school +[b]	937	1,348	2,285
Total	1,114	1,744	2,858
IV			
Less than high school[a]	—	120	120
High school +[b]	136	195	231
Total	136	315	351
All groups	$1,250	$2,059	$3,209

[a] Less than high school education.
[b] High school education or more.
[c] Adjusted as described in the text.

mental category. This assumption led to an excess supply of persons with at least a high school education. We assumed that this excess supply would lead to an equal reduction in permitted accessions of category IV persons with less than high school. Such a reduction causes requirements to fall short of current true volunteers; hence, there is no basis to believe that any rent is foregone by the less-than-high school education group.

The estimates presented in Table 7 indicate a total rent foregone by first-term enlisted men of $1.25 billion annually for a 2.5-million-man force at 1964 levels of compensation. The conscription tax (narrow definition) amounts to over $2 billion annually. This latter amount is 48 percent of the estimated civilian earnings foregone by these draftees and reluctant volunteers; in addition, it is estimated that when the personal income tax is added, the total tax is 51 percent, not including the $1.25 billion in rent foregone.

The conscription tax as estimated by the supply function estimate exceeds the estimate of the financial loss by about $600 million. This difference is consistent with the hypothesis that military service is an inferior occupation, requiring a positive premium in pay to make it as attractive as civilian occupations. Due to the differences in the procedures of estimation of the two magnitudes and the rather strong assumptions embodied in the supply function approach, one can tentatively conclude only that the "equalizing differential" is positive for the individuals involved; estimates of the magnitude of that differential will require more refined data and techniques.

C.   The Costs of Collection of the
Conscription Tax

An indirect method for estimation of the conscription tax (narrow definition) and the costs of collection of that tax was outlined in Section II. In the following paragraphs we report on estimates based on that method for the group accounting for the bulk of the tax – the group falling into mental categories I–III and possessing at least a high school education. Estimates were made under a variety of assumptions concerning the function form of the supply function as well as the parameters of that function.

Let us begin with the constant elasticity supply function and the probability function used in the example in Section II, which are respectively,[14]

$$w(s) = \gamma s^{\rho},\tag{15}$$

$$p = e^{-\beta c}.\tag{4}$$

As annual Selective Service requirements of this group are estimated at 268,076 accessions from a pool of 520,000, the probability function must be such that

$$\int_0^1 p(s)ds = \frac{268{,}000}{520{,}000} = 0.516.\tag{16}$$

Up to a certain point, defined as s^* such that $w^* = w(s^*) = 1 + 1/\beta$ in equation (6), it is true that $p(s) = 1.0$; thereafter $p(s)$ is defined by equation (4). As $p(s)$ is a one-parameter function, it follows that that parameter is determined by

$$\int_{s^*}^1 p(s)ds = 0.514 - s^*,\tag{16'}$$

that is, up to s^* everyone volunteers, and from $s = s^*$ to $s = 1$ we must obtain additional recruits so that accessions equal 51.4 percent of the annual pool. A value of β equal to 3.0 satisfies equation (16); this value implies that $w^* = 1 + 1/\beta$ is equal to 1.333, and from (15), $s^* = .301$.

Reluctant volunteers tend to be concentrated in the range $s = .21$ to $s = s^* = .301$; the conscription tax levied on these people is the difference between supply price and military compensation and is paid with a probability of unity. This component of the tax is approximately $92 million per year. The remaining reluctant volunteers and the draftees will be found in the range $1 = s \geqslant .301$. The tax for these people is the integral of the product of the

---

14 As the elasticity of s with respect to w is assumed to be 1.25, it follows that $\rho = 0.8$; taking military compensation for first-termers as numeraire and as about 21 percent of the group under consideration were true volunteers, we require that $w(.21) = 1.0$; hence, $(.21)^{.8} = 1/\gamma$, so $\gamma = 3.5$.

supply price, net of military pay, and the probability of paying the tax, $p(s)$ — that is,

$$\int_{.301}^{1} [w(s) - 1]p(s)ds. \tag{17}$$

This component of the tax amounts to $1.336 billion; the total tax is therefore $1.428 billion, slightly higher than the $1,348 billion estimate from Part B above.

The cost of collection estimate is obtained from equations (7), (8), and (15) and is $1.836 billion, or 129 percent of the tax proceeds. The ratio of proceeds plus cost of collection to the proceeds is 2.28 — that is, $2.28 are extracted from the affected group for each $1 of tax collected.

A similar computation has been performed under the more conservative assumption that the supply elasticity is unity. The effect of this change is to drastically increase both the tax and the cost of collection. The estimate of the tax rises from $1.428 billion to $2.265 billion; the collection cost rises from $1.836 billion to $3.63 billion. The ratio of tax proceeds plus cost of collection to tax proceeds rises by a modest amount — from 2.28 to 2.60. This ratio is quite stable with respect to assumptions concerning the parameters of the supply function.

Estimates were also made for the well-known complement supply function

$$(1 - s) = aw^{-b}, b > 0. \tag{15'}$$

This function poses special problems, Given our assumed probability function (4), the tax incidence is $p(s)[w(s) - 1]$, which from equation (5) is a constant $1/\beta$, and hence will always be finite. The costs of collection will not, however, be finite when the value of b is less than unity. The elasticity of s with respect to w obtained from (15') is $b(1 - s)/s$, which implies a value of b of .31 for $s = .21$ and an elasticity of 1.25, which in turn implies infinite collection costs owing to the infinite area below the supply curve.

The complement function is concave from above (for $b > 0$) throughout its range, whereas the true supply function may well be convex from above for "small" values of s. Indeed, it is quite possible that the available observations correspond to the convex portion of the supply function — that is, to individuals whose position in the income distribution is below the mode. Such data would impart a strong negative bias to the estimator of b, and this bias would explain why the implicit estimate of b in this study is so low, as was also the case with the earlier study by Oi[5], whereas when the complement function is fitted to the 1965 CPS income data, the estimte of b is consistently greater than unity.[15]

---

15 The complement function was fit to the income distribution data derived from the Current Population Survey tape for 1965, the data being adjusted as was described in Part A of this section. For persons with less than high school, the coefficient corresponding to b in equation (15') above was estimated by least squares as 3.27, with a standard error of 0.28. This estimate was made on the basis of 11 points on the cumulative income distribution. For persons with at least a high school education, for which we had 12 points on the income distribution, the estimate of the coefficient was 3.13, with a standard error of 0.32.

To circumvent the difficulties posed by "implied" estimates of b, we chose a value of unity, as this is the smallest value that yields finite estimates of the cost of collection of the conscription tax. Even so, this implies an elasticity of supply of 3.76 at $s = 0.21$; it remains true, of course, that as s approaches unity, w must approach infinity.

Equation (16) is satisfied in this case by a value of β of 4.3, and the value of s^* is .359. The estimate of the conscription tax (narrow definition) is $942 million, the lowest estimate obtained; the estimate of the costs of collection is $1.754 billion, some 86 percent in excess of the proceeds of the tax. The ratio of tax proceeds plus costs of collection to the proceeds is 2.86.

Finally, a linear nonhomogeneous supply function was assumed. This function, together with the 1.25 elasticity assumption, required a value of β of 3 and s^* of .298. The tax proceeds were estimated at $1.28 billion, and the cost of collection at $2.04 billion, the ratio of tax plus costs to tax being 2.58.

The principal conclusion to be drawn from the results obtained above is that the Selective Service is a very inefficient taxation device, as the costs of collection (the deadweight loss) appear to exceed the proceeds of the tax. These costs of collection are *in addition to* the usual concepts of the inefficiency introduced by conscription.

A second conclusion to be drawn is that the tax itself is substantial. The estimates obtained in this section tend to cluster around those obtained in previous sections in which the approaches were radically different. It seems quite plausible that the conscription tax, even under the narrow definition, imposes a burden of about $2 billion on a small subset of the population and does so in a fashion so discriminatory as to make this tax unique.

IV. The Distribution of the Tax

Data are not available to determine exactly which groups bear the various proportions of the tax, the cost of collection, etc., but an indirect estimate of the incidence of the tax by income groups has been made on the basis of the supply function estimate described under Section III.B above. To obtain that estimate, a probability function was introduced, equation (12), to capture the selectivity of the draft system. The same probability function has been used to estimate the distribution of the tax; in so doing we have assumed that supply price, rather than civilian income, is the relevant "income" variable. Total income is defined relative to an all-volunteer armed force situation – that is, income subject to taxation by conscription is taken to be military pay under an all-volunteer situation or supply price, whichever is greater. Correspondingly the tax is taken to include rents foregone. The computation has been made only for first-termers in mental categories I–III possessing at least a high school education; as is clear from Table 7, this group accounts for over two-thirds of the broad definition of the tax.

Table 8. Distribution of Accessions, Alternative Income, and the
Conscription Tax by Income[a]

	Alternative Income Class by Quintile[b]				
	1st	*2nd*	*3rd*	*4th*	*5th*
Percent of					
Total accessions	38.1	30.0	18.0	9.5	4.4
Alternative income[b]	14.8	14.9	18.0	23.5	28.8
Total conscription tax	28.6	23.4	20.5	16.6	10.9
Tax as a percent of					
Alternative income[c]	40.0	32.0	23.8	14.8	7.9

[a] Refers only to first-termers in mental categories I–III possessing at least a high school education.

[b] See text for definition of alternative income.

[c] Does not include taxes other than the conscription tax.

The calculations are presented in Table 8. The distribution by quintiles, of total accessions, alternative income (as defined above), and share of total tax is presented, together with an estimate of tax as a percent of each group's income. As can be seen from that table, our estimate of the participation rate in the armed forces drops sharply as the supply price rises; over 38 percent of total accessions come from the lowest quintile, whereas only 4.4 percent come from the highest. The highest quintile is estimated to receive about twice the alternative income as does the lowest quintile. The fact that our definition of "income" reflects not civilian income but rather, for the lowest quintile, the income they would receive under all-volunteer army wage rates reduces this ratio below its value for the entire civilian income distribution.

The tax itself is highly regressive in one sense but quite progressive in another. Persons in the highest quintile are estimated to pay only a bit more than one-third of the tax paid by those in the lowest quintile (10.9 percent versus 28.6 percent); hence, the burden of the tax is much greater for the low income *groups* than for their higher income counterparts. In this sense the tax is highly regressive. The magnitude of the regressivity is apparent from the final row of Table 8; the tax rate falls from 40.0 percent to about 8 percent as we move from the lowest to the highest income quintile.[16]

From an individual point of view, however, the tax is progressive. It is progressive in the sense that at the higher end of the income distribution the tax is paid by an unlucky few, and consequently the rates actually paid by those persons are higher than is the case for lower income persons. It is estimated that only 11.6 percent of the persons in the highest income quintile actually serve in

---

16 These rates somewhat overstate the true regressivity of the tax, as the data refer to eligible rather than total population. As is common knowledge, the lower income groups contain higher proportions of persons found ineligible for medical and other reasons than is the case for the higher income groups.

the armed forces; hence, the income foregone by these persons is 3.33 percent of total alternative income (11.6 percent times 28.8 percent). When the income base is adjusted accordingly, we find that the tax *rate* for those in the highest income quintile actually paying the tax is actually 68 percent rather than 7.9 percent. As *all* eligible persons in the lowest income quintile are paying the tax, the rate there is uniformly 40 percent. Thus the tax rate is about 70 percent higher at the uppermost quintile than it is for the lowest quintile *for those that actually serve.*

The effect of conscription, then, is to redistribute income within income groups as well as among them. The poor pay more, in the aggregate, than do their higher income counterparts, but the burden of the tax on the latter is highly concentrated. These conclusions would be modified, of course, when account is taken of costs incurred to avoid conscription. As these costs are borne completely by the upper-income groups, and as all persons in those groups have an incentive to bear the costs, they will tend to be shared more evenly within the groups than is the tax itself. The effect of the cost of collection, then, is to reduce the regressivity of the cost of conscription among income groups.

V. Summary

The results of this study indicate that conscription during the immediate pre-Vietnam period imposed a tax on first-term enlisted personnel of about $2 billion per year. Estimates arrived at by widely divergent methods and different assumptions cluster in a surprisingly tight fashion. The results also indicate that the financial burden of conscription is somewhat less – approximately $1.4 billion per year.

In addition to the tax itself, the coercive nature of conscription is estimated to have deprived first-term enlisted personnel of an additional $1.25 billion of income that they would have received were procurement of first-term enlisted personnel subject to the same rules that guide government procurement in other areas.

Further, the nature of the Selective Service system imposes unnecessary and socially useless costs on all young men – those who escape induction as well as those who do not – in the form of activities undertaken to avoid conscription. These costs are extremely difficult to estimate directly; we have, however, estimated them indirectly. Our procedure is admittedly crude, but it does provide the first available estimate of these costs. Our results indicate that these costs of collection exceed the tax itself, perhaps by as much as 100 percent and very likely by as much as 50 percent. As a tax, conscription under Selective Service is brutally inefficient – virtually in a class by itself.

Finally, the conscription tax falls much more heavily upon lower-income persons than upon the well-to-do, with the lowest-income group paying nearly three times as much tax as persons in the highest-income group. It is true, however, that conscription imposes a higher tax *rate* on the high-income inductee than it does on the true volunteer. That these two statements are consistent is due to the fact that higher income conveys with it greater success in escaping conscription.

References

1. Cutright, P. "Achievement, Military Service, and Earnings." Unpublished manuscript. Social Security Administration, May 20, 1969.
2. Davis, J. R., and N. A. Polomba. "On the Shifting of the Military Draft as a Progressive Tax-in-Kind." *Western Economic Journal* 4, no. 2 (March 1968): 150–153.
3. Fisher, A. C. "The Costs of the Draft and the Cost of Ending the Draft." *American Economic Review*, June 1969, pp. 239–254.
4. Hansen, W. L., and A. Weisbrod. "Economics of the Military Draft." *Quarterly Journal of Economics*, August 1967, pp. 395–421.
5. Karpinos, B. D. "The Mental Test Qualification of American Youth for Military Service and the Relationship to Educational Attainment." Proceedings of the American Statistical Association, Social Statistics Section, 1966.
6. Oi, W. Y. "The Economic Cost of the Draft." *American Economic Review*, May 1967, pp. 39–62.
7. Sjaastad, L. A., and R. W. Hansen. "The Conscription Tax: An Empirical Analysis." In *Studies Prepared for the President's Commission on an All-Volunteer Armed Force*, vol. 11, Washington, D.C.: U.S. Government Printing Office, November 1970.
8. Tax, S., ed. *The Draft*. Chicago: University of Chicago Press, 1967.

4

Implications for Redistribution Policy

The striking neglect, if not disregard, of equity considerations in the operation of many transfer and general expenditure programs suggests some fairly strong policy implications: The explicit consideration of equity criteria or of the distributive effects of many allocation decisions. Contrary to the notion implied by traditional approaches to public finance, the distribution branch of the budget cannot be considered separately from the allocation branch.

The practical outcome of this conclusion points to the adoption of explicit equity norms in the formulation of public policy. Three general areas for the application of such norms are covered by the papers included in Part 4: (a) For explicit transfer programs, the adoption of an income maintenance formula, whether based on break-even income or poverty threshold norms, is suggested. The papers by David and Leuthold discuss the classical proposals for a negative income tax or a guaranteed income, and Lampman and Okner analyze the effects of more recent proposals. (b) For public expenditure decisions or public project selection, McGuire and Garn discuss a method of integrating efficiency with equity criteria. (c) For macroeconomic policy formulation, Hollister and Palmer propose that the distributive consequences of fiscal and monetary policy be considered together with other factors: The implicit tax of inflation does not fall heavily on the poor, whereas the implicit tax of unemployment engendered by anti-inflationary policies falls very heavily on the poor.

Martin David and Jane Leuthold discuss programs proposed for eliminating or alleviating poverty such as negative rates taxation, guaranteed minimum incomes, and family allowances. As all of these approaches subsume a norm reflected in "a mathematical and impersonally administered formula of income transfers," these programs are termed "formula-based income transfers." They examine the formulas implicit in the Friedman Plan, Lampman-Green Plan, Tobin Plan, and the Schwartz-Theobald Income Maintenance Plan. Their major difference from the current welfare systems is that they are aimed solely and explicitly at the poor.

The authors simulate the consequences of alternative plans on hand of a sample of poor families. They conclude: "The Exemption and Minimum Standard Deduction (EX-MSD) (Friedman-type) Plan provides maximum benefits for the retired. The employed receive nearly as large benefits. The plan

309

fills 35 percent of the poverty-income gap of the retired, 24 percent of the income gap of the employed, and 23 percent of the income gap of the poverty population. By contrast with the EX-MSD Plan, any plan based on the poverty-income gap will provide a constant share of the income gap to all population groups. The difference in the amount of payment under the two plans can be sizable, although the average payment to all poor adult units is the same under both plans.

Adult units with children or aged members benefit most from the EX-MSD Plan. Young married and young single persons derive substantially less benefits. They would receive barely half of what they would receive under an Income Gap Plan that provides equal benefits to the poor.

They report some surprising findings: "First, some families are poor despite the fact that their educational attainment suggests skills and ability. Second, any plan that places no ceiling on the poverty standard results in extremely high payments to a few large families. Third, combinations of characteristics and their effect on the operation of a formula-based income maintenance plan are not always obvious."

The authors conclude, however, that "a formula-based income maintenance plan can provide aid to groups that are difficult to locate through categorical programs. Any plan that provides benefits on a standard that deviates from a true subsistence line will give some aid to the near poor."

Robert Lampman suggests that a child allowance would be a rational approach to alleviating poverty. He calculates how disposable income would change for the average family in each income bracket for two plans suggested by Vadakin, one by Brazer, the Family Assistance Plan recommended by President Nixon, and the plan recommended by the Presidential Commission on Income Maintenance Programs (the Heineman Commission), even though the latter, strictly speaking, is not a child allowance. He concludes that "increases in income ... vary from a low of $1.1 billion for Vadakin 2 to a high of $8.6 billion for the Heineman plan. The net benefit to the poor is also different among the plans. The Family Assistance Plan does the most for the poor per dollar transferred, and in that sense it may be said to be the most intensively antipoverty plan. None of these plans would confine its benefits to the 23 million persons who are poor." He observes further that "the most redistributive of the plans [expressed by the change in the share of income going to the lowest fifth of households] ... is the Heineman plan."

Benjamin Okner simulates the effect of the two most recent proposals, the Family Assistance Plan (FAP) and the Universal Income Supplement (UIS) program recommended by the Heineman Commission, based on 1967 Survey of Economic Opportunity data. He concludes that "the net federal cost of the Family Assistance Plan is about $4 billion" as compared to the Universal Income Supplement, whose net cost would amount to about $7 billion. "At present, even after receipt of transfer income, there is still a $9.9 billion posttransfer poverty-income gap. Under the Family Assistance Plan, the posttransfer poverty gap is reduced to $6.6 billion with FAP payments filling one-third of the existing gap. The Universal Income Supplement program leaves a posttransfer poverty gap of only $4.3 billion, filling 57 percent of the gap."

Finally, Okner concludes that due to considerations of horizontal efficiency, the Universal Income Supplement is to be preferred over the Family Assistance Plan.

Martin McGuire and Harvey Garn report on "the formulation and implementation of explicit formulae for consolidation of equity and efficiency criteria in the selection of regional development projects. . . ." This integration is based on an "index of need" based on dual criteria. The latter, in turn, incorporate "an appropriate set of weights which reflect the decision-maker's subjective judgments (interpersonal utility comparisons) between communities. . . ." This leads to a decision rule to evaluate all projects by weighting benefit-cost ratios by a welfare index.

The general policy conclusions discussed by Robinson Hollister and John Palmer are not relevant merely to a given economic situation, nor are the issues to which the entire paper is addressed. However, the authors have related the findings in the paper to the current public controversy. They point out that it is useful to inquire about the impact on the poor of inflation, on the one hand, and of anti-inflationary policies on the other. As is indicated in the paper, whereas the "tax of inflation" does not fall heavily on the poor, it is clear that the "tax of unemployment," which is likely to result from anti-inflationary policies, does indeed fall very heavily on the poor. Further, it is suggested that continued tight labor markets are of central importance to the effectiveness of public and private training and employment programs. A rise in unemployment of even 1 percent could wipe out a substantial portion of the gains from such training programs. It is pointed out that as a nation we have had very little experience with a long period with unemployment rates below 4 percent, and it is possible that with continued tight labor markets private industry would learn how to absorb marginal workers more effectively, and a reduction in inflationary pressures could well result.

The authors question whether, having spent a good deal of the past twenty years finding out about the relationship between high levels of unemployment and the price level – at great cost to the poor in terms of unemployment – we cannot as a nation afford to spend more time finding out about the relationship between very low levels of unemployment and the price level. At the very least, it is argued, we should stop pretending that we are stopping inflation to help the poor; this study indicates that the cure for inflation is likely to impose a far heavier burden on the poor than does inflation itself.

17

Martin David and Jane Leuthold:
Formulas for Income Maintenance:
Their Distributional Impact

I.   Introduction

In 1965, $93 billion was spent by public and private organizations to provide income transfers to individuals and households in the United States. Of that amount $5.5 billion was transferred in the form of public assistance; $30.2 billion was transferred through social insurance programs; and $43.1 billion was transferred through other governmental programs. Private direct income payments from welfare agencies amounted to approximately $14.2 billion.[1] In spite of these transfers, which comprise 17.7 percent of personal income, an estimated 34 million individuals were poor according to the standards established by the Social Security Administration and the President's Office of Economic Opportunity, in 1964 (the latest date for which such information is available).

The persistence of poverty and near-poverty conditions has prompted numerous proposals for relief of the symptoms of poverty (i.e., lack of money or the ability to purchase an adequate standard of living). Others are aimed at rehabilitation of the poor (i.e., endowing poor persons with saleable labor market skills and training them to find jobs in the marketplace). During the past year there has been considerable discussion of programs seeking to fill the poverty-income gap of the poor, in other words, the difference between the actual income of poor families and what is required for a decent level of living.

Among the programs proposed for accomplishing this end are negative rates taxation, guaranteed minimum incomes, and family allowances. All of these programs have certain features in common. They consist of a mathematical and impersonally administered formula of income transfer. The payment is determined by a rate of transfer applied against the income deficiency of the family.

From *National Tax Journal*, March, 1968, Vol. XXI, No. 1. Reprinted by permission of The National Tax Association and the authors.

The authors are Professor of Economics, University of Wisconsin, and Assistant Professor of Economics, University of Illinois. The research reported here was supported by funds from the National Science Foundation and by funds granted to the Institute for Research on Poverty at the University of Wisconsin by the Office of Economic Opportunity pursuant to the provisions of the Economic Opportunity Act of 1964. The facilities of the Social Systems Research Institute and the helpful comments of H. W. Watts, G. H. Orcutt, and R. J. Lampman have assisted in the conception and execution of this study. Thae Soo Park assisted ably in the compilation of the tables. Errors, value judgments, and conclusions are the authors' and do not reflect views of the sponsors or our colleagues.

1 Current Operating Statistics," *Social Security Bulletin*, Vol. 29, No. 3 (March 1966), pp. 279–301.

Eligibility is conditioned only on an income and/or asset test. Because of these common characteristics, programs of this type are known as formula-based income transfers.

One of the first formulas for income maintenance was proposed by Milton Friedman.[2] Under the Friedman Plan, the income grant is half of the unused Federal tax exemptions and deductions for the family. A family of four with no income would receive $1,500 (half of the sum of (a) four times the Federal exemption of $600 and (b) the minimum standard deduction of $300 for the taxpayer plus three times $100 for his dependents). This plan is referred to below as the EX-MSD Plan.

A similar plan, but one not tied to the Federal tax system, is the Lampman-Green Plan.[3] Formula income maintenance is accomplished by a rate applied to the amount by which a poverty standard exceeds income for the family. Lampman and Green assumed that the poverty standard could be reasonably well approximated by $1,500 for the family head plus $500 for each dependent. Thus, for a family of four, the poverty standard would be $3,000. If the family had no income and the rate used was ½, then the family would receive $1,500 (½ · $3,000). This plan is referred to subsequently as the Income Gap Plan.

Another income maintenance plan (proposed by Tobin) pays a basic allowance of $500 to every man, woman and child.[4] Under the Tobin Plan, each unit is subject to a $33\frac{1}{3}$ percent tax rate on income other than the allowance up to the income level at which the tax liability equals the tax liability of the present system. For example, the family of four cited above would receive a payment of $2,000. One third of any income earned would be subtracted from the basic $2,000. The family becomes taxable (according to the Federal formula described above) when earnings exceed $3,000; it would pay $33\frac{1}{3}$ percent of earnings in excess of $3,000 as taxes until $\frac{1}{3}$ of earnings exceeds the sum of $2,000 and the tax liability under the present law on those earnings. For example, if a 20 percent rate applies to all taxable income, this break-even point is reached at approximately $10,500 (.2[10,500 − 3,000] = .33[10,500] − 2,000).

An alternative income maintenance plan proposed by Schwartz and Theobald is intended to fulfill the subsistence needs of the poor and still maintain a transfer rate of less than 100 percent.[5] This involves some payment of

---

2 Milton Friedman, *Capitalism and Freedom* (Chicago: University of Chicago Press, 1962), pp. 191–194.

3 Robert J. Lampman, "Prognosis for Poverty," National Tax Association, *Proceedings of 57th Annual Conference* (Pittsburgh, September, 1964), pp. 71–81; Christopher Green, *Negative Taxes and the Poverty Problem,* a conference monograph prepared for the Brookings Institution Studies in Government Finance (June 9–10, 1966).

4 James Tobin, "Improving the Economic Status of the Negro," *Daedalus*, Vol. 94 (Fall, 1965), pp. 889–895.

5 Edward Schwartz, "A Way to End the Means Test," *Social Work,* Vol. 9 (July 1964), pp. 3–12; and Robert Theobald, *Free Men and Free Markets* (New York: C. N. Potter, 1963), pp. 192–197.

benefits to the near-poor. In principle, the Schwartz-Theobald version of income maintenance is equivalent to the plans discussed above but utilizes a higher poverty standard.

Several other plans have been proposed to provide payments to both the poor and the rich. Such payments or "demogrants" are similar to the foregoing plans since the *cost of the transfer must be paid out of the taxable resources of the wealthy* if any net income redistribution is to be accomplished, although the incentive effects of large gross tax revenue and gross transfers might well differ. Figure 1 illustrates this similarity.

Formula-based income transfer differs from the current system of income maintenance in several important dimensions. First, formula income transfers cover all needy persons, while transfers under the current system are directed for the most part at specific categories of the poor. Second, formula transfers can be directed exclusively to the poor while there tend to be substantial payments to the non-poor under the current system. Finally, formula transfers are aimed at the alleviation of poverty while many of the programs under the current system were created for other purposes. It is easy to give examples of such differences between formula income maintenance and existing transfer programs.

Federal public assistance serves as an example of a program limited to specific population groups. With the exception of limited (and recent) modifications, these categorical aid programs are based on characteristics that were thought to justify payments to non-employed persons or heads of families.[6] In contrast, formula transfer programs would pay benefits to all families with an income deficiency.

Veterans' benefits illustrate a program that extends benefits to both the poor and the non-poor. Payments can be made either as a matter of right or on the basis of need. The means test applied to determine whether relatives of veterans are indigent is less severe than the means test used in public assistance. Thus many persons who are not poor according to standards set by the Office of Economic Opportunity profit from veterans' programs.

Another program not intended exclusively for the poor is social insurance. Social insurance provides benefits to persons and families to assure that anyone with some work experience is entitled to some income (and medical services) when he becomes disabled, unemployed, or when he retires after age 62. Although this program aids poor and non-poor alike, two-fifths of the aged are poor even after the receipt of Social Security according to standards established by Mollie Orshansky. Moreover, Social Security benefits account for 30 percent of the income of families with aged heads.[7]

---

6 When Social Security legislation was enacted in 1935, Aid to the Blind, Aid to the Permanently and Totally Disabled, Old-Age Assistance, and Aid to Families with Dependent Children (originally ADC) were all extended to those families in which the primary (and often the only) breadwinner was incapable of finding remunerative work in the labor market or was prevented from leaving the home to seek work. General assistance was extended to other claimants for relief, but was locally financed and typically extremely limited in duration and scope.

7 Lenore A. Epstein, "Income of the Aged in 1962: First Findings of the 1963 Survey of the Aged," *Social Security Bulletin*, Vol. 27, No. 3 (March 1964), p. 3.

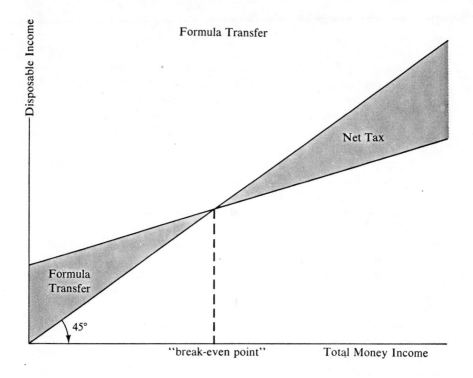

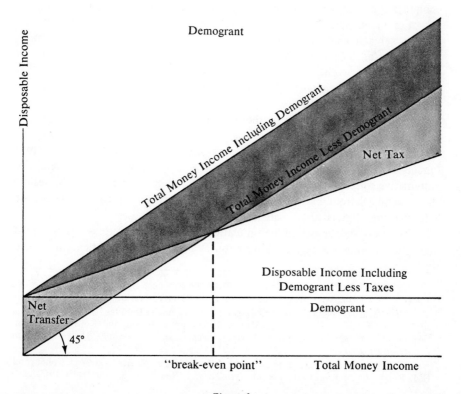

Figure 1.

As a consequence of the mixed character of the public and private programs, only half of the total transfers extended during 1963 were received by families whose pre-transfer income was below the poverty line. Only 10 percent of all families were lifted out of poverty by these transfers.[8] Some may regard such a fraction as a sign of inefficiency, but it should be noted that many of the programs that result in income transfers were established for purposes other than eliminating poverty. Social Security, for example, was originally construed as a program of lifetime income redistribution in which individuals would benefit on the basis of their own past contributions. In actual operation, the program has preserved only a tenuous connection between the individual's past contributions and the benefits he received. Today, benefits from the plan redistribute income rights among beneficiaries and the program has been more closely tied to subsistence than to lifetime redistribution of income.

In summary, formula income transfers were proposed for the purpose of aiding all the poor. They were conceived of as a means to alleviate the symptoms of poverty without paying substantial benefits to the non-poor.

A single formula income payment may not meet the immediate needs of all the poor. The poor are extremely heterogeneous. Their poverty may be situational, it may derive from labor market discrimination, or it may be caused by personal traits, emotional disorders, and so forth.[9] A successful balance between income maintenance programs and rehabilitation may require a more complex system of formula income payments than will be discussed here.

For example, generous support could be given to families whose poverty is situational and who are therefore unable to participate in the labor market. (Examples of these are aged and totally disabled persons.) Assistance to the broken family might call for an alternative approach so that labor market participation is not inhibited by the operation of the transfer program. Persons or families whose full-time earnings are not sufficient to place them above the poverty line may require still another form of supplement.

Many questions concerning the potential success of formula income transfers remain unanswered because such programs have not yet been put into practice in the United States. This paper attempts to analyze the effectiveness of alternative formula-based programs and to judge their comparative costs. Results were obtained from a series of simulation experiments in which formula income transfers were extended to a sample of poor families.

The sample data used in the simulation are a 3,396 unit cross-section sample compiled by the Survey Research Center at the University of Michigan.[10] The

---

8 Robert J. Lampman, "How Much Does the American System of Transfers Benefit the Poor?" Madison, Wis., Institute for Research on Poverty, Reprint 6, 1967.

9 Martin David, "Incomes and Dependency in Coming Decades," *American Journal of Economics and Sociology*, Vol. 23 (July 1964), pp. 249–268; and Robert Lampman, "Approaches to the Reduction of Poverty," *Papers and Proceedings of the American Economic Association*, Vol. LV, No. 2 (May 1965), pp. 521–529.

10 The sample is thoroughly analyzed in J. N. Morgan, M. H. David, W. J. Cohen, and H. E. Brazer, *Income and Welfare in the United States* (New York: McGraw-Hill), 1962.

sample includes observations on a number of demographic and income variables for non-institutional households in the coterminous United States in 1959. Low-income families are represented about twice as frequently as non-low-income families in this sample. In order to prevent bias in statements about the entire population, the sample is weighted, with low-income families receiving the lower weights.

Great care was taken to measure income adequately and to design the questionnaire to overcome response errors and biases in the reporting of financial information by the poor. The sample data were intensively analyzed using multi-variable models of income determination in *Income and Welfare in the United States.* Reports of assistance income were validated in a separate study.[11]

The results of the simulation are crude for several reasons. No allowance is made for the response of the poor and the near-poor to a large increase in transfers. Some change in work, effort and family size would appear to be significant responses. In the simulation no effort is made to forecast the response of state welfare administrations to an income that would be paid directly to the poor by the Federal Government. We view the inclusion of all of these responses as an important sequel to the present computations. Incentive effects and the accommodation in the existing public transfer programs to formula-based income maintenance cannot be quantitatively appraised on the basis of the present study. When more is known, behavior of poor families and administrators could be added to the present simulation to give better insight into the reactions that may be triggered by a new program of income maintenance.[12]

Financing Formula Income Maintenance

Simulation of the distributional effects of formula income maintenance must make some provision for the impact of additional taxation as well as the distribution of net benefits. For plans such as those considered here, ranging from $4 billion to $14 billion, it is obviously extremely important to state explicitly how the expenditure is to be financed.

Fortunately, financing is not as complex a problem as might be imagined. Under both standards of poverty considered here, the population receiving formula income payments is nearly or completely exempt from Federal personal income taxation. If personal income tax rates must be raised to finance the additional transfers, the impact of additional taxes will fall primarily upon the

---

11 M. H. David, "The Validity of Income Reported by a Sample of Families Who Received Welfare Assistance during 1959," *Journal of the American Statistical Association*, 57 (September 1962), pp. 680–685.

12 See, for example, M. David, "Design of Simulation Models of the Household Sector," Madison, Wis.: Social Systems Research Institute, *Household and Labor Market Workshop Paper 6503*, August, 1965 (presented before the First World Congress of the Econometric Society, September, 1965).

non-poor. The distributional impact of a formula income maintenance program on the poor can therefore be assumed to be the same as the gross payment to the poor, if Federal personal income taxes are to be the source of financing.

One additional factor led us to place less emphasis on financing in this simulation than might be considered desirable in the potentially inflationary economic context of 1967. The sample data on which the simulation is based pertain to 1959–1960, a time when substantial unemployment characterized the U.S. economy. That unemployment is naturally reflected in the family incomes reported for 1959. Under those circumstances it would have been quite reasonable to run a Federal deficit to finance additional transfer payments. The economy could have absorbed the simulated transfer programs without inflationary consequences. Of course, that same deficit would have repercussions on total employment and unemployment which would reduce the base upon which formula income transfers are paid.

The simulation that follows shows only the *impact* of additional transfer payments and does not explore the consequences of multiplier effects of a Federal budget deficit on incomes of the poor. The authors felt that the distribution of additional personal income associated with a movement to full employment was sufficiently uncertain so that it would be difficult to adjust gross income and formula income payments received by the poor, the tax liability of the non-poor and the relative numbers of persons in each group to account for multiplier effects.

II.   Fundamental Issues Relating to Formula Income Maintenance Plans

The technique of this simulation involves computing the amounts of the formula income payments for each eligible unit in a sample of low-income families. The amounts of the payments are sensitive to the parameters of the program: the *resource base,* the *standard of poverty,* the *receiving unit,* and the *rate structure.* The logic of formula income maintenance plans is described in detail in the Appendix.

Under a formula transfer program, the unit receives a formula payment if its resources are less than the poverty standard. The payment may be proportional to the income deficiency of the unit or it may be graduated to the size of the income deficiency. The poverty standard, the resources, the rate of payment, and the unit to which the payment is made are critical dimensions of formula income maintenance plans. By altering the definitions of these parameters and examining the distributional results, we are able to analyze the short-run effectiveness of various formulations of formula income transfer programs.

The Formula Income Maintenance Plans chart* presents an overview of the plans discussed in succeeding sections.

---

* See Appendix, p. 340.

We will discuss each of the dimensions presented in the chart briefly. We will show that the measure of resources, the receiving unit, and gradation of rates are important policy issues.

Measure of Resources

The measure of resources used in determining eligibility and the amount of formula income payment should reflect the capacity of the family to meet its subsistence needs. Among the measures suggested for purposes of formula transfer are adjusted gross income (i.e., income excluding transfers and similar to the Federal tax concept) and total money income (i.e., income including transfers but excluding income in kind). Both these measures of resources were used in this simulation. It might also be argued that net worth should be considered in the definition of resources so as to discriminate persons who are destitute from those who are experiencing a drop in money income but are able to use the services of household durables and can cash some part of their net worth for current living expenses. While inclusion of net worth clearly has relevance, an income-cum-wealth measure of resources was not simulated in these initial simulations because: (1) it can be argued that the fungible value of assets is represented in money income; and (2) administrative costs of determining net worth could easily exceed the welfare and equity gains of a system using a definition of resources that includes net worth.[13]

The results of the simulation show that total money income is preferable to adjusted gross income as a measure of the resources of a unit. Adjusted gross income was first proposed as a measure of resources by Friedman in an attempt to link formula income payments to the Federal income tax. The plan that results does not appear desirable to the authors. Payments are distributed to many whose total money income exceeds adjusted gross income by substantial amounts of transfer income. Unless transfer payments are reduced dollar-for-dollar for the amount of formula payment, substantial spill-over of payment to high total money income levels occurs (Table 1). Conversely, benefits are less concentrated on the extremely poor. A plan that uses total money income as a measure of family resources and has the same aggregative cost offers substantially larger payments to families whose total money resources are less than $1,500. (The pattern of mean payments shown in Table 1 holds for any equal cost comparison of the resource definition. If rates were higher the mean payment in each column would simply be increased proportionately to the increase in rates.)

---

13 Incorporating assets into a definition of resources for the purpose of ascertaining consumer welfare has been attempted on numerous occasions. A review of past effort and some assessment of the effect of assets on the apparent well-being of the aged appears in an unpublished paper by Lee Hansen and Burton Weisbrod available from The Institute for Research on Poverty, University of Wisconsin, Madison, Wis. 53706.

Table 1. Simulated Formula Income Maintenance Payment to
Families Under an EX-MSD Plan: Adjusted Gross Income Compared to
Total Money Income as a Measure of Resources within Total
Money Income, 1959

		Mean Amount of Payment	
Total Money Income	Percent of Family Units	TMI-Based Plan 43 Percent Rate	AGI-Based Plan 25 Percent Rate
Negative zero	1%	$648	$377
$ 1–$ 600	3	583	397
601– 1,000	5	530	433
1,001– 1,500	6	437	406
1,501– 2,000	6	323	361
2,001– 2,500	5	342	340
2,501– 3,000	5	230	284
3,001 3,500	4	165	270
3,501· 4,000	5	88	125
4,001– 4,500	5	57	82
4,501– 5,000	5	24	36
5,001– 6,000	11	12	34
6,001– 7,000	9	2	9
7,001– ; 8,000	8	0	2
8,001– 9,000	6	0	4
9,001– 10,000	4	0	0
Over 10,000	13	0	2
Total, average	100%	$139	$138
Number of families	2,800[a]		
Aggregate cost (billions)		$ 7.4[b]	$ 7.4

[a]The payments are computed according to formulas shown in the Appendix and are applied to a representative stratified sample of U.S. families taken in 1960.

[b]Aggregate cost computed by multiplying mean payment by total number of families ($139 x 53.4 mil.).

The Standard of Poverty

The standard of poverty is a parameter of the transfer system, just as personal exemptions are a parameter of our current tax system. In the following discussion the standard is based on family size. It is called the "poverty standard," although we recognize that the standard is not identical with any poverty line or true measure of subsistence costs. It would be desirable for the standard to be correlated with the level of subsistence income, with allowance for departures from a "poverty line" where appropriate. Local variations in subsistence costs and economies of scale might imply a poverty standard that would be administratively awkward or would be an incentive to family actions directed solely toward obtaining maximum transfers.[14]

14 See Harold W. Watts, "The Iso-Prop Index: An Approach to the Determination of Differential Poverty Income Thresholds," *The Journal of Human Resources,* Vol. II, No. 1 (Winter, 1966), pp. 3–18.

   Substitution of total money income for adjusted gross income as a measure of resources does not eliminate difficulties with a plan that uses Federal tax definitions of exemptions and minimum standard deductions as the poverty standard (EX-MSD Plan simulated in Table 1). Table 2 shows that the EX-MSD plan benefits families that are not poor according to a poverty standard proposed by Lampman and Green. That standard is remarkably close to the Orshansky poverty standards, considering its simplicity.[15] Whether spill-over to the non-poor is a serious policy matter depends on whether it is considered important that about 3 percent of the aggregate payments would be made to the non-poor. This payment would go largely to families barely out of poverty (Table 2).

   The Lampman-Green poverty standard for the one-person family with no income equals $1,500. This exceeds the value of unused exemptions and deductions. However, each additional family number increases unused exemptions and deductions by $700, while Lampman and Green assume additional

Table 2. Simulated Formula Income Maintenance Payments Under an EX-MSD Plan with Resources Measured by Total Money Income: Comparison of Payments to Poor and Non-Poor Families within Total Money Income, 1959

Total Money Income	Mean Amount of Payment[a]	
	Poor[b]	Non-Poor
Negative, zero	$377	$0
$ 1–$ 600	339	0
601– 1,000	308	0
1,001– 1,500	258	0
1,501– 2,000	274	c
2,001– 2,500	357	36
2,501– 3,000	348	17
3,001– 3,500	342	3
3,501– 4,000	275	1
4,001– 4,500	526	2
4,501– 5,000	424	2
5,001– 6,000	300	6
6,001– 7,000	0	2
Over 7,000	0	0
Average	$308	$4
Percent of all families	25%	75%

[a]EX-MSD Plan, total money income base, family unit, 25 percent rate.

[b]Poor in the sense that $1,000 + 500S > Y_2$ where S is family size, Y_2 a measure of its resources. See Appendix.

[c]Less than $1.

   15 Mollie Orshansky, "Counting the Poor: Another Look at the Poverty Profile," *Social Security Bulletin*, Vol. 28, No. 1 (January 1965), pp. 3–26.

subsistence cost at $500. For families of five or more persons unused exemptions and deductions exceed the Lampman-Green standard.

Table 3 contrasts the mean formula income maintenance payment for equal cost plans based on these two standards. The plan based on unused exemptions and deductions (EX-MSD) is based on a 25 percent transfer rate. The plan based on the Lampman-Green standard (Income Gap Plan) is based on an equal cost, 28.5 percent flat rate. As would be expected, the mean payment under EX-MSD exceeds the mean payment under the Income Gap Plan for families of five or more persons.

Payments from the EX-MSD Plan exceed the Income Gap payments for families whose head is over 65 years as a result of the additional income tax exemption currently available to any individual of that age (Table 4).

The Receiving Unit

To minimize the cost of a formula transfer program it would be wise to take into account the income in kind that is received by poor persons who live with relatives "doubled up" in the same household. As the value of such income in kind is extremely difficult to measure, it would be natural to apply a formula transfer to the aggregate income of all persons in a family.

Inequities and administrative difficulties could result. Families that undertake to support indigent relatives in their own homes might not obtain a formula payment, while families that support a relative in another household might still be able to obtain formula transfers for the relative.[16] In addition, administrators of a formula income maintenance plan might be plagued by frequent changes in family composition, with the resulting changes in the level of allowable formula transfers.

Another major problem associated with a family unit plan is that it may lead to family fragmentation. If benefits paid to small families are based on a higher per capita transfer than those granted to large families, a family unit plan may be an incentive for families to break up and file several applications for formula income maintenance.[17]

These problems could be solved by using an adult unit (a person 18 or over, his spouse if he is married, and any children under eighteen who live with him and for whom he is responsible) as the basis for computing formula transfers. However, a plan based on the adult unit as the receiving unit is considerably more expensive than a comparable plan based on the family unit. In other

---

16 This would not be technically possible if support payments and income-in-kind received by the dependent were fully reported and included in total money income. It is unlikely that such reporting could be easily enforced.

17 The problem is identical to the income-splitting problem under current Federal tax law. For an excellent discussion see L. Johansen, *Public Economics* (Chicago: Rand McNally, 1966), pp. 281–282.

Table 3. Simulated Formula Income Maintenance to Poor Families:
EX-MSD Plan Compared to a Poverty Income Gap Plan within
Family Size Classes

| Size of Family | Mean Amount of Payment | | Percent of Poor Families | Incidence of Poverty[a] (before receipt of formula transfer) |
	EX-MSD Plan, 25 Percent Rate[b]	Income Gap Plan, 28.5 Percent Rate[b]		
1	$ 131	$207	28%	43%
2	227	208	22	21
3	248	277	10	15
4	324	353	12	17
5	385	365	8	20
6	461	405	9	39
7	718	618	4	35
8	649	481	3	53
9	862	708	3	63
10 or more	1,177	686	1	77
Average for all poor families, total	$ 308	$308	100%	25%
Aggregate cost all families (billions)	$ 4.3[d]	$ 4.1[a]		

[a]Ratio of the number of poor families to the total number of families with this characteristic.

[b]Resources were measured by total money income under both plans.

[c]Aggregate cost computed by multiplying mean payment by total number of poor families ($308 x 13.35 mil.).

[d]See Table 2.

Table 4. Simulated Formula Income Payments to Poor Families:
EX-MSD Plan Compared to a Poverty Income Gap Plan within
Classes Based on Age of Head

| Age of Family Head | Mean Amount of Payment | | Percent of Poor Families | Incidence of Poverty (before receipt of formula transfer) |
	EX-MSD Plan, 25 Percent Rate[a]	Income Gap Plan, 28.5 Percent Rate[a]		
0–24	$166	$258	7%	28%
25–34	398	392	14	19
35–44	448	431	17	18
45–54	309	330	19	23
55–64	175	257	18	27
65–74	273	194	15	39
75–over	329	243	11	65
All	$308	$308	100%	25%
Aggregate cost all families (billions)	$ 4.3	$ 4.1		

[a]Resources were measured by total money income under both plans.

Table 5. Aggregate Expenditure and Rates of Transfer for Various Income Maintenance Plans, 1959[a]

	Equal Rates		Equal Costs		Equal Payments[b]	
	Rate of Transfer	Amount (billions)	Rate of Transfer	Amount (billions)	Rate of Transfer	Amount (billions)
EX-MSD Plan						
Adult unit	25%	$5.6	19%	$4.3	25%	$5.6
Family unit	25	4.3	25	4.3	25	4.3
Poverty Income Gap Plan						
Adult unit	25%	$5.9	18%	$4.3	23%	$5.5
Family unit	25	3.7	29.5	4.3	28.5	4.1

[a]The aggregate base to which these rates apply varies according to the unit to which the plan is administered. Thus a 25 percent rate applied to family units results in a different payment than a 25 percent rate applied to adult units (see the Appendix for the formulas used).

[b]The differences in amounts under "equal payments" in rows 1 and 3 and similarly rows 2 and 4 are due to the fact that under EX-MSD Plan some non-poor are also eligible to receive income payment. Thus $4.3 > $4.1 and $5.6 > $5.5.

words, a family unit plan entitles recipients to a higher rate of transfer than a comparable adult unit plan of equal cost.

Several facets of the aggregate cost of plans using the total money income definition of resources are compared in Table 5. Four distinct formula plans are shown — the EX-MSD Plan administered over adult units, the EX-MSD Plan administered over family units, the Poverty Income Gap Plan administered over adult units, and the Poverty Income Gap Plan administered over family units. In the first two columns of Table 5 the cost of these plans is compared when 25 percent of the discrepancy between the poverty standard and total money income is paid as the formula transfer. Under both EX-MSD and the Poverty Income Gap the aggregate cost is less when administered over family units.

The second pair of columns in Table 5 offers the converse comparison — what rate of transfer could be offered within the framework of a budget, arbitrarily fixed at the cost of the EX-MSD plan over family units? The last pair of columns offer what is probably the most relevant comparison — what is the cost of a given dollar payment to the poor? and what is the rate of transfer consistent with that payment?

In the last two columns the level of payments compared is again somewhat arbitrarily determined. It is the level of payments consistent with a 25 percent rate of transfer under the EX-MSD Plan. Thus the level of payment is $308 per poor family (Tables 3 and 4) and $255 per poor adult unit.

These cost estimates can be compared with Green's estimates for 1964.[18]

18 See Christopher Green, *Negative Taxes and the Poverty Problem* (Washington: The Brookings Institution, 1967), Appendix Table D-1 and Table 9-1, page 141.

Where we estimate that 13.6 million families are poor in 1959 Green estimates 12.6 million for the later year. The percentage of poor families declined from the 25 percent level of 1959 to 20.3 percent in 1964. The overall poverty income gap was $14.6 billion in 1959 and $12.3 in 1964.

The Rate Structure

Figure 2 illustrates three possible patterns of graduation of the rate structure for a family of four members whose poverty standard is $3,000. All plans lead to the same payment to units with no resources. Plans B and C are graduated rate structures. Plan B pays greater benefits to the marginal poor than the flat rate plan. Plan C approaches the benefit level of the flat rate plan only for the "poorest" poor.

Of the three plans, Plan B is the most expensive, Plan C is the least expensive. The schedule of graduated rates used with Plan B is a function of the ratio of the poverty-income gap to the poverty standard. If the family's poverty-income gap is less than one-third of its poverty standard, any increment in resources reduces the formula payment by .75 of the increment. If the ratio is greater than $\frac{1}{3}$ but less than $\frac{2}{3}$, the formula payment is reduced by half the movement. Finally, if the poverty-income gap is more than $\frac{2}{3}$ of the standard, the formula payment is reduced by .25 of any increment in resources. As a

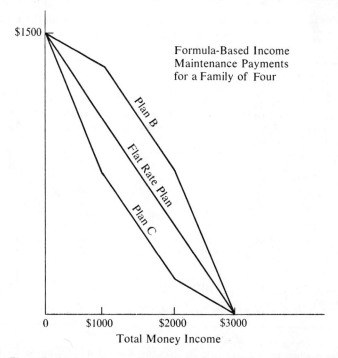

Figure 2. Alternate Income Gap Plans for Formula Income Maintenance

Table 6. Simulated Formula Income Payments to Poor Families Under an Income Gap Plan: A Comparison of Flat and Graduated Rate Plans of Equal Revenue Cost within Total Money Income, 1959*

Total Money Income	Mean Amount of Payment				Percent of Poor Families	Incidence of Poverty before Formula Transfer
	Flat 65 Percent Rate Plan A	Graduated Rate Plan B	Graduated Rate Plan C	Flat 35 Percent Rate Plan D		
Less than 0	$1,163	$895	$895	$626	2%	100%
$ 0–$ 600	982	851	660	529	12	100
601– 1,000	817	782	476	440	19	100
1,001– 1,500	591	608	302	318	23	98
1,501– 2,000	554	586	267	298	16	68
2,001– 2,500	761	816	355	410	11	51
2,501– 3,000	668	736	292	360	7	35
3,001– 3,500	585	663	237	315	5	27
3,501– 4,000	342	394	132	184	3	18
4,001– 6,000	399	460	153	215	2	10
Over 6,000	0	0	0	0	0	0
Average, total	$ 701	$698	$381	$378	100%	25%
Aggregate cost† (billions)	$ 9.4	$ 9.3	$ 5.0	$ 5.1		

*Resources were measured by total money income.
†Discrepancies due to rounding transfer rate.

Table 7. Simulated Formula Income Payments to Poor Adult Units Under an Income Gap Plan: A Comparison of Flat and Graduated Rate Plans of Equal Cost within Adult Unit Size, 1959*

Size of Unit	Mean Amount of Payment				Percent of Poor Adult Units	Incidence of Poverty before Formula Transfer
	Flat 60 Percent† Rate Plan A	Graduated Rate Plan B	Graduated Rate Plan C	Flat 40 Percent Rate Plan D		
1	$ 583	$ 554	$ 419	$389	54%	54%
2	507	536	309	338	15	20
3	658	679	418	439	8	19
4	779	836	462	519	8	21
5	822	890	480	548	6	23
6	951	1,023	561	634	4	36
7	1,138	1,244	653	758	2	33
8	1,182	1,312	658	788	1	46
9	1,785	1,855	1,120	1,190	2	72
10	‡	‡	‡	‡	‡	‡
Average, total	$ 664	$ 671	$ 436	$442	100%	33%
Aggregate cost (billions)	$ 14.2	$ 14.3	$ 9.3	$ 9.4		

*Resources were measured by total money income.
†Rate attached to this plan is lower than that illustrated in the previous table because this plan applies to the adult rather than family unit.
‡Insufficient observations for a reliable estimate.

result, the family with no resources received 50 percent of the poverty-income gap as a formula transfer under Plan B.

Plan C is the mirror image of Plan B. Increases in resources under this plan lead to a reduction in the formula transfer at rates of .25 and .75 as the ratio of the poverty-income gap to the poverty standard increases from less than one-third to more than two-thirds. Like Plan B, a unit with no resources receives 50 percent of the poverty-income gap as a formula transfer.

Plans B and C are compared in Table 6. Each is also compared to a flat rate plan of equal cost. For families with incomes of less than $1,000, the mean income gap payment from the graduated rate (Plan B) is less than the payment from an equal cost, flat rate plan (Plan A). This situation is reversed for families with income greater than $1,000. Comparison of Plan C and its equal cost, flat rate equivalent (Plan D), shows the reverse situation.

Table 7 compares mean payments under the four plans for *adult units* of different sizes. The aggregate cost is more than in Table 6, in spite of the fact that adult units contain fewer persons than family units. This finding reflects the fact that many poor adult units live with a unit that is not poor. The resources of the family as a whole are adequate, while those of the dependent are not.[19]

The distribution of formula payment both by adult unit size and by life cycle indicate that large units benefit the most in absolute dollar amounts from the gradation proposed in Plan B. The least benefits go to the older couple and single person (see Table 8).

Incentive Effects

It is likely that any work effort changes resulting from formula payments will depend on the effective marginal income that an individual can obtain from additional work. The marginal income can be expressed as

$$\tilde{w}(1 - p - r)$$

where w is the wages, p is the rate of payroll taxes and r is the transfer rate. The larger r, the smaller the return to additional effort and the greater the probability that the plan will cause a shift in the labor supply as a function of gross wages.

To the extent that changes in work effort arise from high rates r, the three rate structures differ substantially. Plan B creates the greatest incentive to alter work effort for the marginal poor. Whether such incentives prove a serious

---

19 Some qualifications are in order. The dependent and the supporting units may prefer doubling up to other housing arrangements. For example, unmarried sisters may prefer living together. One assumes responsibilities for keeping house and the other earns income. In that case lack of income earned by the "dependent" sister does not necessarily imply inability to maintain herself out of poverty. In the data used here some imputed income from food and housing has been assigned to the dependent adult unit. However, the amount assigned is not included in the total money income measure as it could not easily be used as the basis for a formula transfer.

Table 8. Simulated Formula Income Payments to Poor Adult Units
Under an Income Gap Plan: A Comparison of Flat and Graduated
Rate Plans of Equal Cost within Life Cycle, 1959*

Life Cycle	Plan A Flat 60 Percent Rate	Plan B Graduated Rate	Percent of Poor Adult Units	Incidence of Poverty Before Formula Transfer
1. No spouse present, no children, under 45	$650	$599	22%	50%
2. Married, spouse present, no children, wife under 45	441	475	2	11
3. Married, spouse present, children, some under 6, wife under 45	885	961	14	21
4. Married, spouse present, children, none under 6, wife under 45	788	860	4	13
5. Married, spouse present, children, some under 6, wife 45 or older	842	892	6	30
6. Married, spouse present, children, none under 6, wife 45 or older				
7. Married, spouse present, no children, wife 45 or older	477	517	10	20
8. No spouse present, no children, 45 or older	537	523	32	57
9. No spouse present, but children	870	884	10	60
Average, total	$664	$671	100%	33%
Aggregate cost (billions)	$ 14.2	$ 14.3		

*Resources were measured by total money income.

problem depends on the degree of labor force attachment of such persons and the latitude for absenteeism, short hours, and discretionary overtime in their place of employment. At the same time, Plan B offers the least incentive to change work habits to those with no income. Whether that is desirable depends on the likelihood that persons with no income from other sources could be pulled into employment under any circumstances. By graduating the rate structure, changes in work effort can be concentrated on those who are already earning income (as in Plan B) or on those who are not in the labor market at all (as in Plan C).

Some insight into the disincentive issue can be obtained by examining the reported labor force status of the poor (Table 9). Among the poor, 41 percent are employed and 10 percent are unemployed. More than a third of the poor do not consider themselves in a position to work even when no formula income maintenance plan is available. These non-labor force poor include two disparate populations – persons who subsist on their own resources, and a small minority who receive assistance payments. For the former, introduction of a formula income maintenance program may reduce the incentive to search for work, an incentive that is already too blunt to bring these adult unit heads into the labor market. For those on assistance, introduction of formula maintenance will provide a positive force to seek work. The effect of such incentives on the labor force participation of these non-labor force groups remains an open question.

Table 9. Distribution and Incidence of Poverty among Adult Units by Labor Force Status of the Head*

Labor Force Status of the Adult Unit Head	Percent of Adult Units		Incidence of Poverty
	Poor	All	
Employed	41%	71%	19%
Unemployed	10	6	60
Retired	14	10	49
Student	9	4	32
Housewife	20	8	79
Other	6	1	—
Total average	100%	100%	33%

* These data hold for the sample of families for whom formula income maintenance plans were simulated, hence data pertain to March-April, 1960 rather than a more recent date.

For those *in* the labor force it is unclear how much latitude for the expression of such incentives to change work habits exists under present employment practices. To what extent working habits and desires can be modified by a promise of support at less than the margin of subsistence is again an open question.

Preliminary work by one of the authors using a work-leisure choice model indicates that changes in work effort resulting from a formula transfer program would be minimal. For certain workers in large families or with low wage rates, however, the change in work effort could be substantial. Heads of adult units and spouses with fewer than two children tend to increase hours worked, while spouses with two or more children tend to decrease hours worked for an increase in the rate of formula transfer.[20]

20 Possibilities arise for increases as well as decreases in work effort in response to changes in the transfer rate. One of the authors is in fact attempting estimates of potential changes in work effort in the context of a work-leisure choice model. See Jane H. Leuthold, "Formula Income Transfers and the Work Decision of the Poor: An Application of a Work-Leisure Choice Model," Unpublished Ph.D. Diss., University of Wisconsin, 1967.

III.   The Distribution of Benefits to
Various Population Groups

In the previous section, we discussed some aspects of the various income measures, rate structures, receiving units, and poverty standards. In this section we examine certain population groups to see how they are affected by the specification of the formula income maintenance plan.

Table 10 shows the distribution of benefits according to the labor force status of the head of the adult unit. (Those who have never worked or who are disabled and not working have been excluded from the table because they represent such a small fraction of the population.)

As one would expect, the EX-MSD Plan provides maximum benefits for the retired. The employed receive nearly as large benefits. The plan fills 35 percent of the poverty-income gap of the retired, 24 percent of the income gap of the employed, and 23 percent of the income gap of the poverty population. The plan favors the retired because it offers a double exemption for the aged. The large payment for the employed is a bit harder to explain. It may be associated with double exemptions, accruing in this case to aged at work; alternatively, large families may account for a large EX-MSD amount.

By contrast with the EX-MSD Plan, any plan based on the poverty-income gap will provide a constant share of the income gap to all population groups. As comparison of columns 2 and 3 of Table 10 indicates, the difference in the amount of payment under the two plans can be sizeable, although the average payment to all poor adult units is the same under both plans.

The last column of the table shows the average amount of transfers to each group from public assistance and from other aids, including private charities. Substitution of formula income maintenance for these existing programs would increase the poverty-income gap in column 1 by a like amount and would increase payments by a fraction of the existing transfer – 25 percent for the EX-MSD Plan and 23 percent for the Income Gap Plan. The amount of such transfers is underreported in the sample, so that the list column indicates an order of magnitude as well as a likely upper limit to the adjustment to formula income maintenance that might occur with the phasing out of existing public assistance measures.

The formula income maintenance programs compared in Tables 10–13 provide equal payments to the poor, as defined by the Lampman-Green standard. Since EX-MSD payments spill over to the non-poor, that program is more expensive per dollar of benefit to the poor. Readers interested in equal cost comparisons may use the conversion percentages in Table 5 to recalculate these tables on the basis of equal cost or fixed rates of transfer.

Even greater disparity in the performance of the EX-MSD and the Income Gap Plans can be observed between adult units at different stages in the life cycle. In Table 11 adult units with children or aged members benefit most from the EX-MSD Plan. Young married and young single persons derive substantially less benefit. They would receive less than 60 percent of what they would receive under an Income Gap Plan that provides equal benefits to the poor.

Table 10. Simulated Formula Income Payments to Poor Adult Units: Mean Payments Under EX-MSD, Income Gap Plans, and Disposable Income within Labor Force Status of Head. 1959

Labor Force Status	Poverty Income Gap	Amount of Payments[a]		Disposable Income[b]		Percent of Poverty Income Gap Met by EX-MSD Plan[e]	Public Non-contributory Transfers[f]
		EX-MSD Plan (25 Percent Rate)	Income Gap Plan (23 Percent Flat Rate)	EX-MSD Plan (25 Percent Rate)	Income Gap Plan (23 Percent Flat Rate)		
Employed	$1,132	$273	$261	$1,804	$1,792	24%	$ 66
Unemployed	1,222	243	282	1,176	1,215	20	147
Retired	786	276	182	1,285	1,191	35	229
Student	1,186	158	273	495	610	13	16
Housewife	1,101	243	254	874	883	22	241
All poor	$1,107	$255	$255	$1,301	$1,301	23%	137
Aggregate cost (in billions)		$ 5.6[c]	$ 5.5[d]				$ 2.95

[a]Resources were measured by total money income.

[b]Total money income + formula transfer — estimated Federal income tax — estimated Federal payroll tax (OASDI).

[c]Ratio of EX-MSD Plan (25 percent rate) to poverty income gap.

[d]Under Income Gap Plan about 33.2 percent of adult units are poor (21,460 million units). Aggregate cost of $5.47 billion is derived by multiplying the average payment of $255 by 21,460 million poor units.

[e]Under the EX-MSD Plan about 2.04 percent (1,319 million units) of non-poor adult units are also eligible to receive income payment (average amount of $80.89 per unit). Total income payment of $107 million to non-poor is added to $5.47 billion.

[f]Include public assistance, gifts from private charities and free medical care.

Table 11. Simulated Formula Income Payments to Poor Adult Units: Mean Poverty Income Gap, Mean Payments Under EX-MSD and Income Gap Plans, and Disposable Income within Life Cycle. 1959

Life Cycle of Head of Adult Unit	Poverty Income Gap	Amount of Payments[a]		Disposable Income[b]		Percent of Poverty Income Gap Met by EX-MSD Plan	Public Non-contributory Transfers[f]
		EX-MSD Plan (25 Percent Rate)	Income Gap Plan (23 Percent Rate)	EX-MSD Plan (25 Percent Rate)	Income Gap Plan (23 Percent Rate)		
No spouse present:							
(a) Under 45, no children	$1,084	$134	$249	$527	$610	12%	$23
(b) 45 or older, no children	895	187	206	781	800	21	153
(c) Children present	1,451	349	334	1,635	1,620	24	400
Married, spouse present, wife under 45:							
(a) No children	734	100	169	1,322	1,391	14	56
(b) Children, some under 6	1,474	446	339	2,710	2,603	30	111
(c) Children, none under 6	1,314	356	302	2,283	2,230	27	58
Married, spouse present, wife 45 or older:							
(a) Children, some under 6	1,777	551	409	2,776	2,634	31	326
(b) Children, none under 6	1,341	365	308	2,007	1,950	27	199
(c) No children	795	294	183	1,489	1,378	40	112
All poor	$1,107	$255	$255	$1,301	$1,301	23%	$137
Aggregate cost (in billions)		$ 5.6[c]	$ 5.5[d]				$ 2.95[e]

[a] Resources were measured by total money income.

[b] Total money income + EX-MSD transfer − estimated Federal income tax − estimated Federal payroll tax (OASDI).

[c] See footnote c in Table 10.

[d] See footnote d in Table 10.

[e] Total public non-contributory transfers including poor and non-poor amount to $4.63 billion. The figure is derived by multiplying average contributory transfer of $71.59 by the total family units of 64.6 million.

[f] Include public assistance, gifts from private charities, and free medical care.

Table 12. Simulated Formula Income Payments to Poor Family Units: Mean Poverty Income Gap, Mean Payments Under EX-MSD and Income Gap Plans, and Disposable Income with Earning Power Potential of Head of Family, 1959

Earning Power Potential of Family Head	Amount of Payments[a]			Disposable Income[a]		Percent of Poverty Income Gap Met by EX-MSD Plan	Public Non-contributory Transfers[f]
	Poverty Income Gap	EX-MSD Plan (25 Percent Rate)	Income Gap Plan (28 Percent Rate)[b]	EX-MSD Plan (25 Percent Rate)	Income Gap Plan (28 Percent Rate)		
1. Retired or disabled and not working	$1,046	$314	$298	$2,013	$1,997	30%	$256
2. Non-retired:							
(a) Negro	1,168	312	333	1,713	1,734	27	187
(b) White farmer	1,125	357	350	2,006	1,999	29	292
3. Non-retired, white non-farmers 18–34 years old:							
(a) 1–11 years of education	930	259	266	1,856	1,863	28	217
(b) Completed high school	990	269	283	1,627	1,641	27	226
(c) Some college training	1,020	255	291	1,587	1,623	25	146
4. Non-retired, white non-farmers 35-years or older:							
(a) 1–11 years of education	1,041	298	297	1,900	1,899	29	163
(b) Completed high school	1,207	357	345	1,826	1,814	30	209
(c) Some college training	1,010	325	288	2,063	2,026	32	150
All poor	$1,079	$308	$308	$1,862	$1,862	28.5%	$194
Aggregate cost (in billions)		$ 4.3*	$ 4.1[d]				$ 2.63[e]

[a] Resources were measured by total money income.

[b] Exact rate used is 28.55 percent.

[c] Total number of poor family units is 13.553 million. Aggregate cost of public non-contributory transfer including poor and non-poor is $4.65 billion. The figure is the product of total family unit (53.4 million) and average public non-contributory transfer ($87.04).

[d] Total number of poor family units is 13.553 million, about 28.38 percent of all family units. The aggregate cost of $4.13 billion is the product of average transfer payment under Income Gap Plan ($308) and total number of poor family units.

[e] Under EX-MSD Plan about 1,383 million of additional non-poor family units are eligible to receive income payment (about 2.59 percent of all family units) averaging $102.31 per unit. The aggregate cost of $4.27 is the sum of the transfer payment to the poor ($4.13 billion) and to the non-poor ($142 million).

[f] Include public assistance, gifts from private charities, and free medical care.

Table 12 shows the distribution of benefits when the family, rather than the adult unit, is the receiving unit. The EX-MSD Plan fills approximately the same percent of the poverty-income gap of each subclass of the working population. Few large differences appear between groups based on education and age of the head.

The ratio between payments under the EX-MSD Plan and the Poverty Income Gap rises substantially when adult units are aggregated into families. This is the result of the fact that family size must equal or exceed adult unit size. As we indicated earlier, the increment in unused exemptions and deductions exceeds the increment in the income gap for an additional family member. Moreover, the aggregation of units causes a larger reduction in the Lampman-Green standard than in unused deductions and exemptions, because $1,000 of poverty gap is erased for each adult unit head who can be considered a dependent (rather than the head) of a family. Only $200 disappears from the total under the EX-MSD calculation.

Somewhat surprising is the finding that the poverty-income gap shows so little correlation with education. (Compare categories 3a, 3b, and 3c, and categories 4a, 4b, and 4c in Table 12.) This finding is corroborated by Table 13. The evidence suggests that hazards which create poverty are present in all population groups and that we may be misled by the typical data on mean incomes which are influenced by large values in a skewed distribution. Median incomes are also misleading as the dispersion of income-earning experience has little influence on that statistic. All education groups have some casualties who become poor and who are likely to exhibit similar income deficiencies.

The choice of the poverty standard makes little difference to the size of payments for various levels of educational attainment except for families whose head has had no education. For these families the EX-MSD payment is larger than the Income Gap payment. Perhaps this occurs because these families have more members. However, a more likely explanation is that this educational group contains a higher percentage of aged persons and they obtain the double exemption for persons over 64 years of age.

IV.   Interpretation and Summary

The development and execution of this simulation experiment provides several useful insights into the operation of formula-based income maintenance programs. We summarize the findings of earlier sections under four headings: (1) distribution of benefits, (2) anticipated relationships, (3) theoretical contributions, and (4) policy uses.

Distribution of Benefits

Three facets of the distribution of benefits highlight the facts that poverty is the result of extreme circumstances, and that the usual statistical information on

Table 13. Simulated Formula Income Payment to Poor Family Units: Mean Poverty Income Gap, Mean Payments Under EX-MSD and Income Gap Plans, and Disposable Income within Education of the Family Head, 1959

Education (years)	Poverty Income Gap	Amount of Payments		Disposable Income[3]		Percent of Poverty Income Gap Met by EX-MSD Plan
		EX-MSD Plan (25 Percent Rate)	Income Gap Plan (28.5 Percent Flat Rate)[1]	EX-MSD Plan (25 Percent Rate)	Income Gap Plan (28.5 Percent Flat Rate)	
None	$ 908	$321	$259	$1,791	$1,729	35%
1–8	1,114	316	317			28
9–11	1,013	284	289	1,726	1,731	28
12	1,243	354	354			29
(a)	1,049	302	290			29
(b)	1,015	305	289	1,672	1,680	30
(c)	1,015	283	289			28
(d)	939	278	268			30
N.A.	0	0	0			0
All poor	$1,079	$308	$308			28.5%
Aggregate cost (billions)		$ 4.3[2]	$ 4.1			

(a) High school plus non-college training, i.e., business college, trade school, etc.

(b) College, no degree.

(c) College, Bachelor's degree or no advanced degree mentioned.

(d) College, advanced degree.

[1] Only 28.5 percent of poverty-income gap is met under this plan.

[2] See footnote in Table 7.

[3] Total money income plus EX-MSD or income gap transfer less estimated Federal income and payroll taxes.

central tendencies for large groups is not always a reliable indicator of what may happen under a program designed to aid the poor.

First, some families are poor despite the fact that their educational attainments suggest substantial skills and ability. Other factors intervene to prevent marketing those skills at the expected rate of pay. These poverty-stricken families will require formula-based income payments on the same order of magnitude as families whose educational attainments suggest minimal skills and marketable talents (see Table 13).[21]

Second, any plan that places no ceiling on the poverty standard results in extremely high payments to a few large families. This may be desirable, but only if the poverty standard is an acceptable gauge of the need of those large families and if the measure of resources truly reflects their ability to purchase subsistence. If the poverty standard departs from a subsistence level, the resulting formula payment will be a windfall to the large family. This appears to be the case when the poverty standard is based on exemptions and minimum standard deductions. Similarly, if adjusted gross income is used as the measure of the family's resources there will be a few who benefit by large formula-based payments in spite of the fact that their total resources exceed the poverty lines (see Table 1).

Third, combinations of characteristics and their effect on the operation of a formula-based income maintenance plan are not always obvious. Thus it is clear that under the EX-MSD Plan greater benefits accrue to the aged than to persons under 65 years of age because of the double exemption granted to the aged. What is less obvious is that enough persons over 65 are at work for the EX-MSD Plan to reduce the size of the poverty gap by more for the employed than for the unemployed, whose poverty gap is greater. The unemployed are younger, on the average, than the employed, since aged persons who become unemployed are quite likely to drop out of the labor market.

Anticipated Relationships

The simulations show clearly that a formula-based income maintenance plan can provide aid to groups that are difficult to locate through categorical programs. The employed poor, the educated poor, and poor with large families and little earning power will all receive benefits.

Any deviation from a constant per capita standard produces a concentration of formula-based income maintenance payments in that direction. For that reason the Lampman-Green poverty line formula gives greater benefits to small families than does the EX-MSD Plan, while the EX-MSD Plan provides greater benefits to the aged.

---

21 These findings were also stressed by the Council of Economic Advisers in their *Economic Report* for 1963 and are implicit in Census income distributions by educational attainment.

Any plan that provides benefits on a standard that deviates from a true subsistence line will give some aid to the near-poor. However, such spill-over of benefits may be associated with greater administrative simplicity, reduction of disincentives, and greater acceptability of the formula-based plan. In addition, if the rate of transfer is low, the aggregate amounts paid to the non-poor may not be large (see Table 2).

We anticipated that gradation of transfers could be used to concentrate benefits at various levels of poverty. A plan that focuses on the extreme poor (Plan C) will cost less than the flat rate plan that provides the same dollar payment to units with no resources. Conversely, a plan that provides the greatest benefits to the marginal poor costs more than the flat rate plan that provides equal benefits to those with no resources. This latter plan (Plan B) has some interesting anticipated consequences, however. Large families with spouse and young children appear to benefit most. This may be socially desirable. Unfortunately, the plan implies a substantial discontinuity in the rate of taxation of additional income just above and just below the poverty line. Those in extreme poverty are taxed at a low rate on any increments to their earnings.

Theoretical Framework for Formula-Based Plans

The Appendix to this paper presents an analytical framework within which it is useful to discuss all formula-based income maintenance and the associated finance problems. While we have not done so here, the framework can be extended to discuss universal per capita grants, the present rent subsidy legislation, and family allowances. In all these programs, increased transfers must be financed with increased taxation so that the effects can be visualized as some standard payment with income offsets just as in the Income Gap of EX-MSD Plans. The disposable income estimates in Tables 10–14 are based on 1959 tax rates and law. In effect this implies that formula income maintenance could have been financed by an increased deficit. This assumption would not hold for full-employment years.

Policy Uses of the Simulation

The data presented in any of the tables that use a *flat rate* plan can be adjusted to show benefits under alternative rates. For example, in Table 3 the first column is actually 25 percent of the average unused exemptions and deductions of each age group; doubling the rate simply doubles the average benefit shown in the column. Column 2 is 28.5 percent times the average poverty-income gap of the family and can be adjusted in the same fashion.

The simulation indicates clearly that substantial additional costs are associated with use of the adult unit as the unit over which benefits are calculated (see Table 5). The cost could possibly be reduced by imputing income to those who share living arrangements with others. The simulation results presented show true budgetary costs only if families do not respond to the value of "transfer splitting" that results from large initial payments to the first member of a household and smaller payments to succeeding members. To the extent that families do respond to that incentive, costs will move to the same level as was simulated for adult units. As we have not incorporated available evidence on undoubling of families in response to income, policy makers will need to judge whether the savings in costs are worth the inequity that results from some families receiving greater benefits than others merely because they are willing and able to rearrange their housing.[22]

The cost and inequity or spill-over to the non-poor of a program based on adjusted gross income must also be weighed subjectively against the likely effect of alternative rates of transfer on work effort. This simulation provides only either a dollar measure of the difference in cost between two programs using the same rate and different measures or resources, or, alternatively, the difference in rates required for equal cost programs.

Lastly, the results constitute food for thought on the desirability of graduating rates. Arguments can be adduced for either lower-than-average rates to the extreme poor or higher-than-average rates to the extreme poor. The likely work effort effects of grants at different levels of poverty would appear to be an important consideration in the choice of gradations; again we can offer no solution but can illustrate the distributional impact of benefits under whatever program is desired.

Summary of Distributional Effects

Table 14 summarizes several aspects of the formula income maintenance payments simulated. The distribution of such payments according to the extent of the income deficiency of the adult unit is shown separately for units headed by an employed person and for all others. Differences in the distribution of payments among the poor and the spill-over to the non-poor are indicated in columns 3 and 4 of the table. Columns 5 and 6 provide estimates of the Federal taxes paid by the poor. (Income taxes were simulated without a minimum standard deduction option, per 1959 law, which partially accounts for the positive tax liabilities for units with a poverty-income gap.) The mean Social Security benefits reported by adult units give some indication of the extent to which social insurance aids the poor, while the last column shows the amount of money income to which formula income payments would be added.

Among the employed one can infer that a poverty gap beyond $500 results from increasing family size and need; resources appear to be relatively constant

---

22 Some estimates of these disincentives are included in Morgan *et al.*, *Income and Welfare in the United States*, Chapter 14.

Table 14. Simulated Formula Income Payment to Poor Adult Units: Mean Poverty Income Gap, Mean Payment under Income Gap Plan, Social Security Tax and Benefit Federal Income Tax Liability, and Disposable Income within Labor Force Status and Size of Poverty Income Gap, 1959

Labor Force Status of Adult Unit Head[2]	Poverty Income Gap	Distribution of Income Gap (Percent)	Amount of Payments		Average Social Security Tax	Average Federal Tax Liability	Average Social Security Benefit	Total Money Income Less Estimated Federal Taxes[3]
			EX-MSD Plan (25 Percent Rate)	Income Gap Plan (23 Percent Rate)				
Employed	$ 0	81%	$ 1	$ 0	$104	$783	$ 22	$6,315
1–$ 500		5	47	57	38	8	68	2,029
501– 1,000		5	139	185	26	1	20	1,430
1,001– 2,000		6	342	331	22	0	16	1,292
Over 2,000		3	838	664	20	0	11	1,325
Mean (employed)	$ 219	100%	$ 53	$ 50	$ 89	$632	$ 24	$5,389
All others[1]	$ 0	33%	$ 11	$ 0	$ 35	$249	$523	$3,988
1–$ 500		12	93	39	7	4	463	1,494
501– 1,000		18	182	177	4	1	245	927
1,001– 2,000		35	287	323	3	0	49	325
Over 2,000		3	691	593	8	0	14	770
Mean (all others)	$ 730	100%	$167	$168	$ 15	$ 82	$288	$1,790
Aggregate cost			$ 5.6	$ 5.5				

[1] Include unemployed, retired, student, housewife, never worked, disabled and not working, and status not ascertained.

[2] At time of interview in March and April, 1960.

[3] Total money income less estimated Federal income and payroll taxes.

at about \$1,300–\$1,400 for families whose poverty gap exceeds \$500. Among the non-employed a somewhat greater drop in income occurs as the poverty gap rises to \$2,000, suggesting a combination of more mouths to feed and fewer resources. Clearly social security plays a major role in maintaining income levels for the small non-employed family, a larger role than is suggested by public noncontributory transfers shown in Table 10. Equally clear, a F.I.M. program of modest cost and low rates of transfer will not eliminate income deficiencies, nor will it obviate the need for support from existing transfer programs.

Appendix
Mathematics of the Formula Payment Program

Notation:

N = amount of formula payment
t = transfer rate
Y = resources
B = poverty standard
S = family size
E = earnings
R = transfer income
A = annuity value of assets
X = tax liability
D = disposable income
a, b, c are constant

Identities:

$$Y_1 = E + R + A, \; Y_2 = E + R, \; Y_3 = E \tag{1}$$

$$D_{ijk} = Y_2 + N_{ijk} - X \tag{2}$$

For all programs

$$N_{ijk} = t_k(B_j - Y_i) \quad \text{if } B > Y \tag{3}$$
$$= 0 \qquad\qquad B < Y$$

$$i = 1, 2, 3 \quad j = 1, 2$$
$$k = 1, 2$$

The subscript i refers to alternative income concepts; j refers to alternative poverty standards; k refers to alternative rate schedules for the income maintenance payment. For both the EX-MSD and the Income Gap Plan

$$B_j = B_j(S) = a_j + b_j S \quad j = 1, 2 \tag{4}$$

For a plan with graduated rates

$$t_1 = t_1(B_j - Y_i) \quad j = 1, 2 \quad i = 1, 2, 3 \tag{5}$$

Otherwise in a flat rate plan

$$t_2 = C \tag{6}$$

Some insight into disincentives can be obtained by taking derivatives of N_{ijk} with respect to Y_i and differences with respect to family size S. For example:

$$\frac{\partial D_{2j2}}{\partial E} = \frac{\partial D_{2j2}}{\partial R} = 1 - t$$

or disposable income increases by only a fraction of earnings or categorical assistance payments.

Given the form of B_j, if $a_j \neq 0$, then it is clear that dissolution of a family of S members into two sub-families sizes S_1 and $S - S_1$ will be advantageous. The family payment will be

$$N_{ijk}^{(f)} = t_k(2a_j + b_j S - Y_i).$$

If a_j is sufficiently large the difference between $N^{(s)}$ and $N^{(f)}$ may induce family dissolution. However, if the formula transfer formula recognizes S as the appropriate administrative unit the form of living arrangement will not affect the amount of the payment. $N^{(s)}$ will be paid in any case.[23]

Formula Income Maintenance Plans

Dimension of the Formula	Options Simulated	
A. *Resources*	A 1	Adjusted Gross Income (excluding transfers and similar to the Federal tax concept)
	A 2	Total Money Income (including transfers, excluding income in kind)
B. *Standard of Poverty*	B 1	EX-MSD (Friedman-type)
	B 2	Poverty Income Gap (Lampman-Green type)
C. *Receiving Unit*	C 1	Families (related individuals occupying a dwelling unit)
	C 2	Adult Units (individuals 18 years of age or older, their spouse, and children under 18)
D. *Rate*	D 1	Flat rate
	D 2	Graduated rate, decreasing with increases in the income deficiency (Plan B)
	D 3	Graduated rate, increasing with increases in the income deficiency (Plan C)

23 See L. Johansen, *op. cit.*, pp. 224–225, for an interesting illustration from the Norwegian income tax structure.

18

Robert J. Lampman: Discussion of New
Transfer Plans

The question is persistent: Why, in a rich country having a large and rapidly growing redistributive system, can we not make some adjustment that will simply eliminate the poverty that remains? The dimensions of the problem seem small — only about 23 million people are poor and their poverty-income gap of under $10 billion is only 1 percent of gross national product. The most direct way to eliminate poverty would be to introduce a negative income tax with guarantees at the poverty lines. If all other income were subject to a special offset tax of 50 percent up to break-even points equal to twice the poverty lines for each family size, this would cost $27 billion in benefits and income tax forgiveness over and above what we are now spending on transfers.[1] These net benefits would go to some 88 million people, leaving the upper 120 million to pay the $27 billion on top of the taxes they are now paying.[2] Worry about subjecting working people to a 50 percent marginal tax rate -- and note that we are talking not about a few categorical poor but about 40 percent of the population — leads some to advocate lowering the offset tax rate to, say, 33.3 percent, thereby raising the break-even points to three times the poverty lines, and placing the whole tax load, which would then be expanded to cover about $50 billion of net new transfers to the lower two-thirds of the population, on the upper one-third. That amount would require a near doubling of the money-transfer now being done by all public and private sources. In any event, what may look at the outset like an easy problem takes on greater scope as one surveys the alternatives. Certainly it is a major disservice to rational discourse to suggest, as many have done, that the United States could eliminate poverty if the government were only willing to transfer an additional $10 billion to the poor. There is no way to get that $10 billion into the hands of the poor without spending far more than that.

Realization of this — and some sense of the gradualness of change — has

From "Transfer Approaches to Distribution Policy," *American Economic Review*, May 1970. Reprinted by permission of the American Economic Association and the author.

1 The President's Commission on Income Maintenance, *Poverty Amid Plenty: The American Paradox*, preliminary copy, mimeographed (Washington, D.C.: November, 1969), p. 18.

2 It is interesting to recall Harry G. Johnson's 1964 comments on a transfer of this amount. He said that it "... may well be politically unacceptable; but is really small potatoes as war finance goes, if war on poverty is really what has been declared" ("Discussion on the Economics of Poverty," American Economic Review, May 1965, pp. 543–45).

prompted many to offer less radical departures. Perhaps the least radical would modify existing programs. The transfer program now paying out the most cash to the poor is Old Age, Survivors, and Disability Insurance. This could be – and likely will be – expanded, but each extra dollar in benefits tends to yield only ten to twenty cents for the poor; these benefits do not reach the noncategorical poor; and the payroll tax puts a heavy burden on the working poor. The second largest source of public transfer funds for the poor is the categorical public assistance programs dominated by Aid to Families with Dependent Children (AFDC). We could improve the status of many of the categorical poor by setting a federal floor under the benefits, now determined by the several states. This would cost relatively little, but it would not reach many of the poor – most of the poor are not in the categories – and would exacerbate the inequity between the working poor at low earned incomes and the categorical poor at relatively high benefit levels. The only way to remedy that inequity via transfers is to drop the age-old principle that receipt of transfers and employability must be mutually exclusive. And one way to broach the contrary principle is to pay benefits to all children. Because most of the nonwelfare poor are in families with children, a child allowance, which is a common type of transfer in other nations, would seem to have time and place utility for the United States.

There are numerous varieties of child allowance plans, but like all transfers, they take from some and give to others, most obviously transferring income from households without children to those with children. They also tend to alter the distribution of income among families with and without children. Benefits can be conditioned in various ways and can be financed, at least in part, by offsetting reductions in existing ways of changing disposable income such as cash transfers and the exemptions for children in the income tax. In order to see how plans differ from one another, it is useful to do, as Dorothy S. Projector[3] has done, a calculation of how disposable income would change for the average family in each income bracket. Table 1 shows some of her calculations for 1967 for four plans; namely two suggested by Vadakin,[4] one by Brazer,[5] and the Family Assistance Plan (FAP) recommended by President Nixon and introduced by Congressman John Byrnes as H.R. 14173. We have added parallel calculations for 1966 for the plan recommended in November 1969 by the Presidential Commission on Income Maintenance Programs (the Heineman Commission),[6] even though their plan would pay benefits to unrelated individuals and families with and without children and hence is not a child allowance. We would like to

---

3 D. S. Projector, "Children's Allowance and Welfare Reform Proposals: Costs and Redistributive Effects," mimeographed paper prepared for meeting of the National Tax Association, October 2, 1969.

4 J. C. Vadakin, *Children, Poverty, and Family Allowances* (New York: Basic Books, 1968).

5 H. E. Brazer, "The Federal Income Tax and the Poor: Where Do We Go from Here?" *California Law Review*, March 1969, pp. 442–49.

6 The President's Commission on Income Maintenance, *Poverty Amid Plenty*.

Table 1. Average Amount of Change in Disposable Income for Families and Unrelated Individuals, by Total Money Income, Four Children's Benefit Plans, 1967, and Heineman Plan, 1966

Total Money Income	Vadakin 1	Vadakin 2	Brazer	Family Assistance Plan	Heineman
Under $3,000	$ 49	$ 47	$ 260	$ 127	$ 417
$3,000–4,999	78	30	345	75	184
$5,000–6,999	78	2	139	−9	−7
$7,000–9,999	63	−15	−132	−29	−151
$10,000–14,999	3	−30	−211	−49	−246
$15,000–24,999	−159	−59	−346	−102	−457
$25,000 and over	−845	−147	−949	−347	−1517

Sources: Columns 1–4, Projector, "Children's Allowances and Welfare Reform Proposals: Costs and Redistributive Effects," Table 5; Column 5, N. D. McClung, "Problems in the Development of Data Bases for the Static Microsimulation of Income Transfer Program Direct Effects," mimeographed staff paper for the President's Commission on Income Maintenance Programs report, *Poverty Amid Plenty.*

include a wage subsidy in this comparison but do not know of a carefully spelled out plan of that type.[7]

The several plans are briefly sketched as follows. To achieve comparability, we assume with Projector that each plan is to be financed, to the extent new tax revenue is needed, by a surtax on personal and corporate income.

Vadakin 1: $120 per year allowance per child; retain child exemption in the income tax; finance by making allowance taxable and adding a 7.4 percent surtax on personal and corporate income.

Vadakin 2: $120 per year allowance per child; finance by eliminating child exemption and making allowance taxable (no surtax needed).

Brazer: $1,400 per year allowance for first child, $900 for second, $600 for third, $400 for each added child; finance by eliminating child exemptions, taxing adjusted gross income by a special child allowance tax at marginal rates around 33 percent but varying both by income and family size, reducing federal contribution to AFDC, and adding a surtax of about 6 percent on personal corporate income.

Family Assistance Plan: Benefits restricted to families with children; $500 per year for first two persons, $300 for each additional person; finance by taxing other income by a special offset tax at a zero rate on first $720 of earnings and at a 50 percent rate beyond that, eliminating federal contribution to AFDC, adding a surtax of about 2.5 percent on personal and corporate income.

Heineman: Benefits not restricted to families with children; $750 per year for each of first two adults, $450 for each other person; finance by taxing other income by a special offset tax at a 50 percent rate, eliminating federal

---

7 For a discussion of the issues, see J. Kesseman, "Labor Supply Effects of Income, Income-Work, and Wage Subsidies," *Journal of Human Resources,* Summer 1969.

contribution to food stamps and to all categorical assistance programs, adding a surtax of about 12 percent on personal and corporate income. (The latter surtax is equivalent to a surtax of 18 percent on personal income only. These surtax rates are for 1966 and would be lower for 1967).

Table 1 demonstrates the similarity in basic design of all child allowance and negative income tax plans in changing disposable income by income bracket. The break-even points differ, ranging from around $15,000 in the Vadakin 1 plan to $5,000 in the Family Assistance Plan. The amount of gain and the distribution of that gain, as well as the amount and distribution of loss, vary among the several plans. Further insight into the variations of the plans is offered by Table 2, which shows the total increases in disposable income occasioned by the introduction of the plans. It should be noted that these estimates take no account of possible reductions in work effort nor of changes in family size or

Table 2. Comparison of Four Children's Benefit Plans, Based on 1967 Income, and the Heineman Plan, Based on 1966 Income

Characteristic	Vadakin 1	Vadakin 2	Brazer	Family Assistance Plan	1966 Heineman
1. Amount "transferred"[b] (billions of dollars)	2.5	1.1	7.5	2.5	8.6
2. Income level above which average change in disposable income is negative (see Table 8)	15,000	7,000	8,000	5,000	6,000
3. Effect on those without children					
(a) Receive benefit	No	No	No	No	Yes
(b) Pay tax	Yes	No	Yes	Yes	Yes
4. Net benefits to households with under $3,000 income (billions of dollars)	0.6	0.6	3.6	1.8	5.6
5. Increase in share (was 4.1 percent) of income going to the lowest fifth of households (percent)	0.1	0.1	0.4	0.3	1.2
6. Marginal tax rates below break-even income (percent)	_b	_b	30–40	0–50	50

[a] In this case, *transfer* means change in disposable income. The total amount of such change below the levels shown in line 2 is matched by an offsetting amount above the line.

[b] Surtax only.

Source: On the Heineman plan see R. Harris, "Role of Taxes and Grants in Income Maintenance," mimeographed paper prepared for meeting of the National Tax Association, October 2, 1969; McClung, "Problems in the Development of Data Bases for the Static Microsimulation of Income Transfer Program Direct Effects." On the other plans, calculated from data in Projector, "Children's Allowance and Welfare Reform Proposals: Costs and Redistributive Effects."

composition which might result from the plan. These increases in income, which are matched by decreases above the line, vary from a low of $1.1 billion for Vadakin 2 to a high of $8.6 billion for the Heineman plan. The net benefit to the poor also is different among the plans. The Family Assistance Plan does the most for the poor per dollar transferred and in that sense may be said to be the most intensively antipoverty plan. A proponent of child allowances has commented on this point as follows: "It will be said that a child allowance wastes money on children who are not poor. . . . A child allowance designed carefully in relation to the income tax system would waste little money. In any event, that money is well wasted that purchases a sense of its rightness. . . . [Moreover] because it is not related to income it quite avoids interfering with the incentive to work."[8] (Note, however, the high guarantee and high marginal tax rates in the Brazer plan.) None of these plans would confine its benefits to the 23 million persons who are poor. FAP would add 14 million persons to those in benefit status, some of whom already have incomes above the poverty lines. The Heineman plan would reach 36.8 million persons in 1971, almost half of whom would not be poor in the absence of the benefits.

Deciding on how to rank these plans in terms of desirability may well turn, for each citizen, on a complex set of considerations. It may lend perspective to relate the amount that would be transferred under these plans to the amount now transferred. (According to calculations made in a paper presented earlier in the volume, the total amount of money transfers in 1967 was $59.1 billion.[9] So the largest amount listed here, the Heineman plan's cost for 1966 of $8.6 billion, is about one-seventh of the total. (The amount needed to finance that plan in 1971 is estimated to be only $6 billion.) A similar consideration is suggested by the question, How much change in the share of income going to the lowest fifth of households would follow from each plan? The most redistributive of the plans by this measure is the Heineman plan which would change that share from 4.1 to 5.3 percent; i.e., a 30 percent increase (see Table 2, line 5).

There are, then, certain broad issues to be weighed. How much total transfer, how to divide transfers between cash and in-kind, how much emphasis on children, how intensely to concentrate on poverty reduction, how high a marginal tax rate, what existing transfers should be reduced to help finance any new benefit? But even after those issues are resolved, there are numerous somewhat more technical issues to be settled. A simple family allowance plan, such as Vadakin 1 or 2, does not have to contend with some of these issues, but the other three plans discussed do. We have space here only to list some of them: (1) Should the plan have a work test associated with it, as does FAP? Should the work test apply to all adults? Should the penalty for failing to work less than full time be severe? (2) Should the income subject to the special offset tax be

---

8 A. L. Schors, "Alternatives in Income Maintenance," *Social Work*, July 1966, pp. 22–29.

9 See R. J. Lampman, "Public and Private Transfers as Social Process," in this volume, pp. 15–40.

defined broadly (as in FAP) or narrowly (as in the Brazer plan)? Should Social Security benefits be included and taxed? Should work expenses and child care expenses be deductible? (3) Should the family be defined so as to leave choice as to what persons, and hence whose incomes, are to be included in calculating a family's benefits? (4) What income period should be used in determining benefits? Most negative income tax analysts have assumed a year would be the period, but public assistance administrators use a month. (5) How should a new benefit be articulated with existing public assistance programs? The Heineman proposal is silent on this point, but FAP has a complicated scheme to ensure maintenance of effort while discouraging increases of relatively high benefits by the states for those in the dependent children categories. It also enforces conformity with FAP upon the states in defining income and income period, family, and resource and work tests for eligibility. It also sets maximum combined tax rates for those families simultaneously on FAP and a state benefit program. (6) How should the new cash benefit be related to in-kind benefits such as food stamps and Medicaid? If food stamps are priced inversely to income, they take on the basic characteristic of a negative tax and hence have a marginal tax rate associated with them. That marginal tax rate could combine with other tax rates to raise the overall tax rate on some families to very high levels. Should the food stamp bonus be calculated after the FAP benefit but before the state supplementary payment, or after both? The Heineman Commission urges that all food stamps be dropped and that the funds be diverted to financing their more generous negative income tax. (7) How should the plan be administered and by whom? Should it be handled by the states or by the federal government? If the latter, should it be done by the Internal Revenue Service, the Social Security Administration, or a new agency? Brazer nominates the Internal Revenue Service; FAP points to the Social Security Administration.

Those seven questions indicate the complexity of introducing a new type of income-conditioned benefit into the existing system of transfers. Economists, tax lawyers, welfare administrators, and other scholars and experts can help to inform the debate now going on concerning President Nixon's Family Assistance Plan and alternatives to it.

Regardless of how that debate comes out, economists have more to do before they fully understand the set of changing institutions by which they can and do modify the preredistribution income, the goals of redistribution (of which poverty reduction is only one), and the consequences, costs, and benefits of such redistribution.

19

Benjamin A. Okner: Alternatives for
Transferring Income to the Poor:
The Family Assistance Plan and
Universal Income Supplements

Since the present system of transfers does such an inadequate job of aiding a very large segment of our poor population, there have recently emerged a wide variety of proposals for vastly overhauling or replacing many aspects of the system.[1] There are many defects embedded in the public assistance programs, but probably most serious is the large gap that exists between those in need and those eligible for aid. Less than a fifth of poor families headed by a person under age 65 receive any help from public assistance. If you are poor and single, or poor and married with no children, or poor and married and have children and your husband resides with you, you fall "through the cracks" in the welfare system (in most localities) and are ineligible for any financial help. The same is true if you have a handicap other than blindness, or if you have a handicap not judged to be "permanent and total."

The proposed income maintenance programs are aimed at those now bypassed and would help to establish more uniform and adequate levels of financial aid for all the poor. In the remainder of this section we examine two of the new programs – the Nixon administration's Family Assistance Plan (FAP), and the Universal Income Supplement (UIS) program recommended by the Heineman Commission. Although many details of both plans are still unresolved, sufficient information is available to estimate their effect (at 1966 income and poverty levels) and to compare them with existing grants.[2] All these estimates are derived from computer simulations and were prepared on an individual family basis, using data from the 1967 Survey of Economic Opportunity.

Presented at the Symposium on the Grants Economy held between the Association for the Study of the Grants Economy and the American Association for the Advancement of Science in December, 1969, in Boston, Mass. All rights reserved. Used by permission of the author. The author is a member of the Economic Studies staff of the Brookings Institution. The views expressed are his own and do not purport to represent the views of the other staff members, officers, or trustees of the Brookings Institution. The study was financed under a research grant to the Brookings Institution from the U.S. Office of Economic Opportunity.

1 The most comprehensive reference on this subject is the recently published report of the President's Commission on Income Maintenance Programs, *Poverty Amid Plenty: The American Paradox* (Washington, D.C.: November 1969). The commission (and its report) is often referred to here as the Heineman Commission (Report), after its chairman Ben W. Heineman.

2 Details concerning the simulations are given in the Appendix. The assessment is confined only to first-order effects of the proposals, and there is no attempt to estimate induced behavioral changes that might alter the pretax, pretransfer amounts, or sources of income received by families. All tax or transfer changes are assumed to be accompanied by compensating fiscal action so that the budget balance is left unchanged.

Both the Family Assistance Plan and the Universal Income Supplement involve an allowance paid to all people based only on family size. This allowance is then reduced by 50 cents for each dollar earned by the family[3] so that people are always better off financially if they earn additional income (as opposed to the present dollar-for-dollar reduction under public assistance programs). Under the administration's FAP, a husband, wife, and two children are entitled to a basic allowance of $1,600; under the commission's UIS, their basic allowance is $2,400. In addition to the 50 percent greater basic allowance under the UIS, the commission proposal pays benefits to all persons, whereas the FAP is limited to families with children.[4] Another difference between the two plans is that under the FAP, the first $720 earned by the family is ignored in computing the 50 percent offset to its basic allowance. Thus, a four-person family in which the husband earns, say, $2,500, receives a net payment of $710 under the Family Assistance Plan; under the Universal Income Supplement, the same family receives a net benefit of $1,150.[5] The break-even point — that is, the earned income level where the net benefit equals zero — is $3,920 for this family under the FAP, under the UIS, the break-even point is $4,800.

Estimated gross payments under the Family Assistance Plan are about $6.4 billion, and the plan also involves reduced income tax collections of about $300 million,[6] for a total gross cost of $6.7 billion. However, against this there is offset the present federal share of public assistance payments of about $2.0 billion plus over $1.0 billion of veterans' pensions (that no longer would be contributed). Thus, the net federal cost of the Family Assistance Plan is about $4 billion. The more comprehensive Universal Income Supplement program involves federal payments of $9.8 billion plus income tax reduction of $750 million, for a gross cost of $10.6 billion. From this the full federal share of existing public assistance programs, $2.6 billion plus the more than $1.0 billion of veterans' pensions, is subtracted to yield a net federal cost of about $7 billion.[7]

---

3 Under the Heineman Commission proposal there would also be a small offset to the basic allowance amount based on the value of the family's net assets. See the Appendix for details.

4 The administration welfare program also includes a proposal for setting a national minimum of $65 per month for the present old age assistance, aid to the blind, and aid to the disabled public assistance categories. These minima are included in the simulation estimates.

5 Under the FAP, the family's first $720 of earnings is ignored and the $1,600 basic allowance is reduced by $890 (50 percent of $2,500 less $720) to yield its net benefit of $710. Under the UIS proposal, the basic allowance of $2,400 is reduced by $1,250 (50 percent of $2,500) to yield the net benefit of $1,150.

6 Income tax collections are reduced because of the method used to integrate the plans with the individual income tax. Details are given in the Appendix.

7 These estimates include a downward adjustment of roughly 10 percent (FAP) to 15 percent (UIS to take account of income underreporting in the survey data. The detailed estimates presented in the remainder of this section do not include these adjustments. The estimated costs exceed the published figures for both plans mainly because our data apply to 1966, whereas the published ones refer to 1970 or 1971.

What results can we expect from the adoption of these new income maintenance programs? Simplified administration, elimination of different eligibility and payments standards in various jurisdictions, diminution of the built-in disincentives to earn — all of these are significant changes that would accompany both of the new programs. But — most important of all — that plans make available many more dollars to the large number of poor families now bypassed by our programs of money grants.

Under existing programs, 9.9 million families classified as poor on the basis of their nontransfer income are still poor after transfers. Of these families, over 4 million receive no transfer income from any source. Under the Family Assistance Plan, the number of families who remain in poverty is reduced to 9.0 million, and the proportion of poor families who receive no transfer is reduced to 14 percent (from 27 percent under existing programs). The number of families who remain poor after Universal Income Supplements falls to 7.6 million, and some UIS benefits are received by all but 4 percent of the pretransfer poor.[8] While 11.0 million of the pretransfer poor receive some income transfer under existing programs, FAP payments increase the number of poor families receiving any transfer by 2.1 million, and UIS payments raise the number by 3.5 million.

The new grants programs do more than merely extend some aid to many of the poor families now ineligible to receive any payments. They also substantially increase the amount of income distributed to the poor. The amounts paid, while still well below the levels that would completely fill the pretransfer poverty-income gap, are considerably higher than are now paid under welfare programs in most areas. At present, even after receipt of transfer income, there is still a $9.9 billion posttransfer poverty-income gap. Under the Family Assistance Plan, the posttransfer poverty gap is reduced to $6.6 billion, with FAP payments filling one-third of the existing gap. The Universal Income Supplement program leaves a posttransfer poverty gap of only $4.3 billion, filling 57 percent of the gap.

Overall, the FAP removes an additional 900,000 families containing 4.1 million persons from poverty, while the UIS moves 2.3 million additional families across the poverty line. Under both programs, most of those removed from poverty are nonaged and married.[9] Of the 900,000 families removed from poverty by FAP payments, about 500,000 are intact families with children (husband, wife, and children) and 200,000 are families headed by a female.

---

8 The 4 percent of poor families who receive no UIS payments are primarily those with sufficient net assets to reduce their basic allowance to zero. It is also possible that some of those counted as nonrecipients do benefit financially from the UIS through reduced income tax liability. However, the recipient figure includes only families who receive positive UIS payments.

9 Under the FAP, single individuals are ineligible for payments and therefore cannot benefit from the program. Although single individuals are eligible for UIS payments, it is impossible for them to receive sufficient benefits to move out of poverty. This is because the income level at which payments cease is determined by the basic allowance and tax rate; with a $750 allowance and 50 percent tax rate, payments fall to zero at $1,500. However, the poverty line for nonfarm single individuals under age 65 is $1,749 — well above the UIS break-even level.

The same general picture is true for families removed from poverty by UIS payments. The only significant differences are that under UIS a small number of husband-wife families receive sufficient benefits to be moved across the poverty line and more families with children move out of poverty because of UIS payments (1.6 million under UIS as compared with 700,000 under FAP).

While both of the new plans are of benefit mainly to families with children, they also aid single individuals and childless couples. Families with no children (including single individuals) can benefit from the Family Assistance Plan if they are now public assistance recipients and receive less than $780 per year in benefits. Under the Universal Income Supplement, however, even though benefits are too low to move any single individuals out of poverty, such people do receive significant help. For example, only 17 percent of single people receive no UIS benefits – a sizable drop from the current nonrecipient rate of 70 percent. Even though such individuals are still poor, they receive an average UIS payment of almost $400 per year. And the number of UIS recipients among childless couples who are still poor after existing transfers is doubled. Almost one-third of such couples have sufficient income after their UIS payment to move out of poverty.

It is not surprising that these plans which dispense higher benefits to the large number of poor families now ineligible for aid have a significant poverty-reducing impact. But are these additional sums allocated efficiently under the new program? The "target efficiency" criterion posited by Weisbrod provides a useful framework within which to consider this question for the FAP and UIS proposals.[10] Target efficiency considers both "vertical efficiency," a measure of the extent to which a program assists *only* the intended target group; and "horizontal efficiency," a measure of the degree to which a program assists *everyone* in the target group. Horizontal efficiency has two subdimensions, defined by the proportion of people in the target group who are affected by the program and by the adequacy of benefits in meeting the needs of the beneficiaries.

When applied to a comparison of the Family Assistance Plan and the Universal Income Supplement, the target efficiency criteria yield ambiguous results. The FAP would be favored on the basis of vertical efficiency because only 11 percent of its benefits go to the nonpoor, whereas under the UIS 15 percent of the benefits are paid to the nonpoor. However, using the horizontal efficiency measure, the Universal Income Supplement is clearly preferable. Under the UIS, 96 percent of the pretransfer poor receive payments, as compared with 86 percent under the FAP program. In addition, the Universal Income Supplement more adequately aids the poor by filling almost 60 percent of the present posttransfer poverty gap, whereas the FAP fills only one third of it.

10 B. A. Weisbrod, "Collective Action and the Distribution of Income: A Conceptual Approach," in *The Analysis and Evaluation of Public Expenditures: The PPB System*, a compendium of papers submitted to the U.S., Congress, Subcommittee on Economy in Government of the Joint Economic Committee, 91st Cong., 1st sess., 1969, vol. 1.

Overall, it seems reasonable to give the vertical efficiency measure a relatively lower weight in comparing the two programs because any definition separating the poor and the nonpoor is somewhat arbitrary. And this is surely true of the current poverty-income levels. Therefore, it is unlikely that anyone would seriously object to a proposal that aids a family whose earnings are a few dollars above the level labeled "the poverty line." Because of the much higher degree of horizontal efficiency in the Universal Income Supplement than in the Family Assistance Plan, there would seem to be little question about the greater efficiency of the proposed UIS program.

Conclusion

In examining the two new proposals for transferring income to the poor, we find that when benefits are increased and eligibility is extended to families with children, as under the Family Assistance Plan, it is possible to move a large number of such families across the poverty-income thresholds. If even more money is spent and benefit eligibility extended generally, as under the Universal Income Supplement, it is possible to aid even more poor families. Within a reasonable range, if more is spent there will be fewer poor.

Redistributing income from the nonpoor to the poor is feasible, and it need not be too painful. Even though both the FAP and UIS programs involve increased transfers of $4 to $7 billion, these sums are so small as compared with total income that they would have an insignificant impact on the overall distribution of income. Overall, the programs would raise the after-tax, after-transfer share of income of the pretransfer poor – and reduce the income share of the nonpoor – by only one percentage point.

There are many ways to finance the cost of new grants for the poor. The various alternatives can be grouped into either reducing other expenditures or foregoing tax reductions that otherwise might have taken place. Given a federal tax system that annually produces a fiscal dividend of about $8 billion, the choice is really how to divide these funds between additional federal expenditures and future tax cuts.

During the past thirty years we have developed programs of money transfers that now "accidentally" remove over 5 million families from poverty. It would be strange if we could not enact others to aid the 10 million families who are still poor.

Appendix: Methodology for Income Maintenance Simulations

The basic procedures for calculating the family benefit under the Administration's Family Assistance Plan (FAP) and the Heineman Commission's Universal Income Supplement (UIS) are quite similar. Under both plans, the family's net benefit is equal to a basic allowance which is then reduced by 50 percent for each dollar of "other income," and under the UIS it is further reduced on the basis of the family's net assets. However, the populations eligible for receipt of payments and the amount of basic allowance differ under the two programs. In the remainder of this section we explain the assumptions used in simulating the two plans and how they would be integrated with the individual income tax.

Family Assistance Plan

Family assistance benefits are paid only to families with children under 18. Another part of the administration welfare proposal establishes a national floor for the "adult" public assistance categories.

For families with children, the basic allowance is equal to $500 each for the first two adults, and $300 for each additional family member, up to a maximum of seven. Thus, the largest possible gross benefit is $2,500 for a family consisting of two parents and their five children.

In calculating the offset to the family's basic allowance, the first $720 of positive earned income – wages, nonfarm business, and farm income – is ignored. If earned income is negative, it is set equal to $0. The amount of offset is then equal to 50 percent of total family income exclusive of public assistance and minus the $720 earned-income exclusion. The offset must always be positive; if income is negative, the offset is set equal to $0.

The family's potential FAP payment is then equal to the gross benefit less the amount of offset (which can yield a negative FAP amount). It is assumed that the family will continue to take (actually, continue to pay the negative FAP amount) the FAP payment until it is more advantageous to pay individual income tax. In the small number of instances where reported public assistance exceeds the FAP benefit, the FAP payment is set equal to public assistance.

For families now receiving aid under the adult public assistance programs (old age assistance, aid to the blind, and aid to the disabled) there is established a federal minimum of $65 per month ($780 per year). If the public assistance amount reported is less than the minimum, it is set equal to $780 in the FAP simulation.

Two unusual situations can occur under the FAP. When FAP is either zero or negative, public assistance income is reported, and the family is liable for federal income tax. If a family is ineligible for FAP (i.e., FAP = $0), its financial situation should not be affected by the program. In this instance, then, income tax as calculated is used and reported, and public assistance income is not changed (unless it is less than $780, in which case it is raised to that amount if the family qualifies). If the FAP payment is negative, the family is eligible to participate in the program. The tax payment is set equal to the calculated tax or negative FAP, whichever is lower. The amount of reported public assistance is retained.

The same procedures are used in the UIS simulation described below. Under both plans, a family cannot pay income tax *and* receive a FAP or UIS payment. For any family eligible to receive a positive payment, federal income tax is set equal to zero.

Universal Income Supplement

Universal income supplements are paid to all families, regardless of whether there are any children present. The basic allowance is equal to $750 each for the first two adults in the family and $450 for each additional member. There is no limit on the total gross benefits to which a family is entitled.

The family's basic allowance is reduced by 50 percent of its total income, exclusive of money received from means-tested transfer programs. Public assistance is such a program and is always excluded in calculating the offset. Veterans' pensions are also means tested. If veterans' benefits are reported by an aged family, it is assumed that these were pensions and the amount is excluded in calculating the offset. Veterans' benefits reported by nonaged families are assumed to be disability compensation, which is not subject to an income means test.

Under the UIS, the basic allowance is also reduced by 10 percent of the family's net assets to prevent making large payments to families with substantial assets but little or no current income. The value of net assets is calculated as the difference between the family's total assets and its liabilities. If net assets are negative, they are set equal to $0 (as is also the case for income if it is negative).

The family's potential UIS payment is then equal to its gross benefit less the offset amount (which can yield a negative UIS amount). As under the FAP program, it is assumed that the family will continue to take (to pay the negative UIS) the UIS until it is more advantageous to pay income tax. In the small number of cases where reported public assistance exceeds the family's UIS benefit, the UIS is set equal to public assistance.

Calculation of Federal Income Tax

The first step in calculating federal income tax liability for each family in the SEO is to estimate their tax-filing status on the basis of family size, age of members, composition, and sources of income. Married couples whose estimated adjusted gross income is greater than the $600 ($1,200) filing requirement are assumed to file joint returns, while the type of return filed by other families is determined on the basis of marital status and number of dependents. In many instances, there are two or more tax returns formed for members of the same family. This would be the case, for example, for a couple with children who have taxable wages.

For each tax return, there is estimated the total adjusted gross income based on the income reported in the survey. Adjusted gross income is equal to the sum of wages, farm and nonfarm business income, rent, interest, dividends, and government and private pensions. Since respondents were not asked about income from the sale of assets, adjusted gross income does not include capital gains.

In calculating the amount of taxable income on each return, the number of dependents is based on the number of members in the family and their relationship to the person filing. A $600 exemption is allowed for each exemption. Taxpayers aged 65 and over are each allowed an additional $600 exemption, but no additional exemptions for blindness are allowed. On all returns with adjusted gross income of $10,000 or less a standard deduction of 10 percent of income, or the minimum standard deduction of $200 + $100 for each exemption, whichever is greater, is used. For returns with adjusted gross income greater than $10,000, itemized deductions equal to 16 percent of income are used. Tax liability is then calculated on the basis of computed taxable income and the appropriate rate schedule depending on the taxpayer's marital status. If there is more than one tax return for the family, the total tax liability of all filers in the family is aggregated to get the family total.

The total number of tax returns estimated and the number in each marital status category compares favorably with the Internal Revenue Service's published statistics.[1] The estimates suffer because it was impossible to include capital gains income in the computation of adjusted gross income. Also, the assumption that no returns with income under $10,000 have itemized deductions is known to be incorrect;[2] the same is true of the assumption that all returns with incomes above $10,000 itemize their deductions and that the average of 16 percent is applicable for all returns.[3]

The known deficiencies in calculating federal individual income tax liability probably do not seriously distort the simulation results because they are used only to determine whether a family will pay income tax or receive a negative income maintenance benefit. The most serious shortcoming is the omission of capital gains income. But since such income is largely concentrated among high-income taxpayers, it probably would have very little influence on the family's crossover decision (see "Integration" section below).

Because most families file only a single tax return, and also because information on almost all income components was collected on a family basis, in the simulations we assume that the family is the recipient unit for both the FAP

---

1 Internal Revenue Service, *Statistics of Income, 1966, Individual Income Tax Returns*, 1968.

2 Actually, about 30 percent of returns with adjusted gross income under $10,000 *do* itemize their deductions.

3 About 25 percent of all returns with income above $10,000 do not have itemized deductions. The average itemized deductions of 16 percent of income is remarkably stable in most income classes. However, this average obscures a great deal of variation among returns within any income class.

and UIS programs. Therefore, for determining whether the family chooses to receive a payment, total liability for all tax returns in the family is compared with the family's potential FAP or UIS payment.

Integration with Present Income Tax

It is assumed that under both the FAP and UIS proposals, families will continue to receive benefits — which might be either plus or minus — until it is financially advantageous for them to move out of the FAP or UIS and merely pay the tax required under the federal individual income tax. It will be to their advantage to make such a move when their income less federal income tax is greater than their income after receipt of a (negative) FAP or UIS payment. Under the FAP, the crossover point is at $4,355 for a four-person family; it is at $5,559 under the UIS. Several examples of how such a family would fare at different income levels under the two proposals are shown in Table A–1.

This merge procedure is the one recommended by the Heineman Commission[4] and is an easy way to assure that people are not faced with inordinately high marginal tax rates as family income rises sufficiently to be subject to the

Table A–1. Comparison of Family Assistance Plan and Universal Income Supplement Benefits at Various Income Levels for a Four-Person Family

				Final Income		
				(Initial Income + Net Benefit)		
	Net Benefit (+)		Tax (−)			
Initial Income	UIS	FAP	1966 Tax Law[c]	UIS	FAP	1966 Income Tax Law
$ 0	$2,400	$1,600	0	$2,400	$1,600	$ 0
2,000	1,400	960	0	3,400	2,960	2,000
3,920	440	0	−159	4,360	3,920	3,761
4,355[a]	222	−218	−218	4,577	4,137	4,137
4,800	0	-440	−260	4,800	4,360	4,540
5,000	−100	−540	−290	4,900	4,460	4,710
5,500	−350	-790	−370	5,150	4,710	5,130
5,559[b]	−379	−820	−379	5,180	4,739	5,180
6,000	−600	−1,040	−450	5,400	4,960	5,550

[a]Family will switch from FAP to individual income tax at this income level.

[b] Family will switch from UIA to individual income tax at this income level.

[c] Computed with 10 percent standard deduction; figures shown are the negatives of 1966 federal individual income tax liability.

4 *Heineman Commission Report*, pp. 153–54. For a detailed explanation, see J. Tobin, J. A. Pechman, and P. Mieszkowski, "Is a Negative Income Tax Practical?" *Yale Law Journal* 77 (November 1967).

federal income tax. In effect, the procedure means that before the crossover point, the family is subject to a marginal tax rate of 50 percent on its earned income. However, once past the crossover income level, rather than rising, the marginal tax rate drops substantially. Assuming that the initial 50 percent rate does not result in disincentives against earning additional income, the sharp drop in the marginal tax rate at the crossover point should provide a strong incentive to continue earning.

20

Martin C. McGuire and Harvey A. Garn:
The Integration of Equity and Efficiency
Criteria in Public Project Selection[1]

1

Recent efforts by Maass, Marglin, Mera, Freeman [1, 2, 3, 4] and others have called attention to hitherto neglected equity considerations in project analysis. In the United States grants-in-aid to state, city and other local governments for such projects have become an increasingly important form of Federal expenditure policy. About $17 billion of the Federal budget in fiscal year 1968 was for such grants-in-aid. Unlike Musgrave's [5] allocation and distribution branches, which can separate considerations of efficiency from equity, policy for Federal grant programmes must integrate both factors either explicitly or implicitly. In this situation how is the economist to assist the policy-maker in establishing generally applicable project selection criteria, when the objectives include equity as well as more familiar efficiency aspects? How are these criteria to be made operationally useful in the selection of projects?

This paper reports on the formulation and implementation of explicit formulae for consolidation of equity and efficiency criteria in the selection of regional development projects in the United States. The programmes we concern ourselves with are "area specific" or "region specific" Federal grants, such that choosing one project over another bears resemblance to choosing one area over another. In effect, therefore, this note is concerned with the construction and application of Bergsonian-type welfare functions in an operational context.

A decade ago Eckstein [6] set forth the basic economics of public project selection. That analysis dealt exclusively with efficiency objectives, and

From *The Economic Journal*, Vol. 83, December 1969, pp. 44–59. Reprinted by permission of the Royal Economic Society and the authors.

1 We are indebted to Professor Donald Farrar, Mr. John Flory and Dr. Robert Raynsford for their assistance in the preparation of this paper.

concluded that subject to a constraint of appropriations plus reimbursable expenses, public projects should be selected from highest benefit - cost ratio to lowest until the available funds are exhausted. Benefits were defined for each community as

$$\lambda^i(pB^i - C^i)$$

with λ^i = i's marginal utility of money, assumed to be constant (and set equal to 1 for simplicity);

B^i = physical benefit accruing to i;

p = market price of B^i;

C^i = i's contribution to the cost of the project;

i = an identifiable group which is assumed to capture all the benefits of the project.

While similar in approach, our analysis differs from Eckstein's in the following respects:

1. All costs are assumed to be borne by the central budget authority, i.e., no local cost contribution; $C^i = 0$.[2]
2. No market prices exist and no proxies for them can be found to express physical benefits to dollar terms; p unknown.
3. A single project usually produces two or more sorts of incommensurable benefits.
4. Marginal utilities, λ^i, vary from community to community, depending upon the welfare level as indicated by a number of welfare criteria.

These differences between Eckstein's analysis and ours give rise to two basic problems for the analyst to resolve and then integrate. These problems involve alternative distributional objectives and efficiency-equity outcomes.

First, one is obliged to deal with the fact that no single unambiguous measure of "poverty" or "community need" exists. Often, a single government programme may be directed against diverse, more or less uncorrelated conditions of economic (or social) distress. This calls for the construction of specific formulae to develop and express the decision-maker's preferences, so as to allow both for explicit trade-off comparisons between one distributional objective and another and for articulation of judgments as to *how much more* needy or deserving one group is than another, on equity grounds. Second, a basic conflict between equity and efficiency choice criteria derives from the fact that poor people and poor communities are generally less efficient at producing goods

---

2 For the treatment of cost-sharing aspects of public projects see [7].

publicly than richer people and richer communities.[3] The resolution of this conflict requires a transformation curve between the equity and efficiency pay-offs from the particular set of projects under consideration, where equity pay-offs stem from the express judgments of relative need just mentioned.

This paper discusses and illustrates our treatment of these issues on an experimental basis for the United States Economic Development Administration, an agency which makes grants-in-aid (and loans) to economically depressed localities in the United States. The primary legal criteria for being "depressed" in this case are that a locality (usually a United States county) has an unemployment rate greater than 6% or has a (1959) median family income which is 50% of the national median or less. (Other secondary tests qualify some localities not eligible under either of the above primary criteria.)

II.   Construction of a Welfare Index

This section describes the creation of an "index of need" for use in E.D.A. project evaluation — an index based upon the dual criteria of local economic distress, low family income and high unemployment rate.

The index to be developed will take on a set of values, $\lambda^1, \lambda^2, \ldots \lambda^n$, as in Eckstein's formulation. Hence the problem for the analyst is to determine an appropriate set of weights which reflect the decision-maker's subjective judgments (interpersonal utility comparisons) between communities.[4] In the construction of such a marginal utility index one must be concerned both with the range of values the function may take on, and with the trade-offs among the arguments of that function.

In view of the fact that project benefit—cost ratios will be multiplied by or weighted by differing values of λ^i, the range of values that the multiplier can take on may be critical. The range of marginal utility weights, if great enough, will completely dominate efficiency as a criterion; if relatively small, will exert no influence on final project ranks; and if the weights, λ^i, are selected so as to

---

3 Empirical evidence developed in connection with grant problems of the Economic Development Administration suggests positive correlation between community affluence and efficiency in public project design and implementation. Also, Mera [3] has illustrated that on theoretical grounds it is unlikely that the most efficient distribution of inputs between regions will also produce what is judged to be the most equitable inter-regional income distribution.

4 In theory, the decision-maker might agree to specify a set of weights in the abstract and to choose projects in accord with those weights — expressed by establishing scale, origin and functional forms for λ^i. More likely, he will wish to see the effects of alternative marginal utility assumptions on the outcome in terms of project approvals. The object of this procedure is to assist in the establishment of operational rules for classifying projects by such broad categories as "reject," "approve" and "borderline." The point is not to generate some particular reasonable community welfare function (let alone a "true" one); rather, it is to discover and express the manager's preference in a communicable form. Hence, reference to the inherent plausibility of the underlying welfare function derivable from a manager's preferences can only provide a general check against absurdities.

correlate perfectly (inversely) with benefit-cost ratios all projects will end up with the same final welfare[5] score except for the influences of errors in cost and benefit estimates.

Since the Economic Development Administration is legally empowered to make grants-in-aid to areas on the basis of high unemployment rates and/or low incomes relative to national averages, we used employment rates and income levels as sub-indicators of area need or marginal utility. The following table gives the multiple distribution of areas eligible for EDA assistance, classified by the statistics which determined eligibility in 1966.

As shown in Table 1, there is a significant variation in income levels in low-employment-rate areas, and vice versa. Therefore a welfare function should take these variations into account, making the trade-offs between income and employment explicit; that is: we require a marginal utility function to be of the form

$$\lambda^i = \lambda^i(E^i, Y^i)$$

with E^i indicating the area's employment rate and Y^i indicating its median family income.

Operating with a population of roughly 300 projects with total cost of roughly \$300 million, we explored a variety of functional forms, sought out administrators' preferences and arrayed projects in order of desirability by alternate preference functions. The functional form provisionally settled upon was one for which the marginal utilities of additional income and additional jobs are independent and therefore additive.

$$\lambda^i = a\left(\frac{\bar{E}}{E^i}\right) + b\left(\frac{\bar{Y}}{Y^i}\right)^{\beta \times 6}$$

---

5 Our terminology throughout this paper will be to refer to the *physical* outputs of projects as "benefits" and to these outputs multiplied by a marginal utility weight as "welfare pay-offs" or "welfare scores."

6 The derivation of this formula is as follows:

We assume that the relevant aspects of the welfare level of each community can be expressed as a sort of composite average of the employment level and average family income.

$$U = Lf(E) + Ng(W)$$

where L = size of labor force;
$E = e/L$ = employment rate;
e = employment in the community;
N = number of families in the area, including single individual "families";
$W = w/N$ = average family (personal) income;
w = total personal income in the area.

Then

$$\Delta U = \frac{\delta f}{\delta E} \Delta e + \frac{\delta g}{\delta W} \Delta w$$

We next assume that the ratio of average to median family income is roughly constant from county to county.

λ^i = area need indicator;
$\bar{E}$ = national average employment rate;
E^i = area employment rate;
$\bar{Y}$ = national median family income;
Y^i = area median family income.

The parameters in this expression can be set to reflect different value judgments about the welfare implications of area employment and income statistics. More specifically, the parameters determine: (1) how income and unemployment trade off in the decision-maker's scheme of values along any fixed "indifference curve" (*i.e.*, for a given value of λ); and (2) the gradient of λ, that is, the rate at which the decision-maker is willing to trade off efficiency for distributional objectives. For example, if one thought that the creation of a new job was just as important in areas with low unemployment rates as in areas with high rates one would set $\alpha = 0$. In our experiment the following conditions were selected as a better reflection of the decision-maker's preferences.

Hence, if

$$Y = \text{median family income}$$
$$W = \theta Y$$

Then

$$U = Lf(E) + Ng(\theta Y)$$

and

$$\Delta U = f_E \Delta e + \frac{1}{\theta} g_Y \, \Delta w$$

In particular, let

$$f(E) = K_1 - \frac{\bar{E} a}{\alpha - 1} \, (\bar{E}/E)^{\alpha - 1} \quad \text{and} \quad f_E = a(\bar{E}/E)^{\alpha}$$

$$g(W) = K_2 - \frac{b}{\beta} \left(\frac{\theta \bar{Y}}{\theta Y}\right)^{\beta} \quad \text{and} \quad \frac{g_Y}{\theta} = \frac{b}{\theta Y} \left(\frac{\bar{Y}}{Y}\right)^{\beta + 1}$$

In practice, it was impossible independently to estimate income and employment impacts of prospective projects. Generally, wages for publicly stimulated employment were about the same as wages already obtained in the area in question. In practice, the best estimate possible was that each new job would generate as much income as the average family in the community already earned.
That is

$$\Delta U = \left[f_E + \frac{\theta Y g_Y}{\theta} \right] \Delta e = \left[a\left(\frac{\bar{E}}{E}\right)^{\alpha} + b\left(\frac{\bar{Y}}{Y}\right)^{\beta} \right] \Delta c$$

The expression in brackets is the term for λ shown in Table 2. We also experimented with forms which allow for inter-dependent marginal utilities of incremental jobs and income, such as

$$U = [f(E) + g(Y)]^{\alpha}$$

but we found the exponent outside brackets to be of little assistance, and the inter-dependence of marginal utilities to confront decision-makers with too many and too complex value judgments.

Table 1. Areas Qualified (in 1966) for Economic Development Administration Grants Distributed by Income and Unemployment Rate

1965 Unemployment Rate	1959 Median Family Income, $/year						
	7,500– 6,500	6,500– 5,500	5,500– 4,500	4,500– 3,500	3,500– 2,500	2,500– 1,500	1,500– 500
0–6%†	18*	52*	120*	106*	207	226	48
6–8%	5	25	64	75	73	29	
8–10%	1	11	22	34	32	25	
10–12%	2	6	13	9	22	10	
12–14%	2	2	2	5	11	10	
14–15%			2	1	14	7	
Over 16%	1			3	13	14	3

* Many of these areas are eligible despite low unemployment and "high" income because they had qualified in earlier years on unemployment grounds.

† Areas known to have low reported unemployment rates; for some of these areas precise current unemployment data are not available.

1. An area with national average unemployment rate and median family income equal to the national family income[7] should receive a weight of $1; \lambda^a = 1$.[8] This establishes an origin.

2. The "worst-off" areas should have a handicap of 15; $\lambda^w = 15$. The range $1-15$ was necessary to give effective weight to equity considerations. This establishes a scale.

3. In an area with national average unemployment rate and median family income equal to the national median, adding 1 job is as important as adding $\$\overline{Y}$ of income.

4. In an area with very high unemployment rates ($E^w = 0.85$) and very low incomes ($Y^w = \$1,850$) adding 1 job is as important as adding $\$1,850$ of income.

5. At high income levels and high unemployment rates jobs are more important than income, while at low income and low unemployment rates income is more important than jobs. This is a diminishing marginal substitution assumption.

These five conditions determine the parameters as follows:

$$\lambda^i = 0.5 \left(\frac{0.96}{E^i}\right)^{22.4} + 0.5 \left(\frac{5,600}{Y^i}\right)^{2.5}$$

The following table and diagram show alternative levels of income and employment which have the same λ^i using these parameters.

7 When we developed this (1966) the national average unemployment rate was 4% and the national median family income which could be compared with area incomes was $5,600 (1958 prices).

8 The practical meaning of this assumption is that, among projects competing for grant funds from such areas, efficiency should be the sole criterion of choices.

Table 2.

	15	10	5
Y^1	$1,600	$1,850	$2,300
E^1	0.87	0.90	0.96
Y^2	$1,850	$2,200	$2,900
E^2	0.85	0.87	0.90
Y^3	$2,200	$2,900	$5,600
E^3	0.84	0.85	0.88

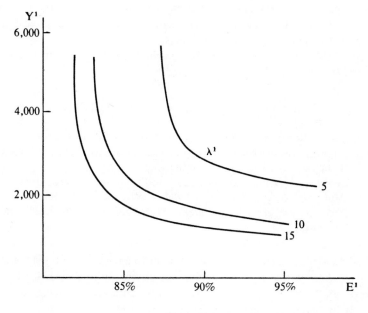

Figure 1.

The parameters can easily be adjusted to take account of such factors as: changes in the distribution of benefit–cost ratios; the discovery that allowing $\lambda^w = 15$ produces more loss of efficiency than is desired or too little boost to projects from neediest areas: or that the particular trade-offs between employment and income overemphasise one at the expense of the other.

The particular parameters displayed above result in very large marginal rates of substitution for communities which suffer from low income only or high unemployment only. This is founded on no theoretical analysis on our part but rather on a sense that project decision-makers have a saturation point in their evaluation of the demands of equity — beyond which point changes in a complementary form of economic distress call forth little further normative response.

III.   Integrating Equity and Efficiency –
An Illustration

The preceding section described a means for constructing an explicit welfare index for use in project selection. This was contrasted with the traditional analysis which tended to deal exclusively in efficiency objectives. This section of the paper illustrates an application of our approach with an example derived from a typical choice situation in the Economic Development Administration.

Normally, the decision-maker is faced with: (1) a larger set of legally acceptable projects than can be funded from the available budget; (2) a wide variation in expected benefits among the projects; (3) a wide variation in the relative need of the communities proposing the projects; and (4) projects from poor areas which have, generally, but not uniformly, lower benefit–cost[9] ratios than projects from relatively better-off areas.

Faced with such choices, what rules might a manager develop to guide his decisions? Various rules have been suggested.

1.   Ignore questions of need and exhaust the budget on the most efficient projects.
2.   Ignore efficiency and give the grant to those who most need it.
3.   Establish a minimum efficiency and select according to need; look at the outcome and re-evaluate the constraints.
4.   Establish a minimum level of need and select according to efficiency; look at the outcome and re-evaluate the constraints.
5.   Develop an explicit preference function between need and efficiency.

The first two of these five choice rules amount to a rejection of project grants as a tool for *both* efficiency and equity objectives. Rules 3 and 4 have been proposed by Marglin [2] as an iterative procedure for balancing equity and efficiency in long-range planning.

For three reasons, however, we argue that development of an explicit set of preferences will result in better choice criteria than any of the four other alternatives. Our experience confirms that the conflict between the redistributive spirit of welfare legislation and the administrative pressures to show results by selecting "good" projects can only reach a systematic resolution if groups of projects are compared to each other in terms of the relative loss of project efficiency entailed by choices which respond to community need. But this is a way of asking the decision-maker to articulate the extent to which he is willing to forego efficiency for distribution objectives. Much of the appeal of imposing constraints is to avoid doing this. Where a decision-maker is not prepared to do this, opportunity gains and losses will fall out of the choices rather than become consistent choice criteria. Second, iterative adjustment of constraints is most

---

9 Benefits refer to physical benefits.

appropriate in adjusting long-range, large-scale plans for a small number of regions. The problem we are addressing involves shorter-range, smaller-scale projects for a very large number of areas. Third, the articulation of an explicit inter-personal utility function enables the decision-maker to test the effects of maximizing an objective function containing both equity and efficiency variables against choices which allow for only one or the other. As our example demonstrates — for Economic Development Administration projects in any case — the choice of decision rule makes a considerable difference in which projects from those available are selected.

As explained in Section II of this paper, the one common quantitative benefit by which E.D.A. projects could be compared was the estimated number of permanent jobs added by the project to the community in question. We will show how different decision rules altered the outcome of projects selected out of a universe of 37 candidate projects with a total cost of $17.9 million, a total job creation potential of slightly more than 8,000 and a range of marginal utility weights of 7.0–2.5.[10] It will be useful first to trace some of the implications of these alternative decision rules by reference to a diagram which shows the general relationships which prevail among observed project sets when the following data are available for each project:

C = the cost of the project
B = jobs created
λ = marginal utility multiplier

Fig. 2 shows a schedule of alternative total welfare additions and corresponding total physical benefits which a *fixed total expenditure* will

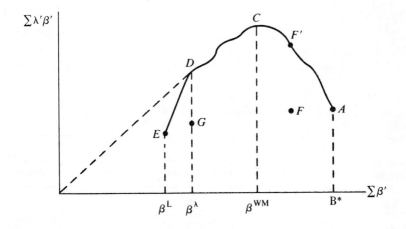

Figure 2.

---

10 The data presented here reflect analysis of projects for one E.D.A. region (including six states) for one three-month period during 1966.

generate as alternative subsets of projects are chosen. Particular combinations of ΣB and $\Sigma \lambda B$ are singled out as follows:

Point A (B^*, W^{BM}) Total physical benefits and welfare additions when benefits are maximized, $i.e.$, efficiency is the sole criterion.

Point C (B^{WM}, W^*) Total physical benefits and welfare additions when welfare is maximized.

Point D (B^λ, W^λ) Total physical benefits and welfare additions when the (weighted) average value of λ is maximized.

Point E (B^L, W^{BL}) Total physical benefits and welfare additions when benefits are minimized.

The curve, labelled $W(B)$, represents a frontier of welfare additions achievable, for a fixed expenditure level. (Some sets of project choices are possible which lie beneath the frontier.) This display is useful as an indication to the decision-maker of the costs (regrets) of not choosing projects which are consistent with his own equity-efficiency judgments. (For internal or external political or bureaucratic reasons, decision-makers are often urged to follow someone else's preferences.) As Fig. 2 suggests, the decision-maker may argue against "efficiency" advocates who urge a choice such as point F by demanding, at least, point F'. He may argue against "equity" advocates who urge point G by pointing out that, by his own equity criteria the most "progressive" choice is point D, where the average (weighted) need of areas served is greatest. In short, Fig. 2 displays the trade-offs which most policy-makers are forced to make between their own subjective judgments and other pressures for particular decisions.

Tables 3 and 4 show these trade-offs for the E.D.A. project population referred to above.

As expected, the employment potential of projects from the neediest areas is very low compared to the most efficient choice (the choice made by choosing from highest benefit–cost ratio to lowest). The choice which maximizes the sum

Table 3. Cumulative Employment Potential (ΣB) of Projects Selected by Different Decision Rules

Expenditure $ million	Most efficient Choice, Max. ΣB	Projects from Neediest Areas	Highest scoring Projects, Max. $\Sigma \lambda B$	Actual[11] choices
1.0	1,805	625	1,535	1,725
2.0	2,960	1,320	2,915	2,525
3.0	3,730	1,710	3,230	3,050
4.0	4,335	2,330	4,225	3,475
5.0	4,835	2,535	4,800	3,800

11 Arranged from highest benefit case ratio to lowest among a larger list of projects actually selected.

Table 4. Cumulative Welfare Potential of Projects Selected by
Different Decision Rules

Expenditure, $ million	Most Efficient Choice, Max. ΣB	Projects from Neediest Areas	Highest Scoring Projects, Max. ΣλB	Actual Choices
1.0	6.6	3.7	7.2	7.0
2.0	11.2	6.5	11.6	9.8
3.0	13.6	7.6	14.9	11.9
4.0	16.9	10.9	17.7	13.4
5.0	19.1	11.2	19.9	14.5

of project scores (where the score equals the benefit-cost ratio times λ^i) results in sacrificing some employment potential relative to the most efficient choice, but improves considerably in this respect over a choice constrained to those projects from the most needy areas.

Table 4 shows these same choices from a welfare point of view, where welfare potential is defined as benefits times λ^i.[12]

It is clear from Table 4 that both the most efficient choice and the selection from the poorest areas fall short of the selection using welfare scores.[13] It should be noted that, in this experiment, the range and scale of λ^i tended to produce welfare choices heavily weighted in favor of efficiency. This outcome is not necessary, of course. If the decision-maker desired to place greater emphasis on equity the range of values for λ^i could have been expanded. As suggested by Fig. 2 and by Tables 3 and 4, the actual choices to emerge from the project decision process for which these techniques were developed were not consistent, entirely, with the efficiency and welfare criteria we developed. This discrepancy was due to three factors: (1) many legitimate non-quantifiable factors other than equity and efficiency (as data forced us rather narrowly to define "efficiency") must enter into project selection decisions; (2) no single decision-maker in fact existed; group decisions were common, and as is well known, group decisions are likely to be inconsistent; (3) even if single policy-makers had dominated project decisions, it is very difficult for a person to accept his own predetermined value judgments as final and to act on them in all specific cases; since these equity judgments are strictly intuitive, one's tendency is to rely on intuition case by case and to suspect any generalizations, even one's own.

---

12 The numbers in Table 4 represent utility pay-offs (measured in "utils") to various decision rules. As such, these figures have no intrinsic or objective meaning. In so far as they are based on operational (although subjective) value judgments by the decision-maker (as reflected by the marginal utility function $\lambda^i (E^i, Y^i)$), they do allow the decision-maker to observe how much he must sacrifice by his own standards to select projects inconsistent with his own criteria.

13 For each expenditure level a plot of the values from Tables 3 and 4 would show welfare vs. employment trade-offs roughly similar to Fig. 2.

Table 5 shows the losses implied by deviations from the maximum welfare choice; three deviations are presented, the actual choices, the maximum efficiency or benefit choices and the choice of serving the neediest areas. The table shows losses for an expenditure of $5 million.[14]

Table 5. Losses from Not Choosing Projects to Maximize Welfare

	Amount of Loss: Measured from Maximum Welfare Choice		
	If Projects Chosen		
Type of Loss	Serve Neediest Areas	Maximize ΣB	Actual Choices
Welfare change	−8.7	−0.8	−5.4
Σ benefits change	−2,265	+35	−1,000
Average λ change	+0.3	−0.2	−0.3

As can be seen from Table 5, the actual choices produced lower values of welfare, benefits and weighted average of λ than the choice which would have maximized welfare. At the same time the actual choices were considerably better on welfare and efficiency grounds than the choice of projects from the neediest areas. A selection using the combined efficiency – equity measure would have improved performance in terms of both major objectives.

In summary, trade-offs between equity and efficiency in Federal grant programmes cannot be eliminated by ignoring them. Project choices will have both equity and efficiency implications whether or not these are treated systematically. Our analysis indicates that the trade-off should be explicitly treated in project selection. This leads to a decision rule to evaluate all projects by weighting benefit – cost ratios by a welfare index. Following Eckstein, projects can then be selected by maximizing the sum of scores subject to a budget constraint. This assists the programme administrator by providing him with a generally applicable, operational project-selection system which is flexible enough to take into account significant variations in project quality, in his preferences between efficiency and equity and in the trade-offs he is willing to make between various categories of need.

---

14 Throughout this paper we have considered a single-choice situation with a known universe of projects and a prior allocation of funds to be spent on some set of these projects. We have not dealt with questions relating to handling of project inventories, project development over time or timing of total fund allocations. These and related questions will be discussed in a forthcoming paper.

References

1. Arthur Maass, "Benefit–Cost Analysis: Its Relevance to Public Investment," *Quarterly Journal of Economics*, Vol. LXXX, No. 2, May 1966, pp. 205–26.
2. Stephan A. Marglin, *Public Investment Criteria* (M.I.T., 1967).
3. Koichi Mera, "Tradeoff Between Aggregate Efficiency and Inter-regional Equity: A Static Analysis," *The Quarterly Journal of Economics*, November 1967, pp. 658–74.
4. A. M. Freeman III, "Income Distribution and Public Investment," *American Economic Review*, Vol. LVII, No. 8, June 1967, pp. 495–508.
5. Richard Musgrave, *The Theory of Public Finance* (McGraw-Hill, 1959).
6. Otto Eckstein, *Water Resource Development, The Economics of Project Evaluation* (Harvard, 1958), especially pp. 70–80.
7. Martin C. McGuire and Harvey A. Garn, "Problems in the Cooperative Allocation of Public Expenditures," *Quarterly Journal of Economics*, Vol. LXXXIII, February 1969, pp. 44–59.

21

**Robinson G. Hollister and John L. Palmer:
The Implicit Tax of Inflation and
Unemployment: Some Policy Implications**

As has been noted repeatedly, the public discussion of inflation and the policy issues related to it have been pervaded by the general presumption that the poor are hurt by inflation. At the very least, our evidence[1] makes it clear that this has been a presumption and not a proven fact; we feel the evidence indicates that the presumption should be that the poor are *not* hurt by inflation.

One might conjecture that the idea that the poor are hurt by inflation has gained currency because of a tendency to generalize from piecemeal considerations and isolated cases. If the money incomes of the poor are fixed, then price rises will cause a deterioration in their economic well-being. But one must go the next step and consider whether the same process that generates the rise in prices is not likely to generate rises in the income of the poor that are as great or greater than the rises in prices. Similarly, although some poor families are living on incomes from fixed value assets or pensions, which are vulnerable to inflation, it should not be concluded that the majority of the poor are in this circumstance.

Both of these considerations are particularly important when the use of

---

1 See Hollister and Palmer, "The Impact of Inflation on the Poor," in this volume.

policy instruments with a broad impact is being considered, e.g., fiscal and monetary policy. With respect to the first consideration, it might be concluded that the policy instrument (reduced aggregate demand or tighter money) might be adequate to stop rising prices, but is it not likely to also generate processes which will reduce the incomes of the poor, perhaps by more than the reduction in price rises? Regarding the second consideration, if there are special situations of inequity within a subgroup of the population, then one should try not to use broad policies to deal with those relatively isolated cases. More particularistic policies can usually be found to deal with particular circumstances. For example, as we suggested above, if it should happen to be a subgroup of the poor receiving a particular type of transfer payment whose incomes are deteriorated by inflation, then it makes little sense to use fiscal and monetary policy in order to stop inflation for their benefit alone (this example may seem ludicrous, but we suggest that a careful examination of much of the arguments about anti-inflationary policies reduce to this sort of reasoning). It seems eminently sensible instead to make a policy decision to raise automatically their transfer payments to keep pace with the price rises.

For these reasons, it is important when assessing the impact of economic phenomena like inflation to try to be comprehensive, to try to weigh all the likely losses and all the probable gains in the balance. This kind of balance in assessment is necessary not only in the sense of determining the impact of inflation but also in estimating the losses and gains from anti-inflationary policies. It is not enough to inquire whether the inflationary processes create some inequities; one must *also* ask whether the cures proposed do not create even greater inequities.

We want to be clear that the tenor of our arguments should not be taken to be one of advocating a purposeful policy of generating strong inflation. We merely wish to attempt to correct what has struck us as an extraordinary imbalance in the public and academic discussion of these issues. The presumption that inflation necessarily hurts the poor simply is not supported by evidence in the recent United States experience. The possibility that the economic well-being of the poor improves as a result of the processes generally associated with inflation should at least be seriously entertained by those concerned with the policy-making process. If, given the imperfect policy instruments at hand and the structure of the economy, we must err in keeping the economy in perfect balance, should we not at least *seriously consider* whether it is better to err on the side of inflation?

Policy Considerations

For some time it has been common to talk about inflation as a tax. Given people's money income, a rise in prices reduces their real income in a fashion quite similar to the reduction in real disposable income which occurs when there is an increase in taxes; this is the sense of the "expenditure effects" discussed in

"The Impact of Inflation on the Poor." Our study indicates that the "tax of inflation" has fallen relatively less heavily on the poor. The incidence of the tax of inflation is not clear and we have not tried to assess its impact on other population groups.

If we are going to talk about the tax of inflation, it might be useful also to talk about the "tax" imposed by unemployment. If, through government policy, we can adjust aggregate demand so as to foster more or less inflation and more or less unemployment, then it seems reasonable to think of unemployment as a cost of government policy, a "tax" imposed through unemployment. We might ask therefore, On whom does the tax of unemployment fall? It falls very heavily on the poor. Surely if middle or upper income people were asked if *they* themselves were willing to bear the tax of unemployment in order to remove the tax of inflation, they would answer resoundingly no! It is very clear that the tax of unemployment is a very inequitable tax; it is not clear that the tax of inflation falls extraordinarily heavily on *any* population group; its impact may be spread rather broadly across the population.

Many people have talked about the necessity of having a "slight rise in unemployment" or even a "slight recession" in order to halt the current inflation. They sometimes point to "slight recessions" in the past which have "shaken out" the inflationary factors in the economic structure. We would like to point out that there is a tendency to define a recession solely in terms of what happens to the rate of growth of output. In these terms the recession of 1957–58 looks slight and short-lived – the rate of growth of output returned to a normal level in the next year. But a recession could also be defined in terms of the unemployment rate, and on those grounds the 1957–58 recession was substantial and lasted nearly eight years – unemployment rates did not return to their 1957 levels until late in 1965.

In the past few years we have seen increasing emphasis put upon public and private training and hiring programs for the poor. These are important programs, but their effectiveness is highly dependent on the existence of tight labor markets, which provide the incentives to employers to undertake extraordinary efforts on behalf of the poor. We have certainly accumulated enough information to indicate that in the past employers have had little experience in employing the hard-core poor; the stories about the special problems of these types of employees and the special efforts employers have had to make to deal with these problems are adequate evidence that employers have not in the past learned on their own how to train marginal workers.

It seems evident that if every time some inflationary pressure appears, a rise in unemployment is going to be generated to halt it, employers are not going to feel that the pains of training and learning to deal with marginal workers are worthwhile. Thus, even a slight rise in unemployment is likely to seriously threaten these manpower training programs, which have been so painfully launched. Just to get an idea of how important a "slight" rise in unemployment is, if we take the estimates from our regressions (which are commensurate with the Mooney and Metcalf results), a "slight" rise of 1 percent in the unemployment rate is likely to put one and a half million people into poverty who would not otherwise have been there. The National Alliance of Businessmen's JOBS program for hiring the hard-core poor has a three-year goal of 500,000 jobs. Thus, if for every job three persons are lifted out of poverty, it would seem that a 1 percent rise in unemployment would wipe out the entire gains of the three-year JOBS program.

We would like to suggest that a *long-term* commitment to tight labor markets, even in the face of some inflation, may be a key to the development by private-sector employers of effective programs to cope with training and employment problems of the hard-core poor. Although there is no hard evidence yet, there are some reasons to hope – and certainly sufficient grounds to explore the possibilities – that with a clear national commitment to a long-term policy of tight markets, even the hard-core poor can be effectively absorbed into the private sector labor force without excessively high training costs or lower productivity. In the past we have only tightened labor markets down to near the 3 percent level for short periods of time. It is not surprising therefore that employers do not have much experience in training marginal workers; they have had little incentive to learn how to do so. By the same token, it is not surprising that they find that the hard-core poor have only slight and highly variable job experience and are therefore more difficult to deal with. With continued tight labor markets we should expect improved performance on both sides; the employer will have improved his training skills and the workers will have overcome that initial difficult experience of adjustment to regular employment.

Furthermore, the European experience in the early 1960s of absorbing immigrant workers into the employed labor force without greatly lowered productivity is promising. The evidence on this experience is very sketchy, but it does suggest that large numbers of difficult-to-train workers can be rapidly converted into effective workers. In the early 1960s Germany was recruiting over 100,000 foreign workers annually. These workers were largely unskilled and had major language problems, and yet they seem to have been absorbed rather rapidly with relatively short periods of training.[2] Labor productivity in Germany continued to grow.[3] Switzerland has absorbed foreign workers to such an extent that they make up nearly one-third of her labor force. It is hard to believe that the problems of absorbing unskilled workers speaking a different language are less difficult than those of dealing with the hard-core poor. The United States equivalent of the German absorption of 100,000 marginal workers a year would be roughly 300,000 jobs per year, about twice the annual rate set as a goal of the JOBS program. We repeat, however, that if every time markets began to really tighten and prices rise the government uses fiscal and monetary policy to cause labor markets to slacken, then employers will take slack markets as the norm

---

2 See C. P. Kindleberger, *Europe's Postwar Growth: The Role of Labor Supply*, Center for International Affairs Series, 1967, pp. 186–91.

3 Kindleberger, *ibid.*, Figure II–I, p. 29.

and will not feel it worthwhile to invest their time and money in learning to make effective workers out of those on the margins of the labor force.

Much of the public policy discussion centers on arguments about the character of the relationship between the level of unemployment and rises in the price level (one form or another of the Phillips curve). We have a considerable amount of experience with the relationship between price level rises and unemployment rates above 4 percent, but we have very little experience with the relationship at levels well below 4 percent. Yet many of these who engage in the public policy arguments talk as if they *knew* what the relationship at levels of 3 percent and below are. We have suggested some reasons why one might expect that with continued unemployment at 3 percent or below more effective absorption of marginal workers would begin to occur. If this does occur, then over the longer term lower levels of unemployment can be maintained without productivity losses and, therefore, one would expect, with less inflationary pressure; if marginal workers can become effective workers inflationary pressures are reduced.

It is hard to believe that as a nation we cannot afford to explore the relationship between lower levels of unemployment and changes in price levels over a longer period of time rather than to continue to make policy on the basis of unsubstantiated conjectures – on either side – about the nature of the relationship. We have spent a great deal of time in the last two decades exploring the relationship between high levels of unemployment and price level changes, and we have imposed a very heavy cost upon the poor in order to carry out that exploration. Can we really show clearly that we cannot afford the cost (which has never been very well specified) of finding out about how the relationship between unemployment and the price level works at low levels of unemployment? And whatever the costs, is it not legitimate to ask groups other than the poor to bear the costs for a while so that we can have sounder grounds for making these important social and economic decisions? Should we not consider whether, if higher unemployment is regarded as absolutely necessary, some means might be found to redistribute the burdens of such a policy?[4]

In closing, it is our hope that we have made the facts sufficiently clear in this paper so that if national policy makers decide that they will not explore further, but will allow unemployment to rise in hopes of stopping inflation, they will at least no longer be able to claim that they are trying to stop inflation in order to protect the poor. If any such policy is made, let it be done with the explicit recognition that, far from helping the poor, it imposes on them a very special and heavy burden.

---

4 For example, if a negative income tax were in existence, rising unemployment would require higher transfer payments and perhaps with the costs thus made more explicit the policy would be examined more carefully.

5

Conclusion

The concluding part is concerned with a long-run, broad view of the likely results of changes in the public grants economy, as described in Michael Taussig's paper. From the results of a government-financed income maintenance experiment – the Graduated Work Incentives Experiment (GWIE), often termed the New Jersey Experiment – designed to assess the effects of guarantee levels and implicit tax rates on "other income" accruing to a family, the costs of a national income maintenance program can be estimated. Of primary interest is the effect the income maintenance programs are likely to have on the work behavior of the recipients. Taussig marshals experience gained from existing programs for use in the task of estimating such effects.

He concludes that "the long view effects of these [Social Security, retirement and AFDC] programs on our society have proved to be pervasive and profound. At the same time, we now see clearly in retrospect the failure of Congress and academic social scientists in the thirties to anticipate and prepare adequately for the subsequent social problems. . . . [Turning to the proposed income maintenance reforms] and taking a pessimistic view ... I shall pay particular attention to the potential disintegrative effects of expanded income maintenance on our society. . . . The proposed negative income tax alternative to AFDC is explicitly a program directed at black families. . . . "The momentum toward further racial disintegration is already manifestly powerful today, perhaps even irresistible, even in the absence of a comprehensive income maintenance program."

Taussig notes that while he favors a negative income tax, he still feels that "the crux of the problem is to alter fundamental factors in our society that generate the present gross inequalities in the distributions of income and wealth."

In the final comments, the editors point out some of the areas not covered by the present volume, such as the whole-life implications of the distribution of income, the dynamics of the distribution of property in society, the role of interest in redistribution, a greater exploration of redistribution in regard to various categories of people, the role of the private grants economy, and the relationship between the grants economy and the integrative structure of society.

22

Michael K. Taussig: Long-Run
Consequences of Income Maintenance
Reform

After some thirty years of neglect by academic economists, the subject of income maintenance reform became fashionable once again in the middle of the 1960s as an important part of the revival of interest in social welfare policies in general. Today economists of all political persuasions appear to give overwhelming support to a negative income tax or to some similar program which would provide substantially improved cash benefits to all the poor. The Nixon administration, while content in its first years in office to tread water on most domestic issues, uncharacteristically advanced the truly revolutionary Family Assistance Plan (FAP), a limited, modified version of a comprehensive negative income tax program. At this juncture in history the desirability of *some* reform of the existing income maintenance structure in the United States is a surprisingly uncontroversial issue, and only the very tough details involved in devising a work program remain subjects of widespread controversy.

Much of this current controversy centers on the alleged merits and shortcomings of alternative new transfer approaches to the problems of poverty — the negative income tax, children's allowances, the FAP, and others. I shall assume in this essay, however, that all of the relevant alternatives today have enough essential details in common that they can be usefully discussed generically. The problem on which I wish to focus here is how government decision-makers can best predict and anticipate the long-run consequences of significant income maintenance reform. Very little thought has been devoted to this problem. Instead, the FAP or some other similar scheme is usually proposed and defended as an emergency feasible solution of the welfare "crisis" in the United States. Perhaps because the subject is so new to academic economists, and also perhaps because of the generally ahistorical approach of the applied social sciences, the longer run implications of reform have been slighted.

I would expect little dissent from the general proposition that the long-run consequences of income maintenance reform should be of controlling importance. What is extremely difficult, however, is to move beyond this almost empty generalization to specific long-range predictions. This essay is an attempt to provide a framework for beginning to think seriously about this problem by considering alternative bodies of more or less relevant evidence. The paper is in

Presented at the Symposium on the Grants Economy held between the Association for the Study of the Grants Economy, The Public Choice Society, and the American Economics Association in December, 1969, in New York, New York. All rights reserved. Used by permission of the author. Mr. Taussig is from Rutgers University.

three parts. The first considers the usefulness of the evidence to be provided by current income maintenance experiments and, more generally, by any feasible experiments in the future. The second takes up the natural, historical evidence provided by this country's experience with the income maintenance programs that have been in operation since the Social Security Act of 1935. (For lack of space and knowledge, I am compelled to omit consideration of still a third body of relevant evidence — experience with income maintenance programs in foreign countries.) The final section summarizes important points and attempts to draw some tentative conclusions.

The Appropriate Role of Income Maintenance Experiments

Government-financed income maintenance experiments are currently attempting to obtain evidence relevant to the design of new federal income maintenance programs. At the present time, one such experiment — the New Jersey Negative Income Tax Experiment — is in full operation in cities in New Jersey and Pennsylvania.[1] A rural counterpart to the urban experiment in New Jersey has also begun operations, and other, similar projects are under way in at least the planning stage. These experiments are pioneering efforts in social science research, and because of their immediate policy relevance, the results are awaited as eagerly by concerned government officials as by academic social scientists.

The New Jersey and other income maintenance experiments were devised by the Office of Economic Opportunity as a response to the many proposals in the 1960s for drastic new alternatives to the old public assistance approach to income maintenance. Both the advocates of these new proposals and their adversaries were soon frustrated by the apparent insufficiency of natural evidence on the likely effects of the implementation of any given scheme. The specific issue which involved the greatest immediate budgetary unknown for any of the alternative proposals was the possible impact of expanded income maintenance on the work effort of the low-income population. Economic theory suggests at best the kinds of evidence relevant to this issue, but without empirical evidence, very little progress could be made in narrowing the huge gap between estimates of the budgetary cost of various income maintenance alternatives.

The Office of Economic Opportunity rejected — perhaps too quickly — the option of subjecting available cross-sectional data to more intensive study, and chose instead to supply the required empirical information by means of elaborate and expensive experiments. Two experimental parameters were

---

1 For a full description of this experiment, see H. W. Watts, "Graduated Work Incentives: An Experiment in Negative Taxation," *American Economic Review, Papers and Proceedings* 59, no. 2 (May 1969): 463–72.

selected as the key structural features crucial to the work response of any income maintenance program. The first is the guarantee level, or the highest benefit payable to families with no other income. The second is the implicit tax rate that reduces the size of the guarantee or maximum benefit by some percentage of each dollar of other income accruing to a family. A probability sample of low-income families in four northeastern urban areas was selected to participate in the experiment, and most of these families were randomly assigned to negative income tax plans combining one of several guarantee levels (standardized for family size) and one of several tax rates. Other families in the experiment were randomly assigned to a control group, in effect being given a tax plan with a zero guarantee and a zero tax rate. The experimental design provided sufficient independent variation between the guarantee level and the tax rate to allow estimation of the independent effect of each parameter on the work effort of families in the experiment over a three-year period. Ideally, the results of the experiment will enable government planners to estimate the cost of a national income maintenance program covering a wide range of combinations of guarantee levels and tax rates, including combinations not actually tested and observed in the course of the experiment.

Preliminary results from the New Jersey experiment indicate, surprisingly, *no* work disincentive effects.[2] These results are limited to less than half of the full sample and extend over a time period of only about one of the three years of the experiment, but they are nevertheless apparently very strong findings. In addition to these preliminary results, the experiment has yielded as a byproduct a wealth of practical experience bearing on both substantive and administrative problems of negative income taxation. Before the actual experimental effort could go into the field, the many researchers on the project first had to devise workable solutions to such problems as the definition of income, the definition of the family unit, the income accounting period, the construction of a responsive payments mechanism, and many others.

Thus far, then, the New Jersey experiment has proved its value as a pilot project and has yielded some tantalizing preliminary experimental results. What can be said about the usefulness of the potential final experimental findings in shaping decisions about the future of government welfare programs? A recurring criticism of the New Jersey experiment has been that its planned three-year duration is too short a time for an experiment, and that the most the results can be expected to show is the short-run or transitory labor supply response to a negative income tax, and not the long-run or permanent effects.[3] An appraisal of

---

2 Office of Economic Opportunity, "Preliminary Results of the New Jersey Graduated Work Incentive Experiment" (Washington, D.C.: U.S. Government Printing Office, February 1970), and H. W. Watts, "Adjusted and Extended Preliminary Results from the Urban Graduated Work Incentive Experiment," discussion paper (Madison, Wis.: Institute for Research on Poverty, University of Wisconsin, June 1970).

3 Actually, distinguishing cycle from trend on the *demand* side may be the real difficulty in analysis, depending on the state of aggregate demand over the three-year period.

this criticism is especially pertinent to the subject of this essay. First, however, an important distinction between two possible interpretations of the "long run" is necessary. The most common interpretation is that the long run is a period of time long enough for all households to adjust fully to the quasi-permanent change in their work-leisure-income opportunities brought about by the introduction of a national negative income tax. This traditional interpretation takes tastes as given, but assumes that the process of full substitution of work and leisure takes an unspecified "long" period of time. A second possible interpretation of the long run is a period of time long enough for all *preferences* to adjust to any change in the household or socioeconomic environment that may result from the prior transformation of opportunities. Economic theorists have traditionally assumed the independence of opportunities and preferences in their analysis of rational decision-making, but such an assumption has always been a matter of faith, justified principally by the use of a partial equilibrium and static framework. But it is conceivable that enactment of a national negative income tax might gradually transform traditional, prevailing attitudes toward work and leisure. Conlisk has formally demonstrated this point by constructing a simple and plausible dynamic model which shows that the static result of a net work-disincentive effect of a negative income tax may not hold if preferences are allowed to vary over time as a function of income maintenance benefits.[4]

If the only problem of short-run–long-run distinctions in the New Jersey experiment involved perceptions of the degree of permanence of the change in opportunities engineered by the experimental design, then some confidence could be expressed in the ability of the researchers on the experiment to estimate the "true" time-paths of work-leisure response. If, instead, the problem of distinguishing the long run involves consideration of the transformation of preference patterns through dynamic effects of expanded income maintenance either directly on affected families or indirectly through induced changes in the socioeconomic environment, then clearly such effects lie beyond any conceivable experimental horizons. Indeed, the full work-behavior response may not become fully apparent until a whole new generation free of ingrained work-leisure attitudes grows up in a radically altered socioeconomic climate.[5]

---

4 J. Conlisk, "Simple Dynamic Effects in Work-Leisure Choice: A Skeptical Comment on the Static Theory," *The Journal of Human Resources* 3, no. 3 (Summer 1968): 324–26.

5 This same point applies to the interpretation of the growing number of cross-sectional findings that have become available since the inception of the New Jersey experiment. All of these studies indicate varying amounts of net work disincentive effects in response to the implementation of a negative income tax type of program. Presumably such effects are the long-run equilibrium adjustments for a set of preferences existing at some point in time. See, for example, C. Green and A. Tella, "Effect of Nonemployment Income and Wage Rates in the Work Incentives of the Poor," *Review of Economics and Statistics* 54, no. 4 (November 1969): 399–408; R. E. Hall, "Wages, Income and Hours of Work in the U.S. Labor Force," Working Paper no. 62, Department of Economics, Massachusetts Institute of Technology, August 1970; and E. D. Kalachek and F. Q. Raines, "Labor Supply of Low Income Workers," The President's Commission on Income Maintenance Programs, *Technical Studies* (Washington, D.C.: U.S. Government Printing Office, 1970), pp. 159–85.

In addition, the New Jersey Experiment and probably all other similar experiments will be designed primarily to investigate work-behavior response. Data on other effects of expanded income maintenance, including possible impact on family size and structure, consumption patterns, and investment in education and training, will be obtained only incidentally to the main experimental objective. No conceivable experiment can fully probe into the family size and structure response, moreover, because of the time span involved — thirty years or so instead of three — and because some aspects of the problem cannot satisfactorily be simulated by the drawing of a sample of feasible magnitude. As I shall indicate in the following section, these non-work-behavior aspects of income maintenance reform which lie beyond the scope of experimental investigation appear to be of the utmost importance in assessing the long-run significance of existing welfare programs in this country. Thus, my view is that the value of income maintenance experiments, beyond their usefulness as demonstration or pilot projects, is largely as an aid in estimation of the immediate budget impact of the introduction of some given national income maintenance reform program. The significant contribution of the experiments in this important role should not be confused, however, with the very limited help they provide in predicting the longer run consequences of new income maintenance legislation.

United States Experience with Income Maintenance Programs

The natural evidence thrown up by historical experience is in some respects clearly inferior to the evidence that can be obtained from a well-designed income maintenance experiment. In attempting to predict the likely work effort response to a new negative income tax, for example, the limited, poor-quality time-series data available allow us only to construct proxy variables for guarantee levels and tax rates, but these proxies in general vary so closely over time with each other and with other variables likely to affect labor supply that they are of little use for predictive purposes. On the other hand, I shall argue that only historical evidence garnered from lengthy experience with domestic or foreign income maintenance program is relative to the crucial long-run issues involved in welfare reform. Since the United States has now had more than thirty years of experience with the various programs enacted in the Social Security Act of 1935, a critical reexamination of some aspects of this experience may now be fruitful.

The two general classes of programs initiated in 1935 are the social insurances and the public assistances, or "welfare" programs. The history of each suggests important lessons applicable to decisions concerning present welfare reforms. Consider first the social insurances, which include both the state unemployment insurance programs and the massive federal government Old Age, Survivors, Disability, and Hospital Insurance (OASDHI) programs. Of all these, the Old Age, or retirement, program dominates in budgetary magnitude and in the public consciousness. In fiscal year 1969 retirement and survivors benefits for some 22 million aged beneficiaries amounted to almost $25 billion.[6] Debate about the merits of the retirement program is almost nonexistent today; Congress argues only about the precise amount and distribution of the frequent increases in retirement benefits. In a country in which social welfare policies are generally sadly deficient, the history of the Social Security retirement program appears to be an exceptional income maintenance success story.

The first question to be asked of the history of this program, then, is an explanation of the extraordinarily generous financing it has received. The overly simple answer is to point to the obvious *quid pro quo* elements built into the program. The Social Security Administration has successfully sold the concept of an "insurance" program to the public, with the implication that a Social Security tax liability today for a young worker is just a payment for his guaranteed insurance benefit at retirement. Such an explanation is only partially satisfactory, however, for it leaves unanswered the political acceptability of the payment of full benefits to retired workers soon after the inception of the retirement program, despite the fact that these first retirees had contributed virtually nothing to the Social Security trust funds. As the Social Security system has matured, the discrepancy between the value of benefits and contributions has narrowed, but it still persists today. Beyond this anomaly is the point that much popular support for the retirement program does not appear to depend on the insurance rationalization. Thus, a full answer to the financial success of the retirement program requires a deeper analysis of the role the program plays in our society.

The key to understanding the development of Social Security in the United States lies, I believe, in observing that the aged, retired population is well along in the process of becoming a separate society with only tenuous links to the larger society. This essay is not the place to attempt a full documentation of this point. Some aspects of the increasing isolation of the aged in our society are easily verifiable, as, for example, the very low and still declining labor force activity of the population aged sixty-five and over and the continuing trend toward splitting off grandparents from the primary family unit. Other less tangible aspects of the alienation of the aged are not readily susceptible to the usual hypothesis testing methodology of the social sciences. Given this interpretation of the evolving status of the aged, the Social Security retirement program appears to serve as the mechanism for financing the growing separation of the aged and the larger societies, and the political success of the program can be attributed to the willingness by people in both age groups to allow this split to occur. In this interpretation, the high level of Social Security taxes is politically acceptable to the young *not* because these taxes are regarded as payments for their *own* annuities sometime in the future, but instead because

---

6 *Economic Report of the President, 1969* (Washington, D.C.: U.S. Government Printing Office, 1969), p. 164.

they are recognized as payments in lieu of direct personal support today for aged parents.[7] The crucial difference between the two means of supporting the aged is, of course, that Social Security provides cash incomes which enable both age groups to maintain separate domiciles, whereas previously in our history the aged were commonly forced to depend on the largely in kind income provided by children or other relatives as part of a larger household unit.

The widespread desire for independent households by both young and old probably long predated the 1935 Social Security Act. Society's ability to accommodate these desires simply lagged, the typical case for all varieties of private and public goods and services that require significant amounts of scarce resources. The lesson that can be drawn from this experience has, then, both a positive and a normative side. The positive implication is that family structure may be a very malleable social variable, in the sense of being highly elastic in the long run to changes in financial opportunities resulting from government income maintenance intervention. The normative implication is that society must anticipate as best it can the consequences of any proposed welfare innovation on family structure and attempt to make a collective judgment about the desirability of the probable consequences. The status of the aged in our society has evolved since 1935 as the result of individual decisions made in a situation of apparently expanded financial opportunities. The economist's visceral reaction is to accept the sum of these millions of individual decisions as self-evidently socially desirable. But it is doubtful that most people today, even most economists, are comfortable with the status of the aged in our society. The segregation of the aged, as under present social arrangements, diminishes the value of life by distorting the natural progression of youth, maturation, and death that exists in a truly integrated society.

This point has even greater force if the assumption of expanded financial opportunities for the aged is seriously questioned. Whereas the Social Security retirement program has certainly improved the nonwork alternatives of the aged, it may also have had some effect in encouraging the growth of institutions and attitudes that hamper the labor force activities of older workers. Such practices as compulsory retirement rules treat all persons above some arbitrary age as an undistinguishable mass, thus limiting the opportunities of the most vigorous oldster according to the present average capabilities of his cohort. To the extent that Social Security has encouraged such practices, it has limited opportunities as well as expanded them.

Other useful lessons can be derived from our experience with Social Security. The most relevant one is perhaps the potential long-run labor force impact of an income maintenance program on a segment of the population which has weak labor force attachments. The explanation of the very sharp decline of the labor

---

7 For a fuller exposition of this view, see J. A. Pechman, H. J. Aaron, and M. K. Taussig, *Social Security: Perspectives for Reform* (Washington, D.C.: The Brookings Institution, 1968), ch. 4.

force participation of the aged in the last thirty years involves many disparate factors that cannot be fully separated because of the limitations of available evidence. One part of the explanation is simply that aged workers with weak desires to continue unattractive work were able to retire once Social Security benefits were made available to them. The earnings test provisions of the Social Security law possibly added to the total work disincentive impact. These pure supply effects have been augmented by pressures on the demand side from employers who have reasons, good and bad, to presume that the productivity of aged workers is low relative to that of substitute factors of production available at equal cost. Such factors as seniority rules, the relative educational and training disadvantages of older workers, the increased availability of relatively inexpensive female labor, and changes in the occupational structure of the labor force are all forces that may lie behind the demand side of the picture. Whatever the details of the full explanation, the steady secular decline in the labor force participation of the aged has resulted in a much larger social cost of the retirement program than could have been anticipated in the 1930s under much different labor force circumstances.

Consider next the history of public assistance programs in this country since 1935, with special attention to the controversial Aid to Families with Dependent Children (AFDC) program. The common evaluation today of ADFC is that it has been a dismal failure, in contrast to the great success of the social insurances. My own view is that the history of AFDC is remarkably similar in important respects to that of OASDHI, and that both programs involve ambiguous elements of success and failure. The one essential difference between AFDC and the Social Security retirement program is, of course, that the latter program has been budgeted relatively generously, whereas AFDC has been financially starved in all but a very few states and cities.

The most important consequence of AFDC, entirely unanticipated in 1935, has been to finance the creation of another, virtually separate society within the larger society. To characterize this new subsociety succinctly at the cost of important qualifications, it consists of urban black families and family fragments without working heads. To accept this consensus evaluation of the historical AFDC, it is not necessary to rely on the crudest versions of the theory of the effects of the program on family mobility and family disintegration. The existence of AFDC has never been shown rigorously to have affected individual decisions to migrate to particular northern cities, but even without such proof, it seems intuitively plausible that the persisting concentration of migrant southern rural black families in specific locations in the urban North depends at least indirectly on the availability of last-ditch AFDC support. Similarly, the well-documented fragmentation of urban black families can probably be attributed in part to the long-run adjustment of family living arrangements to the change in financial opportunities caused by AFDC, although again the process may have been much more indirect and subtle than the crudest theories suggest. If I am wrong in this assessment of the situation, most other economists today are also wrong, and much of the support for welfare reform is based on incorrect premises.[8]

For the purposes of this essay, let me stress some important similarities in the histories of AFDC and the Social Security retirement program. Over the long run, both programs have apparently financed a dramatic revolution in American family structure and the concomitant isolation of new, virtually separate subsocieties. Aged families on Social Security retirement and black, female-headed families on AFDC are alike in being largely out of the labor market and consequently isolated from the shared experiences of the larger society around them. Too much attention to the relatively generous benefits payable under Social Security retirement and to some perverse administrative aspects of AFDC obscures this essential similar element in the two programs. The role of Social Security and AFDC in these developments should not be assigned a primary causal role; the labor market problems of the aged and of nonwhites and preexisting weaknesses in the traditional family structure are surely the more fundamental causal factors. But the role of the government income maintenance programs was probably not an insignificant, independent factor, and only through such programs does the government have a convenient vehicle for intervention in developments that shape the socioeconomic environment.

The history of AFDC also teaches some invaluable lessons about facets of the administration of income maintenance programs. The sad experience of AFDC points clearly to the definition of the family unit and the subsequent enforcement of a given definition as crucial to the success of a program in achieving its welfare goals. The very complex problems of the definitions of income and wealth are relatively simple in contrast. The dilemma that AFDC has revealed is the choice between the old welfare practice of a rigid definition of the family unit that assigns ultimate financial responsibilities to a male head and the very loose definitions incorporated in some of the recent negative income tax proposals. The deficiencies of the old AFDC rules are clear enough today, but alternative definitions of the family unit present other problems of unknown magnitude. Some current negative income tax proposals, for example, would have built-in incentives for legal separations for tax purposes with de facto sharing of earned incomes and negative income tax benefits by family fragments. Beyond the family unit problem, the history of AFDC suggests strongly that making benefits available only when tied to the receipt of social work services and giving administrative responsibilities for any income maintenance program to state and local governments are fundamental mistakes. The Nixon administration's Family Assistance Plan legislation, as it stands at the time this paper is written, ignores both of these hard-earned lessons of AFDC history.

---

8 See, for example, J. Tobin, "On Improving the Economic Status of the Negro," *Daedalus*, Fall 1965, p. 890. As a reading of this article and other sources will show, support for welfare reform depends not just on the allocational or incentive effects mentioned in the text, but also on considerations of horizontal equity and humanitarian concern with the dismally low level of the average benefit under present AFDC programs.

Is it likely that well-designed income maintenance experiments prior to 1935 could have predicted some of the consequences of the Social Security retirement and AFDC programs over the last three and a half decades? I grant immediately that it is difficult even to speculate about the details of the appropriate experiments for this purpose in the depressed economy of the thirties. Such speculation leads me, nonetheless, to the conclusion that even ideally planned and executed experiments of reasonable duration would have yielded only limited results. Good experiments would probably have given the government a long head start in solving administrative problems and avoiding some mistakes and might also have indicated potentially large work-disincentive effects for both programs, especially in the face of the weak demand for labor at the time. (Analysis of suitable bodies of cross-sectional data would probably have been more useful, however, for predicting the long-run labor reply response to the new programs.) It seems fair to conclude, then, that even the best experiments would not have helped social scientists to predict the vast changes in social structure with respect to the state of the aged and of urban blacks that we all now see clearly today — with the invaluable advantage of hindsight — as the crucial products of the 1935 legislation.

Conclusions

To summarize some previous points briefly, we can now see clearly in retrospect the failure of Congress and of academic social scientists to anticipate the full consequences of the new social welfare programs enacted in 1935. The main defect of the Social Security retirement program was the failure to go beyond the provision of cash benefits for retired workers by establishing complementary programs that would help to develop new, meaningful roles for the aged in an industrialized and urbanized society. Programs that would enable the aged to make fuller use of their potential capabilities both within and beyond the market system can and should be developed at the present time, but much inertia has developed since 1935, and, at best, too many years have already been wasted, with the best opportunities already foregone. Similarly, the deficiencies of AFDC can be traced to short-sighted, paternalistic policies which failed to anticipate the destructive long-run consequences of providing cash benefits for the poor only under conditions which maximized perverse labor market and family structure incentives. With the benefit of hindsight, we now recognize that in addition to the Social Security retirement and AFDC programs, Congress should in 1935 have enacted simultaneously complementary programs to strengthen the labor market incentives of the aged and of blacks and other racial minorities.

What can we now anticipate about the long-run consequences of an adequately funded negative income tax-type reform of the present income maintenance structure? The first section of this essay argued that the results of even the best designed income maintenance experiments, supplemented by analysis of the natural evidence available in cross-sectional data, will not be sufficient to answer this question. In addition, even a most detailed study of the past history of income maintenance programs in the United States and abroad should not be expected to yield reliable conclusions about the quite different problems that confront us at the present time; history in its perversity does not repeat itself in sufficient regularity. In all humility, we can do more than to indulge ourselves in more or less intelligent speculation on this problem, perhaps consciously taking the pessimistic view appropriate to government officials accustomed to searching for policies for which the main criterion of success is the avoidance of outright disaster.

The historical experience cited in this paper does suggest, at a minimum, that income maintenance reform should not be viewed as a substitute for badly needed programs to upgrade the labor market opportunities available to the poor, and especially to poor blacks and other racial minority groups. Such programs may require unprecedented government intervention in the operation of private labor markets if our society is to succeed in counteracting the forces that generate the present gross inequalities in the distribution of wealth. The opposite point of view has been cogently argued by Milton Friedman in his pioneering advocacy of a negative income tax.[9] Friedman strongly implies that a negative income tax with adequate benefits would free the government of all other responsibilities for the poor. In his view of the world, the whole maze of present government programs that are now largely justified as indirect subsidies for particular classes of low-income families and individuals would become superfluous once a negative income tax went into effect. My interpretation of the history of the income maintenance in programs enacted in 1935 leads me to just the opposite conclusion: income maintenance reform should be the occasion of concurrent expansion of government efforts in complementary social welfare programs.

The danger I foresee in using the enactment of the FAP or of any alternative income maintenance reform as an excuse for inaction on our fundamental social problems is that it may push us in the direction of a new, profoundly objectionable socioeconomic status quo. Some characteristic features of the new society of the future may include an average unemployment rate much higher than in the recent past (a "natural" unemployment rate?) accepted as the price of avoiding inflationary pressures; a comprehensive income maintenance program providing cash benefits for all those who cannot find work in such loose labor markets; and perhaps even a volunteer army virtually guaranteed recruits at modest monetary incentives from the ranks of active young men unable to find jobs and unwilling to accept idleness cum negative income tax benefits. Perhaps it is needless to add that such a society would be even less well integrated along social class and racial lines than our present society. Unfortunately, there are indications that we are well along in the process of drifting toward such a society, with all its attendant waste of human and natural resources.

---

9 M. Friedman, *Capitalism and Freedom* (Phoenix Books, 1962), pp. 190–95.

23   Kenneth E. Boulding and Martin Pfaff:
Future Directions

The papers of this volume came pretty close to describing the "state of the art" in the two major fields — explicit public grants and implicit public grants. It is important perhaps to indicate here what they do *not* cover. These are the studies that are left to the future.

There is little discussion anywhere in the literature of the whole-life implications of the distribution of income. Suppose, for instance, that we had a society in which everybody was poor when they were young and rich when they were old, so that everybody's income increased with age. The distribution of income, as we usually think of it, would appear as extremely unequal, whether measured either by simple measures, such as the Gini coefficient, or the Beta-distribution. The whole-life distribution of income, however, might be exactly equal, with everybody getting the same total income over his whole life. Whole-life incomes, of course, can only really be measured by longitudinal studies. These are seldom done as nobody would ever get promoted for a study that would not come to fruition for fifty years. Further cross-sectional studies, however, about the age distribution of income would at least throw some light on possible whole-life patterns, and these very much need to be done. The problem is further complicated by dynamic disequilibria in age distribution by age cohort, in which we might find, for instance, that people born in 1910 have a much lower whole-life income and benefit less from redistributions than people born, say, in 1940 or 1950. The problem of justice in distribution becomes much more difficult when we look at these whole-life patterns. Under conditions of economic growth, for instance, the children and young people of today are likely to have a much higher whole-life income than parents or grandparents, and it is at least not an absurd question to ask whether they should not compensate for this through redistributions. These extremely difficult questions are barely touched on in this volume, but they nevertheless underline much of the evaluation of the facts which are revealed here.

Another question that is not treated in these papers is that of the forces which underly the dynamics of the distribution of property in society, including that property in minds and bodies which produces labor income. The distribution of what might be called nongrants income — that is, income which is derived from the processes of production and exchange — depends on two principal factors — the distribution of property, the ownership of which gives claim to income, and the price for services of the property, which determines how much income is derived per unit of property. Whether income is distributed equally or unequally depends in the first case on the equal or unequal distribution of property and would depend also to a rather less degree on the relative price system, in the sense that income will be more equal if those forms of property which are very unequally distributed have a low price for their services, whereas forms of property which are equally distributed have a high price. Thus, nonhuman property is probably distributed more unequally than is human property, that is, property in minds and bodies, which in a nonslave society is distributed rather evenly. Then a shift in the price structure which increases wages at the expense of profits would result in the more equal distribution of income. A very difficult and as yet largely unsolved problem is that of the forces and decisions of society which in fact determine the distribution of the national product as between labor income and property income. The proportions of this distribution are in fact remarkably stable, but why they are stable, why they may be subject to slow secular change as they seem to be, with a rising proportion of national income going to labor and a shrinking proportion to capital, is again the kind of long-run study the papers of this volume do not touch on.

There seems to be no general model in economic literature of the processes of change in the distribution of property over time. Certain variables are intuitively relevant, such as the character of inheritance taxation, the provisions of inheritance laws – whether they encourage primogeniture or wide distribution of property among descendants – the nature of marriage customs and assortative mating – that is, do the rich only marry the rich; the relative fertility of the rich and the poor; the propensity to form charitable foundations; the relative expectations of life of men and of women, and so on. We know of no historical-quantitative models, however, which show exactly how these variables interact to produce the dynamic processes of change in the distribution of property. Societies differ markedly in this respect. This would make a useful topic for future study.

Another factor affecting distribution which is very little explored is the impact of the rate of interest and more generally of the financial structure and the opportunities for credit. It may well be that the gradual democratization of credit over the last hundred years, extending it down to the middle class and the poor, is one of the most important factors affecting the distribution of income in the long run. The actual level of the rate of interest is also an important factor. We do not really know, for instance, how many of the people who pay interest are richer or poorer than the people who receive it, so that we really do not know whether a rise even in the nominal rate of interest redistributes income toward the rich or toward the poor. It is very difficult, therefore, to evaluate the distributional impact of monetary policy. The impact of the rate of interest, of course, is complicated by the further impact of inflation. The pioneering papers on the impact of inflation on the poor and on the effects of alternative public policy instruments included in this volume are the beginning of what should be a very extensive series on the whole distributional effect of inflation and of public policy measures designed to combat inflation and other macroeconomic ills on all classes and income levels. Inflation, of course, to some extent counteracts high rates of interest, as if the nominal rate of interest is 8 percent and the rate of inflation is 5 percent, the real rate of interest is only about 3 percent. It may be, therefore, that one of the major impacts of inflation on the distribution of income lies through its indirect effect on real rates of interest. The effect of inflation on the relative price structure is also very important, but this may vary from case to case and from time to time.

Another very important area in the study of the distribution of income, which we are only just beginning to explore, is distribution in regard to various categories of people. The most obvious category, of course, is race. There are many other categories, however, which are still inadequately explored: distribution by sex (which we know something about), by age (which is still largely unexplored, as we noticed earlier), by religious or political affiliation, by amount and type of education, by type of family, by marital status, and by life style. These are all for the future. The same nominal, or even real income, for instance, means very different things for a hippie commune, a monastery, a ghetto family, an aged rural couple, and a blue-collar worker. We have explored these aspects of income distribution very little, and yet politically these may be very important configurations.

The role of private contributions from individuals, families, and corporations, of foundation grants and of transfers in kind from various types of nonprofit institutions have not been discussed, apart from an overall discussion of some types of transfers by Lampman's introductory paper. Moreover, the alleged role of philanthropy in American life would lead one to ponder questions of the following type: How large is the redistributive effect of intrafamily and interfamily giving? Are private gifts to churches and other nonprofit institutions but a means for providing benefits which will largely accrue to the donor group? What are the net effects of corporate giving? One suspects that foundation grants benefit immediately the middle-income and upper-income classes and only indirectly benefit the poor. Private nonprofit institutions, say private hospitals and schools, again may benefit more the higher income groups when compared with the corresponding public institutions financed from tax revenues.

Data on individual and corporate giving are available due to the tax-deductibility of contributions; hence, the distributive pattern of the sources of these transfers by individual and corporate income classes can be estimated rather easily.[1] However, when their uses are traced to foundations — who act as grantor-intermediaries — or to nonprofit institutions the pattern becomes rather blurred. More thorough investigations are required to cover this twilight zone of seemingly private activities which have significant public effects. In any case, the implicit public grants conveyed to various types of nonprofit institutions under

---

1 See Martin Pfaff and Anita Pfaff, with an introduction by Kenneth E. Boulding, *Transfers in an Urbanized Economy* (Belmont, Calif.: Wadsworth Publishing Company, forthcoming).

the tax laws should be scrutinized more closely and subjected to closer public control wherever such action appears desirable.

We have not considered the distributive effect of forced transfers taking place through the operation of the criminal economy – the economic consequences of theft, robbery, assault, misappropriation, and so on. The magnitude of this economy is estimated at $51 billion for the year 1970 – a staggering figure by any standard of comparison. Whatever data are available suggest that crime is *not* an instrument that enhances income equalization. On the contrary, it appears to have a regressive effect, hurting those who are already worse off more than others.

Yet another aspect of private giving – the distributive consequences of political contributions – is a largely unexplored subject. Its net effect may or may not be progressive, depending on the relative magnitude of low-income contributors and the use to which the funds are put.

The great unanswered, and perhaps, unanswerable, question in the theory of the grants economy is the extent to which the total amount and the distribution of grants is determined by changes in the integrative structure, by changes in the internal threats system, or, of course, by both, and in what proportions. The striking rise in the total of redistribution toward the poor even in the last twenty years, coming as it did in a period of a general increase in income that has brought large numbers of people out of poverty simply through the operations of the exchange system, is easier to take for granted than it is to explain. Part of it, as Myrdal pointed out in *An American Dilemma*,[2] is a perception of a gap between professed ideals and revealed realities, which creates a certain crisis of national identity. The "liberty and justice for all" of the Pledge of Allegiance to the Flag, which almost all American children repeat every day, sits uncomfortably with the realities of racial discrimination and the pockets of obvious poverty in the slums and less obvious poverty in rural areas that constantly confront the urban commuter or the rural traveler. There is a sense also perhaps that, whereas in the past poverty has been an insoluble problem, today it has the appearance at least of a soluble problem in a rich society. The comfortable (for the rich) doctrine that the poverty of the poor is their own fault suffered a very severe blow during the Depression. Furthermore, for the United States there may also be some impact from abroad. The image of a world leader in a world in which the majority of people are not white, and are also not rich, creates anxieties about the national image which can only ultimately be assuaged by changing the national reality. Thus we encounter an apparent paradox, that as poverty diminishes, it also becomes politically less acceptable, even to the rich and powerful. There also may be a rising internal threat as the poor get better organized, more self-conscious, and more concentrated in the cities, which intensifies the political demand to eliminate poverty. These speculations, however, are far beyond the scope of this volume, which sticks pretty closely to the meat and potatoes of measurable economic data.

---

2 Gunnar Myrdal, *An American Dilemma* (New York: Harper & Row, Publishers, 1958).

Grants Economics Series

Transfers in an Urbanized Society
Theory and Effects of the Grants Economy

edited by Kenneth E. Boulding, Martin Pfaff,
and Anita B. Pfaff (Wayne State University)

Contents

Chapter 4   Tax Transfers and Educational Policy

Chapter 5   Transfers as Instruments of Urban Ecological Policy

Chapter 6   Conclusion

The Economy of Love and Fear:
A Preface to Grants Economics

Kenneth E. Boulding

Contents

The Grants Economy

Martin Pfaff